Seneca's
MORAL EPISTLES

Selected and Edited with
Introduction, Notes, and Vocabulary

by
Anna Lydia Motto

BOLCHAZY CARDUCCI PUBLISHERS, INC.
Wauconda, Illinois

General Editor:
Laurie Haight Keenan

Contributing Editor:
D. Scott VanHorn

Cover and Text Design:
Cameron Marshall

Cover Illustration:
Roman Bridge leading to Cordoba, Spain
from *Wanderings in Spain,* by Augustus J. C. Hare

Typesetting:
Charlene Hernandez, Green Tree Design

Latin text © Oxford University Press 1965.
Reprinted from **Seneca: Epistulae Morales** edited by L. D. Reynolds
(Oxford Classical Texts, 1965) by permission of Oxford University Press.

Bolchazy-Carducci Publishers, Inc.

1000 Brown Street
Wauconda, IL 60084 USA
http://www.bolchazy.com

Printed in the United States of America
2001
by John S. Swift Co.
ISBN: 0-86516-487-8

Library of Congress Cataloging-in-Publication Data

Seneca, Lucius Annaeus, ca. 4 b.c.–65 a.d.
  [Epistulae morales ad Lucilium. Selections]
  Seneca's Moral epistles / selected and edited with introduction, notes, and vocabulary
by Anna Lydia Motto
      p. cm.
  Rev. ed. of: Seneca Moral epistles. c1985.
  Epistles in Latin.
  Includes bibliography references (p.).
  ISBN 0-86516-487-8
    1. Conduct of life -- Early works to 1800. 2. Ethics--Early works to 1800. I. Motto,
Anna Lydia. II. Title.

PA6661.E7 M6 2001
876'.01--dc21   2001037979

Seneca's
MORAL EPISTLES

TO: P. H. EPPS

Nullius boni sine socio iucunda possessio est.

CONTENTS

PREFACE

Seneca's Moral Epistles is a selection of forty of Seneca's *Epistulae Morales* that portray the *humanitas*, the deep sentiment, and the profound thought of this renowned Philosopher/Statesman of the Neronian Age. Living in an era of corruption and tyranny, Seneca came forth as a *Seelenartz*, a physician of souls, eager to impart to his fellow men the ethical and moral precepts that would enable them to overcome their weaknesses and attain *vera felicitas.*

The volume, designed primarily as a college textbook, contains some of Seneca's most exemplary letters together with commentary and running vocabulary on facing pages of the text. The student is thus saved from the tedium of having to flip back and forth from text to vocabulary to notes. With most necessary information accompanying the Latin text itself, one can read with greater rapidity and ease. A full vocabulary is provided at the end of the book and an introduction at the beginning gives an account of Seneca's life and work, of his philosophy and style.

The content of the forty letters deals with topics pertinent to the concerns of human beings in all epochs and in every society: epistles on friendship, on old age, on the value of time, on philosophy as the guide of life, on God, on the benefits of virtue and good deeds, on self-improvement, on proper exercise, on how to overcome boredom and despair, on the debunking of warfare, on the condemnation of slavery, on the denunciation of the gladiatorial combats, on valuing the human being for his inner rather than his outer possessions.

These short moral epistles readily lend themselves to philosophical discussion, to critical interpretation, and to literary analysis. As the reader completes one letter after another, he gains confidence in his use of the language as well as in his knowledge of literature and life.

My Latin text is that of L. D. Reynolds, *L. Annaei Senecae Ad Lucilium Epistulae Morales* (1965), published in the Oxford Classical Text series and reprinted here with permission.

I wish to thank *The Classical Bulletin* and also the Twayne Publishers for granting me permission to incorporate the following material into the introduction of this edition: "*Ingenium Facile et Copiosum:* Point and Counterpoint in Senecan Style," *The Classical Bulletin* 52: 1–4; given sentences from pages 35, 36, 41, 50, 59, 60, 63, 64, and 67 of my book *Seneca* (Twayne's World Authors Series, New York, 1973).

In addition, I am most grateful to Professor Preston H. Epps, who shared his notes with me regarding several of the Epistles in this volume. It was his generosity and encouragement that inspired me to edit the *Epistulae Morales* of Seneca. It is to this devoted teacher, scholar, and friend that I dedicate this book.

INTRODUCTION

In the first century A.D., during the early years of the Empire, Rome's despots regularly rewarded intimates, intellectuals, and courtiers alike with exile and extermination. Tacitus records, with superb irony, that "about this time, Lucius Piso, member of the pontifical order, died a natural death—a rare occurrence for one in so high a rank" (*Annals* 6.10). Social distinction, natural talents, and rational capacities were clearly disadvantageous. Into such a dangerous arena did our unusually able author set foot.

Seneca the philosopher was a polymath, a writer adept in innumerable fields— virtually a Renaissance Man. He is best known to us for his intense tragedies of blood, his consummate essays of philosophic advice, his pointed, level-headed moral epistles, and his questioning scientific treatises. His opinions, as well, are equally broad-minded and various. We laud him today as one who extolled humanitarianism in an era of slavery, who stoutly championed clemency in a period of stark brutality, who urged stoic self-restraint in a society devoted to effete lasciviousness, and who counseled potent frankness in a world consumed by adulation and obsequiousness.

Although living in an era of universal corruption and highhanded tyranny and forced to share his destiny with the Emperor Nero, this wealthy courtier and accomplished orator not only transmitted Stoic philosophy to posterity but so altered and enhanced it that it became more personal and humane. His own candid self-confrontations, his polished rhetoric, his deep sentiment, his profound thought—all have influenced men in every age and have duly earned for him a niche in an eternal Hall of Fame.

Seneca's Life and Work

Lucius Annaeus Seneca was born in Cordova, Spain, around 4 B.C., of a wealthy and erudite family. His father, Seneca the Elder (or "the Rhetor"), was a distinguished rhetorician, and his mother, Helvia, was a woman of intellect—well-trained in philosophy and the liberal arts. They had three sons: Novatus, the oldest, who pursued a political career; Mela, the youngest, who won fame as the father of the Roman poet Lucan; and Lucius Annaeus, renowned philosopher, orator, and statesman.

In infancy, Seneca traveled with his parents from Spain to Rome, where they established permanent residence. There, when Seneca came of age, he received training in grammar, rhetoric, and philosophy. He was bored by the teachings of pedantic, unimaginative grammarians, captivated by the training he received from well-known masters of rhetoric, and fascinated most by the wise precepts which he heard discussed by the leading philosophers of the day. By combining philosophical training with rhetorical skill, the young Seneca pursued equally the *vita contemplativa* and the *vita activa*.

His active political life, however, was interrupted by ill health, which he had endured from early childhood. He often refers in his epistles to general ill health as well as to specific ills—fever, asthma, and catarrh. As a result of his infirmity, he decided to visit Egypt, where his maternal aunt, wife of the governor, through diligence and care, helped him regain his strength. To this unusual relative Seneca owed the first significant step in his political career. Through her influence, he obtained the quaestorship in Rome about A.D. 33, perhaps becoming aedile or tribune of the plebs about 36 or 37.

During these years of political advancement, Seneca's reputation as lawyer, philosopher, and writer likewise continued to grow, not only winning for him fame and wealth but also the envy of the mad emperor Caligula (A.D. 37–41), who even contemplated putting the sickly philosopher to death.

Having almost lost his life, Seneca decided to give up his perilous oratorical career and to devote himself more and more to literature and philosophy. It is very likely that he wrote at this time the *Consolation to Marcia* and the dialogue *On Anger*, which contains scathing remarks against Caligula.

In 41 Caligula was assassinated and his uncle Claudius ascended the throne. Seneca, who was on intimate terms with the princesses Julia Livilla and Agrippina, sisters of Caligula and nieces of Claudius, incurred the animosity of the jealous empress Messalina, Claudius' third wife. Regarding Seneca as a dangerous opponent, she accused him of an illicit intrigue with Julia. On this unfounded charge, Julia was exiled without trial and shortly afterward put to death; on the same unproved charge, Seneca was exiled to the barbaric, desolate island of Corsica, where he was to spend eight years of his life (A.D. 41–49).

Prior to his public misfortune, Seneca had been heavily burdened by domestic tragedies—the deaths of his wife, his son, and two of his nephews. To console himself and to alleviate his mother's sorrow, he addressed to her the *Consolation to Helvia* (c. A.D. 41–42), in which he discouraged her grief by setting before her those lofty philosophic precepts that fortify one against the cruel blows of fortune. True happiness, he argues, depends upon a mind that is not enslaved by fickle fortune's gifts. For such a mind, exile is but a change of place (*Ad Helv.* 6.1). Unfortunately, however, as time passed, Seneca began to lose, in exile, his philosophic calm. In fact, he became so despondent that in A.D. 43–44 he addressed to Polybius, Claudius' powerful secretary who had recently lost his brother, a consolation, in which, in sharp contrast to the *Consolation to Helvia,* he openly admits his misery and, in his eagerness to obtain his recall from exile, overtly flatters Polybius and the Emperor Claudius. If this was a failing on the philosopher's part, yet it was a distinctively human one. Seneca frequently recalls that he himself was far from being the ideal Stoic *sapiens* of moral perfection, that all men are flawed (*De Clementia* 1.6.3), and that all men display a kind of madness (*Ep.* 70.3). About himself he was ever candid as well as ambivalent: *virtutes discere vitia dediscere est* (*Ep.* 50.7), he counsels. Vice comes naturally; virtue must, after a contest, be imposed. Seneca well knows that Man must insist upon striving for the virtuous, while finding it difficult to eradicate vice.

But, whatever his motives and foibles, the *Ad Polybium* did not deliver Seneca from exile, as the philosopher had hoped. Such release came five years later through changes in the imperial court. Messalina, denounced by Claudius' freedmen for her debaucheries and for conspiracy against the Emperor, was executed with her lover in 48.

Agrippina, Claudius' niece and fourth wife, as well as Nero's mother by Domitius, promptly recalled the philosopher from exile, bestowing upon him the tutorship of her twelve-year-old son. Soon, indeed, Nero would become the Emperor's adoptive son. Agrippina also awarded Seneca the praetorship and a place in the Senate. Thus, in 49, after eight years in exile, at the age of fifty-three, Seneca returned to Rome to play once more a dominant political role.

To assist Seneca in educating Nero, Agrippina had selected the rough but honest and ready soldier Burrus, later elevated by her to the post of prefect of the Praetorian Guard. Seneca and Burrus experienced an unusual friendship as they united day by day in restraining Nero's excesses and in controlling Agrippina's lawless spirit and her lust for power. After the Emperor Claudius' murder in 54 by Agrippina, who served him a dish of poisoned mushrooms, the two tutors and guides became prominent indeed, and under their tutelage the early principate of the young Nero came to be known as the *Quinquennium Neronis* (A.D. 54–59), a period marked by clemency in government. Divorced from misrule, this period was later proclaimed by the Emperor Trajan as the golden age of Imperial Rome.

This era, however, of equity and kindness was soon to end. The Empress Agrippina, coveting for herself supreme control of the state, became annoyed by the humane and just administration of Seneca and Burrus. Fearful of losing her power and inflamed with a jealous hatred, she threatened to give the throne to Britannicus, son of Claudius by Messalina. Agrippina's open support of the young prince filled Nero with dread, and he ordered Britannicus to be put to death by a poisonous drink. After Britannicus' murder, the hostility between mother and son as well as between tutor and pupil continued to mount. Increasingly, Nero succumbed to the influence of unprincipled men like Suillius, who, envious of Seneca's prestige and power, were anxious to eradicate his leadership. These unscrupulous men, together with Poppaea, Nero's new mistress, urged the Emperor to rid himself not only of his domineering mother but also of Seneca and Burrus. After several unsuccessful attempts to poison Agrippina and an attempt to drown her at sea, Nero had her bludgeoned to death with club and sword in her bedroom.

Although Seneca realized the dangerous waters upon which he was afloat, he did not abandon the ship of state. He continued to sail along for another three years until Burrus' death in 62 (whether by illness or by poisoning remains uncertain). But when Burrus was replaced by the debauched and licentious Tigellinus, Seneca became convinced that he could no longer play a leading role in the complex drama of the Neronian court. As a result, disillusioned and depressed by long, frustrating experience, the philosopher, at sixty-five, confronted his former pupil, asking permission to retire so that he might devote the remainder of his life to studies. Moreover, being perfectly willing to eliminate envy and to purchase freedom at the highest price, he offered to return the millions of his wealth that the Emperor had bestowed upon him. Yet, leaders are not permitted to retire from a totalitarian state. When Nero refused to grant Seneca's request for withdrawal from public life, the philosopher boldly, on his own, assumed the posture of retirement: he avoided the court and the city, eschewed all factions and crowds, and embraced a life of self-exile, reclusion, and study.

What the cause of civilization here lost in the political realm, it certainly gained in philosophy and literature. For these years of retirement, A.D. 62–65, constitute the *anni mirabiles* of Seneca's literary career. To them can be assigned with certainty his *maximum opus*, the 124 *Moral Letters* (*Epistulae Morales*), as well as the seven books of *Natural Questions* (*Quaestiones Naturales*). To this same fruitful period, scholars involved in the insoluble problem of dating the Senecan corpus have often attributed the seven books *On Benefits* (*De Beneficiis*), the dialogues *On Leisure* (*De Otio*) and *On Providence* (*De Providentia*), along with several other works.

Though ensconced in the tranquillity of thought and composition, Seneca was nevertheless constantly harassed by an aura of impending doom. Since Nero had never officially released him from court, the shadow of imperial tyranny continued to haunt his retirement. By A.D. 65, three years after his attempted seclusion, he was accused of complicity in the so-called Pisonian conspiracy—a conspiracy that had as its object the murder of Nero and the transfer of supreme power to Piso. What role Nero's former teacher actually played in this conspiracy remains uncertain, but now Nero had found an excuse to liquidate his mentor. Like so many others implicated in the conspiracy, Seneca was instructed by military officers to commit suicide.

Tacitus (*Annals* 15.62–64) has left us a moving description of Seneca's last hours—detailing his courage in the face of death. Here Seneca is presented as recalling his sad friends from tears to fortitude by that very philosophy that had so strongly and for so long molded his own character. "Where," he asks his companions, "were the precepts of wisdom? Where was that rationality developed over the years to help us face adversity?" Thereafter, Seneca speaks on a more personal note: "Who was, after all, unfamiliar with Nero's cruelty? There was nothing left for one who had murdered his brother and his mother but to slaughter his teacher and guide." Why should his friends be surprised? Rather, they should accept the predictable and continue to regulate their lives despite the evils and mischance present in this world. Seneca himself, it is implied, had pursued such a pattern: he had directed his pinnace in open seas and political waters when that was possible, and he had steadied his craft in studious streams and standing pools when that was possible. No such life, successful upon the various tides, could possibly have been in vain.

Forbidden, as Tacitus details, to make his last will, Seneca turns to his friends and observes that, prevented from rewarding their merit in the public coin, he could only leave to them his "richest" possession—"the image of his life" (*Annals* 15.62). As with Socrates before him, his "private coin" constitutes the wealth of a generous philosophic tradition. Such was his legacy to posterity.

Seneca's Philosophy

Seneca collects and collates his philosophic precepts from all sources, binding himself to the dogmas of no particular school. As a young man, he had come under the influence of philosophers from the various sects—Sotion the Pythagorean, Attalus the Stoic, Demetrius the Cynic. Although he allied himself to the Stoics more closely than to any other group of philosophers, yet his writings reveal him as an eclectic—one who was willing to assemble useful precepts from any school of thought. He writes: "I can dispute with Socrates, doubt with Carneades, achieve tranquillity with Epicurus, conquer human nature with the Stoics, exceed it with the Cynics" (*De Brev. Vit.* 14.2). Thus, Seneca was no sectarian dogmatist, but rather a seeker after truth:

> "Epicurus," you say, "said this. What have you to do with the philosophy of another school?" What's truth is mine. (*Ep.* 12.11)

Unlike earlier philosophers, who had equally stressed three branches of study—ethics, physics, and dialectic—the Stoics (and particularly Seneca) primarily emphasized ethics alone. To be sure, the two most popular schools of philosophy in Imperial Rome were the Stoic and Epicurean—philosophies devoted to ethical conduct. Men like Seneca, in quest of intellectual freedom and tranquillity of mind, found the fundamental ethical teachings of these two schools very similar. The Stoics taught that virtue was the highest good; the Epicureans believed that pleasure was the *summum bonum*. But the Epicurean view of pleasure, as expounded by its founder, was by no means the later distorted idea of wine, women, and song. Since Epicurus taught that one cannot lead a life of pleasure without leading a life of honor, prudence, and justice, nor lead a life of honor, prudence, and justice which is not also a life of pleasure, the basic moral goals of Stoicism and Epicureanism seemed one and the same.

The cultural era of Rome under the early Empire was surprisingly modern, strikingly like our own. Local religions and provincial pieties had failed; an era of mass communications and of mass-man had ensued. If it was an age of cosmopolitan sophistication, yet it was also a period of personal crisis and individual loneliness. The advances of bureaucratic man only enhanced private isolation, indecision, and *Angst*.

In such a society, Seneca dedicated his every energy and devoted his entire life in an effort to impart to his fellow men the philosophic precepts of personal regulation, self-reliance, and control. He had acquired a deep understanding of human ignorance, misery, and sorrow, and he was eager to furnish harassed contemporary man with some remedy for his mental weaknesses and vacillations.

The mass of men, Seneca believes, are irresolute, ambitious, dubious, greedy, and impious, ready and willing to destroy one another in their selfish quest for material acquisitions. Yet, the spectacle of human greed and vice should not cause us to hate our fellow men. The wise man, Seneca insists, will seek to reform rather than oppose the vicious. He will look with kindness upon the crowd, regarding them as sick men in need of a physician. Seneca was strongly committed to the belief that even those who have plunged heavily into depravity can, through proper guidance, progress along the path of virtue. His philosophic writings display deep insight into human frailties, together with an ardent zeal to salvage and elevate the moral tone of mankind.

Man, Seneca maintains, possesses a double nature—a physical nature which animals also enjoy and a rational nature which is man's distinguishing characteristic. The more the individual perfects his reason, the closer he comes to "nature," which is synonymous with God, who is "perfect reason." In fact, Seneca and the Stoics argue that to live "according to nature" is to live according to reason, the highest achievement of man.

Thus, every individual rises or falls on the scale of humanity and happiness as he succeeds or fails in harmonizing his actions with nature and reason. The more perfect his reason, the more fully does he possess that Stoic virtue which alone can give man everlasting joy. Only that which is absolutely good (*virtus*) can be considered a good, and only that which is absolutely bad (*turpitudo*) can be considered an evil. Such was the traditional Stoic teaching, which further distinguished all things which lie outside the categories of good and evil as being *indifferentia*. Among such "indifferent things," it is true, some (health and riches) are advantageous, while others (poverty and disease) are disadvantageous. However desirable or influential the former may be, Seneca and the Stoic school sharply distinguish between their purely relative value and the absolute value of virtue. Such virtue is man's sole and supreme good. It offers him a life that is consistent and a happiness that can be neither increased nor diminished by indifferent things and external conditions.

Men's sins and follies spring from unreason, from the pursuit of worldly possessions, such as riches, power, and sensual pleasure—Fortune's deceptive gifts. The wise man will detach himself from those extraneous possessions and will enjoy an unalterable serenity of mind. The reforming force that brings about such tranquillity is man's own spark of divine reason. Any man who cultivates his reason may obtain some degree of virtue. Consequently, Seneca and the Stoics avidly maintain that virtue can be developed within each individual human being. Since perfect reason and virtue are the same and since children do not possess reason, it follows that virtue is obtained by art, not by nature, by teaching and hard work, not by inheritance. Those who have not yet reached the ideal state of perfection should not despair but should continue persevering, confident that by training they will come day by day nearer to their goal. Every meaningful human life, according to Seneca, must be a journey, a progress.

Seneca distinguishes three classes of *proficientes,* persons traveling along the path of moral progress. First, there are those who have eliminated some vices but not all—avarice, for example, but not anger. Second, there are those who have overcome the worst passions but are not secure against relapse. Third, there are those who have eradicated vices and passions but who, failing to test themselves, lack the confidence of the ideal Stoic *sapiens.* Men, therefore, proceed by degrees on the path of progress. Seneca is fully aware that "no one is strong enough to emerge from folly by himself; someone must lend him a hand, someone must lead him out" (*Ep.* 52.2). Again and again, Seneca insists upon man's duty to aid his fellow man. Everywhere he recommends mercy, tolerance, kindness, and generosity to all: "Let us teach man to offer his hand to the shipwrecked, to show the road to the wanderer, to share his bread with the hungry" (*Ep.* 95.51). Such *humanitas* leads our philosopher to condemn anger, cruelty, warfare, and the ferocity of the gladiatorial combats. Moreover, his deep sentiment for mankind is further illustrated by his attitude toward slavery, toward the treatment of women, and toward the experience of friendship. Regarding slaves he writes:

> "They are slaves" [claims the *adversarius*]. On the contrary, men. "They are slaves." On the contrary, comrades. "They are slaves." On the contrary, modest friends. "They are slaves." On the contrary, fellow-slaves, if you reflect that fortune has equal power over all. . . . Remember that he whom you call your slave sprang from the same seed, enjoys the same sky, lives, breathes, and dies in the same way as yourself! . . . Live with your slave benignly, affably, and admit him into your conversation, into your counsels, into your feasts. . . . Let some dine with you because they are worthy; others, that they may become so. (*Ep.* 47.1, 10, 13, 15)

To Seneca, friendship is the expression of a natural instinct, a need for commitment: "For what reason do I seek a friend? To have someone to follow into exile, someone for whom I would risk my life" (*Ep.* 9.10). Related to the bond of friendship is a new and forceful note in Seneca's writings extolling women. He frequently makes serious appeal for the rights of women, renouncing the trite commonplaces that regard them as physically and morally weak: "But who said that nature has dealt spitefully with women's talent and narrowly confined their virtue? Believe me: should they wish it, they have an equal amount of vigor, an equal capacity for the performance of good deeds; they endure grief and suffering equally with men if they have been trained to it." (*Ad Marc.* 16.1)

Seneca's creed, therefore, is both leveling and lofty, restrictive and inclusive. It recognizes only one claim to rank or nobility—the capacity for and the attainment of virtue. It embraces in the universal commonwealth all human souls, freeborn or slave, male or female, emperor or peasant, heedless of how they might be classed by accident or by fortune.

Not only did Seneca devote his energies to assisting his fellow men and to conjoining them in a universal cosmopolis, but he also sought to plead God's cause. Seneca, like the Stoics, believed that in the universe there is one supreme power, God, who appears under different names as Nature, Fate, or Reason. This deity, however described by human speech, is not an anthropomorphic, angry figure, but rather a divine, coherent principle that controls all things. Together with the Stoics, Seneca is a pantheist. Like them, he regards God as the "rational principle" that penetrates everything and is present everywhere. Such pantheism embraces also the concept that every soul is of divine origin, a part of and a representative of God. Just as God is the secret power in nature that creates unity, so he is the hidden force in man that produces virtue: "Do you wonder that man goes to the gods? God comes to men; rather, what is closer, he comes into men; there is no good mind without God" (*Ep.* 73.16). God is our guide and our protector, whose spirit resides in our hearts.

Since God dwells in our hearts rather than in temples, man needs no prayer or organized worship. Seneca mocks empty superstition and denounces ritual and religious sacrifice. God does not seek such adoration. Rather. he is ever eager to serve and to aid men. Our sole duty to God is to believe in him as the creator and ruler of the universe and to imitate his benevolence. By progressing on the path of perfection, man becomes more virtuous, more like God. In fact, the ideal Stoic *sapiens* is similar to God in everything except his mortality. What is more, he even excels God, since "God is fearless through nature's beneficence, the wise man through his own efforts" (*Ep.* 53.11). Such a man returns to Nature a better life than he received from her. Having rid himself of all fears, he confronts life and death with Stoic serenity and control.

Seneca is concerned not only with teaching men how to live well but also how to die well. To him, conduct in life and the preparation for death are of primary importance. Again and again he urges us to meditate upon death. Death is the final act of one's life and reveals the strength and nature of one's soul. Indeed, Seneca presents death as a harbor which everyone must enter at the close of life's journey. Not only should man accept death, but, should circumstances require, he should even summon it. Suicide guarantees for man freedom of the human soul: "He who denies the right of committing suicide obstructs the road to liberty" (*Ep.* 70.14). Yet, only those, he tells us, oppressed by dire circumstances—extreme weakness in old age, incurable disease, insanity, debilitating poverty, or the inescapable tyranny of a despot—can rightfully resort to such a mode of exodus. Those, however, who commit suicide to escape the common ills of life are morally derelict and weak.

This attention to suicide and death often evokes powerful statements from our philosopher: "Death pursues me, life escapes me; teach me something that will help!" (*Ep.* 49.9). To guide men, to teach them how to face life's end with serenity, he, like Socrates, offers them one of two alternatives: death is either painless annihilation, non-existence, with no infernal punishments, a return to that condition in which we were before birth, or it is a release of the soul from the prison of the body and the soul's rising to the ethereal regions where it will enjoy the freedom, tranquillity, and happiness of the heavenly life.

To learn the difficult art of living nobly and of dying nobly, man must, according to the whole work of Seneca the philosopher, dedicate himself to the study of Philosophy. She alone can show man how to live without fear, how to overcome adversities, and how to extend kindnesses to his fellow men. She alone can rouse man from error and teach him the art of living well, i.e., of living according to nature or reason. Thus, Seneca writes, and writes conclusively: "There is no philosophy without virtue, nor virtue without philosophy" (*Ep.* 89.8).

The philosopher was as good as his word. Even at the moment of dying, as Tacitus records, Seneca continued to exhort and to console his friends, still in pursuit of that rational, contemplative goddess.

Seneca's Style

Seneca distinguished himself not only as an erudite eclectic philosopher who, borrowing and amalgamating ideas from every school, rendered them into a unity of his own, but also as an original. terse, and striking stylist, a master of word and phrase. Seneca once affirmed (*Ep.* 53.11), ". . . magni artificis est clusisse totum in exiguo" ("...it is characteristic of a great artist to have enclosed all things in a little place"). This expression may be aptly applied to his own stylistic art. Epigrammatic brevity, concentration, balance, and antithesis are typical of Seneca's type of prose. a type that French critics have designated the *style coupé*. In fact, Seneca's buoyant, pointed style became most popular in his own era. Quintilian, the Roman critic of the first century A.D., remarked a few decades after the philosopher's death that virtually Seneca alone among authors was being read by the younger generation. He refers to Seneca's "multae claraeque sententiae" and "minutissimae sententiae." Similarly, Abraham Cowley in the seventeenth century speaks of "the dry chips of short lung'd Seneca," and Erasmus observes that "truly from Seneca's reflections you can find something to imitate more easily than from others where maxims are neither frequent nor striking."

Seneca was not the first to develop the pointed, laconic, clipped, epigrammatic style that is diametrically opposed to the long, rhythmic, eloquent, periodic sentences of Ciceronian prose. But, it must be observed that Seneca is master of this pointed style, the first distinguished philosopher to write with such wit, sparkle, and conciseness.

Let us consider a few examples:

Bona mens nec commodatur nec emitur. (*Ep.* 27.8)
(A good mind is neither borrowed nor bought.)

Effugere non potes necessitates, potes vincere. (*Ep.* 37.3)
(You cannot flee necessities, you can conquer them.)

Non continuo sibi vivit qui nemini. (*Ep.* 55.5)
(He who lives for no one does not necessarily live for himself.)

Here we witness instances of one of Seneca's strongest features, the use of the *sententia*, the neat and nearly proverbial saying. Moreover, his expression is concrete and earthy. The imagery in the first selection is taken from the marketplace, that of the second from warfare. The last instance suggests Seneca's play of mind, which joys in ironic indirection and understatement.

Seneca is also sensitive to the very sounds of words and their patterned arrangement on the page:

Haec in animo voluta, quae saepe audisti, saepe dixisti. (*Ep.* 24.15)
(Turn over in your mind these things which you have often heard, have often said.)

Multis timendi attulit causas timeri posse. (*Ep.* 14.10)
(Many a man who inspires fear has himself reasons to fear.)

Habui enim illos tamquam amissurus, amisi tamquam habeam. (*Ep.* 63.7)
(For I had them [dead friends] as if I were going to lose them, I lost them as if I have them [still].)

Levis es si ferre possum; brevis es si ferre non possum. (*Ep.* 24.14)
(You are light, if I can bear you; you are brief, if I cannot bear you.)

. . . cum his versare qui te meliorem facturi sunt, illos admitte quos tu potes facere meliores. (*Ep.* 7.8)
(. . . go with those who will make you better, bring in those whom you can make better.)

Notice the assonance in the first passage (*haec . . . quae saepe . . . saepe*), together with the rhyme (*audisti . . . dixisti*). Alliteration is dominant in the second selection (*timendi . . . timeri*), and a neat inversion of parts in the third (*Habui . . . tamquam amissurus, amisi tamquam habeam*), where the well-balanced repetition permits the sentence literally to turn back upon itself. Senecan style similarly illustrates "copiousness," as in the patterned repetitiveness of the first passage ("these things which you have often heard, have often said"). A similar type of repetitive inversion is again to be observed in the last selection, where the generation of words is balanced and precise.

Together with such witty and neatly turned expressions, moreover, Seneca is often very close to one of his favorite devices—the paradox:

Mihi crede, verum gaudium res severa est. (*Ep.* 23.4)
(Believe me, true joy is a severe thing.)

Multa bona nostra nobis nocent. (*Ep.* 5.9)
(Our many blessings harm us.)

Multis ad philosophandum obstitere divitiae: paupertas expedita est, secura est. (*Ep.* 17.3)
(Wealth has hindered many from attaining wisdom: poverty is unimpeded and free from care.)

. . . infirmi animi est pati non posse divitias. (*Ep.* 5.6)
(. . . it is characteristic of a weak mind not to be able to endure wealth.)

Seneca's paradoxes (literally, contrary to common opinion) regularly shock the reader into paying greater attention. Thus, joy is a severity; blessings are harmful; poverty liberates, whereas wealth confines. The last example presents a particular kind of paradox, what the Greeks termed *para prosdokian*, the injecting at the end of a thought that which is unexpected. In this case, the reader might well have anticipated that an infirm mind could not endure poverty or some other stroke of ill fortune; yet, with a jolting reversal, he is informed that it is riches that the weakling cannot sustain. Seneca's prose, in short, ever crackles with neat twists, bold strokes, turns, and tergiversations. For Seneca, sound thinking, right thinking, is hard work; he will not allow his audience passively to relax; the audience must be forced to participate in any Stoic or Herculean labor. Jonathan Swift explains to his audience a very similar tactic: he intends his raillery "to nettle," to irritate his readers, because such provocation

Sets your Thoughts upon their Mettle:
Gives Imagination Scope,
Never lets your Mind elope:
Drives out Brangling, and Contention,
Brings in Reason and Invention.
　　　　　　　("Epistle to a Lady," lines 218–22)

In any case, it is precisely these backstrokes, bounds, and returns in Senecan prose that continually offer his reader solid and lasting pleasure.

Finally, to obtain an overview of Seneca's performance, we should stand back and consider somewhat longer passages:

Pauper fiam: inter plures ero. Exul fiam: ibi me natum putabo quo mittar. Alligabor: quid enim? Nunc solutus sum? Ad hoc me natura grave corporis mei pondus adstrinxit. Moriar: hoc dicis, desinam aegrotare posse, desinam alligari posse, desinam mori posse (*Ep.* 24.17).

(I'll become poor: I shall be among the many. I'll be exiled: I shall think that I was born in that place to which I'm sent. I'll be imprisoned: What of it? Am I free right now? Nature has bound me to this heavy weight, my body. I'll die: you mean this, I shall cease to be able to be sick, I shall cease to be able to be imprisoned, I shall cease to be able to die.)

This present sample is typical of a great deal of Senecan practice in the *Epistulae Morales*. The passage is chatty at the same time that it is rhetorical; Seneca prided himself upon his ability to deliver ideas in high oratorical tones, yet he also considered his letters to be informal—conversations. There is, in effect, a distinctive tension obtained by thus yoking together the *genus grande* with the *genus humile*. Some critics have indeed claimed that such a mixture renders his style at war with itself. But such tensions are obviously deliberate and seem devised to create vigor, electricity, and pace.

But there is another, more dominant strategy revealed by this passage, that is frequently invoked in his prose, that is, the presence of a contest or debate. On either side of the colons appear two adversaries—almost, if you will, two parts of Seneca. The first, of course, is a neophyte, a non-Stoic, uttering clichés of popular reasoning: it's a bad thing, this person pronounces again and again, to lose one's money, to be exiled, to be tossed into prison, or to die. Responding to this generalized, protesting voice, Seneca answers with bold and confident philosophic strokes. In any event, the presence of such a generalized *adversarius* provides the passage with a remarkable back-and-forth tension of conflict, and the prose comes across to us with the race and force of a tennis match:

'Servi sunt.' Immo homines. 'Servi sunt.' Immo contubernales, 'Servi sunt,' Immo humiles amici, 'Servi sunt.' Immo conservi, si cogitaveris tantundem in utrosque licere fortunae (*Ep.* 47.1).

("They're slaves." On the contrary, men. "They're slaves." On the contrary, comrades. "They're slaves." On the contrary, modest friends. "They're slaves." On the contrary, fellow-slaves, if you reflect that fortune has equal power over all.)

Here again is the contest, and the *adversarius,* unidentified, is nonetheless more clearly identifiable as the *vox populi,* as the crowd's commonplace, stubbornly orthodox, and conservative opinion. The drama here becomes more apparent, for although the *adversarius* remains constant, never altering his opinion, Seneca's argument alters and progresses to a climax; for while he merely holds, at the beginning, that slaves are human beings, he concludes by perceiving, with a sharp reversal. that we the freeborn are the slaves, caught in life's and in fickle fortune's web. In brief, Seneca's prose takes spark and positive fire when a contender steps forward to do battle with him.

Sed iam debeo epistulam includere. 'Sic' inquis 'sine ullo ad me peculio veniet?' Noli timere: aliquid secum fert. Quare aliquid dixi? multum. Quid enim hac voce praeclarius quam illi trado ad te perferendam? 'Malum est in necessitate vivere, sed in necessitate vivere necessitas nulla est.' Quidni nulla sit? Patent undique ad libertatem viae multae, breves, faciles. Agamus deo gratias quod nemo in vita teneri potest: calcare ipsas necessitates licet. 'Epicurus' inquis 'dixit: quid tibi cum alieno?' Quod verum est meum est: perseverabo Epicurum tibi ingerere. (*Ep.* 12.10–11)

(But now I must close my letter. You say, "Will it come to me thus without any allotment?" Fear not; it brings something with it. Why have I said something? Rather, a great deal. For what is more brilliant than this saying which I entrust to it, to be sent along to you: "It is a bad thing to live in need, but there is no need to live in need." Why is there no need? On all sides, many paths, short, easy, lie open to liberty. Let us give thanks to God that no one can be held in life. One may trample upon those very needs. "Epicurus."

you say, "said this. What have you to do with the philosophy of another school?" What's truth is mine. I shall continue to heap Epicurus upon you.)

In this last passage, the contest becomes more concrete, for the contestant materializes into Lucilius himself. Some of the most forceful moments in the *Epistulae* occur when this takes place. Throughout the letters, Seneca repeatedly, insistently addresses Lucilius as if he were present upon the scene. Indeed, when Seneca is not debating, as we have seen, with himself or with society and public opinion, an imaginary Lucilius is virtually omnipresent upon the stage, as the stubborn *interlocutor,* as a questioner or outright challenger of Seneca's arguments. Thus, he functions openly as *adversarius,* as recalcitrant opponent to Seneca himself.

We have not yet finished with altercation and contention, for there is *another* voice present in this passage—that of Epicurus, founder of the chief rival school to Stoicism. Seneca had, early in the letters, promised to "deliver" in each epistle some little saying from the divine wisdom of the past. It most frequently turns out to be a maxim by Epicurus or his followers. Here, then, is another rich source for skirmish and scrimmage. Seneca is doing much more than providing himself with one more paradoxical antagonist; he is giving himself the opportunity in the letters to generate a host of new voices that fill up the page. His terse, pointed prose is best served when cast in a dramatic arena, and his writing is remarkable, ultimately, for supplying so much of this tournament and collision.

Thus, Seneca is able to supply us with philosophy in a new key. While, it is true, his letters are always marked by a moral argument and a hortatory tone, they also, as short, experimental flights upon a variety of topics, surprise us as the nearest thing to our modern essays: Michel de Montaigne, the innovator in the genre of *essais,* refers to Seneca repeatedly, and Francis Bacon, his English counterpart, in his original dedication of his *Essays,* acknowledges a considerable debt to Seneca the philosopher.

Yet, Seneca's epistles ultimately go beyond being merely argument, philosophy, and essay. As we have shown, the rapid cut and thrust of his argument in these last-cited passages remind us that his work is vitally something more. For, with the incessant play of voices and the clash of contest, his epistles finally become a type of creative drama—the rich acting out of ideas in conflict. Perhaps it is the overall drama of Senecan prose—its tensions, its combat, its passionate note—that will continue to earn for him the highest and the most lasting praise.

HISTORICAL CHRONOLOGY

31 B.C.–A.D. 14

Reign of Augustus
Seneca born, c. 4 B.C., at Cordova, Spain. Brought to Rome when a young child.

A.D. 14–37

Reign of Tiberius
Seneca visits Egypt, c. A.D. 19–20.
Returns to Rome in 31.
Commences active public career: Quaestor, c. 33, possibly
Tribune or Aedile, c. 36 or 37.

A.D. 37–41

Reign of Caligula
Seneca as renowned orator, lawyer, and writer.

A.D. 41–54

Reign of Claudius
Seneca exiled to Corsica, 41–49.
Recalled to Rome in 49 by Agrippina, to become
Nero's tutor. Praetor and Senator.

A.D. 54–68

Reign of Nero
Quinquennium Neronis, 54–59.
Death of Burrus in 62.
Semi-retirement, 62–65; Seneca composes *Epistulae Morales.*
Pisonian Conspiracy, 65. Seneca's suicide.

CHRONOLOGY OF SENECA'S EXTANT WORKS

Scholars have labored long to establish a precise chronology for Seneca's writings, but accurate dating has never been accomplished. After each title, I simply suggest a likely date.

Epigrammata super exilio (authorship doubtful) c. 41–49

Tragedies c. 45–55
    Agamemnon
    Hercules Furens
    Medea
    Oedipus
    Phaedra
    Thyestes
    Troades
    Hercules Oetaeus (authorship in doubt)
    Octavia (not by Seneca)
    Phoenissae (fragment—possibly by Seneca)

The so-called "Dialogues"[1]: c. 40–64

    Ad Marciam de Consolatione (Dial. VI) c. 40–41
    De Ira libri tres (Dial. III, IV, V) Bks. I–II c. 41; Bk. III c. 49
    Ad Helviam Matrem de Consolatione (Dial. XII) c. 41–42
    Ad Polybium de Consolatione (Dial. XI) c. 43–44
    De Brevitate Vitae (Dial. X) c. 49
    De Constantia Sapientis (Dial. II) c. 54–56
    De Vita Beata (Dial. VII) c. 58–59
    De Tranquillitate Animi (Dial. IX) c. 59–61
    De Otio (Dial. VIII) c. 62
    De Providentia (Dial. I) c. 63–64

Apocolocyntosis [*Ludus de Morte Claudii*] (authorship questioned) c. 54

De Clementia c. 53–56

De Beneficiis c. 58–63

Quaestiones Naturales c. 62–64

Epistulae Morales ad Lucilium c. 62–65

---

[1]Dialogue numeration follows the Ambrosian MS.

SELECTED BIBLIOGRAPHY

1. LATIN TEXTS
   Reynolds, L. D., ed. *Annaei Senecae, Ad Lucilium Epistulae Morales,* 2 vols. Oxford: Clarendon Press, 1965.
   Summers, W. C., ed. *Select Letters of Seneca.* London: Macmillan, 1910.

2. ENGLISH TRANSLATIONS
   Barker, E. P. *Seneca's Letters to Lucilius,* 2 vols. Oxford: Clarendon Press, 1932.
   Campbell, R. *Seneca, Letters from a Stoic: Epistulae Morales ad Lucilium.* Baltimore: Penguin Books, 1969.
   LOEB CLASSICAL LIBRARY SERIES:
   Basore, J. W., ed. *Seneca, Moral Essays,* 3 vols. New York: G. P. Putnam's Sons: Cambridge, Mass.: Harvard University Press: London: William Heinemann, 1928–1935.
   Corcoran, T. H., ed. *Seneca, Natural Questions,* 2 vols. Cambridge, Mass.: Harvard University Press: London: William Heinemann, 1971.
   Gummere, R. M. , ed. *Seneca, ad Lucilium Epistulae Morales.* 3 vols. New York: G. P. Putnam's Sons: London: William Heinemann, 1917–1925.

3. BIBLIOGRAPHY
   Motto, A. L. and J. R. Clark. *Seneca: A Critical Bibliography, 1900–1980.* Amsterdam: Adolf M. Hakkert, 1989.

4. SCHOLARLY STUDIES
   Arnold, E. V. *Roman Stoicism.* Cambridge: Cambridge University Press, 1911.
   Edelstein, L. *The Meaning of Stoicism.* Cambridge: Harvard University Press, 1965.
   Gould, J. B. *The Philosophy of Chrysippus.* Leiden: Brill, 1970.
   Griffin, M. T. *Seneca: A Philosopher in Politics.* Oxford: Clarendon Press, 1976.
   Grimal, P. *Sénèque ou la conscience de l'empire.* Paris: Belles Lettres, 1978.
   ———. *Sénèque, sa vie, son oeuvre, sa philosophie.* Paris: Presses Universitaires de France, 1948.
   Gummere, R. M. *Seneca the Philosopher and His Modern Message.* Boston: Marshall Jones, 1922.
   Holland, F. *Seneca.* London: Longmans, Green, 1920.
   Knoche, U. *Der Philosoph Seneca.* Frankfurt: V. Klostermann, 1933.
   Marchesi, C. *Seneca.* Milan: Giuseppe Principato, 1934.
   Motto, A. L. *Seneca Sourcebook: Guide to the Thought of Lucius Annaeus Seneca.* Amsterdam: A. M. Hakkert, 1970.
   ———. *Seneca.* New York: Twayne Publishers, 1973.
   Motto, A. L. and J. R. Clark. *Essays on Seneca.* Frankfurt am Main: Peter Lang, 1993.
   Motto, A. L. *Further Essays on Seneca.* Frankfurt am Main: Peter Lang, 2001.
   Pohlenz, M. *Die Stoa, Geschichte einer geistigen Bewegung.* 2 vols. Göttingen: Vandenhoeck and Ruprecht, 1948–49.

Rist, J. M. *Stoic Philosophy*. Cambridge: Cambridge University Press, 1969.
Sandbach, F. H. *The Stoics*. London: Chatto and Windus, 1975.
Waltz, R. *Vie de Sénèque*. Paris: Librairie Académique, 1909.
Zeller, Eduard. *Stoics, Epicureans and Sceptics*, trans. O. J. Reichel, Rev. ed. London: Longmans, Green, 1879.

NOTE TO READERS

Running vocabularies are provided on pages opposite the Latin text. Since some teachers might not assign all the letters in order of sequence, each letter is presented as a complete unit, and the same vocabulary is sometimes repeated in various letters.

In the vocabulary glosses, adjectives formed from the perfect passive participle of verbs (e.g. **doctus, -a, -um** from **doceo, -ere, docui, doctus**) are listed as participial adjectives and marked *p. adj.*

The positive form of the corresponding adjective is usually given for adverbs. For example, the comparative adverb **indecentius** is glossed as **indecens.**

Alternative spellings of words such as **corroboro** for **conroboro** are supplied to familiarize students with both forms.

Seneca's
MORAL EPISTLES

1 **SENECA LVCILIO SVO SALVTEM (DICIT):** "Seneca sends (lit., says) greetings to his Lucilius" was a felicitous combination of formal and informal address in letter writing among the Romans. Lucilius was Seneca's friend, to whom the philosopher addressed the *Epistulae Morales,* the *De Providentia,* and the *Naturales Quaestiones.* Born at Pompeii of humble origins, Lucilius advanced himself through diligence and hard work. He became a Roman knight as well as procurator in Sicily. He was also a devotee of philosophy and literature.

2 **fac:** an irregular imperative like *dic, duc, fer.*

7 **agentibus:** supply *nobis;* either dative of separation or ablative absolute.

8 **aliud:** "something different from what we should be doing."

12 **quidquid . . . est:** the object of *tenet; aetatis* is genitive of the whole.

13 **quod . . . scribis:** this clause is the object of *fac;* quod is used frequently in Latin where one would expect the fuller *id quod.*

13–14 **ut . . . pendeas:** the Latin said, more logically than we do, depend or be dependent from rather than upon.

14 **hodierno . . . inieceris**: *hodierno* is dative with the compound verb; *manum inicio* is a technical term meaning "to lay one's hand upon and thus claim as one's own." Runaway slaves were thus legally reclaimed.

17–18 **ex qua . . . vult:** "from which [possession] anyone who desires evicts us"; i.e., if we do not carefully guard our time, people will snatch it from us.

18–20 **ut . . . patiantur:** *sed* should be understood after this clause; *inputari* is a technical term in accounting. It means "to enter or be charged to one's account." Seneca indicates here that men permit things which are easily replaced to be charged to their account, while time, man's most valuable asset and only possession, is not even recorded in his books.

21 **cum interim:** "when as a matter of fact."

25 **ratio . . . inpensae:** another technical term in accounting. Lit., "the reckoning of the expense to me stands [correct]"; i.e., my account in this matter balances.

32 **sera . . . est:** a Latin proverb meaning "it's too late to be frugal when you reach the bottom of the cask."

2 **vindico,** 1, claim, set free
  adhuc, *adv.,* until now
3 **aufero, auferre, abstuli, abla-tus,** 3, take away, remove
6 **iactura, -ae,** *f.,* a throwing away; loss
7 **adtendo, -ere, -tendi, -tentus,** 3, pay attention
  elabor, -i, -lapsus, 3 *dep.,* slip away
10 **aestimo,** 1, value
  fallo, -ere, fefelli, falsus, 3, deceive
11 **praetereo, -ire, -ivi (-ii),** *irr.,* go by, pass by
13 **complector, -i, -plexus,** 3 *dep.,* embrace
14 **crastinus, -a, -um,** *adj.,* of the morrow, tomorrow's
  crastinum, -i, *n.,* the morrow, tomorrow
  hodiernus, -a, -um, *adj.,* of or relating to today
  hodiernum, -i, *n.,* today
15 **differo, differre, distuli, dilatus,** *irr.,* delay
16 **tantum,** *adv.,* only
17 **lubricus, -a, -um,** *adj.,* slippery
18 **stultitia, -ae,** *f.,* foolishness
19 **inpetro,** 1, obtain
21 **ne. . .quidem,** not. . .even
23 **fortasse,** *adv.,* perhaps
  praecipio, -ere, -cepi, -ceptus, 3, advise, teach
24 **ingenue,** *adv.,* frankly
  apud, *prep. w. acc.,* in the case of
27 **plerique, -aeque, -aque,** *adj.,* very many
28 **inopia, -ae,** *f.,* poverty
  redigo, -ere, -egi, -actus, 3, reduce
  ignosco, -ere, -novi, -notus, 3, pardon
29 **succurro, -ere, -curri, -cursus,** 3, help
30 **supersum, -esse, -fui,** *irr.,* be left, remain
32 **fundus, -i,** *m.,* bottom
33 **imus, -a, -um,** *superl.* (of *inferus*), lowest

Epistle One
THE VALUE OF TIME

Seneca Lucilio Suo Salutem

Ita fac, mi Lucili: vindica te tibi, et tempus quod adhuc aut auferebatur aut subripiebatur aut excidebat collige et serva. Persuade tibi hoc sic esse ut scribo: quaedam tempora eripiuntur nobis, quaedam subducuntur, quaedam effluunt. 5
Turpissima tamen est iactura quae per neglegentiam fit. Et si volueris adtendere, magna pars vitae elabitur male agentibus, maxima nihil agentibus, tota vita aliud agentibus. Quem mihi dabis qui aliquod pretium tempori ponat, qui diem aestimet, qui intellegat se cotidie mori? In hoc enim fallimur, 10
quod mortem prospicimus: magna pars eius iam praeteriit; quidquid aetatis retro est mors tenet. Fac ergo, mi Lucili, quod facere te scribis, omnes horas conplectere; sic fiet ut minus ex crastino pendeas, si hodierno manum inieceris.
Dum differtur vita transcurrit. Omnia, Lucili, aliena sunt, 15
tempus tantum nostrum est; in huius rei unius fugacis ac lubricae possessionem natura nos misit, ex qua expellit quicumque vult. Et tanta stultitia mortalium est ut quae minima et vilissima sunt, certe reparabilia, inputari sibi cum inpetravere patiantur, nemo se iudicet quicquam debere qui 20
tempus accepit, cum interim hoc unum est quod ne gratus quidem potest reddere.

Interrogabis fortasse quid ego faciam qui tibi ista praecipio. Fatebor ingenue: quod apud luxuriosum sed diligentem evenit, ratio mihi constat inpensae. Non possum dicere nihil 25
perdere, sed quid perdam et quare et quemadmodum dicam; causas paupertatis meae reddam. Sed evenit mihi quod plerisque non suo vitio ad inopiam redactis: omnes ignoscunt, nemo succurrit. Quid ergo est ? non puto pauperem cui quantulumcumque superest sat est; tu tamen malo serves 30
tua, et bono tempore incipies. Nam ut visum est maioribus nostris, 'sera parsimonia in fundo est'; non enim tantum minimum in imo sed pessimum remanet. *Vale.*

3 **discurris:** *dis-* and *di-* are the regular particles used in compounds to denote "this way and that," "hither and thither."

11 **ut . . . habeant:** this clause explains the preceding *hoc.*

12 **necesse est:** the subjunctive without *ut* sometimes follows *necesse est.*

   nullius: i.e., of no author.

16 **medicamenta:** i.e., different and various kinds of medicines.

18 **Distringit:** see note to line 3.

21 **evolvere:** the regular and correct verb for this idea, if one recalls the construction of a Roman book.

35 **alieno imminet:** lit., "hangs over," i.e., "yearns for another's property."

4 **inquieto,** 1, disturb
  iactatio, -onis, *f.*, tossing to and fro, restlessness
5 **consisto, -ere, -stiti, -stitus,** 3, stay in one place
6 **moror,** 1 *dep.*, linger
  lectio, -onis, *f.*, reading
9 **nusquam,** *adv.*, nowhere
10 **ubique,** *adv.*, everywhere
  exigo, -ere, -egi, -actus, 3, spend, pass
11 **hospitium, -i,** *n.*, hospitality, inn, hospitable reception
12 **ingenium, -i,** *n.*, genius, mind
13 **transmitto, -ere, -misi, -missus,** 3, pass through
  prosum, prodesse, profui, *irr.*, help
14 **sumo, -ere, sumpsi, sumptus,** 3, take
15 **aeque. . .quam,** equally. . .as
16 **cicatrix, -icis,** *f.*, scar
18 **transitus, -us,** *m.*, passing
  distringo, -ere, -trinxi, -trictus, 3, distract
20 **modo,** *adv.*, now
21 **fastidiens, -entis,** *p. adj.*, squeamish
22 **degusto,** 1, taste
  inquino, 1, pollute
23 **alo, -ere, alui, alitus (altus),** 3, nourish
  quando, *adv.*, at any time
24 **adversus,** *prep. w. acc.*, against
25 **comparo,** 1, prepare, obtain
27 **excerpo, -ere, -cerpsi, -cerptus,** 3, pick out
  concoquo, -ere, -coxi, -coctus, 3, digest
28 **adprehendo, -ere, -hendi, -hensus,** 3, seize upon
  hodiernus, -a, -um, *adj.*, of *or* relating to today
  hodiernum, -i, *n.*, today
29 **apud,** *prep. w. acc.*, in the works of
  nanciscor, -i, nanctus (nactus), 3 *dep.*, come upon, find
30 **tamquam,** *adv.*, as if
  transfuga, -ae, *c.*, deserter
32 **parum,** *adv.*, little
33 **refert, referre, retulit,** *impers.*, it makes a difference
34 **arca, -ae,** *f.*, money box
  horreum, -i, *n.*, granary
  pasco, -ere, pavi, pastus, 3, graze
35 **fenero (faenero),** 1, lend on interest
36 **modus, -i,** *m.*, limit
37 **proximus, -a, -um,** *superl.* (of *propior*), next

Epistle Two
HE IS NOWHERE WHO IS EVERYWHERE

Seneca Lucilio Suo Salutem

Ex iis quae mihi scribis et ex iis quae audio bonam spem
de te concipio: non discurris nec locorum mutationibus
inquietaris. Aegri animi ista iactatio est: primum argumentum compositae mentis existimo posse consistere et secum   5
morari. Illud autem vide, ne ista lectio auctorum multorum
et omnis generis voluminum habeat aliquid vagum et instabile.
Certis ingeniis inmorari et innutriri oportet, si velis aliquid
trahere quod in animo fideliter sedeat. Nusquam est qui
ubique est. Vitam in peregrinatione exigentibus hoc evenit,   10
ut multa hospitia habeant, nullas amicitias; idem accidat
necesse est iis qui nullius se ingenio familiariter applicant
sed omnia cursim et properantes transmittunt. Non prodest
cibus nec corpori accedit qui statim sumptus emittitur; nihil
aeque sanitatem inpedit quam rcmediorum crebra mutatio;   15
non venit vulnus ad cicatricem in quo medicamenta temptan-
tur; non convalescit planta quae saepe transfertur; nihil tam
utile est ut in transitu prosit. Distringit librorum multitudo;
itaque cum legere non possis quantum habueris, satis est
habere quantum legas. 'Sed modo' inquis 'hunc librum   20
evolvere volo, modo illum.' Fastidientis stomachi est multa
degustare; quae ubi varia sunt et diversa, inquinant non
alunt. Probatos itaque semper lege, et si quando ad alios
deverti libuerit, ad priores redi. Aliquid cotidie adversus
paupertatem, aliquid adversus mortem auxili compara, nec   25
minus adversus ceteras pestes; et cum multa percurreris,
unum excerpe quod illo die concoquas. Hoc ipse quoque
facio; ex pluribus quae legi aliquid adprehendo. Hodiernum
hoc est quod apud Epicurum nanctus sum (soleo enim et in
aliena castra transire, non tamquam transfuga, sed tamquam   30
explorator): 'honesta' inquit 'res est laeta paupertas'. Illa
vero non est paupertas, si laeta est; non qui parum habet,
sed qui plus cupit, pauper est. Quid enim refert quantum illi
in arca, quantum in horreis iaceat, quantum pascat aut
feneret, si alieno imminet, si non adquisita sed adquirenda   35
conputat ? Quis sit divitiarum modus quaeris? primus habere
quod necesse est, proximus quod sat est. *Vale.*

9 **hac abierit:** "that's O.K."; lit., "in this way, it will pass."

12 **sed de ipso prius:** "but first [reflect] about [the man] himself."

14 **Theophrasti:** Theophrastus (c. 372–c. 288 B.C.), disciple of Aristotle who succeeded him as head of the Peripatetic School. Theophrastus composed more than 200 treatises on philosophy, natural history, and rhetoric. Besides fragments, his only remaining works are his *Researches on Plants, Causes of Plants,* and his famous *Moral Characters,* a collection of 31 character sketches portraying human weaknesses and foibles.

16 **Cum placuerit fieri:** i.e., *cum tibi placuerit eum amicum fieri.*

18–19 **Tu . . . possis:** i.e., live so honorably that even an enemy could find no fault with you.

22 **docuerunt:** supply *homines* as direct object.

23 **et illi . . . fecerunt:** "and by being suspicious. they have granted [men] the right to commit wrong": *illi* is nom. pl.

37 **apud:** in citing an author, *apud,* "in the works of," "in the writings of," is regularly used. *Pomponium:* possibly Pomponius Secundus, writer of tragedies and epistles, one of Seneca's contemporaries. Pliny the Elder wrote his biography, and Quintilian considered him the best tragic poet of his day. Nothing of his work survives save the title of one of his plays.

37 **animo mandabitur:** supply *a te.*

39–40 **quiescenti . . . agenti:** datives of agent.

2 **perfero, -ferre, -tuli, -latus,** *irr.,* deliver

4 **ne. . .quidem,** not. . .even

7 **quomodo,** *adv.,* in which manner, as

8 **obvius, -a, -um,** *adj.,* meeting, at hand,
obvius, -i, *m.,* one whom we meet
succurro, -ere, -curri, -cursus, 3, occur [to one's mind]
dominus, -i, *m.,* sir

10 **tantundem,** *adv.,* as much
quantum, *adv.,* as

12 **delibero,** 1, weigh carefully, consider

13 **praeposterus, -a, -um,** *adj.,* in a reversed order
permisceo, -ere, -miscui, -mixtus, 2, confuse

15 **an,** *conj.,* whether

18 **committo, -ere, -misi, -missus,** 3, entrust

20 **intervenio, -venire, -veni, -ventus,** 4, come up, happen
arcanus, -a, -um, *adj.,* secret

22 **fallo, -ere, fefelli, falsus,** 3, deceive

24 **coram,** *prep. w. abl.,* in the presence of

25 **tantum,** *adv.,* only

26 **quilibet, quae-, quod-,** *indef. adj.,* any

27 **uro, -ere, ussi, ustus,** 3, burn
exonero, 1, unload
rursus, *adv.,* on the other hand

28 **conscientia, -ae,** *f.,* a sharing of knowledge
reformido, 1, fear

29 **interius,** *comp. adj.,* deep within

30 **uterque, utraque, utrumque,** *adj.,* each

31 **alter. . .alter,** the one. . .the other

32 **reprehendo, -ere, -prehendi, -prehensus,** 3, reprimand

34 **exagitatus, -a, -um,** *adj.,* stirred up, agitated

35 **concursatio, -onis,** *f.,* running about, restlessness

36 **molestia, -ae,** *f.,* annoyance
dissolutio, -onis, *f.,* lethargy

38 **latebra, -ae,** *f.,* hiding, hiding-place, darkness
turbidus, -a, -um, *adj.,* confused.
turbidum, -i, *n.,* confusion

Epistle Three

Epistle Three
ON FRIENDSHIP

Seneca Lucilio Suo Salutem

Epistulas ad me perferendas tradidisti, ut scribis, amico
tuo; deinde admones me ne omnia cum eo ad te pertinentia
communicem, quia non soleas ne ipse quidem id facere: ita
eadem epistula illum et dixisti amicum et negasti. Itaque si   5
proprio illo verbo quasi publico usus es et sic illum amicum
vocasti quomodo omnes candidatos 'bonos viros' dicimus,
quomodo obvios, si nomen non succurrit, 'dominos' saluta-
mus, hac abierit. Sed si aliquem amicum existimas cui non
tantundem credis quantum tibi, vehementer erras et non   10
satis nosti vim verae amicitiae. Tu vero omnia cum amico
delibera, sed de ipso prius: post amicitiam credendum est,
ante amicitiam iudicandum. Isti vero praepostero officia per-
miscent qui, contra praecepta Theophrasti, cum amaverunt
iudicant, et non amant cum iudicaverint. Diu cogita an   15
tibi in amicitiam aliquis recipiendus sit. Cum placuerit fieri,
toto illum pectore admitte; tam audaciter cum illo loquere
quam tecum. Tu quidem ita vive ut nihil tibi committas
nisi quod committere etiam inimico tuo possis; sed quia
interveniunt quaedam quae consuetudo fecit arcana, cum   20
amico omnes curas, omnes cogitationes tuas misce. Fidelem
si putaveris, facies; nam quidam fallere docuerunt dum
timent falli, et illi ius peccandi suspicando fecerunt. Quid est
quare ego ulla verba coram amico meo retraham? quid est
quare me coram illo non putem solum? Quidam quae tantum   25
amicis committenda sunt obviis narrant, et in quaslibet
aures quidquid illos urit exonerant; quidam rursus etiam
carissimorum conscientiam reformidant et, si possent, ne
sibi quidem credituri interius premunt omne secretum.
Neutrum faciendum est; utrumque enim vitium est, et   30
omnibus credere et nulli, sed alterum honestius dixerim
vitium, alterum tutius. Sic utrosque reprehendas, et eos qui
semper inquieti sunt, et eos qui semper quiescunt. Nam illa
tumultu gaudens non est industria sed exagitatae mentis
concursatio, et haec non est quies quae motum omnem   35
molestiam iudicat, sed dissolutio et languor. Itaque hoc quod
apud Pomponium legi animo mandabitur: 'quidam adeo in
latebras refugerunt ut putent in turbido esse quidquid in luce
est'. Inter se ista miscenda sunt: et quiescenti agendum et
agenti quiescendum est. Cum rerum natura delibera: illa   40
dicet tibi et diem fecisse se et noctem. *Vale.*

19 **nostri:** genitive of the whole (partitive genitive) after *nihil*.

21–22 **a qua . . . separabit:** "a lack of similarity [in mores] will prevent us from [keeping] this promise"; *qua = hac*. Recall such phrases as *quae cum ita sint*, translated "since these things are so," where the relative pronoun is used instead of the demonstrative.

24 **secundum naturam vivere:** "to live according to nature" is the keynote of Stoic philosophy. By this phrase, the Stoics mean that one must strive to live according to reason, the highest good in man, the distinguishing characteristic of man and God. To the Stoics, Reason is identical with Nature, God, and Providence. The more man perfects his Reason, the closer he comes to God, who is perfected rationality.

28 **non magno:** ablative of price, "at no great cost."

30 **non incompta:** an example of LITOTES (a figure of speech that asserts the negative of its opposite), lit., "not inelegant" (i.e., "elegant").

38–39 **pati . . . divitias:** an example of PARA PROSDOKIAN (a figure of speech with which an author introduces a turn contrary to what is expected). The reader would have expected *frugalitatem* instead of *divitias*.

---

2 **pertinaciter,** *adv.*, constantly
3 **ago, -ere, egi, actus,** 3, be concerned with
  cotidie, *adv.*, daily
4 **tantum,** *adv.*, only
5 **proficio, -ere, -feci, -fectus,** 3, make progress
  conspicio, -ere, -spexi, -spectus, 3, notice
6 **habitus, -us,** *m.*, appearance
7 **notabilis, -e,** *adj.*, ostentatious
  asper, -era, -erum, *adj.*, rough
  cultus, -us, *m.*, attire
  intonsus, -a, -um, *adj.*, unshorn
8 **barba, -ae,** *f.*, beard
  cubile, -is, *n.*, bed
  humus, -i, *f.*, ground, **humi,** on the ground
9 **ambitio, -onis,** *f.*, ostentation
10 **evito,** 1, avoid
11 **invidiosus, -a, -um,** *adj.*, odious
  consuetudo, -inis, *f.*, custom
12 **excerpo, -ere, -cerpsi, -cerptus,** 3, withdraw
  intus, *adv.*, within
  frons, frontis, *f.*, outward appearance
13 **convenio, -ire, -veni, -ventus,** 4, be suitable
  splendeo, -ere, -ui, 2, shine
14 **caelatura, -ae,** *f.*, carving
17 **alioquin,** *adv.*, otherwise
  emendo, 1, improve
18 **fugo,** 1, put to flight
20 **sensus, -us,** *m.*, feeling
21 **congregatio, -onis,** *f.*, sociability
23 **nempe,** *conj.*, to be sure
25 **torqueo, -ere, torsi, tortus,** 2, twist, torment
  munditia, -ae, *f.*, cleanliness, neatness
26 **vilis, -e,** *adj.*, cheap
27 **taeter, -ra, -rum,** *adj.*, nauseating
  quemadmodum, *adv.*, just as
28 **usitatus, -a, -um,** *adj.*, customary
29 **exigo, -ere, -egi, -actus,** 3, demand
31 **suspicio, -ere, -spexi, -spectus,** 3, look up to, esteem
32 **agnosco, -ere, -novi, -nitus,** 3, understand
33 **intersum, -esse, -fui,** *irr.*, be different
35 **potius,** *adv.*, rather
  quam, *adv.*, than
  suppellex, -lectilis, *f.*, furniture
36 **fictile, -is,** *n.*, earthenware

Epistle Five

Epistle Five
THE GOLDEN MEAN

Seneca Lucilio Suo Salutem

Quod pertinaciter studes et omnibus omissis hoc unum
agis, ut te meliorem cotidie facias, et probo et gaudeo, nec
tantum hortor ut perseveres sed etiam rogo. Illud autem te
admoneo, ne eorum more qui non proficere sed conspici   5
cupiunt facias aliqua quae in habitu tuo aut genere vitae
notabilia sint; asperum cultum et intonsum caput et negle-
gentiorem barbam et indictum argento odium et cubile humi
positum et quidquid aliud ambitionem perversa via sequitur
evita. Satis ipsum nomen philosophiae, etiam si modeste   10
tractetur, invidiosum est: quid si nos hominum consuetudini
coeperimus excerpere? Intus omnia dissimilia sint, frons
populo nostra conveniat. Non splendeat toga, ne sordeat
quidem; non habeamus argentum in quod solidi auri caelatura descenderit, sed non putemus frugalitatis indicium auro 15
argentoque caruisse. Id agamus ut meliorem vitam sequamur
quam vulgus, non ut contrariam: alioquin quos emendari
volumus fugamus a nobis et avertimus; illud quoque efficimus,
ut nihil imitari velint nostri, dum timent ne imitanda sint omnia.
Hoc primum philosophia promittit, sensum communem,   20
humanitatem et congregationem; a qua professione dissimilitudo nos separabit. Videamus ne ista per quae admira-
tionem parare volumus ridicula et odiosa sint. Nempe propositum nostrum est secundum naturam vivere: hoc contra
naturam est, torquere corpus suum et faciles odisse munditias 25
et squalorem adpetere et cibis non tantum vilibus uti sed
taetris et horridis. Quemadmodum desiderare delicatas res
luxuriaest, ita usitatas et non magno parabiles fugere demen-
tiae. Frugalitatem exigit philosophia, non poenam; potest
autem esse non incompta frugalitas. Hic mihi modus placet: 30
temperetur vita inter bonos mores et publicos; suspiciant
omnes vitam nostram sed agnoscant. 'Quid ergo ? eadem
faciemus quae ceteri? nihil inter nos et illos intererit?' Plurimum: dissimiles esse nos vulgo sciat qui inspexerit propius;
qui domum intraverit nos potius miretur quam supellectilem   35
nostram. Magnus ille est qui fictilibus sic utitur quemadmodum argento, nec ille minor est qui sic argento utitur
quemadmodum fictilibus; infirmi animi est pati non posse
divitias.

41   **Hecatonem:** Hecato of Rhodes, Stoic philosopher of the first century B.C., pupil of Panaetius.

41–42   **etiam ad. . .proficere:** "helps also as a remedy against fear."

45   **custodiam et militem:** *custodiam,* in the sense of "prisoner," is a post-Augustan usage. To prevent a prisoner from escaping, a common chain linked together both the prisoner and the soldier who held him in custody.

40   **lucellum, -i,** *n.,* small profit
41   **apud,** *prep. w. acc.,* in the works of
42   **desino, -ere, -sivi (-sii), -situs,** 3, cease
43   **pariter,** *adv.,* alike
44   **dissideo, -ere, -sedi, -sessus,** 2, be different
45   **catena, -ae,** *f.,* chain
     custodia, -ae, *f.,* prisoner
46   **copulo,** 1, link
     pariter, *adv.,* together
47   **uterque, utraque, utrumque,** *adj.,* each
48   **sollicitus, -a, -um,** *adj.,* full of anxiety
49   **quod,** *conj.,* the fact that
50   **apto,** 1, fit, adapt
52   **fera, -ae,** *f.,* wild beast

Sed ut huius quoque diei lucellum tecum communicem,   40
apud Hecatonem nostrum inveni cupiditatum finem etiam
ad timoris remedia proficere. 'Desines' inquit 'timere, si
sperare desieris.' Dices, 'quomodo ista tam diversa pariter
sunt?' Ita est, mi Lucili: cum videantur dissidere, coniuncta
sunt. Quemadmodum eadem catena et custodiam et militem   45
copulat, sic ista quae tam dissimilia sunt pariter incedunt:
spem metus sequitur. Nec miror ista sic ire: utrumque
pendentis animi est, utrumque futuri expectatione solliciti.
Maxima autem utriusque causa est quod non ad praesentia
aptamur sed cogitationes in longinqua praemittimus; itaque   50
providentia, maximum bonum condicionis humanae, in
malum versa est. Ferae pericula quae vident fugiunt, cum
effugere, securae sunt: nos et venturo torquemur et praeterito.
Multa bona nostra nobis nocent; timoris enim tormentum
memoria reducit, providentia anticipat; nemo tantum prae-   55
sentibus miser est. *Vale.*

4–5 Quidni. . .attolli: "why would I not have (i.e., of course I have) many qualities [in me] that should be reorganized—some played down, some played up."

10 illius verae: these words and *illius* in the following line refer to *amicitiae*.

14 honesta: direct object of *cupiendi*.

16 et. . .adversa: "and what's more [they know that they have] adversity [in common]."

17 quantum momenti: "how much change."

20 in hoc: "for this purpose"; *hoc* is accusative.

25 ne. . .inpendas: "in order that you may not expend much effort."

28 in rem. . .oportet: "it is necessary that you go to the circumstances at hand." The subjunctive without *ut* sometimes follows *oportet*.

31 Zenonem. . .expressisset: Zeno (335–263 B.C.), founder of the Stoic School at Athens. Cleanthes (331–232 B.C.), successor to Zeno as head of the Stoic School. Cleanthes reproduces (*exprimit*) the image of his teacher, Zeno.

32–33 observavit. . .viveret: "he (Cleanthes) observed whether he (Zeno) lived according to his own rule." The more usual construction would be: *et observavit, an is ex formula sua viveret.*

35–36 Metrodorum. . .Epicuri: Epicurus (341–270 B.C.), founder of the Epicurean School. Metrodorus, Hermarchus, and Polyacnus were disciples of Epicurus.

37 in hoc: see note to line 20.

37 prosis: supply *mihi.*

40 Hecatonem: Hecato of Rhodes, Stoic philosopher of the first century B.C., pupil of Panaetius.

42 Scito: "know," future imperative of *scio, -ire.*

2 **tantum,** *adv.*, only
3 **supersum, -esse, -fui,** *irr.*, be left, remain
5 **argumentum, -i,** *n.*, proof
6 **translatus, -a, -um,** p. *adj.* (of **transfero**), transferred
  quod, *conj.*, the fact that
  adhuc, *adv.*, up to this point
7 **aeger, -ra, -rum,** *adj.*, sick
10 **fiducia, -ae,** *f.*, confidence
11 **utilitas, -atis,** *f.*, interest
  divello, -ere, -velli, -vulsus, 3, tear asunder
15 **quidni,** *adv.*, why not?, of course
19 **experior, -iri, expertus,** 4 *dep.*, try, test, find
  transfundo, -ere, -fudi, -fusus, 3, pour, heap
20 **disco, -ere, didici,** 3, learn
21 **licet,** although
  eximius, -a, -um, *adj.*, extraordinary
25 **passim,** *adv.*, everywhere
  prosum, prodesse, profui, *irr.*, be useful
26 **protinus,** *adv.*, at once
27 **convictus, -us,** *m.*, intimacy
  oratio, -onis, *f.*, set speech
29 **amplius,** *comp.* (of **ample**), more
31 **tantummodo,** *adv.*, only
33 **diversus, -a, -um,** *adj.*, different
  in diversum, in different directions
36 **contubernium, -i,** *n.*, dwelling together
37 **accerso (arcesso), -ere, -ivi, -itus,** 3, summon
  proficio, -ere, -feci, -fectus, 3, make progress
39 **diurnus, -a, -um,** *adj.*, daily
  mercedula, -ae, *f.*, small reward
40 **apud,** *prep. w. acc.*, in the works of

Epistle Six

Epistle Six
THE JOY OF SHARING ONE'S POSSESSIONS
WITH ONE'S FRIENDS

Seneca Lucilio Suo Salutem

Intellego, Lucili, non emendari me tantum sed transfi-
gurari; nec hoc promitto iam aut spero, nihil in me superesse
quod mutandum sit. Quidni multa habeam quae debeant
colligi, quae extenuari, quae attolli? Et hoc ipsum argumen-   5
tum est in melius translati animi, quod vitia sua quae adhuc
ignorabat videt; quibusdam aegris gratulatio fit cum ipsi
aegros se esse senserunt. Cuperem itaque tecum communicare
tam subitam mutationem mei; tunc amicitiae nostrae certio-
rem fiduciam habere coepissem, illius verae quam non spes,   10
non timor, non utilitatis suae cura divellit, illius cum qua
homines moriuntur, pro qua moriuntur. Multos tibi dabo
qui non amico sed amicitia caruerint: hoc non potest accidere
cum animos in societatem honesta cupiendi par voluntas trahit. Quidni non possit? sciunt enim ipsos omnia habere   15
communia, et quidem magis adversa.

Concipere animo non potes quantum momenti adferre
mihi singulos dies videam. 'Mitte' inquis 'et nobis ista quae
tam efficacia expertus es.' Ego vero omnia in te cupio trans-
fundere, et in hoc aliquid gaudeo discere, ut doceam; nec me   20
ulla res delectabit, licet sit eximia et salutaris, quam mihi uni
sciturus sum. Si cum hac exceptione detur sapientia, ut illam
inclusam teneam nec enuntiem, reiciam: nullius boni sine
socio iucunda possessio est. Mittam itaque ipsos tibi libros,
et ne multum operae inpendas dum passim profutura sectaris,   25
inponam notas, ut ad ipsa protinus quae probo et miror
accedas. Plus tamen tibi et viva vox et convictus quam oratio
proderit; in rem praesentem venias oportet, primum quia
homines amplius oculis quam auribus credunt, deinde quia
longum iter est per praecepta, breve et efficax per exempla.   30
Zenonem Cleanthes non expressisset, si tantummodo audisset:
vitae eius interfuit, secreta perspexit, observavit illum, an ex
formula sua viveret. Platon et Aristoteles et omnis in diversum itura sapientium turba plus ex moribus quam ex verbis
Socratis traxit; Metrodorum et Hermarchum et Polyaenum   35
magnos viros non schola Epicuri sed contubernium fecit. Nec
in hoc te accerso tantum, ut proficias, sed ut prosis; plurimum
enim alter alteri conferemus.

Interim quoniam diurnam tibi mercedulam debeo, quid
me hodie apud Hecatonem delectaverit dicam. 'Quaeris'   40
inquit 'quid profecerim? amicus esse mihi coepi.' Multum
profecit: numquam erit solus. Scito esse hunc amicum
omnibus. *Vale.*

6 **Quod:** the antecedent of *quod* is *hoc* (following line). Latin prefers the relative to the demonstrative pronoun at the beginning of a sentence or clause.

9 **nemo non:** "everyone"; an example of LITOTES.

10 **nescientibus:** dative in agreement with the ind. obj., *nobis.*

16 **meridianum spectaculum:** gladiatorial combats lasted an entire day and to prevent tedium were varied in form. In the morning wild animals fought against wild animals, or men (called *bestiarii*) fought against such animals. In the afternoon, trained gladiators fought one another. In between these morning and afternoon combats, there was a *spectaculum meridianum* which was supposed to relieve the heaviness of the other two by furnishing, as Seneca says, *lusus* ("light entertainment"), *sales* ("wit"), *et aliquid laxamenti* ("some relaxation"). But instead, one came upon even greater butchery. Condemned criminals with no defensive armor were forced into the arena to divert the audience.

18 **ante:** i.e., at the morning spectacle.

22 **ordinariis paribus et postulaticiis:** "to ordinary pairs [of gladiators] and [to pairs] on request": *postulaticiis* refers to unusual fighters kept on reserve to satisfy an audience's demand for encores.

22–23 **Quidni praeferant:** "Why should they not prefer it?" i.e., of course they prefer it.

23 **Quo:** "to what end," "for what purpose"; *quo* is a causal ablative.

26 **iubent:** supply *spectatores* as subject of this verb.

27 **exitus. . .est:** i.e., death was the only thing these fighters might hope for, since each was required to keep fighting until he met his superior.

27–28 **Ferro. . .geritur:** "the whole affair is carried on with sword and fire." These condemned criminals were forced out into the arena with swords and red hot brands.

30 **quid meruisti:** lit., "what have you deserved," where the meaning is "what have you done to deserve" to see this.

31 **Occide, verbera, ure:** commands addressed by the audience to those designated to drive the condemned criminals with sword, lash, and fire into the encounter. See note to lines 27–28.

2 **praecipue,** *adv.,* especially
turba, -ae, *f.,* crowd
3 **nondum,** *adv.,* not yet
tuto, *adv.,* safely
inbecillitas, -atis, *f.,* weakness
5 **compono, -ere, -posui, -positus,** 3, put in order
fugo, 1, put to flight
6 **aeger, -ra, -rum,** *adj.,* sick
usque, *adv.,* all the way
eo, *adv.,* to such a pitch
7 **offensa, -ae,** *f.,* harm
8 **reficio, -ere, -feci, -fectus,** 3, restore
9 **conversatio, -onis,** *f.,* association
10 **adlino, -ere, -levi, -litus,** 3, smear on
utique, *adv.,* certainly
11 **quo. . .hoc = quanto. . .tanto,** the. . .the
12 **damnosus, -a, -um,** *adj.,* harmful
spectaculum, -i, *n.,* show
13 **desido, -ere, -sedi,** 3, settle down
subrepo, -ere, -repsi, -reptus, 3, creep in
15 **immo,** *adv.,* nay, rather
16 **casus, -us,** *m.,* chance, **casu =** **forte,** by chance
lusus, -us, *m.,* entertainment
17 **sal, -is,** *n.* and *m. in sing., m. always in pl.,* salt, wit
laxamentum, -i, *n.,* relaxation
18 **cruor, -oris,** *m.,* blood
19 **nugae, -arum,** *f.,* trifles
merus, -a, -um, *adj.,* pure
20 **ictus, -us,** *m.,* blow
21 **plerique, pleraeque, pleraque,** *adj.,* the majority
23 **galea, -ae,** *f.,* helmet
scutum, -i, *n.,* shield
munimentum, -i, *n.,* protective armor
24 **mora, -ae,** *f.,* delay
mane, *adv.,* in the morning
25 **meridie,** *adv.,* in the afternoon
28 **vaco,** 1, be empty
harena, -ae, *f.,* arena
latrocinium, -i, *n.,* highway robbery
31 **verbero,** 1, lash
32 **parum,** *adv.,* too little, not enough
33 **plaga, -ae,** *f.,* blow
34 **obvius, -a, -um,** *adj.,* exposed

Epistle Seven

Epistle Seven
AVOID THE CROWD

Seneca Lucilio Suo Salutem

Quid tibi vitandum praecipue existimes quaeris? turbam.
Nondum illi tuto committeris. Ego certe confitebor inbecillitatem meam: numquam mores quos extuli refero; aliquid
ex eo quod composui turbatur, aliquid ex iis quae fugavi redit.   5
Quod aegris evenit quos longa inbecillitas usque eo adfecit
ut nusquam sine offensa proferantur, hoc accidit nobis
quorum animi ex longo morbo reficiuntur. Inimica est
multorum conversatio: nemo non aliquod nobis vitium aut
commendat aut inprimit aut nescientibus adlinit. Utique quo   10
maior est populus cui miscemur, hoc periculi plus est. Nihil
vero tam damnosum bonis moribus quam in aliquo spectaculo
desidere; tunc enim per voluptatem facilius vitia subrepunt.
Quid me existimas dicere? avarior redeo, ambitiosior, luxurio-
sior? immo vero crudelior et inhumanior, quia inter homines   15
fui. Casu in meridianum spectaculum incidi, lusus expectans
et sales et aliquid laxamenti quo hominum oculi ab humano
cruore adquiescant. Contra est: quidquid ante pugnatum est
misericordia fuit; nunc omissis nugis mera homicidia sunt.
Nihil habent quo tegantur; ad ictum totis corporibus ex-   20
positi numquam frustra manum mittunt. Hoc plerique
ordinariis paribus et postulaticiis praeferunt. Quidni praeferant? non galea, non scuto repellitur ferrum. Quo munimen-
ta? quo artes? omnia ista mortis morae sunt. Mane leonibus
et ursis homines, meridie spectatoribus suis obiciuntur. Inter-   25
fectores interfecturis iubent obici et victorem in aliam detinent
caedem; exitus pugnantium mors est. Ferro et igne res
geritur. Haec fiunt dum vacat harena. 'Sed latrocinium fecit
aliquis, occidit hominem.' Quid ergo? quia occidit, ille
meruit ut hoc pateretur: tu quid meruisti miser ut hoc   30
spectes? 'Occide, verbera, ure! Quare tam timide incurrit in
ferrum? quare parum audacter occidit? quare parum libenter
moritur? Plagis agatur in vulnera, mutuos ictus nudis et
obviis pectoribus excipiant.' Intermissum est spectaculum:

35 **ne nihil agatur:** lit., "lest nothing be done," i.e., "that there may be no lull" in the excitement.

35–36 **ne. . .intellegitis:** Seneca is addressing the barbarian spectators who are shouting for blood and murder.

37–38 **Agite. . .discere:** Seneca is here employing a striking paradox: the performers in the brutal "show" are innocent, whereas it is the spectators he addresses who are cruel. Thus the meaning of this passage is: thank the gods that these poor men in the arena cannot learn the brutality and cruelty you are attempting to teach them. If they were so low by nature as to learn such lessons readily, the world would be a much worse place to live in than it is.

40 **transitur:** Latin is fond of this passive impersonal use of intransitive verbs. Constructed according to English idiom, it would be: *facile est transire ad plures.*

40 **Socrati:** this and the following datives are datives of separation.

40 **Catoni et Laelio:** Marcus Porcius Cato the Younger (95–46 B.C.) was an arch political opponent of Julius Caesar. When Caesar defeated Pompey in the battle of Thapsus, virtually becoming Emperor, Cato, staunch defender of liberty and the Republic, committed suicide. Seneca repeatedly extols Cato's noble character and often refers to him as the ideal Stoic sage. Gaius Laelius, an erudite man and well-known philosopher, surnamed the "Wise," was the personal friend of Scipio Africanus the Younger, conqueror of Carthage (146 B.C.). To Laelius, Cicero paid special honor by making him the principal speaker in the *De Amicitia.*

41–42 **nemo. . .ingenium:** "no one of us who cultivates his natural power to the greatest extent"; *cum maxime,* a rather frequent expression in Seneca, means "to the greatest extent," "however much," or sometimes "just now"; *concinnamus* agrees logically with *nostrum* rather than grammatically with *nemo.*

46 **candido et simplici:** dative in agreement with the other person implied in the use of *comes.* A dative plural modifying an understood *nobis* would be more in harmony with English idiom.

47 **adfricuit:** a gnomic perfect as if a present. This perfect is used to express a general truth and implies that what has happened once will happen again.

48–49 **aut imiteris aut oderis:** supply *populum* as object.

54 **Non est quod:** "there is no reason why." This expression is frequent in Silver Latin. It occurs again five lines down in this epistle. The verb in the *quod* clause is regularly in the subjunctive. The *non est* is equivalent to *non necesse est.* When it has this meaning, it is generally followed by an *ut* or, as here, *quod* clause. *Quod* may thus be seen beginning its encroachment upon the functions of *ut.*

54–55 **in medium:** supply *populum.*

58–59 **ad intellectum tui:** "to understand you"; *tui* is objective genitive.

35 **iugulo,** 1, cut the throat, kill
    age, come now!
    ne. . .quidem, not. . .even
38 **disco, -ere, didici,** 3, learn
39 **subduco, -ere, -duxi, -ductus,** 3, withdraw
    tener, -era, -erum, *adj.,* tender
40 **excutio, -ere, -cussi, -cussus,** 3, shake out
41 **adeo,** *adv.,* so
43 **comitatus, -us,** *m.,* retinue
44 **convictor, -oris,** *m.,* companion
45 **delicatus, -a, -um,** *adj.,* luxurious
    mollio, 4, soften
46 **quamvis,** *adv.,* however, although
47 **rubigo, -inis,** *m.,* rust
    adfrico, -are, -fricui, -fricatus, 1, rub on
48 **publice,** *adv.,* publicly, i.e., by the crowd
51 **quantum,** *adv.,* as far as
    versor, 1 *dep.,* associate
54 **publico,** 1, make public
    ingenium, -i, *n.,* talent
56 **merx, mercis,** *f.,* merchandise
58 **instituo, -ere, -stitui, -stitutus,** 3, train

Epistle Seven

'interim iugulentur homines, ne nihil agatur'. Age, ne hoc   35
quidem intellegitis, mala exempla in eos redundare qui
faciunt? Agite dis immortalibus gratias quod eum docetis
esse crudelem qui non potest discere.

Subducendus populo est tener animus et parum tenax recti:
facile transitur ad plures. Socrati et Catoni et Laelio excutere   40
morem suum dissimilis multitudo potuisset: adeo nemo no-
strum, qui cum maxime concinnamus ingenium, ferre impetum vitiorum tam magno comitatu venientium potest. Unum
exemplum luxuriae aut avaritiae multum mali facit: convictor
delicatus paulatim enervat et mollit, vicinus dives cupidita-   45
tem inritat, malignus comes quamvis candido et simplici
rubiginem suam adfricuit: quid tu accidere his moribus credis
in quos publice factus est impetus? Necesse est aut imiteris
aut oderis. Utrumque autem devitandum est: neve similis
malis fias, quia multi sunt, neve inimicus multis, quia dissi-   50
miles sunt. Recede in te ipse quantum potes; cum his versare
qui te meliorem facturi sunt, illos admitte quos tu potes
facere meliores. Mutuo ista fiunt, et homines dum docent
discunt. Non est quod te gloria publicandi ingenii producat in
medium, ut recitare istis velis aut disputare; quod facere te   55
vellem, si haberes isti populo idoneam mercem: nemo est qui
intellegere te possit. Aliquis fortasse, unus aut alter incidet,
et hic ipse formandus tibi erit instituendusque ad intellectum
tui. 'Cui ergo ista didici?' Non est quod timeas ne operam
perdideris, si tibi didicisti.   60

62–63 quae occurrunt. . .tria: "three excellent sayings which occur to me concerning approximately the same topic."

63 in debitum: "toward canceling my debt." In Epistle 2, Seneca had promised to share with Lucilius in every letter an outstanding quotation. He is sending three quotations in this letter. One is to pay the present debt, the other two are sent as payment "in advance" (*in antecessum*). Seneca describes the payment of these quotations by many financial terms.

64 Democritus: Democritus (c. 460–c. 360 B.C.), known as the "laughing philosopher," developed fully the atomic theory of matter, reducing everything to atoms and void. Epicurus was greatly indebted to him.

65 Bene et ille: supply *ait*.

66–67 quo. . .perventurae: lit., "whither looked so great attention to an art destined to reach a very few?" I.e., "what was the use of so great attention to an art destined to reach a very few?"

70 multis: supply *scribo*.

73–74 ecquid. . .tibi: "have you any reason why you should be pleased with yourself?"

64 antecessus, -us, *m.*, a going before, **in antecessum,** in advance
pro, *prep. w. abl.*, for, in place of, as good as
65 ambigo, -ere, 3, wander about, doubt, dispute
69 consors, -sortis, *adj.*, sharing in, partaking of
71 condo, -ere, -didi, -ditus, 3, store away
72 contemno, -ere, -tempsi, -temptus, 3, scorn
73 adsensio, -onis, *f.*, agreement, applause
74 introrsus, *adv.*, inwards

Sed ne soli mihi hodie didicerim, communicabo tecum
quae occurrunt mihi egregie dicta circa eundem fere sensum
tria, ex quibus unum haec epistula in debitum solvet, duo
in antecessum accipe. Democritus ait, 'unus mihi pro populo
est, et populus pro uno'. Bene et ille, quisquis fuit (ambigitur   65
enim de auctore), cum quaereretur ab illo quo tanta diligentia
artis spectaret ad paucissimos perventurae, 'satis sunt' inquit
'mihi pauci, satis est unus, satis est nullus'. Egregie hoc
tertium Epicurus, cum uni ex consortibus studiorum suorum
scriberet: 'haec' inquit 'ego non multis, sed tibi; satis enim   70
magnum alter alteri theatrum sumus'. Ista, mi Lucili, con-
denda in animum sunt, ut contemnas voluptatem ex plurium
adsensione venientem. Multi te laudant: ecquid habes cur
placeas tibi, si is es quem intellegant multi? introrsus bona
tua spectent. *Vale.*

7–8 adeo. . .rubor: "so did he blush from deep within."

8 Hic: i.e., rubor.

17–18 illo vitio. . .admonet: "and through that weakness admonishes even the most robust of her power."

23 Sulla: Sulla, distinguished leader of the aristocratic party, opponent of Marius, head of the democratic party. Sulla became dictator at Rome in 82 B.C.

24 Pompei: Gnaeus Pompeius, renowned for his military achievements, was called "Pompey the Great." He became consul in 70 B.C. In 60 B.C. he joined the so-called First Triumvirate—a private coalition formed by Caesar, Crassus, and himself which aimed to shape and to control affairs in Rome.

24–25 numquam non: "always"; an example of LITOTES.

25 Fabianum: Papirius Fabianus, of the Sextian School of philosophy, was one of Seneca's teachers.

28–29 quae. . .pronos: "which even if it does not rattle the inexperienced [yet] affects them [thus] if they are naturally prone to this tendency."

34 cum multum. . .diuque: "however much and however long."

2 **indoles, -is,** *f.,* natural disposition, nature
4 **profectus, -us,** *m.,* progress
gustus, -us, *m.,* taste
6 **subito,** *adv.,* suddenly
deprehendo, -ere, -prehendi, -prehensus, 3, catch off guard
verecundia, -ae, *f.,* modesty
7 **excutio, -ere, -cussi, -cussus,** 3, shake out
8 **quantum,** *adv.,* as far as
9 **exuo, -ere, -ui, -utus,** 3, strip off, shake off
11 **ponuntur = deponuntur**
lenio, 4, assuage
13 **sudor, -oris,** *m.,* sweat
aliter, *adv.,* otherwise
14 **aestuo,** 1, be hot
genu, -us, *n.,* knee
15 **collido, -ere, -lisi, -lisus,** 3, dash together
titubo, 1, falter
labrum, -i, *n.,* lip
16 **usus, -us,** *m.,* experience
18 **rubor, -oris,** *m.,* blushing
19 **subitus, -a, -um,** *adj.,* sudden
adfundo, -ere, -fudi, -fusus, 3, pour on, spread on
20 **tener, -era, -erum,** *adj.,* tender, youthful
frons, frontis, *f.,* brow
nihilominus, *adv.,* nevertheless
22 **erubesco, -ere, erubui,** 3, redden, blush
quasi, *adv.,* as if
23 **effundo, -ere, -fudi, -fusus,** 3, pour out
24 **mollis, -e,** *adj.,* soft
25 **coram,** *prep. w. abl.,* in the presence of
utique, *adv.,* especially
contio, -onis, *f.,* meeting
26 **testis, -is,** *c.,* witness
27 **decet, -ere, decuit,** *impers.,* 2, it fits, it becomes
28 **inexercitatus, -a, -um,** *adj.,* inexperienced
29 **concutio, -ere, -cussi, -cussus,** 3, shake, agitate
31 **cito,** *adv.,* quickly
32 **abigo, -ere, -egi, -actus,** 3, drive away
alioquin, *adv.,* otherwise

Epistle Eleven
WISDOM UNABLE TO SUPPRESS NATURAL EMOTIONS

Seneca Lucilio Suo Salutem

Locutus est mecum amicus tuus bonae indolis, in quo quantum esset animi, quantum ingenii, quantum iam etiam profectus, sermo primus ostendit. Dedit nobis gustum, ad quem respondebit; non enim ex praeparato locutus est, sed subito deprehensus. Ubi se colligebat, verecundiam, bonum in adulescente signum, vix potuit excutere; adeo illi ex alto suffusus est rubor. Hic illum, quantum suspicor, etiam cum se confirmaverit et omnibus vitiis exuerit, sapientem quoque sequetur. Nulla enim sapientia naturalia corporis aut animi vitia ponuntur: quidquid infixum et ingenitum est lenitur arte, non vincitur. Quibusdam etiam constantissimis in conspectu populi sudor erumpit non aliter quam fatigatis et aestuantibus solet, quibusdam tremunt genua dicturis, quorundam dentes colliduntur, lingua titubat, labra concurrunt: haec nec disciplina nec usus umquam excutit, sed natura vim suam exercet et illo vitio sui etiam robustissimos admonet. Inter haec esse et ruborem scio, qui gravissimis quoque viris subitus adfunditur. Magis quidem in iuvenibus apparet, quibus et plus caloris est et tenera frons; nihilominus et veteranos et senes tangit. Quidam numquam magis quam cum erubuerint timendi sunt, quasi omnem verecundiam effuderint; Sulla tunc erat violentissimus cum faciem eius sanguis invaserat. Nihil erat mollius ore Pompei; numquam non coram pluribus rubuit, utique in contionibus. Fabianum, cum in senatum testis esset inductus, erubuisse memini, et hic illum mire pudor decuit. Non accidit hoc ab infirmitate mentis sed a novitate rei, quae inexercitatos, etiam si non concutit, movet naturali in hoc facilitate corporis pronos; nam ut quidam boni sanguinis sunt, ita quidam incitati et mobilis et cito in os prodeuntis. Haec, ut dixi, nulla sapientia abigit: alioquin haberet rerum naturam sub imperio, si omnia eraderet vitia. Quaecumque adtribuit condicio nascendi et corporis temperatura, cum multum se diuque animus composuerit, haerebunt; nihil horum vetari potest, non

5

10

15

20

25

30

35

54 **ad memoriam. . .eius:** "by the recollection of that one," i.e., by calling him to mind.

56–57 **Catonem. . .Laelium:** see *Ep.* 7, note to line 40.

57 **eum:** i.e., aliquem.

58–59 **cuius. . .ipse animum ante se ferens vultus:** lit., "whose face itself revealing the soul before it"; i.e., "whose face itself mirroring the soul within."

60–61 **ad quem. . .corriges:** "following whom our very character may fashion itself; you will not correct what is crooked except with the use of a ruler."

35 **haereo, -ere, haesi, haesus,** 2, cling

36 **accerso (arcesso), -ere, -ivi, -itus,** 3, summon
adfectus, -us, *m.*, emotion

39 **summitto, -ere, -misi, -missus,** 3, lower
figo, -ere, fixi, fixus, 3, fix

41 **adversus,** *prep. w. acc.*, against

42 **proficio, -ere, -feci, -fectus,** 3, help

44 **clausula, -ae,** *f.*, conclusion

46 **diligo, -ere, -lexi, -lectus,** 3, love, esteem

47 **tamquam,** *adv.*, as if

48 **praecipio, -ere, -cepi, -ceptus,** 3, teach

49 **inmerito,** *adv.*, undeservedly

50 **peccatum, -i,** *n.*, sin
tollo, -ere, sustuli, sublatus, 3, lift up, remove

51 **vereor, -eri, veritus,** 2 *dep.*, respect

53 **tantum,** *adv.*, only

57 **remissus, -a, -um,** *p. adj.* (*of* **remitto**), mild

60 **opus est,** there is need

61 **exigo, -ere, -egi, -actus,** 3, measure, weigh

magis quam accersi. Artifices scaenici, qui imitantur adfectus,
qui metum et trepidationem exprimunt, qui tristitiam
repraesentant, hoc indicio imitantur verecundiam. Deiciunt
enim vultum, verba summittunt, figunt in terram oculos et
deprimunt: ruborem sibi exprinlere non possunt; nec pro-   40
hibetur hic nec adducitur. Nihil adversus haec sapientia
promittit, nihil proficit: sui iuris sunt, iniussa veniunt,
iniussa discedunt.

Iam clausulam epistula poscit. Accipe, et quidem utilem
ac salutarem, quam te adfigere animo volo: 'aliquis vir bonus   45
nobis diligendus est ac semper ante oculos habendus, ut sic
tamquam illo spectante vivamus et omnia tamquam illo
vidente faciamus'. Hoc, mi Lucili, Epicurus praecepit;
custodem nobis et paedagogum dedit, nec inmerito: magna
pars peccatorum tollitur, si peccaturis testis adsistit. Aliquem   50
habeat animus quem vereatur, cuius auctoritate etiam secretum suum sanctius faciat. O felicem illum qui non praesens
tantum sed etiam cogitatus emendat! O felicem qui sic
aliquem vereri potest ut ad memoriam quoque eius se com-
ponat atque ordinet! Qui sic aliquem vereri potest cito erit   55
verendus. Elige itaque Catonem; si hic tibi videtur nimis
rigidus, elige remissioris animi virum Laelium. Elige eum
cuius tibi placuit et vita et oratio et ipse animum ante se
ferens vultus; illum tibi semper ostende vel custodem vel
exemplum. Opus est, inquam, aliquo ad quem mores nostri   60
se ipsi exigant: nisi ad regulam prava non corriges. *Vale.*

6 **quid mihi futurum est:** "what is to become of me."

13 **Quod. . .sit:** "let this be between you and me" or "between you and me"; *quod = hoc.* Cf. *Ep.* 5, lines 21–22.

16 **foras. . .spectat:** a comic reference to the Roman custom of placing corpses near the entrance with their feet facing the door to emphasize their exit from life.

   istunc: acc. masc. sing. of *istic, istaec, istuc* (*iste* + deictic enclitic particle *-ce* shortened to *-c*).

17 **alienum mortuum tollere:** "to hoist (for burial) someone else's dead"; i.e., his previous owner should have retained him and assumed responsibility for his burial.

18 **sigillaria:** small images or figures presented to children as gifts during the last days of the Saturnalia, a Roman winter festival similar to Christmas.

21 **dentes. . .cadunt:** "his teeth are just now falling out." Seneca is jestingly referring to second childhood. For the expression *cum maxime*, see *Ep.* 7, line 42.

27 **summam manum:** "the finishing touch."

30 **in extrema tegula:** "on the edge of the roof."

34 **tam seni. . .quam iuveni:** inverted for *tam iuveni. . .quam seni.* Seneca is being paradoxical here; one would expect the old to be more fully mindful of death than the young.

35 **citamur ex censu:** "summoned from the censor's list." The census was a register of Roman citizens, ranking them as either *seniores* or *iuniores.*

---

2 **argumentum, -i,** *n.,* proof
3 **suburbanum, -i,** *n.,* suburban villa
   queror, -i, questus, 3 *dep.,* complain
   inpensa, -ae, *f.,* expense
4 **dilabor, -i, -lapsus,** 3 *dep.,* fall down
   vilicus, -i, *m.,* steward
5 **vitium, -i,** *n.,* fault
8 **stomachor,** 1 *dep.,* be angry *or* vexed
   platanus, -i, *f.,* plane-tree
9 **nodosus, -a, -um,** *adj.,* knotty
   retorridus, -a, -um, *adj.,* dried up
11 **circumfodio, -ere, -fodi, -fosus,** 3, dig
   genius, -i, *m.,* guardian spirit
15 **merito,** *adv.,* deservedly
   ostium, -i, *n.,* entrance
16 **foras,** *adv.,* out of doors, out
   nanciscor, -i, nanctus, 3 *dep.,* get
19 **deliciolum, -i,** *n.,* little darling, pet
20 **pupulus, -i,** *m.,* little boy
   delicium, -i, *n.,* little darling, sweetheart
21 **prorsus,** *adv.,* absolutely
23 **conplector, -i, -plexus,** 3 *dep.,* embrace
25 **pomum, -i,** *n.,* fruit
   decor, -oris, *m.,* charm
26 **dedo, -ere, dedidi, deditus,** 3, give up
   mergo, -ere, mersi, mersus, 3, sink, immerse
28 **differo, differre, distuli, dislatus,** *irr.,* put off, delay
29 **devexus, -a, -um,** *adj.,* sliding downward
   praeceps, -cipitis, *adj.,* fallen
31 **succedo, -ere, -cessi, -cessus,** 3, follow
32 **egeo, -ere, egui,** 2, be in need of

Epistle Twelve
THE ADVANTAGES OF OLD AGE

Seneca Lucilio Suo Salutem

Quocumque me verti, argumenta senectutis meae video.
Veneram in suburbanum meum et querebar de inpensis
aedificii dilabentis. Ait vilicus mihi non esse neglegentiae
suae vitium, omnia se facere, sed villam veterem esse. Haec   5
villa inter manus meas crevit: quid mihi futurum est, si tam
putria sunt aetatis meae saxa? Iratus illi proximam occasionem stomachandi arripio. 'Apparet' inquam 'has platanos
neglegi: nullas habent frondes. Quam nodosi sunt et retorridi
rami, quam tristes et squalidi trunci! Hoc non accideret si   10
quis has circumfoderet, si inrigaret.' Iurat per genium meum
se omnia facere, in nulla re cessare curam suam, sed illas
vetulas esse. Quod intra nos sit, ego illas posueram, ego
illarum primum videram folium. Conversus ad ianuam 'quis
est iste?' inquam 'iste decrepitus et merito ad ostium admotus?   15
foras enim spectat. Unde istunc nanctus es? quid te delectavit
alienum mortuum tollere?' At ille 'non cognoscis me?'
inquit: 'ego sum Felicio, cui solebas sigillaria adferre; ego
sum Philositi vilici filius, deliciolum tuum'. 'Perfecte' inquam
'iste delirat: pupulus, etiam delicium meum factus est?   20
Prorsus potest fieri: dentes illi cum maxime cadunt.'

Debeo hoc suburbano meo, quod mihi senectus mea
quocumque adverteram apparuit. Conplectamur illam et
amemus; plena <est> voluptatis, si illa scias uti. Gratissima
sunt poma cum fugiunt; pueritiae maximus in exitu decor   25
est; deditos vino potio extrema delectat, illa quae mergit,
quae ebrietati summam manum inponit; quod in se iucun-
dissimum omnis voluptas habet in finem sui differt. Iucun-
dissima est aetas devexa iam, non tamen praeceps, et illam
quoque in extrema tegula stantem iudico habere suas volu-   30
ptates; aut hoc ipsum succedit in locum voluptatium, nullis
egere. Quam dulce est cupiditates fatigasse ac reliquisse!
'Molestum est' inquis 'mortem ante oculos habere.' Primum
ista tam seni ante oculos debet esse quam iuveni (non enim
citamur ex censu); deinde nemo tam senex est ut inprobe   35
unum diem speret. . . .

38 **peculio:** *peculium* originally meant "property in cattle"; then it came to have the general meaning "property." Here, in continuation of the business metaphor concerned with quotations, it seems to have the meaning of "allotment" or "allowance."

40 **illi:** "to it"; i.e., to the letter.

41–42 **Quidni nulla sit:** "why is there no need?" i.e., "of course there is no need!"

45 **alieno:** "a philosopher of another school."

42 **pateo, -ere, patui,** 2, lie open
44 **calco,** 1, trample upon
46 **ingero, -ere, -gessi, -gestus,** 3, heap on
47 **aestimo,** 1, value

Sed iam debeo epistulam includere. 'Sic' inquis 'sine ullo ad me peculio veniet?' Noli timere: aliquid secum fert. Quare aliquid dixi? multum. Quid enim hac voce praeclarius quam illi trado ad te perferendam? 'Malum est in necessitate   40 vivere, sed in necessitate vivere necessitas nulla est.' Quidni nulla sit? patent undique ad libertatem viae multae, breves faciles. Agamus deo gratias quod nemo in vita teneri potest: calcare ipsas necessitates licet. 'Epicurus' inquis 'dixit: quid tibi cum alieno?' Quod verum est meum est; perseverabo   45 Epicurum tibi ingerere, ut isti qui in verba iurant nec quid dicatur aestimant, sed a quo, sciant quae optima sunt esse communia. *Vale.*

8 **illam secundam:** supply *valetudinem;* refers to physical health which should come second in importance, mental health coming first.

   quae. . .constabit: an idiomatic expression meaning "which will cost you no great price"; *magno* is an abl. of price with *pretio* understood.

15 **locum laxa:** "make room"; *laxo, -are,* stretch out, expand.

16 **huic. . .curae:** i.e., athletic training.

19 **Accedent:** lit., "approach": here it means "are added" and is a variant for *adice quod* (line 13, above).

   in magisterium: "for instruction"; a rather frequent construction for expressing purpose in Silver Latin. Earlier Latin would have preferred the dative case.

20 **homines:** in apposition with *mancipia* (line 19).

   quibus: dative of agent. With the compound tenses of the passive (as here *actus est*), the dative of agent is often used instead of the ablative of agent.

20–21 **ad votum:** "according to their wish."

22–23 **multum. . .regesserunt:** "they have taken in a large quantity of drink that will go down more deeply during a period of fasting."

23 **cardiaci:** used to describe a man "with heart-burn" or "with stomachache." This ailment was treated by drinking wine or by sweats, or by both. Hence, Seneca's statement here that "drinking and sweating is the life of a man with stomach trouble."

25 **cuius. . .est:** *cuius* refers to *tempori; ratio habenda est* means literally "an account must be considered," where the idiomatic meaning is "account must be taken" of something.

26–28 **saltus. . .fullonius:** the *vel*'s indicate Seneca's triple division of *saltus: qui. . .levat* refers to the high jump; *qui. . .mittit* refers to the broad jump; *saliaris* refers to jumping about like the leaping priests of Mars, called *Salii.* Their festival was celebrated in March. Dressed in costumes and carrying the sacred shields (*ancilia*), they went from place to place singing and dancing; *fullonius* refers to the Roman fuller or laundry man who washed clothes by jumping upon them in a tub of water.

29 **usum rude facile:** The daggers indicate a difficulty in the manuscript reading.

35 **ut. . .remittatur:** "that it is not unhinged but relaxed."

---

2 **usque,** *adv.,* right up to
5 **demum,** *adv.,* at length, precisely
6 **furiosus, -a, -um,** *adj.,* mad, furious
   furiosus, -i, *m.,* madman
   freneticus, -a, -um, *adj.,* frantic
   freneticus, -i, *m.,* frantic man
7 **praecipue,** *adv.,* especially
9 **stultus, -a, -um,** *adj.,* foolish
   minime, *superl. adv.,* not at all
10 **litteratus, -a, -um,** *adj.,* learned, liberally educated
   lacertus, -i, *m., generally pl.,* muscles
   cervix, -icis, *f.,* shoulders
11 **latus, -eris,** *n.,* side, lung
   sagina, -ae, *f.,* stuffing
12 **torus, -i,** *m.,* muscle
   opimus, -a, -um, *adj.,* fat
13 **adicio, -ere, -ieci, -iectus, 3,** add
   quod, *conj.,* the fact that
   sarcina, -ae, *f.,* burden
14 **elido, -ere, -lisi, -lisus, 3,** shatter, crush
   quantum, *adv.,* as much as
16 **incommodus, -a, -um,** *adj.,* inconvenient
   incommodum, -i, *n.,* inconvenience
   dedo, -ere, dedidi, deditus, 3, give up
17 **exhaurio, -ire, -hausi, -haustus, 4,** drain
   inhabilis, -e, *adj.,* unfit
   intentio, -onis, *f.,* application [to anything]
19 **nota, -ae,** *f.,* mark, note, stamp
   mancipium, -i, *n.,* slave
20 **oleum, -i,** *n.,* oil
21 **desudo, 1,** perspire
24 **lasso, 1,** make weary, exhaust
25 **praecipuus, -a, -um,** *adj.,* special
26 **saltus, -us,** *m.,* jumping
28 **contumeliosus, -a, -um,** *adj.,* insulting, abusive
   quilibet, quae-, quid-, *indef. pron.,* anyone
29 **cito,** *adv.,* quickly
31 **alo, -ere, alui, altus (alitus), 3,** nourish
   frigus, -oris, *n.,* cold
   aestus, -us, *m.,* heat
32 **ne. . .quidem,** not. . .even
33 **inmineo, -ere, 2,** hang over
34 **pugillares, -ium,** *m.,* writing tablets
35 **gestatio, -onis,** *f.,* riding
36 **concutio, -ere, -cussi, -cussus, 3,** shake
   officio, -ere, -feci, -fectus, 3, hinder
37 **ambulatio, -onis,** *f.,* walking

Epistle Fifteen
AGAINST STRENUOUS PHYSICAL EXERCISE

Seneca Lucilio Suo Salutem

Mos antiquis fuit, usque ad meam servatus aetatem, primis epistulae verbis adicere 'si vales bene est, ego valeo'. Recte nos dicimus 'si philosopharis, bene est'. Valere enim hoc demum est. Sine hoc aeger est animus; corpus quoque, etiam   5
si magnas habet vires, non aliter quam furiosi aut frenetici validum est. Ergo hanc praecipue valetudinem cura, deinde et illam secundam; quae non magno tibi constabit, si volueris bene valere. Stulta est enim, mi Lucili, et minime conveniens litterato viro occupatio exercendi lacertos et dilatandi cervi-   10
cem ac latera firmandi; cum tibi feliciter sagina cesserit et tori creverint, nec vires umquam opimi bovis nec pondus aequabis. Adice nunc quod maiore corporis sarcina animus eliditur et minus agilis est. Itaque quantum potes circum-scribe corpus tuum et animo locum laxa. Multa sequuntur   15
incommoda huic deditos curae: primum exercitationes, quarum labor spiritum exhaurit et inhabilem intentioni ac studiis acrioribus reddit; deinde copia ciborum subtilitas inpeditur. Accedunt pessimae notae mancipia in magisterium recepta, homines inter oleum et vinum occupati, quibus ad   20
votum dies actus est si bene desudaverunt, si in locum eius quod effluxit multum potionis altius in ieiuno iturae regesse-runt. Bibere et sudare vita cardiaci est. Sunt exercitationes et faciles et breves, quae corpus et sine mora lassent et tempori parcant, cuius praecipua ratio habenda est: cursus et cum   25
aliquo pondere manus motae et saltus vel ille qui corpus in altum levat vel ille qui in longum mittit vel ille, ut ita dicam, saliaris aut, ut contumeliosius dicam, fullonius: quoslibet ex his elige †usum rude facile†. Quidquid facies, cito redi a cor-pore ad animum; illum noctibus ac diebus exerce. Labore   30
modico alitur ille; hanc exercitationem non frigus, non aestus inpediet, ne senectus quidem. Id bonum cura quod vetustate fit melius. Neque ego te iubeo semper inminere libro aut pugillaribus: dandum est aliquod intervallum animo, ita tamen ut non resolvatur, sed remittatur. Gestatio et corpus   35
concutit et studio non officit: possis legere, possis dictare, possis loqui, possis audire, quorum nihil ne ambulatio quidem vetat fieri. . . .

40 **unum graecum:** the daggers indicate a difficulty in the manuscript reading. Several remedies have been proposed, among which is *munus Graecum* (Haase's conjecture), "a Greek gift."

43 **Babae et Isionis:** Baba and Ision, contemporary court fools. Supply *vitam* with *Babae et Isionis.*

47–48 **ex fortuna pendere:** English idiom says: "depend on fortune."

51 **Quid. . .ceteris:** lit., "what is there to you with others?" i.e., "what have you to do with others?" or "why compare yourself with others?"

60 **prope ab ultimo:** *prope* with *ab* + ablative = near to.

39 **pusillum, -i,** *n.*, small amount
negotium, -i, *n.*, trouble
mercedula, -ae, *f.*, small recompense
40 **accedo, -ere, -cessi, -cessus,** 3, approach, be added
44 **caecus, -a, -um,** *adj.*, blind
48 **subinde,** *adv.*, continually
consequor, -i, -secutus, 3 *dep.*, attain
50 **adversus,** *prep. w. acc.*, to
53 **aliquando,** *adv.*, finally, at some time or other
54 **adsequor, -i, secutus,** 3 *dep.*, attain
55 **impleo, -ere, -plevi, -pletus,** 2, satisfy
haurio, -ire, hausi, haustus, 4, drain
sitis, -is, *f.*, thirst
56 **mittantur = dimittantur**
speciosus, -a, -um, *adj.*, showy
57 **sors, sortis,** *f.*, lot
inpetro, 1, demand
58 **obliviscor, -i, oblitus,** 3 *dep.*, forget
59 **congero, -ere, -gessi, -gestus,** 3, amass [a great quantity]
60 **ut,** *conj.*, although

Detraxi tibi non pusillum negotii: una mercedula et †unum graecum† ad haec beneficia accedet. Ecce insigne 40 praeceptum: 'stulta vita ingrata est, trepida; tota in futurum fertur'. 'Quis hoc' inquis 'dicit?' idem qui supra. Quam tu nunc vitam dici existimas stultam? Babae et Isionis? Non ita est: nostra dicitur, quos caeca cupiditas in nocitura, certe numquam satiatura praecipitat, quibus si quid satis esse 45 posset, fuisset, qui non cogitamus quam iucundum sit nihil poscere, quam magnificum sit plenum esse nec ex fortuna pendere. Subinde itaque, Lucili, quam multa sis consecutus recordare; cum aspexeris quot te antecedant, cogita quot sequantur. Si vis gratus esse adversus deos et adversus vitam 50 tuam, cogita quam multos antecesseris. Quid tibi cum ceteris? te ipse antecessisti. Finem constitue quem transire ne possis quidem si velis; discedant aliquando ista insidiosa bona et sperantibus meliora quam adsecutis. Si quid in illis esset solidi, aliquando et implerent: nunc haurientium sitim con- 55 citant. Mittantur speciosi apparatus; et quod futuri temporis incerta sors volvit, quare potius a fortuna inpetrem ut det, quam a me ne petam? Quare autem petam? oblitus fragilitatis humanae congeram? in quid laborem ? Ecce hic dies ultimus est; ut non sit, prope ab ultimo est. *Vale.*

10 **non opus est:** not in the manuscripts but conjectured by Haase.

14 **non est quod:** "there is no reason why."

18 **est:** "it consists."

39 **illo:** adv., "thither," "to that point."

2 **liqueo, -ere, liqui (licui),** 2, be clear
3 **ne. . .quidem,** not. . .even
4 **ceterum,** *adv.,* but
5 **inchoo,** 1, begin
   cotidianus, -a, -um, *adj.,* daily
8 **robur, -oris,** *n.,* strength, vigor
11 **proficio, -ere, -feci, -fectus,** 3, go forward, make progress
12 **fictus, -a, -um,** *p. adj.* (*of* **fingo**), feigned
14 **cito,** *adv.,* quickly
15 **excutio, -ere, -cussi, -cussus,** 3, shake out, examine
18 **adhibeo, -ere, -ui, -itus,** 2, summon, employ
19 **oblectatio, -onis,** *f.,* pleasure, amusement
20 **dispono, -ere, -posui, -positus,** 3, arrange
22 **anceps, -ipitis,** *adj.,* uncertain
25 **prosum, prodesse, profui,** *irr.,* be of use, help
34 **tueor, -eri, tuitus,** 2 *dep.,* defend, protect
35 **contumaciter,** *adv.,* obstinately
38 **inligo,** 1, fasten, bind
39 **subitus, -a, -um,** *adj.,* sudden
40 **delabor, -labi, -lapsus,** 3 dep., fall down

Epistle Sixteen
PHILOSOPHY: LIFE'S GUIDE

Seneca Lucilio Suo Salutem

Liquere hoc tibi, Lucili, scio, neminem posse beate vivere,
ne tolerabiliter quidem, sine sapientiae studio, et beatam
vitam perfecta sapientia effici, ceterum tolerabilem etiam
inchoata. Sed hoc quod liquet firmandum et altius cotidiana   5
meditatione figendum est: plus operis est in eo ut proposita
custodias quam ut honesta proponas. Perseverandum est et
adsiduo studio robur addendum, donec bona mens sit quod
bona voluntas est.

Itaque <non opus est> tibi apud me pluribus verbis aut   10
adfirmatione tam longa: intellego multum te profecisse. Quae
scribis unde veniant scio; non sunt ficta nec colorata. Dicam
tamen quid sentiam: iam de te spem habeo, nondum fiduciam.
Tu quoque idem facias volo: non est quod tibi cito et facile
credas. Excute te et varie scrutare et observa; illud ante   15
omnia vide, utrum in philosophia an in ipsa vita profeceris.
Non est philosophia populare artificium nec ostentationi
paratum; non in verbis sed in rebus est. Nec in hoc adhibetur,
ut cum aliqua oblectatione consumatur dies, ut dematur otio
nausia: animum format et fabricat, vitam disponit, actiones   20
regit, agenda et omittenda demonstrat, sedet ad gubernaculum et per ancipitia fluctuantium derigit cursum. Sine hac
nemo intrepide potest vivere, nemo secure; innumerabilia
accidunt singulis horis quae consilium exigant, quod ab hac
petendum est. Dicet aliquis, 'quid mihi prodest philosophia,   25
si fatum est? quid prodest, si deus rector est? quid prodest,
si casus imperat? Nam et mutari certa non possunt et nihil
praeparari potest adversus incerta, sed aut consilium meum
occupavit deus decrevitque quid facerem, aut consilio meo
nihil fortuna permittit.' Quidquid est ex his, Lucili, vel si   30
omnia haec sunt, philosophandum est; sive nos inexorabili
lege fata constringunt, sive arbiter deus universi cuncta dis-
posuit, sive casus res humanas sine ordine inpellit et iactat,
philosophia nos tueri debet. Haec adhortabitur ut deo libenter
pareamus, ut fortunae contumaciter; haec docebit ut deum   35
sequaris, feras casum. Sed non est nunc in hanc disputationem
transeundum, quid sit iuris nostri si providentia in imperio
est, aut si fatorum series inligatos trahit, aut si repentina ac
subita dominantur: illo nunc revertor, ut te moneam et
exhorter ne patiaris impetum animi tui delabi et refrigescere.   40
Contine illum et constitue, ut habitus animi fiat quod est
impetus.

47   **Istuc:** an alternative form of *istud.*

48   **ad naturam vives:** see *Ep.* 5, line 24.

52   **eo:** adv., "to such a pitch," "to such a point."

61   **progresso:** supply *tibi;* translate "for you having advanced far."

49   **exiguus, -a, -um,** *adj.,* little, small

50   **locuples, -etis,** *adj.,* wealthy, rich

53   **tantum,** *adv.,* only

54   **calco,** 1, tread upon

56   **disco, -ere, didici,** 3, learn

57   **desino, -ere, -sivi (-sii), -situs,** 3, cease, stop

58   **extremus, -a, -um,** *adj.,* extreme, last

     extremum, -i, *n.,* end

61   **alicubi,** *adv.,* somewhere, anywhere

Iam ab initio, si te bene novi, circumspicies quid haec epistula munusculi adtulerit: excute illam, et invenies. Non est quod mireris animum meum: adhuc de alieno liberalis sum. Quare autem alienum dixi? quidquid bene dictum est   45
ab ullo meum est. Istuc quoque ab Epicuro dictum est: 'si ad naturam vives, numquam eris pauper; si ad opiniones, numquam eris dives'. Exiguum natura desiderat, opinio immensum. Congeratur in te quidquid multi locupletes possederant; ultra privatum pecuniae modum fortuna te   50
provehat, auro tegat, purpura vestiat, eo deliciarum opumque perducat ut terram marmoribus abscondas; non tantum habere tibi liceat sed calcare divitias; accedant statuae et picturae et quidquid ars ulla luxuriae elaboravit: maiora cupere ab his disces. Naturalia desideria finita sunt: ex falsa   55
opinione nascentia ubi desinant non habent; nullus enim terminus falso est. Via eunti aliquid extremum est: error immensus est. Retrahe ergo te a vanis, et cum voles scire quod petes, utrum naturalem habeat an caecam cupiditatem, considera num possit alicubi consistere: si longe progresso   60
semper aliquid longius restat, scito id naturale non esse. *Vale.*

2 **December:** during this month, from the 17th to the 23rd, was celebrated the Saturnalia, a festival in honor of Saturn, the god of agriculture, who, as the father of Jupiter, was considered to be the patron of a pristine Golden Age. The Saturnalia was a period of rejoicing and good will similar to our Christmas season. Gifts were exchanged, schools were closed, war was not declared, and slaves, temporarily freed, were permitted to criticize their masters and to speak with liberty on any subject; all was merriment and unrestrained mirth.

2–3 **Ius. . .datum est:** "the right of extravagance has been openly granted."

4–5 **tamquam. . .agendarum:** "as if there were any difference between the Saturnalia and working days."

10 **exuendam togam:** during the Saturnalia the toga was taken off and a showy dressing-gown, called *synthesis,* was put on.

10–12 **Nam. . .mutavimus:** translate *voluptatis. . .mutavimus* first, then *quod. . .solebat; in tumultu* refers to civil uprisings or wars; *tristi tempore,* to public misfortunes.

13 **arbitri. . .functus:** "having played the role of judge [in this matter]."

14 **pilleatae:** *pilleatus, -a, -um,* adj., wearing the *pilleus.* The *pilleus* was a felt cap worn by the Romans at festivals and entertainments, especially during the Saturnalia; it was also given to slaves at their manumission as a sign of their freedom.

16 **solus:** i.e., the soul (*animo,* line 15).

17 **capit:** *animus* is the subject.

18 **nec. . .abducitur:** "neither goes [of its own volition] nor is led."

Hoc: explained by *siccum ac sobrium esse.*

29 **decurrit:** a technical military term, "goes through military exercises."

vallum iacit: "he throws up a fortification."

30 **necessario:** supply *labori.*

---

2 **sudo,** 1, sweat
3 **apparatus, -us,** *m.*, preparation
5 **adeo,** *adv.*, so, to such an extent
6 **olim,** *adv.*, once, formerly
7 **hic,** *adv.*, here
  libenter, *adv.*, gladly
9 **dissideo, -ere, -sedi, -sessus,** 2, be at variance
10 **exuo, -ere, -ui, -utus,** 3, take off
14 **forte,** *adv.*, by chance
16 **procumbo, -ere, -cubui, -cubitus,** 3, fall, sink
17 **blandus, -a, -um,** *adj.*, enticing
20 **excerpo, -ere, -cerpsi, -cerptus,** 3, separate
  insignio, 4, distinguish one's self
21 **licet, -ere, licuit,** *impers.*, 2, it is permitted
23 **ceterum,** *adv.*, but
24 **praecipio, -ere, -cepi, -ceptus,** 3, teach
25 **interpono, -ere, -posui, -positus,** 3, set aside
  aliquot, *indec. adj.*, several
  vilis, -e, *adj.*, cheap
26 **horridus, -a, -um,** *adj.*, coarse
29 **supervacuus, -a, -um,** *adj.*, superfluous
30 **lasso,** 1, make weary, exhaust
  sufficio, -ere, -feci, -fectus, 3, be fit for
32 **prope,** *adv.*, near, close to
33 **expavesco, -ere, -pavi,** 3, fear
  disco, -ere, didici, 3, learn

Epistle Eighteen

Epistle Eighteen
ON PRACTICING POVERTY

Seneca Lucilio Suo Salutem

December est mensis: cum maxime civitas sudat. Ius luxuriae publice datum est; ingenti apparatu sonant omnia, tamquam quicquam inter Saturnalia intersit et dies rerum agendarum; adeo nihil interest ut <non> videatur mihi errasse qui dixit olim mensem Decembrem fuisse, nunc annum. Si te hic haberem, libenter tecum conferrem quid existimares esse faciendum, utrum nihil ex cotidiana consuetudine movendum an, ne dissidere videremur cum publicis moribus, et hilarius cenandum et exuendam togam. Nam quod fieri nisi in tumultu et tristi tempore civitatis non solebat, voluptatis causa ac festorum dierum vestem mutavimus. Si te bene novi, arbitri partibus functus nec per omnia nos similes esse pilleatae turbae voluisses nec per omnia dissimiles; nisi forte his maxime diebus animo imperandum est, ut tunc voluptatibus solus abstineat cum in illas omnis turba procubuit; certissimum enim argumentum firmitatis suae capit, si ad blanda et in luxuriam trahentia nec it nec abducitur. Hoc multo fortius est, ebrio ac vomitante populo siccum ac sobrium esse, illud temperantius, non excerpere se nec insignire nec misceri omnibus et eadem sed non eodem modo facere; licet enim sine luxuria agere festum diem.

Ceterum adeo mihi placet temptare animi tui firmitatem ut ex praecepto magnorum virorum tibi quoque praecipiam: interponas aliquot dies quibus contentus minimo ac vilissimo cibo, dura atque horrida veste, dicas tibi 'hoc est quod timebatur?' In ipsa securitate animus ad difficilia se praeparet et contra iniurias fortunae inter beneficia firmetur. Miles in media pace decurrit, sine ullo hoste vallum iacit, et supervacuo labore lassatur ut sufficere necessario possit; quem in ipsa re trepidare nolueris, ante rem exerceas. Hoc secuti sunt qui omnibus mensibus paupertatem imitati prope ad inopiam accesserunt, ne umquam expavescerent quod saepe didicissent.

34–36 **Timoneas. . .ludit:** Timon was a renowned Athenian misanthrope of the fifth century who lived in the forest and led a life withdrawn from his fellow men; the phrase *pauperum cellas* refers to small rooms in which the poor lived. Wealthy men, imitating the poor, often included in their luxurious abodes a small, simple room whither the worn out *dives* could withdraw from the glitter of extravagance; *per. . .ludit:* "through which luxury (i.e., luxurious men), because of boredom of wealth, amuses itself" or "through which the extravagance of wealth amuses its boredom."

37 **sordidus:** this adjective not only means "dirty" but also "small," "paltry"; *panis durus et sordidus* is best translated "bread hard and small in quantity." This meaning is supported by the words *maligne famem extingueret* and *gloriatur non toto asse <se> pasci* in lines 49 and 53.

     triduo et quatriduo: "for three or four days." Seneca frequently uses an ablative rather than an accusative to express duration of time.

39 **dipondio:** "on a penny"; *dipondium* was a Roman coin worth two asses.

41 **dabit et irata:** "[fortune] even when angered will give."

45 **palum:** "a stake." Roman soldiers learned to fight by attacking a stake set in the ground.

51 **an. . .pensaret:** "whether [what was lacking] was worthy of someone's purchasing it with great effort"; *dignum [erat] quod. . .pensaret:* the adjectives *dignus, indignus, aptus,* and *idoneus* are followed by a descriptive relative clause in the subjunctive. The verb *penso, -are* here has the Silver Latin meaning to "purchase."

52 **Charino magistratu:** "when Charinus was in office": Charinus was archon in 308–307 B.C. Athenian government had a board of nine principal magistrates (*archontes*), the chief of whom (the *archon eponymos*) gave his name to the year in which he held the office.

53 **Polyaenum:** Polyaenus, a mathematician who followed the tenets of Epicurus.

54 **Metrodorum:** Metrodorus, a disciple and intimate friend of Epicurus.

61–62 **sepositos. . .pascit:** "he who is going to kill those set aside for capital punishment does not feed [them] so meagerly."

63 **ad extrema. . .decretis:** "by those condemned to death."

68–69 **aude. . .deo:** Vergil, *Aeneid* 8.364–365. When Aeneas enters the humble dwelling of Evander, the king utters these words to the Roman hero after mentioning that Hercules, the great victor, had also graced that house.

36 **grabattus, -i,** *m.,* pallet, small couch
     sagum, -i, *n.,* coarse cloak
37 **interdum,** *adv.,* sometimes
43 **nomen, -inis,** *n.,* account (*lit.* name)
     suspicio, -ere, -spexi, -spectus, 3, look up to
45 **aliquando,** *adv.,* now and then
49 **maligne,** *adv.,* hardly, scarcely
53 **glorior,** 1 *dep.,* boast
     pasco, -ere, pavi, pastus, 3, feed
54 **proficio, -ere, -feci, -fectus,** 3, make progress
55 **victus, -us,** *m.,* food
     saturitas, -atis, *f.,* fullness, satiety
56 **subinde,** *adv.,* constantly
     reficio, -ere, -feci, -fectus, 3, restore
57 **polenta, -ae,** *f.,* barley
58 **frustum, -i,** *n.,* piece
     hordeacium, -i, *n.,* barley
63 **ne. . .quidem,** not. . .even
64 **praeoccupo,** 1, seize beforehand, forestall
66 **destino,** 1, choose, appoint
68 **contemno, -ere, -tempsi, -temptus,** 3, scorn
69 **fingo, -ere, finxi, fictus,** 3, mould

Non est nunc quod existimes me dicere Timoneas cenas et
pauperum cellas et quidquid aliud est per quod luxuria   35
divitiarum taedio ludit: grabattus ille verus sit et sagum et
panis durus ac sordidus. Hoc triduo et quatriduo fer, interdum pluribus diebus, ut non lusus sit sed experimentum:
tunc, mihi crede, Lucili, exultabis dipondio satur et intelleges
ad securitatem non opus esse fortuna; hoc enim quod necessi-   40
tati sat est dabit et irata. Non est tamen quare tu multum
tibi facere videaris (facies enim quod multa milia servorum,
multa milia pauperum faciunt): illo nomine te suspice, quod
facies non coactus, quod tam facile erit tibi illud pati semper
quam aliquando experiri. Exerceamur ad palum, et ne   45
inparatos fortuna deprehendat, fiat nobis paupertas familiaris;
securius divites erimus si scierimus quam non sit grave pau-
peres esse. Certos habebat dies ille magister voluptatis
Epicurus quibus maligne famem extingueret, visurus an
aliquid deesset ex plena et consummata voluptate, vel quan-   50
tum deesset, et an dignum quod quis magno labore pensaret.
Hoc certe in iis epistulis ait quas scripsit Charino magistratu
ad Polyaenum; et quidem gloriatur non toto asse <se> pasci,
Metrodorum, qui nondum tantum profecerit, toto. In hoc
tu victu saturitatem putas esse? Et voluptas est; voluptas   55
autem non illa levis et fugax et subinde reficienda, sed stabilis
et certa. Non enim iucunda res est aqua et polenta aut
frustum hordeacii panis, sed summa voluptas est posse capere
etiam ex his voluptatem et ad id se deduxisse quod eripere
nulla fortunae iniquitas possit. Liberaliora alimenta sunt   60
carceris, sepositos ad capitale supplicium non tam anguste
qui occisurus est pascit: quanta est animi magnitudo ad id
sua sponte descendere quod ne ad extrema quidem decretis
timendum sit! hoc est praeoccupare tela fortunae. Incipe
ergo, mi Lucili, sequi horum consuetudinem et aliquos dies   65
destina quibus secedas a tuis rebus minimoque te facias
familiarem; incipe cum paupertate habere commercium;

  aude, hospes, contemnere opes et te quoque dignum
  finge deo.

78   **necesse est scias:** *necesse est* often takes the subjunctive without *ut.*

83   **maximum:** supply *ignem.*

71   **interdico, -ere, -dixi, -dictus,** 3, forbid

75   **complico,** 1, fold up

77   **numeratio, -onis,** *f.*, payment
     quam, *adv.*, how

78   **in,** *prep. w. acc.*, against

79   **adfectus, -us,** *m.*, emotion

81   **interest,** *impers.*, it matters

82   **refert,** *impers.*, it matters

83   **rursus,** *adv.*, on the other hand

84   **scintilla, -ae,** *f.*, spark
     foveo, -ere, fovi, fotus, 2, nourish
     usque, *adv.*, right up to

85   **exitus, -us,** *m.*, outcome

Nemo alius est deo dignus quam qui opes contempsit; quarum 70
possessionem tibi non interdico, sed efficere volo ut illas intrepide possideas; quod uno consequeris modo, si te etiam
sine illis beate victurum persuaseris tibi, si illas tamquam
exituras semper aspexeris.

Sed iam incipiamus epistulam complicare. 'Prius' inquis 75
'redde quod debes.' Delegabo te ad Epicurum, ab illo fiet
numeratio: 'inmodica ira gignit insaniam'. Hoc quam verum
sit necesse est scias, cum habueris et servum et inimicum. In
omnes personas hic exardescit adfectus; tam ex amore nascitur
quam ex odio, non minus inter seria quam inter lusus et iocos; 80
nec interest ex quam magna causa nascatur sed in qualem
perveniat animum. Sic ignis non refert quam magnus sed quo
incidat; nam etiam maximum solida non receperunt, rursus
arida et corripi facilia scintillam quoque fovent usque in
incendium. Ita est, mi Lucili: ingentis irae exitus furor est, 85
et ideo ira vitanda est non moderationis causa sed sanitatis. *Vale.*

2 **istis:** i.e., those who encourage Lucilius to pursue worldly glory.

10–11 **ascenditur:** "is a step upwards."

12 **alieno:** supply *luce,* "with another's light," i.e., "with borrowed light."

16 **Idomeneo**: Idomeneus (c. 325–c. 270 B.C.), friend of Epicurus and Greek biographer and historian from Lampsacus who wrote a life of Socrates and a history of Samothrace.

18–19 **regiae. . .tractantem:** "at that time a minister endowed with regal power and [one] handling important matters."

21 **Idomenea:** masc., acc., sing. of the Greek consonant declension.

22–23 **megistanas et satrapas:** masc., acc., pl. of the Greek consonant declension.

23–24 **ex. . .petebatur:** "from whom Idomeneus' glory was being sought."

24 **Nomen Attici:** Atticus, the intimate friend of Cicero to whom the orator addressed one of his four collections of letters. Atticus' daughter married Agrippa, minister of Augustus. Their daughter Vipsania Agrippina married Tiberius, to whom she bore Drusus Caesar who, in A.D. 23, met death at an early age, the victim of Sejanus, Tiberius' wicked minister. Had not the letters of Cicero preserved the name of Atticus, that name would have perished in spite of Atticus' inimacy with the imperial family.

35–38 **fortunati. . .habebit:** Vergil, *Aeneid* 9.446–449. The passage refers to Nisus and Euryalus, Trojans who came to Italy with Aeneas and who sacrificed their lives together to warn Aeneas of the Rutilian attack. Their loyalty and friendship to each other were proverbial.

---

2 **negotium, -i,** *n.,* trouble
6 **parum,** *adv.,* too little, not enough
  dispicio, -ere, -spexi, -spectus, 3, see
9 **fulgor, -oris,** *m.,* glitter, glory
  tamquam, *adv.,* as if
12 **niteo, -ere,** 2, shine
13 **extrinsecus,** *adv.,* from without
  percutio, -ere, -cussi, -cussus, 3, strike
17 **speciosus, -a, -um,** *adj.,* showy
21 **mentior, -iri, -itus,** 4 *dep.,* lie, cheat
22 **incido, -ere, -cidi, -cisus,** 3, cut into, engrave
  megistanes, -um, *m.,* grandees
23 **titulus, -i,** *m.,* a title, a title of honor, glory, honor
25 **sino, -ere, sivi, situs,** 3, allow
  gener, -eri, *m.,* son-in-law
26 **progener, -eri,** *m.,* granddaughter's husband
  pronepos, -otis, *m.,* great-grandson
27 **adplico, -are, -avi (-ui), -atus (-itus),** 1, attach
28 **ingenium, -i,** *n.,* genius, man of genius
29 **exero (exsero), -ere, -erui, -ertus,** 3, thrust out
  quandoque, *adv.,* at some time or other
32 **gratia, -ae,** *f.,* favor
  duro, 1, last, remain
34 **praesto, -are, -stiti, -status (-status),** 1, fulfill, keep one's promise
36 **eximo, -ere, -emi, -emptus,** 3, remove
39 **medium, -i,** *n.,* the midst of all, the public
40 **vigesco, -ere, vigui,** 3, become vigorous, thrive

Epistle Twenty-One
A LASTING MONUMENT

Seneca Lucilio Suo Salutem

Cum istis tibi esse negotium iudicas de quibus scripseras?
Maximum negotium tecum habes, tu tibi molestus es. Quid
velis nescis, melius probas honesta quam sequeris, vides ubi
sit posita felicitas sed ad illam pervenire non audes. Quid sit   5
autem quod te inpediat, quia parum ipse dispicis, dicam:
magna esse haec existimas quae relicturus es, et cum propo-
suisti tibi illam securitatem ad quam transiturus es, retinet
te huius vitae a qua recessurus es fulgor tamquam in sordida
et obscura casurum. Erras, Lucili: ex hac vita ad illam ascen-   10
ditur. Quod interest inter splendorem et lucem, cum haec
certam originem habeat ac suam, ille niteat alieno, hoc inter
hanc vitam et illam: haec fulgore extrinsecus veniente percussa est, crassam illi statim umbram faciet quisquis obstiterit:
illa suo lumine inlustris est. Studia te tua clarum et nobilem   15
efficient. Exemplum Epicuri referam. Cum Idomeneo scri-
beret et illum a vita speciosa ad fidelem stabilemque gloriam
revocaret, regiae tunc potentiae ministrum et magna tractan-
tem, 'si gloria' inquit 'tangeris, notiorem te epistulae meae
facient quam omnia ista quae colis et propter quae coleris'.   20
Numquid ergo mentitus est? quis Idomenea nosset nisi
Epicurus illum litteris suis incidisset? Omnes illos megistanas
et satrapas et regem ipsum ex quo Idomenei titulus petebatur oblivio alta suppressit. Nomen Attici perire Ciceronis
epistulae non sinunt. Nihil illi profuisset gener Agrippa et   25
Tiberius progener et Drusus Caesar pronepos; inter tam
magna nomina taceretur nisi <sibi> Cicero illum adplicuisset.
Profunda super nos altitudo temporis veniet, pauca ingenia   √√
caput exerent et in idem quandoque silentium abitura obli-
vioni resistent ac se diu vindicabunt. Quod Epicurus amico   30
suo potuit promittere, hoc tibi promitto, Lucili: habebo
apud posteros gratiam, possum mecum duratura nomina
educere. Vergilius noster duobus memoriam aeternam pro-
misit et praestat:

      fortunati ambo! si quid mea carmina possunt,   35
      nulla dies umquam memori vos eximet aevo,
      dum domus Aeneae Capitoli immobile saxum
      accolet imperiumque pater Romanus habebit.

Quoscumque in medium fortuna protulit, quicumque mem-
bra ac partes alienae potentiae fuerant, horum gratia viguit,   40

41–42 post. . .defecit: "after them memory [of them] quickly disappeared."

46 de suo: "from his own account."

47 Pythoclea: masc., acc., sing. of the Greek consonant declension. Pythocles was a friend of Idomeneus.

63–65 ut. . .probent: "so that they (i.e., the *egregia dicta Epicuri*) may prove."

65–66 quocumque. . .vivendum: i.e., no matter what school of philosophy men follow, they must live honorably.

67 et inscriptum hortulis: The daggers indicate a difficulty in the manuscripts reading.

42 **dignatio, -onis,** *f.,* reputation
tantum, *adv.,* only
43 **adhaereo, -ere, -haesi, -haesus,** 2, cling to
44 **excipio, -ere, -cepi, -ceptus,** 3, receive, welcome, continue
45 **gratis,** *adv.,* free of charge, gratis
46 **redimo, -ere, -emi, -emptus,** 3, pay for
47 **locuples, -etis,** *adj.,* rich
publicus, -a, -um, *adj.,* common, ordinary
48 **anceps, -ipitis,** *adj.,* ambiguous, dangerous
50 **apertus, -a, -um,** *adj.,* open, obvious
51 **disertus, -a, -um,** *p. adj. (of* **disero**), well-spoken
57 **impleo, -ere, -plevi, -pletus,** 2, fill, make full
60 **censeo, -ere, -sui, -sus,** 2, express an opinion
63 **eo,** *adv.,* therefore
libenter, *adv.,* willingly, gladly
egregius, -a, -um, *adj.,* distinguished
64 **velamentum, -i,** *n.,* cover, screen
67 **hortulus, -i,** *m.,* garden
69 **polenta, -ae,** *f.,* barley
70 **ecquid = nonne**
73 **consenesco, -ere, -senui,** 3, grow old
75 **desino, -ere, -sivi (-sii), -situs,** 3, cease
76 **licet,** *impers.,* it is permitted
differo, -ferre, distuli, dilatus, *irr.,* postpone
77 **commonefacio, -ere, -feci, -factus,** 3, admonish
78 **inpendo, -ere, -pendi, -pensus,** 3, expend
80 **modo,** *adv.,* only

domus frequentata est, dum ipsi steterunt: post ipsos cito
memoria defecit. Ingeniorum crescit dignatio nec ipsis tantum honor habetur, sed quidquid illorum memoriae adhaesit
excipitur.

Ne gratis Idomeneus in epistulam meam venerit, ipse eam   45
de suo redimet. Ad hunc Epicurus illam nobilem sententiam
scripsit qua hortatur ut Pythoclea locupletem non publica
nec ancipiti via faciat. 'Si vis' inquit 'Pythoclea divitem facere,
non pecuniae adiciendum sed cupiditati detrahendum est.'
Et apertior ista sententia est quam <ut> interpretanda sit,   50
et disertior quam ut adiuvanda. Hoc unum te admoneo, ne
istud tantum existimes de divitiis dictum: quocumque trans-
tuleris, idem poterit. Si vis Pythoclea honestum facere, non
honoribus adiciendum est sed cupiditatibus detrahendum; si
vis Pythoclea esse in perpetua voluptate, non voluptatibus   55
adiciendum est sed cupiditatibus detrahendum; si vis Pythoclea senem facere et implere vitam, non annis adiciendum
est sed cupiditatibus detrahendum. Has voces non est quod
Epicuri esse iudices: publicae sunt. Quod fieri in senatu solet
faciendum ego in philosophia quoque existimo: cum censuit   60
aliquis quod ex parte mihi placeat, iubeo illum dividere
sententiam et sequor quod probo.

Eo libentius Epicuri egregia dicta commemoro, ut istis
qui ad illum confugiunt spe mala inducti, qui velamentum
ipsos vitiorum suorum habituros existimant, probent quo-   65
cumque ierint honeste esse vivendum. Cum adieris eius
hortulos †et inscriptum hortulis† 'HOSPES, HIC BENE MANEBIS,
HIC SVMMVM BONVM VOLVPTAS EST', paratus erit istius domi-
cilii custos hospitalis, humanus, et te polenta excipiet et
aquam quoque large ministrabit et dicet, 'ecquid bene acce-   70
ptus es?' 'Non inritant' inquit 'hi hortuli famem sed extin-
guunt, nec maiorem ipsis potionibus sitim faciunt, sed naturali
et gratuito remedio sedant; in hac voluptate consenui.' De
his tecum desideriis loquor quae consolationem non recipiunt,
quibus dandum est aliquid ut desinant. Nam de illis extra-   75
ordinariis quae licet differre, licet castigare et opprimere,
hoc unum commonefaciam: ista voluptas naturalis est, non
necessaria. Huic nihil debes; si quid inpendis, voluntarium
est. Venter praecepta non audit: poscit, appellat. Non est
tamen molestus creditor: parvo dimittitur, si modo das illi   80
quod debes, non quod potes. *Vale.*

4–5 verba quaerentium: equivalent to our "groping about for subjects of conversation."

7 ne gaudeas: the second person present and perfect subjunctives are sometimes used in commands and prohibitions instead of the more usual imperative mood.

28 in alto: "deep."

32–33 quod. . .introrsus: "[a joy] which reveals more the deeper you go"; or "[a joy] which reveals more when you get to the inside or heart of it."

34 felicem: supply *te.*

37 te. . .parte: these are in apposition to *tuo.*

41 stat: supplied by Madvig to complete the meaning of the clause.

---

2 **quam,** *adv.,* how
3 **remissus, -a, -um,** *p. adj. (of remitto),* mild
4 **ineptiae, -arum,** *f.,* absurdities
5 **prosum, prodesse, profui,** *irr.,* help, be of use
8 **culmen, -inis,** *n.,* summit, height
10 **sollicitus, -a, -um,** *adj.,* anxious, troubled
11 **prorito,** 1, incite, tempt
 licet, although
13 **disco, -ere, didici,** 3, learn
14 **summoveo, -ere, -movi, -motus,** 2, remove
15 **oblectamentum, -i,** *n.,* delight
 devito, 1, avoid
 immo, *adv.,* nay, nay rather
16 **contra,** *adv.,* on the contrary
 desum, -esse, -fui, -futurus, *irr.,* fail, be lacking
17 **modo,** *adv.,* only
18 **impleo, -ere, -plevi, -pletus,** 2, fill
19 **forte,** *adv.,* by chance
20 **alacer, -cris, -cre,** *adj.,* cheerful
21 **quisquam, quae-, quid- (quic-),** *indef. pron.,* anyone, anything
22 **contemno, -ere, -tempsi, -temptus,** 3, scorn, despise
24 **frenum, -i,** *n.,* bridle, reins
25 **verso,** 1, turn, turn over, consider
25 **blandus, -a, -um,** *adj.,* enticing, tempting
26 **deficio, -ere, -feci, -fectus,** 3, fail
 semel, *adv.,* once
27 **levis, -e,** *adj.,* trifling, of small value
 metallum, -i, *n.,* mine, quarry
 fructus, -us, *m.,* profit, yield
28 **summum, -i,** *n.,* surface
29 **fodio, -ere, fodi, fosus,** 3, dig
30 **perfusorius, -a, -um,** *adj.,* slight, superficial
31 **invecticius, -a, -um,** *adj.,* imported, not genuine
34 **praesto, -are, -stiti, -status (-status),** 1, show, display, render
 dissicio, -ere, -ieci, -iectus, 3, throw aside
 conculco, 1, trample upon
39 **suggero, -ere, -gessi, -gestus,** 3, furnish, supply
41 **praeceps, -cipitis,** *n.,* precipice, extreme danger

Epistle Twenty-three

Epistle Twenty-three
TRUE JOY IS A STERN MATTER

Seneca Lucilio Suo Salutem

Putas me tibi scripturum quam humane nobiscum hiemps
egerit, quae et remissa fuit et brevis, quam malignum ver sit,
quam praeposterum frigus, et alias ineptias verba quaerentium? Ego vero aliquid quod et mihi et tibi prodesse possit   5
scribam. Quid autem id erit nisi ut te exhorter ad bonam
mentem? Huius fundamentum quod sit quaeris? ne gaudeas
vanis. Fundamentum hoc esse dixi: culmen est. Ad summa
pervenit qui scit quo gaudeat, qui felicitatem suam in aliena
potestate non posuit; sollicitus est et incertus sui quem spes   10
aliqua proritat, licet ad manum sit, licet non ex difficili
petatur, licet numquam illum sperata deceperint. Hoc ante
omnia fac, mi Lucili: disce gaudere. Existimas nunc me
detrahere tibi multas voluptates qui fortuita summoveo, qui
spes, dulcissima oblectamenta, devitandas existimo? immo   15
contra nolo tibi umquam deesse laetitiam. Volo illam tibi
domi nasci: nascitur si modo intra te ipsum fit. Ceterae
hilaritates non implent pectus; frontem remittunt, leves sunt,
nisi forte tu iudicas eum gaudere qui ridet: animus esse debet
alacer et fidens et supra omnia erectus. Mihi crede, verum   20
gaudium res severa est. An tu existimas quemquam soluto
vultu et, ut isti delicati loquuntur, hilariculo mortem contemnere, paupertati domum aperire, voluptates tenere sub
freno, meditari dolorum patientiam? Haec qui apud se
versat in magno gaudio est, sed parum blando. In huius   25
gaudii possessione esse te volo: numquam deficiet, cum semel
unde petatur inveneris. Levium metallorum fructus in
summo est: illa opulentissima sunt quorum in alto latet vena
adsidue plenius responsura fodienti. Haec quibus delectatur
vulgus tenuem habent ac perfusoriam voluptatem, et quod-   30
cumque invecticium gaudium est fundamento caret: hoc de
quo loquor, ad quod te conor perducere, solidum est et quod
plus pateat introrsus. Fac, oro te, Lucili carissime, quod
unum potest praestare felicem: dissice et conculca ista quae
extrinsecus splendent, quae tibi promittuntur ab alio vel ex   35
alio; ad verum bonum specta et de tuo gaude. Quid est
autem hoc 'de tuo'? te ipso et tui optima parte. Corpusculum
quoque, etiam si nihil fieri sine illo potest, magis necessariam
rem crede quam magnam; vanas suggerit voluptates, breves,
paenitendas ac, nisi magna moderatione temperentur, in   40
contrarium abituras. Ita dico: in praecipiti voluptas <stat>,

47 **unam prementis viam:** a strong way of expressing the consistency necessary to the attainment of a *mens bona*.

50 **suspensi. . .vagi:** adjectives agreeing with the subject of *possunt*.

57 **aeris alieni:** *aes alienum,* "another's coin," is the regular word in Latin for "debt."

64 **cum maxime:** "just now." Cf. *Ep.* 7, lines 41–42.

44 **tutus, -a, -um,** *adj.,* safe
48 **transilio, -ire, -ivi (-ui),** 4, leap across
ne. . .quidem, not. . .even
51 **dispono, -ere, -posui, -positus,** 3, arrange
53 **veho, -ere, vexi, vectus,** 3, carry
54 **torrens, -entis,** *p. adj. (of* **torreo**), rushing
59 **modo,** *adv.,* just now, lately
64 **ordior, -iri, orsus,** 4 dep., begin
65 **propemodum,** *adv.,* almost, nearly
66 **desino, -ere, -sivi (-sii), -situs,** 3, cease, stop

ad dolorem vergit nisi modum tenuit; modum autem tenere
in eo difficile est quod bonum esse credideris: veri boni
aviditas tuta est. Quod sit istud interrogas, aut unde subeat?
Dicam: ex bona conscientia, ex honestis consiliis, ex rectis   45
actionibus, ex contemptu fortuitorum, ex placido vitae et
continuo tenore unam prementis viam. Nam illi qui ex aliis
propositis in alia transiliunt aut ne transiliunt quidem sed
casu quodam transmittuntur, quomodo habere quicquam
certum mansurumve possunt suspensi et vagi? Pauci sunt   50
qui consilio se suaque disponant: ceteri, eorum more quae
fluminibus innatant, non eunt sed feruntur; ex quibus alia
lenior unda detinuit ac mollius vexit, alia vehementior rapuit,
alia proxima ripae cursu languescente deposuit, alia torrens
impetus in mare eiecit. Ideo constituendum est quid velimus   55
et in eo perseverandum.

    Hic est locus solvendi aeris alieni. Possum enim tibi vocem
Epicuri tui reddere et hanc epistulam liberare: 'molestum est
semper vitam inchoare'; aut si hoc modo magis sensus potest
exprimi, 'male vivunt qui semper vivere incipiunt'. 'Quare ?'   60
inquis; desiderat enim explanationem ista vox. Quia semper
illis inperfecta vita est; non potest autem stare paratus ad
mortem qui modo incipit vivere. Id agendum est ut satis
vixerimus: nemo hoc praestat qui orditur cum maxime vitam.
Non est quod existimes paucos esse hos: propemodum omnes   65
sunt. Quidam vero tunc incipiunt cum desinendum est. Si
hoc iudicas mirum, adiciam quod magis admireris: quidam
ante vivere desierunt quam inciperent. *Vale.*

8 **pudebit:** supply *te*, "it will make you ashamed."

11 **magno:** ablative of price; translate "at a high price."

19 **infra:** supply *diem*, "below the sun"; *dies* not only means "day" but also "daylight," "sun."

21 **continget. . .cessatur. . .festinetur:** Seneca (somewhat artfully) employs here the impersonal construction instead of the more blunt personal construction with *tu* as the subject. Latin uses intransitive verbs impersonally more freely than English does. With *continget* supply *tibi; non quidem. . .festinetur:* "you, to be sure, have not been idle up till now but you must increase your speed."

23 **res ista:** the development of virtue *ex se sibi.*

24 **aliud litterarum genus:** i.e., other studies as opposed to philosophy.

27 **illi:** dative after *excideret;* translate "escaped him."

30 **nomenclator:** a slave who announced the names of guests at large gatherings. This important gentleman was undoubtedly also called into service at the morning *salutatio.* The *nomenclator* was originally a political attaché who pointed out to the master the voters by name.

30–31 **non reddit sed inponit:** i.e., when he cannot remember a caller's name he makes up one for him.

34 **teneret:** supply *memoria* (abl.).

36 **non invenerat, faciendos locavit:** "if he did not find them, he had them made to order"; *locare* with the gerundive means "to contract for having a thing done." This sentence illustrates well Seneca's tendency to use compound rather than complex sentences. This would have been written as a conditional sentence by earlier writers.

3 **ideo,** *adv.,* for that reason
vaco, 1, have time for, have leisure for

4 **inprobus, -a, -um,** *adj.,* bold
curatio, -onis, *f.,* cure
obeo, -ire, -ivi (-ii), -itus, 4, offer
tamquam, *adv.,* as if

5 **valetudinarium, -i,** *n.,* hospital
iaceo, -ere, iacui, iacitus, 2, lie

8 **exigo, -ere, -egi, -actus,** 3, deliberate, consult

10 **circa,** *prep. w. acc.,* regarding
praesto, -stare, -stiti, -status (-status), fulfill, offer

11 **luo, -ere, lui,** 3, pay for
tantum, *adv.,* only

12 **quemadmodum,** *adv.,* just as

13 **deprehendo, -ere, -prehendi, -prehensus,** 3, detect

16 **potius,** *adv.,* rather

19 **nubes, -is,** *f.,* cloud
modus, -i, *m.,* manner, way,
modo, in the manner of

21 **contingo, -ere, -tigi, -tactus,** 3, befall, fall to one's lot

22 **vigilia, -ae,** *f.,* sleeplessness

23 **inpendo, -ere, -pendi, -pensus,** 3, expend

24 **adiutorium, -i,** *n.,* assistance

27 **beatus, -a, -um,** *adj.,* wealthy
indecens, -entis, *adj.,* unbecoming

28 **modo,** *adv.,* now

30 **vetulus, -a, -um,** *adj.,* old

31 **perperam,** *adv.,* wrongly
tribus, -us, *f.,* tribe, mob

32 **persaluto,** 1, greet one by one
nihilominus, *adv.,* nevertheless

33 **compendiarius, -a, -um,** *adj.,* short
compendiaria, -ae, *f.,* (supply *via*), short cut
emo, -ere, emi, emptus, 3, buy

35 **lyricus, -i,** *m.,* lyric poet

37 **familia, -ae,** *f.,* household of slaves
comparo, 1, prepare

38 **subinde,** *adv.,* continually

39 **refero, -ferre, -tuli, -latus,** *irr.,* repeat
excido, -ere, -cidi, 3, stumble

Epistle Twenty-seven
VIRTUE ALONE GIVES EVERLASTING JOY

Seneca Lucilio Suo Salutem

'Tu me' inquis 'mones? iam enim te ipse monuisti, iam
correxisti? ideo aliorum emendationi vacas?' Non sum tam
inprobus ut curationes aeger obeam, sed, tamquam in eodem
valetudinario iaceam, de communi tecum malo conloquor   5
et remedia communico. Sic itaque me audi tamquam mecum
loquar; in secretum te meum admitto et te adhibito mecum
exigo. Clamo mihi ipse, 'numera annos tuos, et pudebit
eadem velle quae volueras puer, eadem parare. Hoc denique
tibi circa mortis diem praesta: moriantur ante te vitia. Dimitte   10
istas voluptates turbidas, magno luendas: non venturae tantum sed praeteritae nocent. Quemadmodum scelera etiam si
non sunt deprehensa cum fierent, sollicitudo non cum ipsis
abit, ita inprobarum voluptatum etiam post ipsas paenitentia
est. Non sunt solidae, non sunt fideles; etiam si non nocent,   15
fugiunt. Aliquod potius bonum mansurum circumspice;
nullum autem est nisi quod animus ex se sibi invenit. Sola
virtus praestat gaudium perpetuum, securum; etiam si quid
obstat, nubium modo intervenit, quae infra feruntur nec
umquam diem vincunt.' Quando ad hoc gaudium pervenire   20
continget? non quidem cessatur adhuc, sed festinetur.
Multum restat operis, in quod ipse necesse est vigiliam, ipse
laborem tuum inpendas, si effici cupis; delegationem res ista
non recipit. Aliud litterarum genus adiutorium admittit.
Calvisius Sabinus memoria nostra fuit dives; et patrimonium   25
habebat libertini et ingenium; numquam vidi hominem
beatum indecentius. Huic memoria tam mala erat ut illi
nomen modo Ulixis excideret, modo Achillis, modo Priami,
quos tam bene noverat quam paedagogos nostros novimus.
Nemo vetulus nomenclator, qui nomina non reddit sed   30
inponit, tam perperam tribus quam ille Troianos et Achivos
persalutabat. Nihilominus eruditus volebat videri. Hanc
itaque compendiariam excogitavit: magna summa emit servos, unum qui Homerum teneret, alterum qui Hesiodum;
novem praeterea lyricis singulos adsignavit. Magno emisse   35
illum non est quod mireris: non invenerat, faciendos locavit.
Postquam haec familia illi comparata est, coepit convivas
suos inquietare. Habebat ad pedes hos, a quibus subinde cum
peteret versus quos referret, saepe in medio verbo excidebat.

42 **analectas:** *analectae* were slaves who picked up crumbs after a meal. Satellius playfully advises Calvisius to employ *grammaticos analectas* who would not only pick up crumbs but words that his master had forgotten.

43 **centenis millibus. . .constare:** with *centenis millibus* supply *sesterium; constare* with a genitive or (as here) ablative of price was a mercantile technical term. Cf. the English expression "it stood him twenty dollars."

43 **minoris:** genitive of value or indefinite price; translate "at a lesser sum."

46 **hominem:** in apposition to illum.

48 **istuc:** an alternate form of istud.

52 **accipe. . .quod debeo:** see *Ep.* 7, line 63.

40 **adrosor, -oris,** *m.,* gnawer, parasite
41 **adrisor, -oris,** *m.,* fawner, flatterer
42 **derisor, -oris,** *m.,* mocker
44 **totidem,** *indecl. adj.,* just so many, just as many
    scrinium, -i, *n.,* bookcase
46 **luctor,** 1 *dep.,* wrestle
47 **gracilis, -e,** *adj.,* thin
50 **commodo,** 1, lend
    venalis, -e, *adj.,* for sale
51 **cotidie,** *adv.,* daily
52 **ad,** *prep. w. acc.,* according to
53 **compositus, -a, -um,** *p. adj.* (*of* **compono**), arranged, regulated
54 **aliter,** *adv.,* otherwise
    aliter atque aliter, now in one way now in another

Suasit illi Satellius Quadratus, stultorum divitum adrosor   40
et, quod sequitur, adrisor, et, quod duobus his adiunctum est,
derisor, ut grammaticos haberet analectas. Cum dixisset
Sabinus centenis millibus sibi constare singulos servos, 'minoris'
inquit 'totidem scrinia emisses'. Ille tamen in ea opinione
erat ut putaret se scire quod quisquam in domo sua sciret.   45
Idem Satellius illum hortari coepit ut luctaretur, hominem
aegrum, pallidum, gracilem. Cum Sabinus respondisset, 'et
quomodo possum? vix vivo', 'noli, obsecro te' inquit 'istuc
dicere: non vides quam multos servos valentissimos habeas?'
Bona mens nec commodatur nec emitur; et puto, si venalis   50
esset, non haberet emptorem: at mala cotidie emitur.
    Sed accipe iam quod debeo et vale. 'Divitiae sunt ad legem
naturae composita paupertas.' Hoc saepe dicit Epicurus
aliter atque aliter, sed numquam nimis dicitur quod numquam satis discitur; quibusdam remedia monstranda,   55
quibusdam inculcanda sunt. *Vale.*

3–4 **quod. . .mentis:** this clause explains the preceding *hoc.*

7 **terraeque. . .recedant:** Vergil, *Aeneid* 3.72. Aeneas refers to the lands and cities that recede as he and his comrades sail from one place to another encountering different perils.

12 **in inritum cedit:** "is good for nothing," "is of no avail"; *inritus, -a, -um,* in vain, useless.

16 **vatis:** a genitive with *habitum* understood; *vatis* refers to the Cumaean Sibyl or prophetess.

18–19 **bacchatur. . .deum:** Vergil, *Aeneid* 6.78–79. The Cumaean Sibyl or prophetess resists submission to Phoebus and hopelessly tries to shake the god from her breast. But unable to do so and fully inspired, she proceeds to make predictions to Aeneas.

21–23 **sicut. . .demergunt:** "just as a fixed cargo on a ship does not unbalance it [whereas] a cargo that shifts unevenly more readily tilts that side where it has settled"; *minus = non.*

24 **istuc:** an alternate form of *istud.*

27 **quis:** in the sense of *qualis.* This whole clause is the subject of *interest.* Lit., "what sort of a person [you are who have come] rather than where you have come is of importance"; i.e., the condition in which you have come to a place is of greater importance than the place to which you have come.

32–33 **prima. . .crederes:** with *quaeque prima. . .quaeque* supply *regio:* "Every [region you came to] first would have pleased you, if you believed that every [region] was your own." This idea refers to *patria mea totus hic mundus est,* line 30.

37 **disponere se:** "to arrange oneself"; i.e., choose one's environment.

2 **quasi,** *adv.,* as if it were
3 **peregrinatio, -onis,** *f.,* traveling
4 **discutio, -ere, -cussi, -cussus,** 3, shake off
8 **queror, -i, questus,** 3 *dep.,* complain
10 **prosum, prodesse, profui,** *irr.,* be of use, aid
12 **iactatio, -onis,** *f.,* frequent motion, restlessness
15 **habitus, -us,** *m.,* condition, disposition
18 **bacchor,** 1 *dep.,* revel, rave
19 **excutio, -ere, -cussi, -cussus,** 3, shake out
20 **vado, -ere,** 3, go
   insido, -ere, -sedi, -sessus, sit *or* settle down
21 **incommodus, -a, -um,** *adj.,* troublesome
23 **incumbo, -ere, -cubui, -cubitus,** 3, lean upon
24 **eximo, -ere, -emi, -emptus,** 3, take out, remove
26 **quilibet, quae-, quid-,** *indef. adj.,* any
   angulus, -i, *m.,* corner
27 **qualiscumque, qualecumque,** *adj.,* of whatever sort
28 **addico, -ere, -dixi, -dictus,** 3, give up or over, attach
29 **persuasio, -onis,** *f.,* conviction
31 **liqueo, -ere, liqui (licui),** 2, be clear
32 **subinde,** *adv.,* continually
33 **quisque, quaeque, quodque,** *adj.,* whoever or whatever it be, each, every
34 **peregrinor,** 1 *dep.,* travel
36 **turbidus, -a, -um,** *adj.,* tumultuous
38 **procul,** *adv.,* far, at a distance

Epistle Twenty-eight
TRAVEL CANNOT CURE THE SOUL'S MALADIES

Seneca Lucilio Suo Salutem

Hoc tibi soli putas accidisse et admiraris quasi rem novam
quod peregrinatione tam longa et tot locorum varietatibus
non discussisti tristitiam gravitatemque mentis? Animum
debes mutare, non caelum. Licet vastum traieceris mare,   5
licet, ut ait Vergilius noster,

> terraeque urbesque recedant,

sequentur te quocumque perveneris vitia. Hoc idem querenti
cuidam Socrates ait, 'quid miraris nihil tibi peregrinationes
prodesse, cum te circumferas? premit te eadem causa quae   10
expulit'. Quid terrarum iuvare novitas potest? quid cognitio
urbium aut locorum? in inritum cedit ista iactatio. Quaeris
quare te fuga ista non adiuvet? tecum fugis. Onus animi
deponendum est: non ante tibi ullus placebit locus. Talem
nunc esse habitum tuum cogita qualem Vergilius noster   15
vatis inducit iam concitatae et instigatae multumque habentis
in se spiritus non sui:

> bacchatur vates, magnum si pectore possit
> excussisse deum.

Vadis huc illuc ut excutias insidens pondus quod ipsa iacta-   20
tione incommodius fit, sicut in navi onera inmota minus
urgent, inaequaliter convoluta citius eam partem in quam
incubuere demergunt. Quidquid facis, contra te facis et motu
ipso noces tibi; aegrum enim concutis. At cum istuc exemeris
malum, omnis mutatio loci iucunda fiet; in ultimas expellaris   25
terras licebit, in quolibet barbariae angulo conloceris, hospitalis tibi illa qualiscumque sedes erit. Magis quis veneris
quam quo interest, et ideo nulli loco addicere debemus
animum. Cum hac persuasione vivendum est: 'non sum uni
angulo natus, patria mea totus hic mundus est'. Quod si   30
liqueret tibi, non admirareris nil adiuvari te regionum varietatibus in quas subinde priorum taedio migras; prima enim
quaeque placuisset si omnem tuam crederes. Nunc <non>
peregrinaris sed erras et ageris ac locum ex loco mutas, cum
illud quod quaeris, bene vivere, omni loco positum sit. Num   35
quid tam turbidum fieri potest quam forum? ibi quoque
licet quiete vivere, si necesse sit. Sed si liceat disponere se,
conspectum quoque et viciniam fori procul fugiam; nam ut

41   **Dissentio ab his:** Latin says "disagree from," where we say "disagree with."

46   **inquit:** the subject is one of the *his qui* of line 41.

50   **portorium:** here the quotation due Lucilius for each letter (see *Ep.* 7, line 63) is spoken of as "tax" or "duty."

54   **cogitare:** supply *eos* as subject.

39   **gravis, -e,** *adj.*, unwholesome
    valetudo, -inis, *f.*, health
40   **necdum,** *adv.*, and not yet
    convalesco, -ere, -valui, 3, gain strength
41   **parum,** *adv.*, too little
42   **cotidie,** *adv.*, daily
43   **conluctor,** 1 *dep.*, struggle
45   **rixor,** 1 *dep.*, quarrel
48   **contemno, -ere, -tempsi, -temptus,** 3, scorn
    quantuslibet, quanta-, quantum-, *adj.*, however great
49   **turba, -ae,** *f.*, crowd
50   **desino, -ere, -sivi (-sii), -situs,** 3, stop
51   **notitia, -ae,** *f.*, knowledge
    egregie, *adv.*, excellently
53   **deprehendo, -ere, -prehendi, -prehensus,** 3, detect, discover
54   **glorior,** 1 *dep.*, boast
56   **coarguo, -ere, -argui,** 3, convict
    fungor, -i, functus, 3 *dep.*, perform
57   **novissime,** *superl. adv.*, lastly
    deprecator, -oris, *m.*, intercessor
    aliquando, *adv.*, at times
    offendo, -ere, -fendi, -fensus, 3, punish

loca gravia etiam firmissimam valetudinem temptant, ita
bonae quoque menti necdum adhuc perfectae et convalescenti   40
sunt aliqua parum salubria. Dissentio ab his qui in fluctus
medios eunt et tumultuosam probantes vitam cotidie cum
difficultatibus rerum magno animo conluctantur. Sapiens
feret ista, non eliget, et malet in pace esse quam in pugna;
non multum prodest vitia sua proiecisse, si cum alienis rixan-   45
dum est. 'Triginta' inquit 'tyranni Socraten circumsteterunt
nec potuerunt animum eius infringere.' Quid interest quot
domini sint? servitus una est; hanc qui contempsit in quanta-
libet turba dominantium liber est.

Tempus est desinere, sed si prius portorium solvero.   50
'Initium est salutis notitia peccati.' Egregie mihi hoc dixisse
videtur Epicurus; nam qui peccare se nescit corrigi non vult;
deprehendas te oportet antequam emendes. Quidam vitiis
gloriantur: tu existimas aliquid de remedio cogitare qui mala
sua virtutum loco numerant? Ideo quantum potes te ipse   55
coargue, inquire in te; accusatoris primum partibus fungere,
deinde iudicis, novissime deprecatoris; aliquando te offende.
Vale.

6 **aliter. . .quam ut:** "other than that."

13 **hortantem:** supply *me* as subject.

13–15 **Quid illud. . .constat:** "'What of that? you say. 'I'm still willing.' The most important element lies precisely in this [i.e., willingness]; it is not merely, as the proverb has it, that 'Well begun is half done' [for willingness constitutes *more* than *half*]. Such willingness is the essence of the mind."

21 **in recto:** "on the right track."

2 **discutio, -ere, -cussi, -cussus,** 3, shake off
   recalesco, -ere, -calui, 3, become warm, glow
   quotiens, *adv.,* whenever, as often as

4 **olim,** *adv.,* sometime ago
   superiacio, -ere, -ieci, -iectus, 3, outstrip

5 **fetus, -us,** *m.,* breeding, off-spring
   grex, gregis, *m.,* flock

6 **alumnus, -i,** *m.,* pupil
   intueor, -eri, -tuitus, 2 *dep.,* look upon, regard

8 **ingenium, -i,** *n.,* mind
   tener, -era, -erum, *adj.,* young

9 **subito,** *adv.,* suddenly
   adsero, -ere, -serui, -sertus, 3, claim

10 **indoles, -is,** *f.,* nature

11 **lente,** *adv.,* slowly
   subinde, *adv.,* repeatedly, continually

12 **invicem,** *adv.,* in turn

17 **absolutus, -a, -um,** *p. adj.* (*of* **absolvo**), complete

19 **incumbo, -ere, -cubui, -cubitus,** 3, apply *or* devote one's self

20 **congruo, -ere, -grui,** 3, harmonize
   percutio, -ere, -cussi, -cussus, 3, strike, stamp

Epistle Thirty-four
THE TEACHER'S JOY AT HIS PUPIL'S SUCCESS

Seneca Lvcilio Svo Salvtem

Cresco et exulto et discussa senectute recalesco quotiens
ex iis quae agis ac scribis intellego quantum te ipse—nam
turbam olim reliqueras—superieceris. Si agricolam arbor ad
fructum perducta delectat, si pastor ex fetu gregis sui capit   5
voluptatem, si alumnum suum nemo aliter intuetur quam ut
adulescentiam illius suam iudicet, quid evenire credis iis
qui ingenia educaverunt et quae tenera formaverunt adulta
subito vident? Adsero te mihi; meum opus es. Ego cum
vidissem indolem tuam, inieci manum, exhortatus sum,   10
addidi stimulos nec lente ire passus sum sed subinde incitavi;
et nunc idem facio, sed iam currentem hortor et invicem
hortantem. 'Quid illud?' inquis 'adhuc volo.' In hoc plurimum est, non sic quomodo principia totius operis dimi-
dium occupare dicuntur. Ista res animo constat; itaque pars   15
magna bonitatis est velle fieri bonum. Scis quem bonum
dicam? perfectum, absolutum, quem malum facere nulla
vis, nulla necessitas possit. Hunc te prospicio, si persevera-
veris et incubueris et id egeris ut omnia facta dictaque tua
inter se congruant ac respondeant sibi et una forma percussa   20
sint. Non est huius animus in recto cuius acta discordant.
Vale.

2–3 **Quod. . .rogatus es:** "you have taken an oath, you have promised [to be] a good man; this is the mightiest bond regarding a sound mind." The infinitive clause *virum bonum,* which has an *esse* understood with it, is the object of both *promisisti* and *rogatus es.* The *quod* clause is in apposition to this object infinitive clause: *sacramento rogatus es* is a technical military phrase meaning "you have been bound by an oath."

4 **militiam:** i.e., "soldiering [toward virtue]."

6 **uri. . .necari:** this was the cruel oath taken by the gladiator when he made a contract with his master: *uri, vinciri, verberari, ferroque necari patior.* For the butchery of the gladiatorial combats, see *Ep. 7.*

7–8 **edunt. . .reddant:** i.e., these gladiators were well nourished and lived from wages received for fighting in the arena, but sooner or later they had to pay with their blood.

8 **cavetur:** the verb *caveo* is here used impersonally in the sense of "receive bail or security" from a person. The person from whom it is received is in the ablative with *a* or *ab,* and that for which the bail is received is expressed by an *ut* or *ne* clause.

    a te: supply *cavetur.*

10 **misericordiam populi temptare:** the defeated gladiator could appeal to the audience's mercy to spare his life.

15 **Fit via <vi>:** Vergil, *Aeneid* 2.494. In Book 2, Aeneas, at the request of Dido, narrates the fall of Troy. This quotation refers to the incident where the Greeks, led by Achilles' son Pyrrhus, force their way into the palace of Priam, the Trojan king.

18 **contingere:** subject of the verb.

29 **non ire sed ferri:** for an explanation of these words, cf. *Ep. 107,* line 11: *Ducunt volentem fata, nolentem trahunt,* where Seneca is quoting from the Stoic Cleanthes.

4 **mollis, -e,** *adj.,* soft
5 **auctoramentum, -i,** *n.,* oath
6 **uro, -ere, ussi, ustus,** 3, burn
  vincio, -ire, vinxi, vinctus, 4, bind
  neco, 1, slay
7 **loco,** 1, lease or hire out
8 **vel,** *conj.,* even
  invitus, -a, -um, *adj.,* against one's will
9 **libens, -entis,** *p. adj.* (of **libet),** willing, gladly
  summitto, -ere, -misi, -missus, 3, lower
12 **porro,** *adv.,* moreover
  prosum, prodesse, profui, *irr.,* be of use
  lucrifico, 1, gain
  missio, -onis, *f.,* discharge
13 **expedio,** 4, set free, liberate
18 **contingo, -ere, -tigi, -tactus,** 3, attain
  aliter, *adv.,* otherwise
19 **stultitia, -ae,** *f.,* folly
  adfectus, -us, *m.,* emotion
20 **interdum,** *adv.,* sometimes
  alternus, -a, -um, *adj.,* by turns, alternately
  alternis (*abl. pl.,* supply *vicibus*), alternately, by turns
21 **pariter,** *adv.,* together
23 **gradus, -us,** *m.,* step
25 **adgredior, -i, -gressus,** 3 *dep.,* go to, approach
  incido, -ere, -cidi, -casus, 3, fall upon
27 **illo,** *adv.,* to that situation
  impetus, -us, *m.,* impulse
  inpingo, -ere, -pegi, -pactus, 3, drive
29 **subito,** *adv.,* suddenly
  turbo, -inis, *m.,* whirlpool

Epistle Thirty-seven
SOLDIERING TOWARD THE GOOD LIFE

Seneca Lucilio Suo Salutem

Quod maximum vinculum est ad bonam mentem, promisisti virum bonum, sacramento rogatus es. Deridebit te,
si quis tibi dixerit mollem esse militiam et facilem. Nolo te
decipi. Eadem honestissimi huius et illius turpissimi aucto-   5
ramenti verba sunt: 'uri, vinciri ferroque necari'. Ab illis
qui manus harenae locant et edunt ac bibunt quae per
sanguinem reddant cavetur ut ista vel inviti patiantur: a te
ut volens libensque patiaris. Illis licet arma summittere,
misericordiam populi temptare: tu neque summittes nec   10
vitam rogabis; recto tibi invictoque moriendum est. Quid
porro prodest paucos dies aut annos lucrificare? sine missione
nascimur. 'Quomodo ergo' inquis 'me expediam?' Effugere
non potes necessitates, potes vincere.

Fit via <vi>;   15

et hanc tibi viam dabit philosophia. Ad hanc te confer si vis
salvus esse, si securus, si beatus, denique si vis esse, quod est
maximum, liber; hoc contingere aliter non potest. Humilis
res est stultitia, abiecta, sordida, servilis, multis adfectibus et
saevissimis subiecta. Hos tam graves dominos, interdum alter-   20
nis imperantes, interdum pariter, dimittit a te sapientia,
quae sola libertas est. Una ad hanc fert via, et quidem recta;
non aberrabis; vade certo gradu. Si vis omnia tibi subicere,
te subice rationi; multos reges, si ratio te rexerit. Ab illa
disces quid et quemadmodum adgredi debeas; non incides   25
rebus. Neminem mihi dabis qui sciat quomodo quod vult
coeperit velle: non consilio adductus illo sed impetu inpactus
est. Non minus saepe fortuna in nos incurrit quam nos in
illam. Turpe est non ire sed ferri, et subito in medio turbine
rerum stupentem quaerere, 'huc ego quemadmodum veni?'   30
Vale.

6 **consilium:** supply *sed* before the second *consilium* in this line. Seneca frequently employs ASYNDETON (the omission of a conjunction between words, phrases, or sentences).

8 **ubi vero:** "but indeed when."

10 **haerent:** supply *animo:* the subject is *submissiora verba.*

14 **non late. . .crescit:** "it is not largely in evidence, if you look at it; [but] increases with use."

15 **Pauca. . .dicuntur:** cf. *nec enim multis opus est sed efficacibus* (lines 10–11).

19 **ipsa:** i.e., *mens.*

2 **merito,** *adv.*, deservedly
exigo, -ere, -egi, -actus, 3, demand
commercium, -i, *n.*, exchange
3 **frequento,** 1, repeat often
proficio, -ere, -feci, -fectus, 3, help
minutatim, *adv.*, little by little
4 **inrepo, -ere, -repsi, -reptus,** 3, creep into
effundo, -ere, -fudi, -fusus, 3, pour out
5 **strepitus, -us,** *m.*, noise
6 **clare,** *adv.*, in a loud voice
7 **aliquando,** *adv.*, at some time or other
contio, -onis, *f.*, speech
9 **disco, -ere, didici,** 3, learn
submissus, -a, -um, *p. adj. (of* **submitto),** soft
10 **haereo, -ere, haesi, haesus,** 2, cling
11 **modus, -i,** *m.*, manner, way,
modo, in the manner of, like
spargo, -ere, sparsi, sparsus, 3, scatter
12 **quamvis,** *adv.*, however
exiguus, -a, -um, *adj.*, small
idoneus, -a, -um, *adj.*, suitable
13 **explico,** 1, unfold
auctus, -us, *m.*, growth
diffundo, -ere, -fudi, -fusus, 3, spread
15 **excipio, -ere, -cepi, -ceptus,** 3, receive
16 **convalesco, -ere, -valui,** 3, gain strength
exsurgo, -ere, -surrexi, 3, rise up
17 **efficio, -ere, -feci, -fectus,** 3, accomplish
angustus, -a, -um, *adj.*, narrow, small
18 **tantum,** *adv.*, only
19 **invicem,** *adv.*, in turn

Epistle Thirty-eight
THE INTIMACY AND VALUE OF CONVERSATION

Seneca Lucilio Suo Salutem

Merito exigis ut hoc inter nos epistularum commercium fre-
quentemus. Plurimum proficit sermo, quia minutatim
inrepit animo: disputationes praeparatae et effusae audiente
populo plus habent strepitus, minus familiaritatis. Philo-   5
sophia bonum consilium est: consilium nemo clare dat.
Aliquando utendum est et illis, ut ita dicam, contionibus,
ubi qui dubitat inpellendus est; ubi vero non hoc agendum
est, ut velit discere, sed ut discat, ad haec submissiora verba
veniendum est. Facilius intrant et haerent; nec enim multis   10
opus est sed efficacibus. Seminis modo spargenda sunt, quod
quamvis sit exiguum, cum occupavit idoneum locum, vires
suas explicat et ex minimo in maximos auctus diffunditur.
Idem facit ratio: non late patet, si aspicias; in opere crescit.
Pauca sunt quae dicuntur, sed si illa animus bene excepit,   15
convalescunt et exsurgunt. Eadem est, inquam, praecepto-
rum condicio quae seminum: multum efficiunt, et angusta
sunt. Tantum, ut dixi, idonea mens rapiat illa et in se tra-
hat; multa invicem et ipsa generabit et plus reddet quam
acceperit. *Vale.*   20

6 **a te:** Latin says "near from" where the English idiom demands "near to."

13 **quis deus. . .deus:** Vergil, *Aeneid* 8.352. With *quis deus* a *sit* is to be understood. In Book 8, Aeneas seeks the aid of King Evander, a Greek from Arcadia who had founded the small town Pallanteum, which was to become the future site of Rome. Through the mouth of Evander, Vergil points out the historic places of the imperial city. When the King describes the site of the future Capitol in Book 8, he employs the line quoted here.

14–16 **Si tibi. . .summovens:** here Seneca deviates from his usual crisp style with short clauses. This passage is a sample of Seneca's use of the complex sentence in the periodic style; *lucus* is modified by the two adjectives *frequens* and *summovens*. The ablatives *vetustis arboribus. . .egressis* are due to the idea of fullness in *frequens; conspectum* is the object of *summovens,* and the genitive clause *ramorum aliorum alios protegentium* depends upon *densitate: alios* is the object of *protegentium.*

23–25 **coluntur. . .sacravit:** Seneca sometimes changes from the active to the passive and vice versa in the same sentence.

29–30 **quam ut. . .possit:** lit., "than that it can be believed. . . ." i.e., "to be believed similar to this tiny body in which it exists." The subjunctive *possit* is used in a result clause after the comparative degree and is introduced by *quam ut.*

30 **isto:** supply *corpusculo.*

31 **omnia:** object of *transeuntem,* which modifies *animum.*

32 **quidquid. . .optimusque:** object of *ridentem,* which modifies *animum.*

34 **itaque. . .descendit:** "and so, in respect to its greater part it is there [i.e., in heaven] whence it descended"; *maiore. . .parte* is ablative of respect or specification.

36 **in hoc:** "for this purpose."

39 **nostris. . .interest:** "it takes part in our affairs as if it were a superior"; *interest* is here not the impersonal "it concerns" but the personal form of the verb *intersum, -esse,* be present, take part in.

2 **salutaris, -e,** *adj.,* wholesome, beneficial
3 **stultus, -a, -um,** *adj.,* foolish
4 **inpetro, 1,** obtain
5 **aedituus, -i,** *m.,* keeper of a temple
   simulacrum, -i, *n.,* statue
   quasi, *adv.,* as if
9 **prout,** *conj.,* just as
   tracto, 1, treat
12 **unusquisque, unaquaeque, unumquidque,** *indef. pron.,* each one, each
14 **vetustus, -a, -um,** *adj.,* old
   solitus, -a, -um, *adj.,* usual
15 **egredior, -i, -gressus, 3** *dep.,* go beyond
   frequens, -entis, *adj.,* crowded, filled
   lucus, -i, *m.,* grove
16 **protego, -ere, -texi, -tectus, 3,** cover
   summoveo, -ere, -movi, -motus, 2, remove
   proceritas, -atis, *f.,* tallness
17 **secretum, -i,** *n.,* solitude
18 **numen, -inis,** *n.,* divinity
19 **specus, -us,** *m.,* cave
   penitus, *adv.,* deep within
   exedo, -ere, -edi, -esus, 3, eat up
   suspendo, -ere, -pendi, -pensus, 3, support
20 **laxitas, -atis,** *f.,* roominess
21 **excavatus, -a, -um,** *p. adj. (of* **excavo),** hollowed out
   percutio, -ere, -cussi, -cussus, 3, strike
22 **caput, -itis,** *n.,* source
   subitus, -a, -um, *adj.,* sudden
23 **abditum, -i,** *n.,* hiding
   amnis, -is, *m.,* stream
24 **calens, -entis,** *p. adj. (of* **caleo),** hot
   stagnum, -i, *n.,* pool
   opacitas, -atis, *f.,* shade
31 **tamquam,** *adv.,* as if
33 **adminiculum, -i,** *n.,* support
34 **quemadmodum,** *adv.,* just as
35 **radius, -i,** *m.,* ray
   contingo, -ere, -tigi, -tactus, 3, touch
36 **unde,** *adv.,* whence, from where
37 **propior, propius,** *comp. adj.,* nearer, more closely
   conversor, 1 *dep.,* associate
38 **haereo, -ere, haesi, haesus, 2,** cling
39 **nitor, -i, nisus (nixus), 3** *dep.,* strive

Epistle Forty-one
GOD WITHIN YOU

Seneca Lucilio Suo Salutem

Facis rem optimam et tibi salutarem si, ut scribis, per-
severas ire ad bonam mentem, quam stultum est optare cum
possis a te inpetrare. Non sunt ad caelum elevandae manus
nec exorandus aedituus ut nos ad aurem simulacri, quasi   5
magis exaudiri possimus, admittat: prope est a te deus,
tecum est, intus est. Ita dico, Lucili: sacer intra nos spiritus
sedet, malorum bonorumque nostrorum observator et custos; hic prout a nobis tractatus est, ita nos ipse tractat.
Bonus vero vir sine deo nemo est: an potest aliquis supra   10
fortunam nisi ab illo adiutus exsurgere? Ille dat consilia
magnifica et erecta. In unoquoque virorum bonorum

(quis deus incertum est) habitat deus.

Si tibi occurrerit vetustis arboribus et solitam altitudinem
egressis frequens lucus et conspectum caeli <densitate> ra-   15
morum aliorum alios protegentium summovens, illa proceritas silvae et secretum loci et admiratio umbrae in aperto
tam densae atque continuae fidem tibi numinis faciet. Si
quis specus saxis penitus exesis montem suspenderit, non
manu factus, sed naturalibus causis in tantam laxitatem   20
excavatus, animum tuum quadam religionis suspicione per-
cutiet. Magnorum fluminum capita veneramur; subita ex
abdito vasti amnis eruptio aras habet; coluntur aquarum
calentium fontes, et stagna quaedam vel opacitas vel immensa
altitudo sacravit. Si hominem videris interritum periculis,   25
intactum cupiditatibus, inter adversa felicem, in mediis tem-
pestatibus placidum, ex superiore loco homines videntem, ex
aequo deos, non subibit te veneratio eius? non dices, 'ista
res maior est altiorque quam ut credi similis huic in quo est
corpusculo possit'? Vis isto divina descendit; animum excel-   30
lentem, moderatum, omnia tamquam minora transeuntem,
quidquid timemus optamusque ridentem, caelestis potentia
agitat. Non potest res tanta sine adminiculo numinis stare;
itaque maiore sui parte illic est unde descendit. Quemadmodum radii solis contingunt quidem terram sed ibi   35
sunt unde mittuntur, sic animus magnus ac sacer et in hoc
demissus, ut propius [quidem] divina nossemus, conversatur
quidem nobiscum sed haeret origini suae; illinc pendet, illuc
spectat ac nititur, nostris tamquam melior interest. Quis est

41 **aliena:** i.e., the externals or outer possessions of a man.

     eo: "than that man."

44 **mittitur:** supply *in arenam.*

47 **speciosus ex horrido:** i.e., attractive to people from the fear he inspires.

47–48 **non. . .aspici:** this infinitive clause explains the preceding *hic.*

48 **praefertur:** supply "by the bettors."

49 **suo:** used of the internal self as opposed to the external self (see *aliena,* line 41).

50 **pondere. . .eorum quae tulit:** "by the weight of those things which it has borne," i.e., with the weight of the fruit it bears. The *ipsa* in this clause is rather widely separated from its noun, *adminicula.*

51 **cui:** dative after *dependent.*

53 **quod ipsius est:** "which is [characteristic] of himself," i.e., what is peculiar to his own nature; *ipsius* is a predicate genitive of possession.

40 **niteo, -ere,** 2, shine

42 **protinus,** *adv.,* straightway, at once

43 **aureus, -a, -um,** *adj.,* golden
     frenum, -i, *n.,* (*pl.* **freni,** *m. or* **frena** *n.*), bit, bridle
     aliter, *adv.,* differently

44 **iuba, -ae,** *f.,* mane
     contracto, 1, touch, handle

45 **incultus, -a, -um,** *adj.,* unadorned, wild

46 **hic, haec, hoc,** *dem. adj.,* and *pron.,* the latter
     scilicet, *adv.,* of course

47 **speciosus, -a, -um,** *adj.,* good-looking
     decor, -oris, *m.,* glory

48 **bratteatus, -a, -um,** *adj.,* gilded
     glorior, 1 *dep.,* boast

49 **vitis, -is,** *f.,* vine
     palmes, -itis, *f.,* shoot
     onero, 1, load

50 **adminiculum, -i,** *n.,* prop
     deduco, -ere, -duxi, -ductus, 3, lead down, drag

52 **dependeo, -ere,** 2, hang from *or* on
     proprius, -a, -um, *adj.,* special, peculiar

54 **formonsus, -a, -um,** *adj.,* beautiful
     sero, -ere, sevi, satus, 3, sow, plant

55 **fenero,** 1, lend on interest

59 **inpleo, -ere, -plevi, -pletus,** 2, fulfill

62 **trudo, -ere, trusi, trusus,** 3, push

ergo hic animus? qui nullo bono nisi suo nitet. Quid enim   40
est stultius quam in homine aliena laudare? quid eo demen-
tius qui ea miratur quae ad alium transferri protinus possunt?
Non faciunt meliorem equum aurei freni. Aliter leo aurata
iuba mittitur, dum contractatur et ad patientiam recipiendi
ornamenti cogitur fatigatus, aliter incultus, integri spiritus: 45
hic scilicet impetu acer, qualem illum natura esse voluit,
speciosus ex horrido, cuius hic decor est, non sine timore
aspici, praefertur illi languido et bratteato. Nemo gloriari
nisi suo debet. Vitem laudamus si fructu palmites onerat, si
ipsa pondere [ad terram] eorum quae tulit adminicula de-   50
ducit: num quis huic illam praeferret vitem cui aureae uvae,
aurea folia dependent? Propria virtus est in vite fertilitas;
in homine quoque id laudandum est quod ipsius est. Fami-
liam formonsam habet et domum pulchram, multum serit,
multum fenerat: nihil horum in ipso est sed circa ipsum.   55
Lauda in illo quod nec eripi potest nec dari, quod proprium
hominis est. Quaeris quid sit? animus et ratio in animo
perfecta. Rationale enim animal est homo; consummatur
itaque bonum eius, si id inplevit cui nascitur. Quid est
autem quod ab illo ratio haec exigat? rem facillimam, secun-   60
dum naturam suam vivere. Sed hanc difficilem facit communis insania: in vitia alter alterum trudimus. Quomodo
autem revocari ad salutem possunt quos nemo retinet, populus inpellit? *Vale.*

4   **secundae notae:** "of the second class." The following *ille alter* means "that other," i.e., "first class."

6   **ex intervallo:** "after a long interval of time."

10   **At:** "but" introduces Lucilius' supposed objections.

12   **nequitiaest:** "does wickedness have"; *nequitiae* is dative of possession; *nequitiaest = nequitiae est*.

15–16 **non minus. . .aperuit:** "[but] when their own strength has pleased them (i.e., when they are capable of exercising their strength), their vices will be no less daring than those which prosperity has already disclosed."

20   **ut. . .deficitur:** "lacks the favor of fortune [which would enable it] to dare deeds equal to the worst"; i.e., the multitude simply lacks the opportunity to exercise its vices. *Deficio* in the passive means "to be wanting in," "to lack."

21   **eadem. . .volunt:** "you will find out that their desires are the same: [if you] give them power to do whatever they wish." The words in brackets, *subaudi si*, are untranslatable because the text is defective here.

22   **Meministi:** in this paragraph we are given an instance of that type of man mentioned above, who, once he escapes restraint, displays all of his vices and thereby induces his own downfall.

31–32 **quaedam tanti non sunt:** "some things are not of so much worth," i.e., are of less value [than the superfluous things].

---

2   **atqui,** *conj.*, and yet
3   **cito,** *adv.*, quickly
5   **fortasse,** *adv.*, perhaps
     tamquam, *adv.*, like
     semel, *adv.*, once
7   **in,** *prep. w. acc.*, among, regarding
     eximius, -a, -um, *adj.*, extraordinary
8   **adhuc,** *adv.*, still
9   **profiteor, -eri, -fessus, 2** *dep.*, profess
     nondum, *adv.*, not yet
12   **displiceo, -ere, -plicui, -plicitus, 2,** displease
13   **subitus, -a, -um,** *adj.*, sudden
     inpotenter, *adv.*, intemperately
14   **inbecillus, -a, -um,** *adj.*, weak, powerless
17   **explico, 1,** unfold
     tuto, *adv.*, safely
18   **tracto, 1,** handle
     rigeo, -ere, 2, be stiff
19   **torpeo, -ere, 2,** be numb
23   **volaticus, -a, -um,** *adj.*, flighty
24   **pinna, -ae,** *f.*, wing
     mentior, 4 *dep.*, lie
     pluma, -ae, *f.*, feather
25   **remitto, -ere, -misi, -missus, 3,** leave behind
27   **onerosus, -a, -um,** *adj.*, burdensome
28   **supervacuus, -a, -um,** *adj.*, superfluous
29   **adfecto, 1,** strive after
30   **contendo, -ere, -tendi, -tentus, 3,** hasten
     inspicio, -ere, -spexi, -spectus, 3, see
     commodus, -a, -um, *adj.*, advantageous
31   **incommodus, -a, -um,** *adj.*, disadvantageous
33   **consto, -stare, -stiti, -status, 1,** cost
     stupor, -oris, *m.*, stupidity
34   **emo, -ere, emi, emptus, 3,** buy
36   **inpendo, -ere, -pendi, -pensus, 3,** expend
37   **amoenus, -a, -um,** *adj.*, pleasant
     fructuosus, -a, -um, *adj.*, profitable
38   **praedium, -i,** *n.*, estate
39   **iactura, -ae,** *f.*, loss
40   **vilis, -e,** *adj.*, cheap
41   **quotiens,** *adv.*, as often as, whenever
42   **institor, -oris,** *m.*, huckster
     merx, mercis, *f.*, merchandise

Epistle Forty-two
THE RARITY OF THE *VIR BONUS*

Seneca Lucilio Suo Salutem

Iam tibi iste persuasit virum se bonum esse? Atqui vir
bonus tam cito nec fieri potest nec intellegi. Scis quem nunc
virum bonum dicam? hunc secundae notae; nam ille alter
fortasse tamquam phoenix semel anno quingentesimo nasci-   5
tur. Nec est mirum ex intervallo magna generari: mediocria
et in turbam nascentia saepe fortuna producit, eximia vero
ipsa raritate commendat. Sed iste multum adhuc abest ab
eo quod profitetur; et si sciret quid esset vir bonus, nondum
esse se crederet, fortasse etiam fieri posse desperaret. 'At   10
male existimat de malis.' Hoc etiam mali faciunt, nec ulla
maior poena nequitiaest quam quod sibi ac suis displicet.
'At odit eos qui subita et magna potentia inpotenter utun-
tur.' Idem faciet cum idem potuerit. Multorum quia in-
becilla sunt latent vitia, non minus ausura cum illis vires   15
suae placuerint quam illa quae iam felicitas aperuit. Instru-
menta illis explicandae nequitiae desunt. Sic tuto serpens
etiam pestifera tractatur dum riget frigore: non desunt tunc
illi venena sed torpent. Multorum crudelitas et ambitio et
luxuria, ut paria pessimis audeat, fortunae favore deficitur.   20
Eadem velle [subaudi si] cognosces: da posse quantum volunt.
Meministi, cum quendam adfirmares esse in tua potestate,
dixisse me volaticum esse ac levem et te non pedem eius
tenere sed pinnam? Mentitus sum: pluma tenebatur, quam
remisit et fugit. Scis quos postea tibi exhibuerit ludos, quam   25
multa in caput suum casura temptaverit. Non videbat se per
aliorum pericula in suum ruere; non cogitabat quam onerosa
essent quae petebat, etiam si supervacua non essent.

Hoc itaque in his quae adfectamus, ad quae labore magno
contendimus, inspicere debemus, aut nihil in illis commodi   30
esse aut plus incommodi: quaedam supervacua sunt, quaedam tanti non sunt. Sed hoc non pervidemus et gratuita
nobis videntur quae carissime constant. Ex eo licet stupor
noster appareat, quod ea sola putamus emi pro quibus
pecuniam solvimus, ea gratuita vocamus pro quibus nos ipsos   35
inpendimus. Quae emere nollemus si domus nobis nostra
pro illis esset danda, si amoenum aliquod fructuosumve
praedium, ad ea paratissimi sumus pervenire cum sollicitu-
dine, cum periculo, cum iactura pudoris et libertatis et
temporis; adeo nihil est cuique se vilius. Idem itaque in   40
omnibus consiliis rebusque faciamus quod solemus facere quotiens ad institorem alicuius mercis accessimus: videamus hoc

43   **quanti deferatur:** "at what price it is being sold"; *defero* is the technical word for "bring to market to sell."

47   **de. . .agetur:** "it is a question of gain."

55–56   **sed cogitat:** "but he thinks [he feels their loss]."

56–57   **habere se:** subject of *contigit*.

45   **extorqueo, -ere, -torsi, -tortus,** 2, twist out, wrest

47   **verso,** 1, consider

48   **nempe,** *conj.*, to be sure
     adventicius, -a, -um, *adj.*, foreign, external

51   **adsuesco, -ere, -suevi, -suetus,** 3, become accustomed to

54   **damnum, -i,** *n.*, loss

56   **quotus quisque, quotum quidque,** *pron.*, how many; (*ironically*) how few

57   **contingo, -ere, -tigi, -tactus,** 3, fall to one's lot

quod concupiscimus quanti deferatur. Saepe maximum pretium est pro quo nullum datur. Multa possum tibi ostendere
quae adquisita acceptaque libertatem nobis extorserint;   45
nostri essemus, si ista nostra non essent. Haec ergo tecum
ipse versa, non solum ubi de incremento agetur, sed etiam
ubi de iactura. 'Hoc periturum est.' Nempe adventicium
fuit; tam facile sine isto vives quam vixisti. Si diu illud
habuisti, perdis postquam satiatus es; si non diu, perdis   50
antequam adsuescas. 'Pecuniam minorem habebis.' Nempe
et molestiam. 'Gratiam minorem.' Nempe et invidiam. Circumspice ista quae nos agunt in insaniam, quae cum pluri-
mis lacrimis amittimus: scies non damnum in iis molestum
esse, sed opinionem damni. Nemo illa perisse sentit sed   55
cogitat. Qui se habet nihil perdidit: sed quoto cuique habere
se contigit? *Vale.*

5   **hunc locum:** i.e., Rome.

11 **in provincia:** Lucilius was procurator in Sicily.

19–20 **lanitores. . .opposuit:** "our conscience, not our pride, has placed keepers at [our doors]."

20 **deprendi:** predicate after *sit*.

6   **metior, -iri, mensus,** 4 *dep.*, measure
    moror, 1 *dep.*, dwell
7   **emineo, -ere, -minui,** 2, stand out
9   **tollo, -ere, sustuli, sublatus,** 3, raise
    deprimo, -ere, -pressi, -pressus, 3, lower
10 **gubernaculum, -i,** *n.*, rudder
11 **exiguus, -a, -um,** *adj.*, small
    licet, although
    contemno, -ere, -tempsi, -temptus, 3, scorn
12 **quemadmodum,** *adv.*, how
13 **eo,** *adv.*, for that reason, therefore
15 **paries, -etis,** *m.*, wall
    tego, -ere, texi, tectus, 3, protect
16 **plerumque,** *adv.*, for the most part, generally
    tutus, -a, -um, *adj.*, safe
17 **pecco,** 1, sin
18 **vix,** *adv.*, scarcely
    quisquam, quae-, quid- (quic-), *indef. pron.*, anyone, anything
    aperio, -ire, -ui, -ertus, 4, open
19 **ostium, -i,** *n.*, door
20 **subito,** *adv.*, suddenly
21 **prosum, prodesse, profui,** *irr.*, be of use
22 **vito,** 1, avoid
23 **sollicitus, -a, -um,** *adj.*, disturbed
24 **refert,** *impers.*, it matters

Epistle Forty-three
NO ESCAPE FROM ONE'S OWN CONSCIENCE

Seneca Lucilio Suo Salutem

Quomodo hoc ad me pervenerit quaeris, quis mihi id te cogitare narraverit quod tu nulli narraveras? Is qui scit plurimum, rumor. 'Quid ergo ?' inquis 'tantus sum ut possim excitare rumorem?' Non est quod te ad hunc locum respi- 5
ciens metiaris: ad istum respice in quo moraris. Quidquid inter vicina eminet magnum est illic ubi eminet; nam ma-gnitudo <non> habet modum certum: comparatio illam aut tollit aut deprimit. Navis quae in flumine magna est in mari parvula est; gubernaculum quod alteri navi magnum alteri 10
exiguum est. Tu nunc in provincia, licet contemnas ipse te, magnus es. Quid agas, quemadmodum cenes, quemadmodum dormias, quaeritur, scitur: eo tibi diligentius vivendum est. Tunc autem felicem esse te iudica cum poteris in publico vivere, cum te parietes tui tegent, non abscondent, quos 15
plerumque circumdatos nobis iudicamus non ut tutius viva-mus, sed ut peccemus occultius. Rem dicam ex qua mores aestimes nostros: vix quemquam invenies qui possit aperto ostio vivere. Ianitores conscientia nostra, non superbia opposuit: sic vivimus ut deprendi sit subito aspici. Quid 20
autem prodest recondere se et oculos hominum auresque vitare? Bona conscientia turbam advocat, mala etiam in solitudine anxia atque sollicita est. Si honesta sunt quae facis, omnes sciant; si turpia, quid refert neminem scire cum tu scias? O te miserum si contemnis hunc testem! *Vale.* 25

2 **te pusillum facis:** "you are making yourself out [to be] insignificant," "you are disparaging yourself."

2-3 **tecum egisse:** "dealt with you."

8 **quattuordecim:** the fourteen rows of seats at the theater or arena reserved by Roman law for the knights (*equites*). These seats were situated just behind those in the senatorial zone. The knights comprised the second class of Rome's hierarchy, the first class being the senatorial order, the third, the plebeian.

17 **hoc:** explained by the following *a nullo te nobilitate superari.*

23 **ad vetera:** "to ancient times."

27 **fumosis:** "smoky," "full of smoke." The Lares and especially the Penates were traditionally the spirits (of ancestors and gods) sacred to the private home. Their figures were situated in the *atrium* or central room, at the hearth. At every meal, a portion of the food was reserved for the Penates and cast into the flaming hearth—hence Seneca's imagery here.

28-29 **cui. . .licet surgere:** lit., "to which [soul] it is permitted to rise," i.e., "this soul may rise."

32 **non populo auctore:** "not according to the judgment of the crowd."

33 **veniant:** supply *ingenui* as subject.

38 **eius:** i.e., *securitas.*

42 **quo plus. . .hoc. . .magis:** "the more. . .the more."

2 **iterum,** *adv.*, again
3 **eximo, -ere, -emi, -emptus,** 3, take away from, free from
5 **stemma, -atis,** *n.*, pedigree
9 **curia, -ae,** *f.*, senate
12 **quisquam, quae-, quid-(quic-),** *indef. pron.*, anyone, anything
   luceo, -ere, luxi, 2, shine
13 **rigo,** 1, water
   hortus, -i, *m.*, garden
14 **loco,** 1, let out to hire
16 **maiores, -um,** *m. pl.*, ancestors
17 **protinus,** *adv.*, at once
18 **totidem,** *indecl. adj.*, just as many
19 **ultra,** *prep. w. acc.*, beyond
   iaceo, -ere, iacui, 2, lie
20 **orior, -iri, ortus,** 4 *dep.*, spring from
21 **misceo, -ere, miscui, mixtus,** 2, mix
   sursum, *adv.*, upwards,
   deorsum, *adv.*, downwards,
   sursum deorsum, up and down, topsy-turvy
22 **generosus, -a, -um,** *adj.*, noble
23 **intueor, -eri, -tuitus,** 2 *dep.*, look at, consider
   alioquin, *adv.*, otherwise
24 **inde,** *adv.*, from that time
25 **ortus, -us,** *m.*, beginning
   usque, *adv.*, all the way
   in, *prep. w. acc.*, towards, for, regarding
28 **quicumque, quae-, quod-,** *indef. adj.*, any whatever
30 **libertinus, -i,** *m.*, freedman
31 **consequor, -i, secutus,** 3 *dep.*, attain, reach
   ingenuus, -a, -um, *adj.*, free-born
   ingenuus, -i, *m.*, free-born man
33 **unde,** *adv.*, whence
   quo, *adv.*, whither
35 **depravo,** 1, pervert, distort
38 **securitas, -atis,** *f.*, freedom from care
39 **inconcussus, -a, -um,** *adj.*, unshaken
   sollicitudo, -inis, *f.*, anxiety
40 **tantum,** *adv.*, only
   sarcina, -ae, *f.*, burden
42 **inpendo, -ere, -pendi, -pensus,** 3, expend
44 **inplico,** 1, entangle

Epistle Forty-four
PHILOSOPHY NEVER LOOKS TO PEDIGREES

Seneca Lucilio Suo Salutem

Iterum tu mihi te pusillum facis et dicis malignius tecum egisse naturam prius, deinde fortunam, cum possis eximere te vulgo et ad felicitatem hominum maximam emergere. Si quid est aliud in philosophia boni, hoc est, quod stemma non inspicit; omnes, si ad originem primam revocantur, a dis sunt. Eques Romanus es, et ad hunc ordinem tua te per-duxit industria; at mehercules multis quattuordecim clausa sunt, non omnes curia admittit, castra quoque quos ad laborem et periculum recipiant fastidiose legunt: bona mens omnibus patet, omnes ad hoc sumus nobiles. Nec reicit quemquam philosophia nec eligit: omnibus lucet. Patricius Socrates non fuit; Cleanthes aquam traxit et rigando horto locavit manus; Platonem non accepit nobilem philosophia sed fecit: quid est quare desperes his te posse fieri parem? Omnes hi maiores tui sunt, si te illis geris dignum; geres autem, si hoc protinus tibi ipse persuaseris, a nullo te nobili-tate superari. Omnibus nobis totidem ante nos sunt; nullius non origo ultra memoriam iacet. Platon ait neminem regem non ex servis esse oriundum, neminem non servum ex regibus. Omnia ista longa varietas miscuit et sursum deorsum fortuna versavit. Quis est generosus? ad virtutem bene a natura compositus. Hoc unum intuendum est: alioquin si ad vetera revocas, nemo non inde est ante quod nihil est. A primo mundi ortu usque in hoc tempus perduxit nos ex splendidis sordidisque alternata series. Non facit nobilem atrium plenum fumosis imaginibus; nemo in nostram gloriam vixit nec quod ante nos fuit nostrum est: animus facit nobilem, cui ex qua-cumque condicione supra fortunam licet surgere. Puta itaque te non equitem Romanum esse sed libertinum: potes hoc consequi, ut solus sis liber inter ingenuos. 'Quomodo?' inquis. Si mala bonaque non populo auctore distinxeris. Intuendum est non unde veniant, sed quo eant. Si quid est quod vitam beatam potest facere, id bonum est suo iure; depravari enim in malum non potest. Quid est ergo in quo erratur, cum omnes beatam vitam optent? quod instru-menta eius pro ipsa habent et illam dum petunt fugiunt. Nam cum summa vitae beatae sit solida securitas et eius inconcussa fiducia, sollicitudinis colligunt causas et per insidiosum iter vitae non tantum ferunt sarcinas sed trahunt; ita longius ab effectu eius quod petunt semper abscedunt et quo plus operae inpenderunt, hoc se magis inpediunt et feruntur retro. Quod evenit in labyrintho properantibus: ipsa illos velocitas inplicat. *Vale.*

6–7 **tantundem. . .fortunae:** the sentence means "if you will take into consideration how much power fortune has over each of these" (i.e., slave and master). *Fortunae* may be taken as a genitive after *tantundem* or as a dative after *licere.*

8   **quare:** supply *turpe existimant* from the preceding clause. A subjunctive *sit* is to be supplied too with the following *nisi.*

10   **capit:** "holds" or "is able to hold." Cf. the English *capacity.*

13   **in hoc:** "for this purpose." The hapless slaves may not move their lips even in talk, much less in eating.

---

2 **libenter,** *adv.,* willingly, gladly
4 **decet, -ere, decuit,** *impers.,* 2, it fits, it suits
   immo, *adv.,* nay, rather, on the contrary
5 **contubernalis, -is,** *c.,* comrade
6 **conservus, -i,** *m.,* fellow slave
   tantundem, *adv.,* just so much
7 **uterque, utraque, utrumque,** *adj.,* both
   licet, -ere, licuit, *impers.,* 2, it is allowed
9 **consuetudo, -inis,** *f.,* custom
   turba, -ae, *f.,* crowd
10 **edo, -ere, edi, esus,** 3, eat
11 **onero,** 1, load
   venter, -tris, *m.,* stomach
   desuetus, -a, -um, *p. adj.* (*of* **desuesco**), unaccustomed
12 **egero, -ere, -gessi, -gestus,** 3, carry or bring out, vomit
13 **labrum, -i,** *n.,* lip
   ne. . .quidem, not. . .even
14 **virga, -ae,** *f.,* rod
   conpesco, -ere, -pescui, 3, check, restrain
15 **verber, -eris,** *n.,* lash
   tussis, -is, *f.,* coughing
   sternumentum, -i, *n.,* sneezing
   singultus, -us, *m.,* hiccupping
16 **malum, -i,** *n.,* punishment
   interpellatus, -a, -um, *p. adj.,* (*of* **interpello**), interrupted
   luo, -ere, lui, 3, pay for
17 **ieiunus, -a, -um,** *adj.,* hungry
18 **coram,** *prep. w. abl.,* in the presence of
19 **tantum,** *adv.,* only
   os, oris, *n.,* mouth
20 **consuo, -ere, -sui, -sutus,** 3, sew
   porrigo, -ere, -rexi, -rectus, 3, offer
   cervix, -icis, *f.,* neck
21 **convivium, -i,** *n.,* feast
22 **tormentum, -i,** *n.,* torture
23 **iacto,** 1, toss about
   totidem, *indecl. adj.,* just so many
   quot, *indecl. adj.,* how many, **tot. . .quot,** so many. . .as
25 **quod,** *conj.,* the fact that
   tamquam, *adv.,* as if
26 **iumentum, -i,** *n.,* beast of burden
27 **discumbo, -ere, -cubui, -cubitus,** 3, recline
   sputum, -i, *n.,* spit
   detergeo, -ere, -tersi, -tersus, 2, wipe up

Epistle Forty-seven
NOT SLAVES BUT FELLOW SLAVES

Seneca Lucilio Suo Salutem

Libenter ex iis qui a te veniunt cognovi familiariter te
cum servis tuis vivere: hoc prudentiam tuam, hoc erudi-
tionem decet. 'Servi sunt.' Immo homines. 'Servi sunt.'
Immo contubernales. 'Servi sunt.' Immo humiles amici.   5
'Servi sunt.' Immo conservi, si cogitaveris tantundem in
utrosque licere fortunae. Itaque rideo istos qui turpe existimant cum servo suo cenare: quare, nisi quia superbissima
consuetudo cenanti domino stantium servorum turbam cir-
cumdedit? Est ille plus quam capit, et ingenti aviditate   10
onerat distentum ventrem ac desuetum iam ventris officio,
ut maiore opera omnia egerat quam ingessit. At infelicibus
servis movere labra ne in hoc quidem, ut loquantur, licet;
virga murmur omne conpescitur, et ne fortuita quidem
verberibus excepta sunt, tussis, sternumenta, singultus;   15
magno malo ulla voce interpellatum silentium luitur; nocte
tota ieiuni mutique perstant. Sic fit ut isti de domino loquantur quibus coram domino loqui non licet. At illi quibus non
tantum coram dominis sed cum ipsis erat sermo, quorum os
non consuebatur, parati erant pro domino porrigere cervi-   20
cem, periculum inminens in caput suum avertere; in con-
viviis loquebantur, sed in tormentis tacebant. Deinde eiusdem
adrogantiae proverbium iactatur, totidem hostes esse quot
servos: non habemus illos hostes sed facimus. Alia interim
crudelia, inhumana praetereo, quod ne tamquam hominibus   25
quidem sed tamquam iumentis abutimur. [quod] Cum ad
cenandum discubuimus, alius sputa deterget, alius reliquias

31   **nisi quod:** "except for the fact that," "except that." Here the *quod* adds very little and seems hardly necessary.

32   **necessitatis:** supply *causa*.

33–34   **cum aetate luctatur:** the reference is to slaves who were full-grown and male but who were kept youthful and female in appearance. Debauched Roman masters exhibited such slaves to excite the envy of their wayward guests. As Seneca says below, such slaves had to be men in their more private services to their masters and boys in their public services. Seneca's metaphor, then, "that they had to wrestle with their age," is truly apt. The beards of such slaves were kept shaved especially close or were pulled out by the roots.

35   **militari habitu:** "with a soldier's appearance."

40–41   **obsonatores. . .subtilis est:** "the buyers of provisions who have a subtle knowledge of their master's palate"; *obsonatores* were the "purchasers of victuals" and also the makers of the menus. Their task was to keep a close watch upon the fastidiousness and fickleness of their master's palate and keep themselves prepared to administer to it satisfactorily and at once.

44   **sustinet:** an understood *dominus* is the subject of this verb, which here means "to endure." With *his* supply *servis*.

45   **Di melius:** idiomatic in Latin for "God forbid." The full expression is *Di melius velint*.

46   **ex istis:** supply *servis*.

49   **in. . .coniectus:** "thrown into the first group." Slaves put up for sale were grouped into various categories. The first group consisted of the least desirable.

50   **in. . .experitur:** lit., "on whom the crier or auctioneer tries out his voice"; i.e., the auctioneer has to put forth his best sales talk in order to persuade the buyers to purchase slaves of such inferior caliber.

52   **domino. . .Callistus:** "at what cost to the master was Callistus sold"; *domino* is dative of reference: *multa* is not the adjective but a noun in the ablative case (attendant circumstance). Callistus is the subject of *venditus est* understood; *quam* is an adverb.

53   **Vis tu cogitare:** a colloquial expression, "just remember to reflect," or "please reflect." The imperative of *volo* is lacking; this expression substitutes for it.

56   **Variana clade:** "at the time of Varus' disaster." Quintilius Varus was commander of the Roman armies in Germany. He was enticed by the crafty German chief, Arminius, to enter the Teutoburgian forest. There, Varus' army was cut to pieces and Varus himself committed suicide.

56–57   **senatorium. . .gradum:** "commencing to attain senatorial rank through military service."

28   **temulentus, -a, -um,** *adj.*, drunken
     temulentus, -i, *m.*, drunken man
28   **torus, -i,** *m.*, couch
     subditus, -a, -um, *p. adj.* (*of* **subdo**), placed at
29   **scindo, -ere, scidi, scissus,** 3, cut
     clunis, -is, *m. and f.*, rump
     ductus, -us, *m.*, carving
30   **eruditus, -a, -um,** *p. adj.* (*of* **erudio**), skilled
     frustum, -i, *n.*, bit, piece
     excutio, -ere, -cussi, -cussus, 3, cut off
31   **altilis, -e,** *adj.*, fattened
     altilis (supply *avis*), **-is,** *f.*, fowl
     decenter, *adv.*, properly
     seco, -are, secui, sectus, 1, cut
34   **luctor,** 1 *dep.*, wrestle
35   **glaber, -bra, -brum,** *adj.*, beardless
     retritus, -a, -um, *adj.*, rubbed down
     pilus, -i, *m.*, hair
     penitus, *adv.*, thoroughly
     evello, -ere, -velli, -vulsus, 3, tear out
37   **cubiculum, -i,** *n.*, bedroom
38   **censura, -ae,** *f.*, rating
     expecto, 1, wait to see
40   **crastinum, -i,** *n.*, tomorrow
     in crastinum, for tomorrow
42   **nauseabundus, -a, -um,** *adj.*, nauseated
     erigo, -ere, -rexi, -rectus, 3, arouse
43   **fastidio,** 4, cause nausea
     esurio, 4, be hungry, long for
46   **limen, -inis,** *n.*, door
47   **inpango, -ere, -pegi, -panctus,** 3, fix upon
     titulus, -i, *m.*, sales-tag
48   **reiculus, -a, -um,** *adj.*, worthless
     mancipium, -i, *n.*, slave
     produco, -ere, -duxi, -ductus, 3, expose, or put up for sale
50   **invicem,** *adv.*, in turn
     apologo, 1, reject
54   **semen, -inis,** *n.*, seed, origin
     aeque, *adv.*, equally
     spiro, 1, breathe
55   **ingenuus, -a, -um,** *adj.*, free-born
59   **contemno, -ere, -tempsi, -temptus,** 3, scorn

temulentorum <toro> subditus colligit. Alius pretiosas aves
scindit; per pectus et clunes certis ductibus circumferens
eruditam manum frusta excutit, infelix, qui huic uni rei   30
vivit, ut altilia decenter secet, nisi quod miserior est qui hoc
voluptatis causa docet quam qui necessitatis discit. Alius
vini minister in muliebrem modum ornatus cum aetate
luctatur: non potest effugere pueritiam, retrahitur, iamque
militari habitu glaber retritis pilis aut penitus evulsis tota   35
nocte pervigilat, quam inter ebrietatem domini ac libidinem
dividit et in cubiculo vir, in convivio puer est. Alius, cui
convivarum censura permissa est, perstat infelix et expectat
quos adulatio et intemperantia aut gulae aut linguae revo-
cet in crastinum. Adice obsonatores quibus dominici palati   40
notitia subtilis est, qui sciunt cuius illum rei sapor excitet,
cuius delectet aspectus, cuius novitate nauseabundus erigi
possit, quid iam ipsa satietate fastidiat, quid illo die esuriat.
Cum his cenare non sustinet et maiestatis suae deminutionem
putat ad eandem mensam cum servo suo accedere. Di melius!   45
quot ex istis dominos habet! Stare ante limen Callisti dominum suum vidi et eum qui illi inpegerat titulum, qui inter
reicula manicipia produxerat, aliis intrantibus excludi. Ret-
tulit illi gratiam servus ille in primam decuriam coniectus,
in qua vocem praeco experitur: et ipse illum invicem apolo-   50
gavit, et ipse non iudicavit domo sua dignum. Dominus
Callistum vendidit: sed domino quam multa Callistus!
    Vis tu cogitare istum quem servum tuum vocas ex isdem
seminibus ortum eodem frui caelo, aeque spirare, aeque vivere,
aeque mori! tam tu illum videre ingenuum potes quam ille   55
te servum. Variana clade multos splendidissime natos, senatorium per militiam auspicantes gradum, fortuna depressit:
alium ex illis pastorem, alium custodem casae fecit. Contemne
nunc eius fortunae hominem in quam transire dum contemnis
potes.   60

67–68 Bona aetas est: supply *tibi*, "you are still young."

68–70 Hecuba. . .Croesus. . .Darei mater. . .Platon. . .Diogenes: famous free-born personages who at some time in their lives fell into slavery. *Hecuba:* the wife of king Priam, after the fall of Troy, was taken captive and fell to the lot of Odysseus. *Croesus:* the wealthy, renowned king of Lydia, was defeated in 548 B.C. by Cyrus, the Persian king, and fell into the conqueror's hands. *Darei mater:* Sisigambis, the mother of Darius III, the last king of Persia; she was taken prisoner by Alexander the Great. *Platon:* Plato was sold into slavery by Dionysius the Elder, tyrant of Syracuse, who opposed the teachings of the philosopher; he remained only a short time in bondage. *Diogenes:* famous philosopher of the Cynic School; in his old age, while sailing to Aegina, he was captured by pirates, taken to Crete, and put up for sale; he was purchased by a wealthy Corinthian. who, amazed at Diogenes' wit, took him to Corinth and gave him his freedom.

78–79 non quo. . .sed quo utique: i.e., *non ut eo solo die. . .sed ut eo die utique.*

80 ius dicere: "to administer justice."

84 ut puta: "as for instance."

87–88 ex sordida conversatione: "as a result of mean association."

61 **locus, -i,** *m.*, topic
    usus, -us, *m.*, treatment
62 **contumeliosus, -a, -um,** *adj.*, insulting
65 **quotiens,** *adv.*, as often as
66 **tantundem,** *adv.*, just so much
70 **comiter,** *adv.*, affably
71 **convictus, -us,** *m.*, social life
72 **locus, -i,** *m.*, point
73 **deprehendo, -ere, -prehendi, -prehensus,** 3, catch
74 **osculo,** 1, kiss
75 **invidia, -ae,** *f.*, hostility
76 **contumelia, -ae,** *f.*, insult
79 **vescor, vesci,** 3 *dep.*, eat
    utique, *adv.*, in any case, at any rate
80 **pusillus, -a, -um,** *adj.*, tiny
83 **quasi,** *adv.*, as if
84 **mulio, -onis,** *m.*, muleteer
    bubulcus, -i, *m.*, herdsman
85 **ministerium, -i,** *n.*, duty
86 **casus, -us,** *m.*, fate
88 **convictus, -us,** *m.*, association
    excutio, -ere, -cussi, -cussus, 3, shake out

Nolo in ingentem me locum inmittere et de usu servorum
disputare, in quos superbissimi, crudelissimi, contumeliosis-
simi sumus. Haec tamen praecepti mei summa est: sic cum
inferiore vivas quemadmodum tecum superiorem velis
vivere. Quotiens in mentem venerit quantum tibi in servum   65
<tuum> liceat, veniat in mentem tantundem in te domino
tuo licere. 'At ego' inquis 'nullum habeo dominum.' Bona
aetas est: forsitan habebis. Nescis qua aetate Hecuba servire
coeperit, qua Croesus, qua Darei mater, qua Platon, qua
Diogenes? Vive cum servo clementer, comiter quoque, et in   70
sermonem illum admitte et in consilium et in convictum.

Hoc loco adclamabit mihi tota manus delicatorum 'nihil
hac re humilius, nihil turpius'. Hos ego eosdem deprehendam
alienorum servorum osculantes manum. Ne illud quidem
videtis, quam omnem invidiam maiores nostri dominis,   75
omnem contumeliam servis detraxerint? Dominum patrem
familiae appellaverunt, servos, quod etiam in mimis adhuc
durat, familiares; instituerunt diem festum, non quo solo
cum servis domini vescerentur, sed quo utique; honores illis
in domo gerere, ius dicere permiserunt et domum pusillam   80
rem publicam esse iudicaverunt. 'Quid ergo? omnes servos
admovebo mensae meae?' Non magis quam omnes liberos.
Erras si existimas me quosdam quasi sordidioris operae
reiecturum, ut puta illum mulionem et illum bubulcum.
Non ministeriis illos aestimabo sed moribus: sibi quisque dat   85
mores, ministeria casus adsignat. Quidam cenent tecum quia
digni sunt, quidam ut sint; si quid enim in illis ex sordida
conversatione servile est, honestiorum convictus excutiet.

92 **ipsum**: supply *equum*.

104 **pilleum:** a felt cap given to a slave when liberated, as a sign of his manumission.

106 **'Ita' inquit 'prorsus?':** the remark of some incensed objector; "'does he actually mean this?' he says."

111 **verborum castigatione uteris:** lit., "you employ verbal punishment," i.e., you never punish your slave harshly, you merely scold him.

111 **muta:** supply *animalia*.

112 **Non. . .laedit:** non goes with *laedit*. Translate: "whatever irks us does not [necessarily] harm us too."

113 **ut. . .respondit:** "so that whatever does not answer to our will." The preposition *ex* sometimes has the meaning "according to" or "in conformity with."

119 **acceperunt iniuriam:** i.e., they pretend they have received an injury. This is an example of Senecan BRACHYLOGY or conciseness; *acceperunt* refers to *quasi iniuriam acceperint*, line 116.

121 **Hoc:** i.e., the following *placent sibi, permanent.*

89 **tantum,** *adv.*, only
curia, -ae, *f.*, senate-house
91 **cesso,** 1, be idle
artifex, -ficis, *m.*, artist
quemadmodum, *adv.*, just as
92 **stultus, -a, -um,** *adj.*, foolish
emo, -ere, emi, emptus, 3, buy
93 **stratum, -i,** *n.*, saddle
frenum, -i, *n.* (*pl.* = **freni,** *m.* or **frena,** *n.*), bridle
94 **modo,** *adv.*, only
97 **libido, -inis,** *f.*, lust
98 **anicula, -ae,** *f.*, little old woman
99 **ancillula, -ae,** *f.*, maid-servant
mancipium, -i, *n.*, slave
100 **pantomimus, -i,** *m.*, ballet-dancer
102 **hilaris, -e,** *adj.*, cheerful
103 **potius,** *adv.*, rather
105 **fastigium, -i,** *n.*, summit
106 **tamquam,** *adv.*, as if
107 **salutator, -oris,** *m.*, early-morning caller
obliviscor, -i, oblitus, 3 *dep.*, forget
108 **parum,** *adv.*, too little
111 **verber, -eris,** *n.*, lash
112 **rabies, -ei,** *f.*, rage
113 **deliciae, -arum,** *f. pl.*, luxury
114 **induo, -ere, -dui, -dutus,** 3, put on, assume
115 **inbecillitas, -atis,** *f.*, weakness
alienus, -a, -um, *adj.*, another's
excandesco, -ere, -candui, 3, grow hot
116 **saevio,** 4, rage
117 **praesto, -are, -stiti,** 1, render
118 **queror, -i, questus,** 3 *dep.*, complain
120 **moror,** 1 *dep.*, delay
122 **levis, -e,** *adj.*, fickle
malitia, -ae, *f.*, wickedness

Non est, mi Lucili, quod amicum tantum in foro et in curia
quaeras: si diligenter adtenderis, et domi invenies. Saepe   90
bona materia cessat sine artifice: tempta et experire. Quemadmodum stultus est qui equum empturus non ipsum
inspicit sed stratum eius ac frenos, sic stultissimus est qui
hominem aut ex veste aut ex condicione, quae vestis modo
nobis circumdata est, aestimat. 'Servus est.' Sed fortasse liber   95
animo. 'Servus est.' Hoc illi nocebit? Ostende quis non sit: alius
libidini servit, alius avaritiae, alius ambitioni, <omnes spei>,
omnes timori. Dabo consularem aniculae servientem, dabo
ancillulae divitem, ostendam nobilissimos iuvenes mancipia
pantomimorum: nulla servitus turpior est quam voluntaria.   100
Quare non est quod fastidiosi isti te deterreant quominus
servis tuis hilarem te praestes et non superbe superiorem:
colant potius te quam timeant.
    Dicet aliquis nunc me vocare ad pilleum servos et dominos
de fastigio suo deicere, quod dixi, 'colant potius dominum   105
quam timeant'. 'Ita' inquit 'prorsus? colant tamquam clien-
tes, tamquam salutatores?' Hoc qui dixerit obliviscetur id
dominis parum non esse quod deo sat est. Qui colitur, et
amatur: non potest amor cum timore misceri. Rectissime
ergo facere te iudico quod timeri a servis tuis non vis, quod   110
verborum castigatione uteris: verberibus muta admonentur.
Non quidquid nos offendit et laedit; sed ad rabiem cogunt
pervenire deliciae, ut quidquid non ex voluntate respondit
iram evocet. Regum nobis induimus animos; nam illi quoque
obliti et suarum virium et inbecillitatis alienae sic excan-   115
descunt, sic saeviunt, quasi iniuriam acceperint, a cuius rei
periculo illos fortunae suae magnitudo tutissimos praestat.
Nec hoc ignorant, sed occasionem nocendi captant queren-
do; acceperunt iniuriam ut facerent.
    Diutius te morari nolo; non est enim tibi exhortatione   120
opus. Hoc habent inter cetera boni mores: placent sibi,
permanent. Levis est malitia, saepe mutatur, non in melius
sed in aliud. *Vale.*

6–7 **ut. . .facias, ut. . .ponas, ut intellegas:** these clauses are in apposition to *aliud*.

7–8 **intellegas. . .rerum:** "you are realizing that the vices which you thought characteristic of circumstances are your own"; *rerum* here means "circumstances" or "environment," as the following words *locis et temporibus* show.

10 **Harpasten:** Greek acc., sing., fem. Parasites, jesters, and buffoons were frequently in the houses of the great, and were found in the courts of Philip, Alexander, and Eastern potentates. In Roman times, for example, the buffoon Gabba occupied a permanent place in the household of the Emperor Augustus. That such buffoons were sometimes freaks is clear from *prodigiis* in the succeeding sentence.

15 **paedagogum:** this is the regular word in Latin to denote a person assigned to another to lead him wherever he must go. This woman had a "guide" assigned to her after she had gone blind.

migret: *migro* is intransitive here and means "change one's residence or quarters."

4 **valde,** *adv.*, very
6 **cotidie,** *adv.*, daily
7 **ponas** = deponas
9 **quocumque,** *adv.*, wherever
10 **fatuus, -a, -um,** *adj.*, foolish
  fatua, -ae, *f.*, fool
11 **prodigium, -i,** *n.*, monstrosity
12 **quando,** *adv.*, at any time
13 **subito,** *adv.*, suddenly
  desino, -ere, -sivi (-sii), -situs, 3, cease, stop
14 **caecus, -a, -um,** *adj.*, blind
15 **subinde,** *adv.*, repeatedly
16 **tenebricosus, -a, -um,** *adj.*, dark
17 **liqueo, -ere, liqui (licui),** 2, be clear
19 **aliter,** *adv.*, in another way, differently
20 **sumptuosus, -a, -um,** *adj.*, extravagant
21 **inpensa, -ae,** *f.*, expense
  exigo, -ere, -egi, -actus, 3, demand
  iracundus, -a, -um, *adj.*, irascible
22 **nondum,** *adv.*, not yet
  constituo, -ere, -stitui, -stitutus, 3, fix or settle upon
24 **extrinsecus,** *adv.*, outside, external
26 **aegroto,** 1, be sick
  curo, 1, care for, cure
27 **morbus, -i,** *m.*, disease
  discutio, -ere, -cussi, -cussus, 3, dispel

Epistle Fifty
BECOMING BETTER DAILY

Seneca Lucilio Suo Salutem

Epistulam tuam accepi post multos menses quam miseras; supervacuum itaque putavi ab eo qui adferebat quid ageres quaerere. Valde enim bonae memoriae est, si meminit; et tamen spero te sic iam vivere ut, ubicumque eris, sciam quid agas. Quid enim aliud agis quam ut meliorem te ipse cotidie facias, ut aliquid ex erroribus ponas, ut intellegas tua vitia esse quae putas rerum? Quaedam enim locis et temporibus adscribimus; at illa, quocumque transierimus, secutura sunt. Harpasten, uxoris meae fatuam, scis hereditarium onus in domo mea remansisse. Ipse enim aversissimus ab istis pro-digiis sum; si quando fatuo delectari volo, non est mihi longe quaerendus: me rideo. Haec fatua subito desiit videre. In-credibilem rem tibi narro, sed veram: nescit esse se caecam; subinde paedagogum suum rogat ut migret, ait domum tenebricosam esse. Hoc quod in illa ridemus omnibus nobis accidere liqueat tibi: nemo se avarum esse intellegit, nemo cupidum. Caeci tamen ducem quaerunt, nos sine duce erramus et dicimus, 'non ego ambitiosus sum, sed nemo aliter Romae potest vivere; non ego sumptuosus sum, sed urbs ipsa magnas inpensas exigit; non est meum vitium quod iracun-dus sum, quod nondum constitui certum genus vitae: adulescentia haec facit'.

Quid nos decipimus? non est extrinsecus malum nostrum: intra nos est, in visceribus ipsis sedet, et ideo difficulter ad sanitatem pervenimus quia nos aegrotare nescimus. Si curari coeperimus, quando tot morborum tantas vires discutiemus?

5

10

15

20

25

33 **illud:** "the following" is explained by the infinitive clause *posse . . .influere.*

35 **ante:** with *quam* in the following line. This is an example of TMESIS, the separation of parts of a compound word by one or more words set between them.

40 **explicat:** "folds out of" their crookedness, i.e., "straightens."

  natae: supply *trabes.*

49 **eo:** "for that reason"; abl. of cause.

51–52 **Contraria. . .haerent:** "opposites have difficulty in clinging to that which is alien."

58 **cogenda:** supply *mens.*

28 **ne. . .quidem,** not. . .even
  negotium, -i, *n.,* trouble
29 **adhibeo, -ere, -hibui, -hibitus,** 2, call on, summon
  tener, -era, -erum, *adj.,* tender
30 **rudis, -e,** *adj.,* raw, unhardened
31 **deficio, -ere, -feci, -fectus,** 3, revolt
  erubesco, -ere, erubui, 3, blush
33 **despero,** 1, despair of, give up
  casus, -us, *m.,* chance
  casu = forte, by chance
34 **influo, -ere, -fluxi, -fluxus,** 3, flow or rush upon
36 **recorrigo, -ere, -correxi, -correctus,** 3, amend, reform
37 **induresco, -ere, -durui,** 3, harden
  pravitas, -atis, *f.,* depravity
38 **expugno,** 1, conquer
  pertinax, -acis, *adj.,* persistent
  intentus, -a, -um, *p. adj. (of* **intendo**), unceasing
39 **robur, -oris,** *n.,* wood
  rectus, -a, -um, *p. adj. (of* **rego**), right, straight
  rectum, -i, *n.,* straightness
  quamvis, *adv.,* however much
  flexus, -a, -um, *p. adj. (of* **flecto**), bent
40 **trabs, trabis,** *f.,* beam
  calor, -oris, *m.,* heat
  aliter, *adv.,* otherwise
  fingo, -ere, finxi, fictus, 3, fashion
41 **exigo, -ere, -egi, -actus,** 3, demand
42 **umor, -oris,** *m.,* liquid
  obsequens, -entis, *p. adj. (of* **obsequor**), yielding
48 **disco, -ere, didici,** 3, learn
49 **dedisco, -ere, -didici,** 3, unlearn
50 **semel,** *adv.,* once
52 **depello, -ere, -puli, -pulsus,** 3, drive out
  exturbo, 1, thrust out
53 **secundum,** *prep. w. acc.,* according to
54 **infestus, -a, -um,** *adj.,* hostile
  quemadmodum, *adv.,* just as
56 **tutela, -ae,** *f.,* guarding
57 **inbecillus, -a, -um,** *adj.,* weak
  formido, 1, fear
  inexpertus, -a, -um, *adj.,* untried
59 **protinus,** *adv.,* immediately
60 **pariter,** *adv.,* equally, at the same time

Nunc vero ne quaerimus quidem medicum, qui minus negotii
haberet si adhiberetur ad recens vitium; sequerentur teneri
et rudes animi recta monstrantem. Nemo difficulter ad natu-   30
ram reducitur nisi qui ab illa defecit: erubescimus discere
bonam mentem. At mehercules, <si> turpe est magistrum
huius rei quaerere, illud desperandum est, posse nobis casu
tantum bonum influere: laborandum est et, ut verum dicam, ne labor quidem magnus est, si modo, ut dixi, ante   35
animum nostrum formare incipimus et recorrigere quam
indurescat pravitas eius. Sed nec indurata despero: nihil
est quod non expugnet pertinax opera et intenta ac diligens
cura. Robora in rectum quamvis flexa revocabis; curvatas
trabes calor explicat et aliter natae in id finguntur quod usus   40
noster exigit: quanto facilius animus accipit formam, flexibilis et omni umore obsequentior! Quid enim est aliud
animus quam quodam modo se habens spiritus? vides autem
tanto spiritum esse faciliorem omni alia materia quanto
tenuior est. Illud, mi Lucili, non est quod te inpediat quo-   45
minus de nobis bene speres, quod malitia nos iam tenet, quod
diu in possessione nostri est: ad neminem ante bona mens
venit quam mala; omnes praeoccupati sumus; virtutes discere vitia dediscere <est>. Sed eo maiore animo ad emenda-
tionem nostri debemus accedere quod semel traditi nobis boni   50
perpetua possessio est; non dediscitur virtus. Contraria enim
male in alieno haerent, ideo depelli et exturbari possunt;
fideliter sedent quae in locum suum veniunt. Virtus secundum naturam est, vitia inimica et infesta sunt. Sed quemadmodum virtutes receptae exire non possunt facilisque earum   55
tutela est, ita initium ad illas eundi arduum, quia hoc proprium inbecillae mentis atque aegrae est, formidare inex-
perta; itaque cogenda est ut incipiat. Deinde non est acerba
medicina; protinus enim delectat, dum sanat. Aliorum reme-
diorum post sanitatem voluptas est, philosophia pariter et   60
salutaris et dulcis est. Vale.

2 **Quomodo quisque potest:** supply *faciat.*

4 **Messala. . .Valgius:** M. Valerius Messala Corvinus, a renowned author, orator, and literary patron of the Augustan Age. Valgius Rufus was a distinguished poet of the Augustan Age and intimate friend of Horace.

8 **Bais:** Baiae, a much-frequented and luxurious resort in Campania, opposite Puteoli.

18 **Canopum:** Canopus, a city of Egypt, twelve miles from Alexandria, whose inhabitants were known for their dissoluteness and debauchery.

19 **ne Baias quidem:** supply *eliget,* "nor will he choose Baiae either."

26 **quae. . .luxuria:** "which luxury as if loosened from [the restraint of] law."

30 **Hannibalem:** Hannibal, the renowned Carthaginian general of the Second Punic War (218–201 B.C.), son of Hamilcar. The reference is to Hannibal's stay in Capua, where the Carthaginian soldiers, weakened by the pleasures of this luxurious city, forgot how to conquer.

32 **fomenta:** *fomentum, -i,* n., a hot or cold compress applied for medical purposes; *fomenta* here may refer to warm baths. The word also has the figurative meanings, "remedy," "solace," "alleviation."

5 **evomo, -ere, -ui, -itus,** 3, vomit forth
6 **tantum,** *adv.,* only
  editus, -a, -um, *p. adj.* (*of* **edo**), high
  videlicet, *adv.,* clearly
7 **iaceo, -ere, iacui, iacitus,** 2, lie low
  utcumque, *adv.,* however
10 **dos, dotis,** *f.,* gift
  celebro, 1, visit frequently
11 **desumo, -ere, -sumpsi,** 3, take for one's self, choose
13 **aliqua. . .aliqua = alia. . .alia,** one. . .another
17 **secessus, -us,** *m.,* retirement
18 **quamvis,** *adv.,* although
19 **frugi,** indecl. *adj.,* temperate
  deversorium, -i, *n.,* resort, lodging
23 **quemadmodum,** *adv.,* just as
  tortor, -oris, *m.,* torturer
24 **ne. . .quidem,** not. . .either, not . .even
  popina, -ae, *f.,* eating-house
25 **comessatio, -onis,** *f.,* revel
  symphonia, -ae, *f.,* musical performance
26 **strepens, -entis,** *p. adj.* (*of* **strepo**), noisy
28 **inritamentum, -i,** *n.,* incentive
30 **procul,** *adv.,* far
31 **indomitus, -a, -um,** *adj.,* unsubdued
34 **primus, -a, -um,** *superl . adj.,* first
  in primis, especially
35 **saevus, -a, -um,** *adj.,* austere
  ingenium, -i, *n.,* nature
36 **adgredior, -i, gressus,** 3 *dep.,* approach, attack, undertake
38 **calens, -entis,** *p. adj.* (*of* **caleo**), hot
  stagnum, -i, *n.,* bath
  sudatorium, -i, *n.,* sweating-room
39 **siccus, -a, -um,** *adj.,* dry
  exhaurio, -ire, -hausi, -haustus, 4, drain
  sudor, -oris, *m.,* sweat
41 **foveo, -ere, fovi, fotus,** 2, cherish, pamper
42 **operam dare,** give attention to
  desidia, -ae, *f.,* sloth

Epistle Fifty-one
BAIAE AND VICE

Seneca Lucilio Suo Salutem

Quomodo quisque potest, mi Lucili: tu istic habes Aet-
nam, †et illuc† nobilissimum Siciliae montem (quem quare
dixerit Messala unicum, sive Valgius—apud utrumque enim
legi—non reperio, cum plurima loca evomant ignem, non   5
tantum edita, quod crebrius evenit, videlicet quia ignis in
altissimum effertur, sed etiam iacentia), nos, utcumque
possumus, contenti sumus Bais; quas postero die quam
attigeram reliqui, locum ob hoc devitandum, cum habeat
quasdam naturales dotes, quia illum sibi celebrandum lu-   10
xuria desumpsit.

'Quid ergo? ulli loco indicendum est odium?' Minime;
sed quemadmodum aliqua vestis sapienti ac probo viro magis
convenit quam aliqua, nec ullum colorem ille odit sed
aliquem parum putat aptum esse frugalitatem professo, sic   15
regio quoque est quam sapiens vir aut ad sapientiam tendens
declinet tamquam alienam bonis moribus. Itaque de secessu
cogitans numquam Canopum eliget, quamvis neminem
Canopus esse frugi vetet, ne Baias quidem: deversorium
vitiorum esse coeperunt. Illic sibi plurimum luxuria permittit, 20
illic, tamquam aliqua licentia debeatur loco, magis solvitur.
Non tantum corpori sed etiam moribus salubrem locum eli-
gere debemus; quemadmodum inter tortores habitare nolim,
sic ne inter popinas quidem. Videre ebrios per litora errantes
et comessationes navigantium et symphoniarum cantibus   25
strepentes lacus et alia quae velut soluta legibus luxuria non
tantum peccat sed publicat, quid necesse est? Id agere
debemus ut inritamenta vitiorum quam longissime profu-
giamus; indurandus est animus et a blandimentis voluptatum
procul abstrahendus. Una Hannibalem hiberna solverunt et   30
indomitum illum nivibus atque Alpibus virum enervaverunt
fomenta Campaniae: armis vicit, vitiis victus est. Nobis quoque militandum est, et quidem genere militiae quo numquam
quies, numquam otium datur: debellandae sunt in primis
voluptates, quae, ut vides, saeva quoque ad se ingenia rapu-   35
erunt. Si quis sibi proposuerit quantum operis adgressus sit,
sciet nihil delicate, nihil molliter esse faciendum. Quid mihi
cum istis calentibus stagnis? quid cum sudatoriis, in quae
siccus vapor corpora exhausurus includitur? omnis sudor
per laborem exeat. Si faceremus quod fecit Hannibal, ut   40
interrupto cursu rerum omissoque bello fovendis corporibus
operam daremus, nemo non intempestivam desidiam, victori

43 **vincenti:** "one striving for victory"; present participle with conative force.

50 **idem. . .ira:** "both ambition and anger will desire that they have the same amount of jurisdiction over me"; *sibi* is dative of possession.

53–54 **fortunam in aequum deducere:** "to bring fortune down to a level [with yourself]."

54–55 **Quo. . .poterit:** "the day on which I understand that she has more power, she will have no power"; an example of Seneca's use of paradox.

57–58 **nec. . .regio:** "and without doubt one's abode has some power to break one's vigor."

59 **in aspero:** "on harsh ground." Seneca frequently uses adjectives as substantives. Other examples of such usage in this letter are *ex confragoso* (line 61), "from a rugged place," and *ex edito* (line 70), "from a lofty place."

61 **urbanus et verna:** "town-bred"; *verna* is a slave born in his master's house, a homeborn slave.

63 **in primo. . .nitidus:** "the man anointed [with unguents] and glittering [in appearance] is defeated by the first [whiff of] dust."

65 **Literni. . .Scipio:** Publius Cornelius Scipio Africanus Major, who brought the Second Punic War to an end by his victory at Zama (202 B.C.). He then spent his retirement in his estate at Liternum in Campania, where he had withdrawn after having been denounced by enemies at Rome.

65 **quam Bais:** supply *exulavisset*.

65–66 **ruina. . .conlocanda:** "such a fall did not need a setting so soft."

78 **duxisset:** "had constructed."

85 φιλήτας: Greek acc. pl., "thieves," with a pun on φιλητάς, "lovers."

43 **nedum,** *adv.*, not to mention
    merito, *adv.*, rightly
44 **licet, -ere, licuit,** *impers.*, 2, it is permitted
47 **immo,** *adv.*, nay rather
48 **excutio, -ere, -cussi, -cussus,** 3, shake off
51 **adfectus, -us,** *m.*, emotion
    discerpo, -ere, -cerpsi, -cerptus, 3, tear to pieces
56 **intentus, -a, - um,** *p. adj.* (*of* **intendo**), attentive to
57 **amoenitas, -atis,** *f.*, pleasantness
    nimius, -a, -um, *adj.*, too much
58 **quilibet, quae-, quod-,** *indef. adj.*, any
    iumentum, -i, *n.*, beast of burden
59 **ungula, -ae,** *f.*, hoof
60 **paluster, -tris, -tre,** *adj.*, marshy
    pascuum, -i, *n.*, pasture
    saginatus, -a, -um, *p. adj.* (*of* **sagino**), fattened
    cito, *adv.*, quickly
    subtero, -ere, -trivi, -tritus, 3, bruise
61 **segnis, -e,** *adj.*, sluggish
63 **deficio, -ere, -feci, -fectus,** 3, fail
65 **exulo,** 1, live in exile
68 **exstruo, -ere, -struxi, -structus,** 3, construct
69 **iugum, -i,** *n.*, summit
70 **speculor,** 1 *dep.*, examine, explore
72 **excito,** 1, erect
75 **cumba, -ae,** *f.*, boat
76 **convicium, -i,** *n.*, loud noise
77 **vallum, -i,** *n.*, entrenchment
78 **quidni,** *adv.*, why not?, of course
79 **classicum, -i,** *n.*, war-trumpet
81 **persequor, -i, secutus,** 3 *dep.*, pursue, proceed against
    modus, -i, *m.*, limit
83 **lanio,** 1, rend
    aliter, *adv.*, otherwise
    nequeo, -ire, -ivi, -itus, 4, be unable
84 **revello, -ere, -velli, -vulsus (-volsus),** 3, tear out
    exturbo, 1, drive away
85 **invisus, -a, -um,** *adj.*, hateful
    latro, -onis, *m.*, thief
86 **in hoc,** for this purpose
    amplector, -i, plexus, 3 *dep.*, embrace

quoque, nedum vincenti, periculosam, merito reprehenderet:
minus nobis quam illis Punica signa sequentibus licet, plus
periculi restat cedentibus, plus operis etiam perseverantibus.   45
Fortuna mecum bellum gerit: non sum imperata facturus;
iugum non recipio, immo, quod maiore virtute faciendum
est, excutio. Non est emolliendus animus: si voluptati cessero,
cedendum est dolori, cedendum est labori, cedendum est paupertati; idem sibi in me iuris esse volet et ambitio et ira; inter   50
tot adfectus distrahar, immo discerpar. Libertas proposita
est; ad hoc praemium laboratur. Quae sit libertas quaeris?
Nulli rei servire, nulli necessitati, nullis casibus, fortunam in
aequum deducere. Quo die illam intellexero plus posse, nil
poterit: ego illam feram, cum in manu mors sit?   55
    His cogitationibus intentum loca seria sanctaque eligere
oportet; effeminat animos amoenitas nimia, nec dubie aliquid
ad corrumpendum vigorem potest regio. Quamlibet viam iu-
menta patiuntur quorum durata in aspero ungula est: in
molli palustrique pascuo saginata cito subteruntur. Et fortior   60
miles ex confragoso venit: segnis est urbanus et verna. Nullum
laborem recusant manus quae ad arma ab aratro transferun-
tur: in primo deficit pulvere ille unctus et nitidus. Severior
loci disciplina firmat ingenium aptumque magnis conatibus
reddit. Literni honestius Scipio quam Bais exulabat: ruina   65
eiusmodi non est tam molliter conlocanda. Illi quoque ad
quos primos fortuna populi Romani publicas opes transtulit,
C. Marius et Cn. Pompeius et Caesar, exstruxerunt quidem
villas in regione Baiana, sed illas inposuerunt summis iugis
montium: videbatur hoc magis militare, ex edito speculari   70
late longeque subiecta. Aspice quam positionem elegerint,
quibus aedificia excitaverint locis et qualia: scies non villas
esse sed castra. Habitaturum tu putas umquam fuisse illic
M. Catonem, ut praenavigantes adulteras dinumeraret et tot
genera cumbarum variis coloribus picta et fluvitantem toto   75
lacu rosam, ut audiret canentium nocturna convicia? nonne
ille manere intra vallum maluisset, quod in unam noctem
manu sua ipse duxisset? Quidni mallet, quisquis vir est,
somnum suum classico quam symphonia rumpi?
    Sed satis diu cum Bais litigavimus, numquam satis cum   80
vitiis, quae, oro te, Lucili, persequere sine modo, sine fine;
nam illis quoque nec finis est nec modus. Proice quaecumque
cor tuum laniant, quae si aliter extrahi nequirent, cor ipsum
cum illis revellendum erat. Voluptates praecipue exturba et
invisissimas habe: latronum more, quos φιλήτας Aegyptii   85
vocant, in hoc nos amplectuntur, ut strangulent. *Vale.*

13 **Metrodorum:** Metrodorus (331–278 B.C.), a disciple and intimate friend of Epicurus.

15 **bene. . .agitur:** lit., "it is waged well with us," i.e., we are treated or fare well.

21 **color:** i.e., "class."

22 **Hermarchum:** Hermarchus (fl., 341–270 B.C.), disciple of Epicurus and his successor as head of the Epicurean school.

23–24 **alteri. . .suspicit:** "he congratulates the one (i.e., Metrodorus) more, he looks up to the other (i.e., Hermarchus) more."

27 **puram aream:** i.e., a naturally solid foundation.

30–31 **intuentibus. . .latet:** i.e., that which caused the greatest difficulty in erecting one of the buildings is entirely hidden from the sight of observers. The parentheses around *alter* and the three asterisks indicate textual difficulties in the manuscript.

32–33 **manu. . .facienda sunt:** "must be moulded or made by hand," i.e., artificially.

34 **hunc:** supply *sed* before this word. Seneca frequently employs ASYNDETON (the omission of a conjunction between words, phrases, or sentences).

2 **alio. . .alio,** in one direction. . .in another
   tendo, -ere, tetendi, tentus, 3, stretch, aim
3 **eo,** *adv.*, there
   conluctor, 1 *dep.*, struggle, wrestle
4 **semel,** *adv.*, once for all
7 **revello, -ere, -velli, -vulsus (-volsus),** 3, tear away
9 **porrigo, -ere, -rexi, -rectus,** 3, hold forth, offer
12 **indigeo, -ere, -ui,** 2, be in need of
14 **egregius, -a, -um,** *adj.*, excellent, outstanding
   ingenium, -i, *n.*, nature, character
16 **ne. . .quidem,** not. . .even
19 **fastidio,** 4, loathe, despise
20 **tantum,** *adv.*, only
24 **uterque, utraque, utrumque,** *adj.*, each
26 **excito,** 1, erect
27 **excelsus, -a, -um,** *adj.*, lofty, high
28 **protinus,** *adv.*, at once, immediately
   lasso, 1, make weary, exhaust
   mollis, -e, *adj.*, soft
29 **fluvidus, -a, -um,** *adj.*, moist
   humus, -i, *f.*, ground
32 **expeditus, -a, -um,** *p. adj.* (*of* **expedio**), unimpeded, free, easy
34 **negotium, -i,** *n.*, trouble

Epistle Fifty-two
MAN NEEDS A MORAL GUIDE

Seneca Lucilio Suo Salutem

Quid est hoc, Lucili, quod nos alio tendentes alio trahit
et eo unde recedere cupimus inpellit? quid conluctatur cum
animo nostro nec permittit nobis quicquam semel velle?
Fluctuamur inter varia consilia; nihil libere volumus, nihil   5
absolute, nihil semper. 'Stultitia' inquis 'est cui nihil constat,
nihil diu placet.' Sed quomodo nos aut quando ab illa revel-
lemus? Nemo per se satis valet ut emergat; oportet manum
aliquis porrigat, aliquis educat. Quosdam ait Epicurus ad
veritatem sine ullius adiutorio exisse, fecisse sibi ipsos viam;   10
hos maxime laudat quibus ex se impetus fuit, qui se ipsi
protulerunt: quosdam indigere ope aliena, non ituros si nemo
praecesserit, sed bene secuturos. Ex his Metrodorum ait esse;
egregium hoc quoque, sed secundae sortis ingenium. Nos ex
illa prima nota non sumus; bene nobiscum agitur, si in secun-   15
dam recipimur. Ne hunc quidem contempseris hominem qui
alieno beneficio esse salvus potest; et hoc multum est, velle
servari. Praeter haec adhuc invenies genus aliud hominum
ne ipsum quidem fastidiendum eorum qui cogi ad rectum
conpellique possunt, quibus non duce tantum opus sit sed   20
adiutore et, ut ita dicam, coactore; hic tertius color est. Si
quaeris huius quoque exemplar, Hermarchum ait Epicurus
talem fuisse. Itaque alteri magis gratulatur, alterum magis
suspicit; quamvis enim ad eundem finem uterque pervenerit,
tamen maior est laus idem effecisse in difficiliore materia.   25
Puta enim duo aedificia excitata esse, ambo paria, aeque
excelsa atque magnifica. Alter puram aream accepit, illic
protinus opus crevit; alterum fundamenta lassarunt in mollem et fluvidam humum missa multumque laboris exhaustum
est dum pervenitur ad solidum: intuentibus quidquid fecit   30
<alter> * * * alterius magna pars et difficilior latet. Quaedam
ingenia facilia, expedita, quaedam manu, quod aiunt, facienda sunt et in fundamentis suis occupata. Itaque illum ego
feliciorem dixerim qui nihil negotii secum habuit, hunc
quidem melius de se meruisse qui malignitatem naturae suae   35
vicit et ad sapientiam se non perduxit sed extraxit.

40 **ad priores:** "to those of former times," "the ancients."

43 **communes locos volvunt:** "roll out or reel off commonplaces."

43 **circulantur:** *circulor, -ari,* 1 *dep.,* collect people around one's self (as fakers or traveling performers do who extract money from the gullible crowd). The noun *circulator* means "peddler," "quack," "charlatan," "a boastful and unscrupulous pretender to knowledge."

51 **causa:** here separated, somewhat irregularly, from its genitive.

52 **captante clamores:** "striving after shouts of applause."

53 **Tacete. . .praebete:** Seneca is addressing men in general rather than Lucilius alone.

58 **Apud Pythagoram:** *apud* with a proper noun is regular for "at the house or school of." Pythagoras, renowned Greek philosopher of the sixth century B.C., was the founder of the Pythagorean School of philosophy. His disciples had to endure a disciplined and stern initiation which consisted of keeping silence, of subsisting on a frugal vegetable diet, of performing some duty each hour of the day, and of undergoing frequent examinations of the conscience. Pythagoras supported the doctrine of metempsychosis or transmigration of the soul into different bodies, he himself claiming that he recollected the different bodies his own soul had animated before he obtained the identity of Pythagoras. He conceived that the fundamental essence of all things was to be found not in matter but in numbers.

64 **Fabianus:** Fabianus Papirius, teacher of Seneca and philosopher of the Sextian School, founded by Quintus Sextius the Elder in the time of Julius Caesar. Sextius was an original thinker with eclectic tendencies and with Stoic and Pythagorean leanings.

70 **minimis:** supply *rebus.*

71–72 **relatus. . .digitus:** the Romans regarded the scratching of the head with a single finger as an indication of lasciviousness or effeminacy.

42 **praecipito,** 1, throw headlong, hurl, hasten

46 **deprehendo, -ere, -prehendi, -prehensus,** 3, catch, seize

49 **dissero, -ere, -serui, -sertus,** 3, discuss, speak
    modo, *adv.,* only

50 **propositum, -i,** *n.,* purpose

53 **seco, -are, secui, sectus,** 1, cut
    praebeo, -ere, -ui, -itus, 2, offer, furnish

55 **ingemesco, -ere, -ui,** 3, groan

56 **sane,** *adv.,* indeed, to be sure
    licet, -ere, licuit, *impers.,* 2, it is permitted or allowed

57 **quidni,** *adv.,* why not?, of course

61 **inperitus, -a, -um,** *adj.,* inexperienced, ignorant

65 **interdum,** *adv.,* sometimes

66 **molliter,** *adv.,* softly

67 **elabor, -i, elapsus,** 3 *dep.,* slip forth
    intersum, -esse, -fui, *irr.,* be different, make a difference

70 **inpudicus, -a, -um,** *adj.,* lewd, incontinent
    incessus, -us, *m.,* gait

72 **flexus, -us,** *m.,* turning

Hoc durum ac laboriosum ingenium nobis datum scias
licet; imus per obstantia. Itaque pugnemus, aliquorum in-
vocemus auxilium. 'Quem' inquis 'invocabo? Hunc aut illum?'
Tu vero etiam ad priores revertere, qui vacant; adiuvare nos   40
possunt non tantum qui sunt, sed qui fuerunt. Ex his autem
qui sunt eligamus non eos qui verba magna celeritate prae-
cipitant et communes locos volvunt et in privato circulantur,
sed eos qui vita docent, qui cum dixerunt quid faciendum sit
probant faciendo, qui docent quid vitandum sit nec umquam   45
in eo quod fugiendum dixerunt deprehenduntur; eum elige
adiutorem quem magis admireris cum videris quam cum
audieris. Nec ideo te prohibuerim hos quoque audire quibus
admittere populum ac disserere consuetudo est, si modo hoc
proposito in turbam prodeunt, ut meliores fiant faciantque   50
meliores, si non ambitionis hoc causa exercent. Quid enim
turpius philosophia captante clamores? numquid aeger laudat
medicum secantem? Tacete, favete et praebete vos cura-
tioni; etiam si exclamaveritis, non aliter audiam quam si ad
tactum vitiorum vestrorum ingemescatis. Testari vultis ad-   55
tendere vos moverique rerum magnitudine? sane liceat: ut
quidem iudicetis et feratis de meliore suffragium, quidni
non permittam? Apud Pythagoram discipulis quinque annis
tacendum erat: numquid ergo existimas statim illis et loqui
et laudare licuisse?   60
　　Quanta autem dementia eius est quem clamores inperi-
torum hilarem ex auditorio dimittunt! Quid laetaris quod
ab hominibus his laudatus es quos non potes ipse laudare?
Disserebat populo Fabianus, sed audiebatur modeste; erum-
pebat interdum magnus clamor laudantium, sed quem rerum   65
magnitudo evocaverat, non sonus inoffense ac molliter orationis elapsae. Intersit aliquid inter clamorem theatri et
scholae: est aliqua et laudandi elegantia. Omnia rerum
omnium, si observentur, indicia sunt, et argumentum morum
ex minimis quoque licet capere: inpudicum et incessus osten-   70
dit et manus mota et unum interdum responsum et relatus
ad caput digitus et flexus oculorum; inprobum risus, insanum
vultus habitusque demonstrat. Illa enim in apertum per notas
exeunt: qualis quisque sit scies, si quemadmodum laudet,
quemadmodum laudetur aspexeris. Hinc atque illinc philo-   75
sopho manus auditor intentat et super ipsum caput miran-
tium turba consistit: non laudatur ille nunc, si intellegis, sed
conclamatur. Relinquantur istae voces illis artibus quae
propositum habent populo placere: philosophia adoretur.

84 **At:** not found in the manuscripts but supplied by Hense.

    ad rem: "the subject matter," while *verba composita* means "the style," "rhetoric."

89–90 **apud populum. . .apud se:** "in the presence of the people. . .in the presence of one's self" (i.e., the lecturer). Seneca means that a full discussion of the subject would involve the question of what privileges a lecturer should allow himself when lecturing in public and again what license should be allowed the hearers or public when they attend a lecture.

90 **fecisse:** *damnum* with the verb *facere* regularly means "to suffer loss."

91 **in penetralibus:** lit., "in her innermost sanctuary," i.e., for what she really is.

92 **institorem:** "a mere salesman or huckster," while *antistitem* means "a genuine master or high priest."

80 **aliquando,** *adv.*, sometimes
85 **alioquin,** *adv.*, otherwise
87 **differo, differre, distuli, dilatus,** *irr.*, postpone
92 **nanciscor, -i, nanctus (nactus),** 3 *dep.*, find, come upon

Permittendum erit aliquando iuvenibus sequi impetum   80
animi, tunc autem cum hoc ex impetu facient, cum silentium sibi imperare non poterunt; talis laudatio aliquid
exhortationis adfert ipsis audientibus et animos adulescen-
tium exstimulat. <At> ad rem commoveantur, non ad verba
composita; alioquin nocet illis eloquentia, si non rerum cupi-   85
ditatem facit sed sui.

Differam hoc in praesentia; desiderat enim propriam et
longam exsecutionem, quemadmodum populo disserendum,
quid sibi apud populum permittendum sit, quid populo
apud se. Damnum quidem fecisse philosophiam non erit   90
dubium postquam prostituta est; sed potest in penetralibus
suis ostendi, si modo non institorem sed antistitem nancta
est. *Vale.*

3 **Solvi:** supply *navem:* translate, "I set out."

5–6 **Parthenope. . .Puteolos:** Parthenope is the ancient name for Naples. Since Pompeii, Lucilius' birthplace, and Naples are both in Campania, Seneca refers to Parthenope as *tua.* Puteoli, a town of Campania, is between Baiae and Naples.

8 **Nesida:** Nesis, an island on the coast of Campania.

8 **praecisurus. . .sinus:** "for the purpose of cutting off all the curves of the coast."

13 **aspera. . .inportuosa:** adjectives modifying an understood *litora;* "the coast was rugged and without harbors."

14–15 **Peius. . .succurreret:** "I was feeling too ill for danger to occur to me" (lit., "worse than that danger would occur to me"); a result clause after the comparative *peius.*

16–17 **quae. . .effundit:** "which stirs the bile but doesn't throw it off"; i.e., a seasickness which causes dry heaves.

18 **coegi, peteret:** i.e., *coegi ut peteret.*

20 **obvertunt. . .proras:** Vergil, *Aeneid* 6.3. Aeneas and his men reach Cumae and disembark. The reference is to the method of anchoring their ship.

22 **ancora. . .iacitur:** Vergil, *Aeneid* 3.277. In the course of their wanderings, Aeneas and his crew drop anchor at Actium in Acarnania.

23 **frigidae:** supply *aquae.*

28–29 **Ulixem. . .faceret:** "Ulysses was not so destined to an angry sea that he encountered shipwreck everywhere."

30 **vicensimo anno:** it took Ulysses ten years to return home; Seneca will require twice that amount of time whenever he sails.

41 **ubi ut:** "when once."

3 **languidus, -a, -um,** *adj.,* gentle
4 **sordidus, -a, -um,** *adj.,* mean
fere, *adv.,* almost
6 **subripio, -ere, -ripui, -reptus,** 3, steal
quamvis, *adv.,* however much, although
inpendeo, -ere, 2, threaten
7 **protinus,** *adv.,* straightway, at once
8 **derigo (dirigo), -ere, -rexi, -rectus,** 3, set straight out
eo, *adv.,* to that point
10 **aequalitas, -atis,** *f.,* calm
corrumpo, -ere, -rupi, -ruptus, 3, corrupt, entice
11 **inclinatio, -onis,** *f.,* swelling
subinde, *adv.,* continually
12 **gubernator, -oris,** *m.,* pilot
16 **segnis, -e,** *adj.,* sluggish
17 **vellet nollet,** willy-nilly
24 **psychroluta, -ae,** *m.,* cold-water bather
gausapatus, -a, -um, *adj.,* clad in a cloak
25 **erepo, -ere, -repsi,** 3, creep
35 **nedum,** *adv.,* not to mention
eo. . .quo, the. . .the
36 **motiuncula, -ae,** *f.,* attack of fever
37 **exardesco, -ere, -arsi, -arsus,** 3, burn
perpessicius, -a, -um, *adj.,* who has suffered or endured much
38 **articulus, -i,** *m.,* joint
punctiuncula, -ae, *f.,* pricking pain
adhuc, *adv.,* until now
dissimulo, 1, conceal
39 **talus, -i,** *m.,* ankle
41 **talaria, -ium,** *n.,* ankles
intendo, -ere, -tendi, -tentus, 3, stretch out, swell
42 **podagra, -ae,** *f.,* gout

Epistle Fifty-three
TOSSED UPON LAND AND SEA

Seneca Lucilio Suo Salutem

Quid non potest mihi persuaderi, cui persuasum est ut navigarem? Solvi mari languido; erat sine dubio caelum grave sordidis nubibus, quae fere aut in aquam aut in ventum resolvuntur, sed putavi tam pauca milia a Parthenope tua usque Puteolos subripi posse, quamvis dubio et inpendente caelo. Itaque quo celerius evaderem, protinus per altum ad Nesida derexi praecisurus omnes sinus. Cum iam eo processissem ut mea nihil interesset utrum irem an redirem, primum aequalitas illa quae me corruperat periit; nondum erat tempestas, sed iam inclinatio maris ac subinde crebrior fluctus. Coepi gubernatorem rogare ut me in aliquo litore exponeret: aiebat ille aspera esse et inportuosa nec quicquam se aeque in tempestate timere quam terram. Peius autem vexabar quam ut mihi periculum succurreret; nausia enim me segnis haec et sine exitu torquebat, quae bilem movet nec effundit. Institi itaque gubernatori et illum, vellet nollet, coegi, peteret litus. Cuius ut viciniam attigimus, non expecto ut quicquam ex praeceptis Vergilii fiat,

                    obvertunt pelago proras
aut
                    ancora de prora iacitur:

memor artificii mei vetus frigidae cultor mitto me in mare, quomodo psychrolutam decet, gausapatus. Quae putas me passum dum per aspera erepo, dum viam quaero, dum facio? Intellexi non inmerito nautis terram timeri. Incredibilia sunt quae tulerim, cum me ferre non possem: illud scito, Ulixem non fuisse tam irato mari natum ut ubique naufragia faceret: nausiator erat. Et ego quocumque navigare debuero vicensimo anno perveniam. Ut primum stomachum, quem scis non cum mari nausiam effugere, collegi, ut corpus unctione recreavi, hoc coepi mecum cogitare, quanta nos vitiorum nostrorum sequeretur oblivio, etiam corporalium, quae subinde admonent sui, nedum illorum quae eo magis latent quo maiora sunt. Levis aliquem motiuncula decipit; sed cum crevit et vera febris exarsit, etiam duro et perpessicio confessionem exprimit. Pedes dolent, articuli punctiunculas sentiunt: adhuc dissimulamus et aut talum extorsisse dicimus nos aut in exercitatone aliqua laborasse. Dubio et incipiente morbo quaeritur nomen, qui ubi ut talaria coepit intendere et utrosque distortos pedes fecit, necesse est podagram fateri.

43 **Contra evenit:** "the opposite happens."

43–44 **quo. . .minus:** i.e., *quanto peius. . .tanto minus.*

45–46 **et species. . .cogitat:** "both receives visions in his sleep and sometimes when asleep is aware that he is asleep."

55 **precario:** lit., "by entreaty or request"; i.e., when the other matters (cf. *omnibus aliis rebus* of the preceding line) permit, or in your spare time.

58 **in remissione:** "in the midst of your recovery."

62–63 **non est res subsiciva; ordinaria est:** "she is not a thing for one's spare time; she is regular" (i.e., she requires regular attention); *subsicivus, -a -um* literally means "cut off," "left remaining."

67 **Idem. . .omnibus:** "philosophy [says] the same thing in all matters."

80 **laxo sinu eludit:** "she wards them off with the loose fold [of her garment]."

47 **sopor, -oris,** *m.,* sleep
   somnium, -i, *n.,* dream
50 **expergiscor, -i, perrectus,** 3 *dep.,* awake, arouse one's self
51 **coarguo, -ere, -argui,** 3, expose
52 **excutio, -ere, -cussi, -cussus,** 3, shake off
54 **complexus, -us,** *m.,* embrace
58 **quam primum,** as soon as possible
64 **dimidium, -i,** *n.,* half
73 **cludo, -ere, clusi, clusus,** 3, shut, close
   exiguus, -a, -um, *adj.,* little
78 **retundo, -ere, -tudi, -tusus (-tunsus),** 3, beat, blunt
79 **defetigo (defatigo),** 1, weary, fatigue, tire, exhaust
80 **discutio, -ere, -cussi, -cussus,** 3, dash to pieces
81 **respuo, -ere, -spui, -sputus,** 3, spit back

Contra evenit in his morbis quibus adficiuntur animi: quo quis peius se habet, minus sentit. Non est quod mireris, Lucili carissime; nam qui leviter dormit, et species secundum quietem capit et aliquando dormire se dormiens cogitat: gravis sopor etiam somnia extinguit animumque altius mergit quam ut in ullo intellectu sui sit. Quare vitia sua nemo confitetur? quia etiamnunc in illis est: somnium narrare vigilantis est, et vitia sua confiteri sanitatis indicium est. Expergiscamur ergo, ut errores nostros coarguere possimus. Sola autem nos philosophia excitabit, sola somnum excutiet gravem: illi te totum dedica. Dignus illa es, illa digna te est: ite in complexum alter alterius. Omnibus aliis rebus te nega, fortiter, aperte; non est quod precario philosopheris. Si aeger esses, curam intermisisses rei familiaris et forensia tibi negotia excidissent nec quemquam tanti putares cui advocatus in remissione descenderes; toto animo id ageres ut quam primum morbo liberareris. Quid ergo? non et nunc idem facies? omnia inpedimenta dimitte et vaca bonae menti: nemo ad illam pervenit occupatus. Exercet philosophia regnum suum; dat tempus, non accipit; non est res subsiciva; ordinaria est, domina est, adest et iubet. Alexander cuidam civitati partem agrorum et dimidium rerum omnium promittenti 'eo' inquit 'proposito in Asiam veni, ut non id acciperem quod dedissetis, sed ut id haberetis quod reliquissem'. Idem philosophia rebus omnibus: 'non sum hoc tempus acceptura quod vobis superfuerit, sed id vos habebitis quod ipsa reiecero'. Totam huc converte mentem, huic adside, hanc cole: ingens intervallum inter te et ceteros fiet; omnes mortales multo antecedes, non multo te dii antecedent. Quaeris quid inter te et illos interfuturum sit? diutius erunt. At mehercules magni artificis est clusisse totum in exiguo; tantum sapienti sua quantum deo omnis aetas patet. Est aliquid quo sapiens antecedat deum: ille naturae beneficio non timet, suo sapiens. Ecce res magna, habere inbecillitatem hominis, securitatem dei. Incredibilis philosophiae vis est ad omnem fortuitam vim retundendam. Nullum telum in corpore eius sedet; munita est, solida; quaedam defetigat et velut levia tela laxo sinu eludit, quaedam discutit et in eum usque qui miserat respuit. *Vale.*

3 **Quo genere:** "in what way" or " [an illness] of what kind."

5 **Graeco nomine:** i.e., asthma.

13–15 **Tam. . .distulit:** "If I take delight in this result, as if in good health, I'm acting as foolishly as he who thinks he has won [his case] when he has [merely] postponed his trial."

29–30 **quid. . .desinas:** "for what does it matter whether you do not begin or whether you cease [to be]."

31–32 **nam. . .erat:** "since I was in no condition to speak."

34 **remansit:** supply *suspirium* as subject.

36 **eius:** i.e., *spiritus.*

36–37 **Quomodo. . .suspirem:** "[Let it do] whatever it pleases, provided that I do not sigh from my soul"; i.e., provided that the sigh is caused by physical asthma rather than mental grief of soul. Seneca plays with the two meanings of *suspirium.*

38 **nihil. . .toto:** "I make no plans for an entire day."

44 **coactura est:** supply *necessitas* as subject.

2 **commeatus, -us,** *m.*, respite, furlough
  valetudo, -inis, *f.*, health
  repente, *adv.*, suddenly
3 **prorsus,** *adv.*, certainly, absolutely
6 **suspirium, -i,** *n.*, shortness of breath
  valde, *adv.*, very
7 **procella, -ae,** *f.*, storm
  fere, *adv.*, almost
  desino, -ere, -sivi (-sii), -situs, 3, cease
10 **quidni,** *adv.*, why not?
  aegroto, 1, be sick
11 **egero, -ere, -gessi, -gestus,** 3, draw out
12 **aliquando,** *adv.*, at some time or other, finally
  spiritus, -us, *m.*, breath
17 **adquiesco, -ere, -quievi, -quietus,** 3, find comfort in
22 **atqui,** *conj.*, and yet, nevertheless
24 **lucerna, -ae,** *f.*, lamp
26 **utrimque,** *adv.*, on either side
30 **uterque, utraque, utrumque,** *adj.*, both
33 **anhelitus, -us,** *m.*, panting
35 **quamvis,** *adv.*, although
  ex natura, naturally
39 **piget, -ere, piguit,** *impers.*, 2, it displeases, it grieves
41 **hic,** *adv.*, here, in this place
43 **invitus, -a, -um,** *adj.*, unwilling

Epistle Fifty-four
ON SICKNESS AND DEATH

Seneca Lucilio Suo Salutem

Longum mihi commeatum dederat mala valetudo; repente me invasit. 'Quo genere?' inquis. Prorsus merito interrogas: adeo nullum mihi ignotum est. Uni tamen morbo quasi adsignatus sum, quem quare Graeco nomine appellem nescio;   5 satis enim apte dici suspirium potest. Brevis autem valde et procellae similis est impetus; intra horam fere desinit: quis enim diu exspirat? Omnia corporis aut incommoda aut pericula per me transierunt: nullum mihi videtur molestius. Quidni? aliud enim quidquid est aegrotare est, hoc animam   10 egerere. Itaque medici hanc 'meditationem mortis' vocant; facit enim aliquando spiritus ille quod saepe conatus est. Hilarem me putas haec tibi scribere quia effugi? Tam ridicule facio, si hoc fine quasi bona valetudine delector, quam ille, quisquis vicisse se putat cum vadimonium distulit.   15

Ego vero et in ipsa suffocatione non desii cogitationibus laetis ac fortibus adquiescere. 'Quid hoc est?' inquam 'tam saepe mors experitur me? Faciat: [at] ego illam diu expertus sum.' 'Quando?' inquis. Antequam nascerer. Mors est non esse. Id quale sit iam scio: hoc erit post me quod ante me   20 fuit. Si quid in hac re tormenti est, necesse est et fuisse, antequam prodiremus in lucem; atqui nullam sensimus tunc vexationem. Rogo, non stultissimum dicas si quis existimet lucernae peius esse cum extincta est quam antequam accenditur? Nos quoque et extinguimur et accendimur: medio   25 illo tempore aliquid patimur, utrimque vero alta securitas est. In hoc enim, mi Lucili, nisi fallor, erramus, quod mortem iudicamus sequi, cum illa et praecesserit et secutura sit. Quidquid ante nos fuit mors est; quid enim refert non incipias an desinas, cum utriusque rei hic sit effectus, non esse?   30

His et eiusmodi exhortationibus (tacitis scilicet, nam verbis locus non erat) adloqui me non desii; deinde paulatim suspirium illud, quod esse iam anhelitus coeperat, intervalla maiora fecit et retardatum est. At remansit, nec adhuc, quamvis desierit, ex natura fluit spiritus; sentio haesita-   35 tionem quandam eius et moram. Quomodo volet, dummodo non ex animo suspirem. Hoc tibi de me recipe: non trepidabo ad extrema, iam praeparatus sum, nihil cogito de die toto. Illum tu lauda et imitare quem non piget mori, cum iuvet vivere: quae est enim virtus, cum eiciaris, exire? Tamen est   40 et hic virtus: eicior quidem, sed tamquam exeam. Et ideo numquam eicitur sapiens quia eici est inde expelli unde invitus recedas: nihil invitus facit sapiens; necessitatem effugit, quia vult quod coactura est. *Vale.*

3 **seposito:** supply *viro,* "for a man withdrawn."

5 **in. . .adducere:** lit., "can bring the ears to disgust or annoyance"; i.e., "can weary the ears."

12–13 **actum est:** lit., "it has been done"; i.e., "it's all over," "I've had it."

16–17 **alipilum. . .exprimentem:** "think of the hair plucker continually forcing out his slender, shrill voice so that he may be more noticeable [to the customers]."

19–21 **iam. . .vendentis:** supply *cogita,* the direct objects of which are *exclamationes . . .botularium. . .crustularium. . .institores.*

22 **te. . .ferreum. . .surdum:** accusatives of exclamation.

23 **Chrysippum:** Chrysippus (280–207 B.C.), successor of Cleanthes as head of the Stoic School.

24 **perducat ad mortem:** an idiomatic, metaphorical expression, like the English "bores a person to death," "drives a person crazy."

4 **balneum (balineum), -i,** *n.,* bathhouse
6 **plumbum, -i,** *n.,* leaden-weight
7 **gemitus, -us,** *m.,* grunt
  quotiens, *adv.,* as often as
8 **remitto, -ere, -misi, -missus,** 3, let go
  sibilus, -i, *m.,* hissing
  acerbus, -a, -um, *adj.,* harsh, shrill
9 **unctio, -onis,** *f.,* anointing, massage
10 **crepitus, -us,** *m.,* noise
  inlido, -ere, -lisi, -lisus, 3, beat against
  umerus, -i, *m.,* shoulder
11 **prout,** *conj.,* according as
12 **pilicrepus, -i,** *m.,* ball-player
  pila, -ae, *f.,* ball
13 **scordalus, -i,** *m.,* quarrelsome fellow
  fur, furis, *c.,* thief
  deprendo (deprehendo), -ere, -prendi, -prensus, 3, catch
14 **piscina, -ae,** *f.,* pool
15 **salio, -ire, salui, saltus,** 4, leap
16 **rectus, -a, -um,** *p. adj.* (*of* **rego**), right, all right
18 **vello, -ere, vulsi, vulsus,** 3, pluck
  ala, -ae, *f.,* armpit
  pro, *prep. w. abl.,* instead of
19 **biberarius, -i,** *m.,* man selling drinks
  botularius, -i, *m.,* sausage-maker
20 **crustularius, -i,** *m.,* confectioner
  popina, -ae, *f.,* eating-house
  institor, -oris, *m.,* huckster
21 **insignitus, -a, -um,** *p. adj.* (*of* **insignio**), marked, striking
22 **ferreus, -a, -um,** *adj.,* made of iron
  surdus, -a, -um, *adj.,* deaf
23 **consto, -are, -stiti, -status,** 1, stand firm, be unshaken
24 **adsiduus, -a, -um,** *adj.,* continual
  salutatio, -onis, *f.,* good-morning greeting
25 **fremitus, -us,** *m.,* loud noise
  curo, 1, pay attention to
26 **deiectus, -us,** *m.,* fall
  quamvis, *adv.,* although
27 **fragor, -oris,** *m.,* din
28 **avoco,** 1, distract

Epistle Fifty-six
THE PHILOSOPHER IN THE BATHHOUSE

Seneca Lucilio Suo Salutem

Peream si est tam necessarium quam videtur silentium in
studia seposito. Ecce undique me varius clamor circumsonat:
supra ipsum balneum habito. Propone nunc tibi omnia genera
vocum quae in odium possunt aures adducere: cum fortiores   5
exercentur et manus plumbo graves iactant, cum aut labo-
rant aut laborantem imitantur, gemitus audio, quotiens
retentum spiritum remiserunt, sibilos et acerbissimas re-
spirationes; cum in aliquem inertem et hac plebeia unctione
contentum incidi, audio crepitum inlisae manus umeris,   10
quae prout plana pervenit aut concava, ita sonum mutat. Si
vero pilicrepus supervenit et numerare coepit pilas, actum
est. Adice nunc scordalum et furem deprensum et illum cui
vox sua in balineo placet, adice nunc eos qui in piscinam
cum ingenti inpulsae aquae sono saliunt. Praeter istos quo-   15
rum, si nihil aliud, rectae voces sunt, alipilum cogita tenuem
et stridulam vocem quo sit notabilior subinde exprimentem
nec umquam tacentem nisi dum vellit alas et alium pro se
clamare cogit; iam biberari varias exclamationes et botu-
larium et crustularium et omnes popinarum institores   20
mercem sua quadam et insignita modulatione vendentis.

'O te' inquis 'ferreum aut surdum, cui mens inter tot
clamores tam varios, tam dissonos constat, cum Chrysippum
nostrum adsidua salutatio perducat ad mortem.' At mehercules ego istum fremitum non magis curo quam fluctum aut   25
deiectum aquae, quamvis audiam cuidam genti hanc unam
fuisse causam urbem suam transferendi, quod fragorem Nili
cadentis ferre non potuit. Magis mihi videtur vox avocare

29 **animum adducit:** "draws the mind [to it]."

32 **ad Metam Sudantem:** *Meta Sudans* or "Sweating Column," a cone-shaped public fountain from which water issued from various openings; its remains still stand near the Colosseum.

33 **nec cantat sed exclamat:** "he does not play a tune but [merely] blasts notes."

39 **dum. . .non:** Seneca sometimes uses *non* for *ne* in negative clauses of proviso.

43 **Omnia. . .quiete:** A fragment by the Latin poet Varro Atacinus (82–36 B.C.), who translated the *Argonautica* of Apollonius Rhodius (c. 295–215 B.C.). Varro also wrote epigrams, elegies, satires, and an epic poem *De Bello Sequanico* dealing with Caesar's exploits in Gaul.

46 **insomnia:** "dreams": the neuter noun of the second declension, *insomnium, -ii,* n., has two meanings, "sleeplessness" and "dream." The first declension noun, *insomnia, -ae,* f., means "sleeplessness."

50–51 **suspensum. . .ponitur:** "those coming close to him walk on tip-toe." Lit., "the foot-step of those coming close to him is placed in suspense"; *suspensus. -a, -um* figuratively means "suspended," "pressing or touching lightly," "on tiptoe."

57 **nos male habet:** "takes evil hold of us."

60 **vacat:** impers. + dat., "there is time or leisure for a thing."

63 **secessisse:** in post-Augustan authors, the verb *secedo, -ere* has the meaning "retire" from public into private life.

---

29 **crepitus, -us,** *m.,* noise
 tantum, *adv.,* only
30 **impleo, -ere, -plevi, -pletus,** 2, fill
 verbero, 1, beat
 avocatio, -onis, *f.,* distraction
 circumstrepo, -ere, -strepui, -strepitus, 3, make a noise
31 **esseda, -ae,** *f.,* carriage
 faber, fabri, *m.,* carpenter
 inquilinus, -i, *m.,* resident
32 **serrarius, -i,** *m.,* one who saws
 vicinus, -a, -um, *adj.,* near, nearby, neighboring
33 **tubula, -ae,** *f.,* small trumpet
 experior, -iri, -pertus, 4 *dep.,* test
 tibia, -ae, *f.,* flute
 etiamnunc, *conj.,* moreover
34 **subinde,** *adv.,* continually
36 **vel,** *conj.,* even
 pausarius, -i, *m.,* boatswain
 remex, -igis, *m.,* oarsman
37 **modus, -i,** *m.,* measure, beat
38 **foris,** *adv.,* out of doors, outside
39 **rixor,** 1 *dep.,* quarrel
40 **dissideo, -ere, -sedi, -sessus,** 2, sit apart, be at variance
41 **prosum, prodesse, profui,** *irr.,* be of use
42 **adfectus, -us,** *m.,* emotion
 fremo, -ere, fremui, fremitus, 3, roar
46 **insomnium, -i,** *n.,* dream
48 **explico, -are, -plicavi (-plicui), -plicatus (-plicitus),** 1, unfold
 laxus, -a, -um, *adj.,* spacious
50 **turba, -ae,** *f.,* crowd
 conticesco, -ere, -ticui, 3, become silent
51 **nempe,** *conj.,* to be sure
52 **aegritudo, -inis,** *f.,* malady, care
 queror, -i, questus, 3 *dep.,* complain
53 **obstrepo, -ere, -strepui, -strepitus,** 3, roar
54 **conpesco, -ere, -pescui,** 3, check, restrain
55 **iaceo, -ere, iacui, iacitus,** 2, lie down
 interdum, *adv.,* sometimes
60 **distringo, -ere, -strinxi, -strictus,** 3, occupy
61 **discutio, -ere, -cussi, -cussus,** 3, shake off
62 **statio, -onis,** *f.,* position
63 **paenitentia, -ae,** *f.,* dissatisfaction
 latebra, -ae, *f.,* hiding-place, retreat
64 **recrudesco, -ere, -crudui,** 3, break out again

quam crepitus; illa enim animum adducit, hic tantum aures
implet ac verberat. In his quae me sine avocatione circum-   30
strepunt essedas transcurrentes pono et fabrum inquilinum
et serrarium vicinum, aut hunc qui ad Metam Sudantem
tubulas experitur et tibias, nec cantat sed exclamat: etiamnunc molestior est mihi sonus qui intermittitur subinde quam
qui continuatur. Sed iam me sic ad omnia ista duravi ut   35
audire vel pausarium possim voce acerbissima remigibus
modos dantem. Animum enim cogo sibi intentum esse nec
avocari ad externa; omnia licet foris resonent, dum intus
nihil tumultus sit, dum inter se non rixentur cupiditas et
timor, dum avaritia luxuriaque non dissideant nec altera   40
alteram vexet. Nam quid prodest totius regionis silentium,
si adfectus fremunt?

> Omnia noctis erant placida composta quiete.

Falsum est: nulla placida est quies nisi quam ratio composuit;
nox exhibet molestiam, non tollit, et sollicitudines mutat.   45
Nam dormientium quoque insomnia tam turbulenta sunt
quam dies: illa tranquillitas vera est in quam bona mens
explicatur. Aspice illum cui somnus laxae domus silentio
quaeritur, cuius aures ne quis agitet sonus, omnis servorum
turba conticuit et suspensum accedentium propius vestigium   50
ponitur: huc nempe versatur atque illuc, somnum inter
aegritudines levem captans; quae non audit audisse se que-
ritur. Quid in causa putas esse? Animus illi obstrepit. Hic
placandus est, huius conpescenda seditio est, quem non est
quod existimes placidum, si iacet corpus: interdum quies   55
inquieta est; et ideo ad rerum actus excitandi ac tractatione
bonarum artium occupandi sumus, quotiens nos male habet
inertia sui inpatiens. Magni imperatores, cum male parere
militem vident, aliquo labore conpescunt et expeditionibus
detinent: numquam vacat lascivire districtis, nihilque tam   60
certum est quam otii vitia negotio discuti. Saepe videmur
taedio rerum civilium et infelicis atque ingratae stationis
paenitentia secessisse; tamen in illa latebra in quam nos
timor ac lassitudo coniecit interdum recrudescit ambitio.

83–86 **et me. . .timentem:** Vergil, *Aeneid* 2.726–729. Aeneas is describing his emotions when he, carrying his father Anchises on his shoulders and leading his son Ascanius by the hand, flees with them from burning Troy. The word *comiti* refers to his son, the word *oneri,* to his father. Romans traditionally recognized this tableau as exemplary of familial and public duty.

87 **Prior ille:** i.e., the fearless Aeneas of the first two lines.

89 **hic alter:** i.e., the fearful Aeneas of the last two lines.

90–91 **quem. . .deiecit:** "a single sound, whatever it is, taken as the noise [of the enemy], has upset him."

92 **sarcinae:** "burdens." Seneca compares Aeneas, carrying his father Anchises, to luxurious men weighed down by the burden of their wealth.

100–101 **cum. . .invenerit:** Homer, *Odyssey* 12.165–200, describes how Odysseus, on the advice of the sorceress Circe, stopped the ears of his companions with wax so that they might sail past the Sirens and their songs in safety.

65 **excido, -ere, -cidi, -cisus,** 3, cut *or* root out
desino, -ere, -sivi (-sii), -situs, 3, stop
66 **parum,** *adv.*, too little, not enough
cedo, -ere, cessi, cessus, 3, yield
67 **aliquando,** *adv.*, sometimes
cedo, -ere, cessi, cessus, 3, depart
sollicito, 1, disturb
69 **eo. . .quo = tanto. . .quanto,** by so much. . .by how much, the. . .the
73 **simulatus, -a, -um,** *p. adj.* (*of* **simulo**), feigned
74 **subsido, -ere, -sedi, -sessus,** 3, sink, settle down
75 **bona fide,** genuinely, truly
receptus, -us, *m.*, retreat
contemno, -ere, -tempsi, -temptus, 3, scorn
77 **concentus, -us,** *m.*, harmonious music
79 **introsus,** *adv.*, inwards, within
accido, -ere, -cidi, 3, happen
80 **erigo, -ere, -rexi, -rectus,** 3, arouse
81 **conceptus, -a, -um,** *p. adj.* (*of* **concipio**), preconceived
curiosus, -a, -um, *adj.*, full of care, anxious
83 **dudum,** *adv.*, lately, recently
84 **glomero,** 1, gather together
86 **suspensus, -a, -um,** *p. adj.* (*of* **suspendo**), anxious
pariter, *adv.*, equally
87 **vibro,** 1, brandish
arieto, 1, strike violently
88 **inpello, -ere, -puli, -pulsus,** 3, drive on, overthrow
89 **inperitus, -a, -um,** *adj.*, untaught, ignorant
91 **exanimo,** 1, deprive of life, terrify greatly
96 **blandior, -iri, blanditus,** 4 *dep.*, flatter
minor, 1 *dep.*, threaten
98 **convicium, -i,** *n.*, noise

Non enim excisa desiit, sed fatigata aut etiam obirata rebus   65
parum sibi cedentibus. Idem de luxuria dico, quae videtur
aliquando cessisse, deinde frugalitatem professos sollicitat
atque in media parsimonia voluptates non damnatas sed
relictas petit, et quidem eo vehementius quo occultius.
Omnia enim vitia in aperto leniora sunt; morbi quoque tunc   70
ad sanitatem inclinant cum ex abdito erumpunt ac vim sui
proferunt. Et avaritiam itaque et ambitionem et cetera mala
mentis humanae tunc perniciosissima scias esse cum simulata
sanitate subsidunt. Otiosi videmur, et non sumus. Nam si
bona fide sumus, si receptui cecinimus, si speciosa contem-   75
psimus, ut paulo ante dicebam, nulla res nos avocabit, nullus
hominum aviumque concentus interrumpet cogitationes
bonas, solidasque iam et certas. Leve illud ingenium est nec
sese adhuc reduxit introsus quod ad vocem et accidentia
erigitur; habet intus aliquid sollicitudinis et habet aliquid   80
concepti pavoris quod illum curiosum facit, ut ait Vergilius
noster:

> et me, quem dudum non ulla iniecta movebant
> tela neque adverso glomerati ex agmine Grai,
> nunc omnes terrent aurae, sonus excitat omnis   85
> suspensum et pariter comitique onerique timentem.

Prior ille sapiens est, quem non tela vibrantia, non arietata
inter <se> arma agminis densi, non urbis inpulsae fragor
territat: hic alter inperitus est, rebus suis timet ad omnem
crepitum expavescens, quem una quaelibet vox pro fremitu   90
accepta deiecit, quem motus levissimi exanimant; timidum
illum sarcinae faciunt. Quemcumque ex istis felicibus elegeris,
multa trahentibus, multa portantibus, videbis illum 'comiti-
que onerique timentem'. Tunc ergo te scito esse compositum
cum ad te nullus clamor pertinebit, cum te nulla vox tibi   95
excutiet, non si blandietur, non si minabitur, non si inani
sono vana circumstrepet. 'Quid ergo? non aliquando com-
modius est et carere convicio?' Fateor; itaque ego ex hoc
loco migrabo. Experiri et exercere me volui: quid necesse est
diutius torqueri, cum tam facile remedium Ulixes sociis   100
etiam adversus Sirenas invenerit? *Vale.*

5 **nostrorum:** "of our relatives."

   eo. . .felicius: "the more happily they've been realized, the more harmful they are." *eo. . .quo = tanto. . .quanto.*

8 **vocem gratuitam:** i.e., words that ask no favor of the gods.

11–12 **unius mensae instrumentum:** "supplies for a single meal."

18 **quantulum. . .datur:** i.e., nature is satisfied with very little; it is man's greed that covets more than nature requires.

20 **Sallustius:** Sallust, *Catiline* 1.1.

25 **licet:** *ut* is sometimes omitted after *licet.*

   in limine ipso. . .marmori: "on the very marble threshold." Note that *marmori* (a noun) is in apposition to *in timine ipso* and suggests the idea of a tomb.

2 **queror, -i, questus,** 3 *dep.,* complain
3 **nondum,** *adv.,* not yet
7 **execratio, -onis,** *f.,* curse
  quandoque, *adv.,* at some time
8 **quousque,** *adv.,* how long
10 **satio, -onis,** *f.,* planting
11 **meto, -ere, messui,** 3, reap
13 **iugerum, -i,** *n.,* acre
  pascuum, -i, *n.,* pasture
16 **alvus, -i,** *f.,* belly
  modicus, -a, -um, *adj.,* moderate in size
17 **edax, -acis,** *adj.,* voracious
18 **minime,** *superl. adv.,* not at all
19 **venter, -tris,** *m.,* belly
23 **latito,** 1, hide
24 **torpeo, -ere,** 2, be torpid, sluggish
  quomodo, *adv.,* as
  conditivum, -i, *n.,* tomb
25 **licet, -ere, licuit,** *impers.,* 2, it is permitted

Epistle Sixty
MAN'S SUPPLICATION FOR AFFLICTION

Seneca Lucilio Suo Salutem

Queror, litigo, irascor. Etiamnunc optas quod tibi optavit
nutrix tua aut paedagogus aut mater? nondum intellegis
quantum mali optaverint? O quam inimica nobis sunt vota
nostrorum! eo quidem inimiciora quo cessere felicius. Iam   5
non admiror si omnia nos a prima pueritia mala sequuntur:
inter execrationes parentum crevimus. Exaudiant di quandoque nostram pro nobis vocem gratuitam. Quousque pos-
cemus aliquid deos? [quasi] ita nondum ipsi alere nos possumus? Quamdiu sationibus implebimus magnarum urbium   10
campos? quamdiu nobis populus metet? quamdiu unius
mensae instrumentum multa navigia et quidem non ex uno
mari subvehent ? Taurus paucissimorum iugerum pascuo
impletur; una silva elephantis pluribus sufficit: homo et
terra et mari pascitur. Quid ergo? tam insatiabilem nobis   15
natura alvum dedit, cum tam modica corpora dedisset, ut
vastissimorum edacissimorumque animalium aviditatem vin-
ceremus? Minime; quantulum est enim quod naturae datur!
Parvo illa dimittitur: non fames nobis ventris nostri magno
constat sed ambitio. Hos itaque, ut ait Sallustius, 'ventri   20
oboedientes' animalium loco numeremus, non hominum,
quosdam vero ne animalium quidem, sed mortuorum. Vivit
is qui multis usui est, vivit is qui se utitur; qui vero latitant
et torpent sic in domo sunt quomodo in conditivo. Horum
licet in limine ipso nomen marmori inscribas: mortem suam   25
antecesserunt. *Vale.*

5–6 **ut. . .sit:** "so that for me [every] day may be like an entire life."

  6 **rapio:** supply *diem* as object.

  8 **cum maxime:** "just now." See *Ep.* 7, lines 41–42.

9–10 **quia. . .pendeo:** "because I am not too anxious [to know] how long this will last."

12 **Da operam:** "pay attention," "see to it."

19–20 **Satis. . .est:** "life is sufficiently equipped [with necessaries]."

  2 **ago, -ere, egi, actus,** 3, do
  7 **vel,** *conj.,* even
12 **libenter,** *adv.,* willingly
13 **invitus, -a, -um,** *adj.,* unwilling
14 **excipio, -ere, -cepi, -ceptus,** 3, take
17 **exigo, -ere, -egi, -actus,** 3, demand
18 **in primis,** especially, above all
20 **instrumentum, -i,** *n.,* supply, provision

Epistle Sixty-one
LIVE EACH DAY AS IF IT WERE YOUR LAST

Seneca Lucilio Suo Salutem

Desinamus quod voluimus velle. Ego certe id ago <ne> senex eadem velim quae puer volui. In hoc unum eunt dies, in hoc noctes, hoc opus meum est, haec cogitatio, inponere veteribus malis finem. Id ago ut mihi instar totius vitae dies sit; nec mehercules tamquam ultimum rapio, sed sic illum aspicio tamquam esse vel ultimus possit. Hoc animo tibi hanc epistulam scribo, tamquam me cum maxime scribentem mors evocatura sit; paratus exire sum, et ideo fruar vita quia quam diu futurum hoc sit non nimis pendeo. Ante senectutem curavi ut bene viverem, in senectute ut bene moriar; bene autem mori est libenter mori. Da operam ne quid umquam invitus facias: quidquid necesse futurum est repugnanti, id volenti necessitas non est. Ita dico: qui imperia libens excipit partem acerbissimam servitutis effugit, facere quod nolit; non qui iussus aliquid facit miser est, sed qui invitus facit. Itaque sic animum componamus ut quidquid res exiget, id velimus, et in primis ut finem nostri sine tristitia cogitemus. Ante ad mortem quam ad vitam praeparandi sumus. Satis instructa vita est, sed nos in instrumenta eius avidi sumus; deesse aliquid nobis videtur et semper videbitur: ut satis vixerimus, nec anni nec dies faciunt sed animus. Vixi, Lucili carissime, quantum satis erat; mortem plenus expecto. *Vale.*

5

10

15

20

2–3 **qui. . .videri volunt:** "who want it to seem."

8 **abduco:** supply *me.*

9 **quibus. . .congregavit:** "to whom some circumstance has joined me."

10 **cum optimo quoque:** "with all the best"; *optimus quisque* means "every best man," i.e., all the best.

12 **Demetrium:** Demetrius of Sunium, renowned Cynic philosopher, who taught in Rome during Caligula's reign.

13 **relictis conchyliatis:** supply *viris.*

14 **Quidni admirer:** "why should I not admire him?"

18 **tamquam. . . permiserit:** "as if he has surrendered to others the possession of all things." Demetrius, like the Stoic sage, is self-sufficient, fortified against external forces, and therefore does not need material possessions.

2 **mentior, -iri, -itus,** 4 *dep.*, lie
turba, -ae, *f.*, crowd
3 **simulo,** 1, feign, pretend
5 **commodo,** 1, lend
6 **consto, -are, -stiti, -status,** 1, be located, be settled
7 **tracto,** 1, draw, conduct
9 **moror,** 1 *dep.*, linger
13 **conchyliatus, -a, -um,** *adj.*, clothed in purple
15 **contemno, -ere, -tempsi, -temptus,** 3, scorn

Epistle Sixty-two
SCORN RICHES; SEIZE THE WEALTH OF THE AGES

Seneca Lucilio Suo Salutem

Mentiuntur qui sibi obstare ad studia liberalia turbam
negotiorum videri volunt: simulant occupationes et augent
et ipsi se occupant. Vaco, Lucili, vaco, et ubicumque sum,
ibi meus sum. Rebus enim me non trado sed commodo, nec   5
consector perdendi temporis causas; et quocumque constiti
loco, ibi cogitationes meas tracto et aliquid in animo salutare
converso. Cum me amicis dedi, non tamen mihi abduco nec
cum illis moror quibus me tempus aliquod congregavit aut
causa ex officio nata civili, sed cum optimo quoque sum; ad   10
illos, in quocumque loco, in quocumque saeculo fuerunt,
animum meum mitto. Demetrium, virorum optimum,
mecum circumfero et relictis conchyliatis cum illo seminudo
loquor, illum admiror. Quidni admirer? vidi nihil ei deesse.
Contemnere aliquis omnia potest, omnia habere nemo potest: 15
brevissima ad divitias per contemptum divitiarum via est.
Demetrius autem noster sic vivit, non tamquam contempserit
omnia, sed tamquam aliis habenda permiserit. *Vale.*

2 **Moleste fero:** "I am sorry."

11 **in unum. . .diem:** Homer, *Iliad* 19.228–229. In this reference, when Achilles refuses to eat or drink until he has avenged the death of his comrade Patroclus, Odysseus urges him to mourn but one day and to strengthen himself and his comrades with food and drink before returning to battle.

    Niobam: *Iliad* 24.602. When Achilles informs Priam that he will return Hector's corpse, the hero urges the aged king to eat his supper, reminding him that even Niobe, whose twelve children perished in her palace, took thought of food.

18–19 **Non. . .quo:** "I am not putting it off to a period of time longer [than that] by which."

22 **custodienti:** supply *tibi.*

22–23 **eoque. . .desinit:** "the sharper it is, the more quickly it comes to a halt"; *eo. . .quo = tanto. . .quanto.*

28 **Attalus:** Attalus, Stoic philosopher, teacher of Seneca.

4 **contingo, -ere, -tigi, -tactus,** 3, befall

6 **vellico,** 1, sting
    tantum, *adv.,* only
    ignosco, -ere, -novi, -notus, 3, pardon

7 **prolabor, -i, lapsus,** 3 *dep.,* fall
    nimius, -a, -um, *adj.,* too much, excessive

9 **ploro,** 1, wail, lament

11 **dumtaxat,** *adv.,* only

12 **unde,** *adv.,* whence, from what source

13 **argumentum, -i,** *n.,* proof
    desiderium, -i, *n.,* loss

15 **stultitia, -ac,** *f.,* folly
    ambitio, -onis, *f.,* desire for display

17 **iam,** *adv.,* soon

18 **quilibet, quae-, quod-,** *indef. adj.,* some, any

19 **mulceo, -ere, mulsi, mulsus,** 2, soothe

20 **luctus, -us,** *m.,* grief
    resideo, -ere, -sedi, -sessus, 2, quiet down
    cum primum, as soon as

22 **elabor, -i, lapsus,** 3 *dep.,* slip away

23 **desino, -ere, -sivi (-sii), -situs,** 3, cease

25 **sicut,** *adv.,* just as, as

27 **morsus, -us,** *m.,* sting, pain

28 **defungor, -i, functus,** 3 *dep.,* die

29 **quomodo,** *adv.,* in what manner, even as
    pomum, -i, *n.,* fruit

30 **suaviter,** *adv.,* agreeably, pleasantly

31 **amaritudo, -inis,** *f.,* bitterness

32 **ango, -ere, anxi, anctus (anxus),** 3, cause pain

33 **incolumis, -e,** *adj.,* safe and sound
    mel, mellis, *n.,* honey
    placenta, -ae, *f.,* cake

34 **retractatio, -onis,** *f.,* remembrance

41 **interpretor,** 1 *dep.,* interpret
    aufero, auferre, abstuli, ablatus, *irr.,* take away

Epistle Sixty-three
THE MODERATION OF GRIEF

Seneca Lucilio Suo Salutem

Moleste fero decessisse Flaccum, amicum tuum, plus tamen
aequo dolere te nolo. Illud, ut non doleas, vix audebo exigere;
et esse melius scio. Sed cui ista firmitas animi continget nisi
iam multum supra fortunam elato? illum quoque ista res   5
vellicabit, sed tantum vellicabit. Nobis autem ignosci potest
prolapsis ad lacrimas, si non nimiae decucurrerunt, si ipsi
illas repressimus. Nec sicci sint oculi amisso amico nec fluant;
lacrimandum est, non plorandum. Duram tibi legem videor
ponere, cum poetarum Graecorum maximus ius flendi   10
dederit in unum dumtaxat diem, cum dixerit etiam Niobam
de cibo cogitasse? Quaeris unde sint lamentationes, unde
inmodici fletus ? per lacrimas argumenta desiderii quaerimus
et dolorem non sequimur sed ostendimus; nemo tristis sibi
est. O infelicem stultitiam! est aliqua et doloris ambitio.   15
'Quid ergo?' inquis 'obliviscar amici?' Brevem illi apud te
memoriam promittis, si cum dolore mansura est: iam istam
frontem ad risum quaelibet fortuita res transferet. Non
differo in longius tempus quo desiderium omne mulcetur,
quo etiam acerrimi luctus residunt: cum primum te obser-   20
vare desieris, imago ista tristitiae discedet. Nunc ipse custodis
dolorem tuum; sed custodienti quoque elabitur, eoque citius
quo est acrior desinit. Id agamus ut iucunda nobis amissorum fiat recordatio. Nemo libenter ad id redit quod non
sine tormento cogitaturus est, sicut illud fieri necesse est, ut   25
cum aliquo nobis morsu amissorum quos amavimus nomen
occurrat; sed hic quoque morsus habet suam voluptatem.
Nam, ut dicere solebat Attalus noster, 'sic amicorum defunctorum memoria iucunda est quomodo poma quaedam sunt
suaviter aspera, quomodo in vino nimis veteri ipsa nos   30
amaritudo delectat; cum vero intervenit spatium, omne
quod angebat extinguitur et pura ad nos voluptas venit'.
Si illi credimus, 'amicos incolumes cogitare melle ac placenta
frui est: eorum qui fuerunt retractatio non sine acerbitate
quadam iuvat. Quis autem negaverit haec acria quoque et   35
habentia austeritatis aliquid stomachum excitare?' Ego non
idem sentio: mihi amicorum defunctorum cogitatio dulcis
ac blanda est; habui enim illos tamquam amissurus, amisi
tamquam habeam.

Fac ergo, mi Lucili, quod aequitatem tuam decet, desine   40
beneficium fortunae male interpretari: abstulit, sed dedit.
Ideo amicis avide fruamur quia quamdiu contingere hoc

46   **in vivis:** "when they were alive."

51   **qui. . .solacium:** "who are powerless (i.e., if they have no power) to console us for the one who has been buried."

75   **Annaeum Serenum:** to this intimate friend, Annaeus Serenus, Seneca dedicated the dialogues *De Constantia Sapientis, De Otio,* and *De Tranquillitate Animi.*

45   **moror,** 1 *dep.*, delay, loiter
47   **lugeo, -ere, luxi, luctus,** 2, mourn
48   **maereo, -ere,** 2, mourn, lament
49   **serus, -a, -um,** *adj.*, late
     adfectus, -us, *m.*, emotion
53   **quicumque, quae-, quid-,** *indef. rel. pron.*, whoever, whatever
54   **ne. . .quidem,** not. . .even
55   **despolio,** 1, rob
57   **scapulae, -arum,** *f.*, shoulders
58   **effero, efferre, extuli, elatus,** *irr.*, carry out, bury
59   **satius,** *comp.* (*of* **satis**), better
     reparo, 1, acquire
64   **lassitudo, -inis,** *f.*, weariness
65   **quam primum,** as soon as possible
70   **rogus, -i,** *m.*, funeral pile
     revello, -ere, -velli, -vulsus (-volsus), 3, tear away
71   **citus, -a, -um,** *p. adj.* (*of* **cieo**), quick
73   **inmerito,** *adv.*, undeservedly
74   **simulo,** 1, feign
     stultus, -a, -um, *adj.*, foolish
80   **minor, minus,** *comp.* (*of* **parvus**), younger

possit incertum est. Cogitemus quam saepe illos reliquerimus
in aliquam peregrinationem longinquam exituri, quam saepe
eodem morantes loco non viderimus: intellegemus plus nos   45
temporis in vivis perdidisse. Feras autem hos qui neglegen-
tissime amicos habent, miserrime lugent, nec amant quemquam nisi perdiderunt? ideoque tunc effusius maerent quia
verentur ne dubium sit an amaverint; sera indicia adfectus
sui quaerunt. Si habemus alios amicos, male de iis et meremur   50
et existimamus, qui parum valent in unius elati solacium;
si non habemus, maiorem iniuriam ipsi nobis fecimus quam
a fortuna accepimus: illa unum abstulit, nos quemcumque
non fecimus. Deinde ne unum quidem nimis amavit qui plus
quam unum amare non potuit. Si quis despoliatus amissa   55
unica tunica conplorare se malit quam circumspicere quomodo frigus effugiat et aliquid inveniat quo tegat scapulas,
nonne tibi videatur stultissimus? Quem amabas extulisti:
quaere quem ames. Satius est amicum reparare quam flere.

   Scio pertritum iam hoc esse quod adiecturus sum, non   60
ideo tamen praetermittam quia ab omnibus dictum est:
finem dolendi etiam qui consilio non fecerat tempore invenit. Turpissimum autem est in homine prudente remedium
maeroris lassitudo maerendi: malo relinquas dolorem quam
ab illo relinquaris; et quam primum id facere desiste quod,   65
etiam si voles, diu facere non poteris. Annum feminis ad
lugendum constituere maiores, non ut tam diu lugerent, sed
ne diutius: viris nullum legitimum tempus est, quia nullum
honestum. Quam tamen mihi ex illis mulierculis dabis vix
retractis a rogo, vix a cadavere revulsis, cui lacrimae in totum 70
mensem duraverint? Nulla res citius in odium venit quam
dolor, qui recens consolatorem invenit et aliquos ad se
adducit, inveteratus vero deridetur, nec inmerito; aut enim
simulatus aut stultus est.

   Haec tibi scribo, is qui Annaeum Serenum carissimum   75
mihi tam inmodice flevi ut, quod minime velim, inter
exempla sim eorum quos dolor vicit. Hodie tamen factum
meum damno et intellego maximam mihi causam sic lugendi
fuisse quod numquam cogitaveram mori eum ante me posse.
Hoc unum mihi occurrebat, minorem esse et multo minorem—   80
tamquam ordinem fata servarent! Itaque adsidue cogitemus
tam de nostra quam omnium quos diligimus mortalitate.
Tunc ego debui dicere, 'minor est Serenus meus: quid
ad rem pertinet? post me mori debet, sed ante me potest'.

85 **percutio, -ere, -cussi, -cussus,**
3, strike

Quia non feci, inparatum subito fortuna percussit. Nunc   85
cogito omnia et mortalia esse et incerta lege mortalia; hodie
fieri potest quidquid umquam potest. Cogitemus ergo, Lucili
carissime, cito nos eo perventuros quo illum pervenisse mae-
remus; et fortasse, si modo vera sapientium fama est recipit-
que nos locus aliquis, quem putamus perisse praemissus est.   90
Vale.

6–7 **ut parata sint:** "so that they (referring to *quaecumque. . .deposita sunt*) may be ready."

8–9 **Cum. . .moram:** "as soon as I have hope for a longer stay in the same place."

12–13 **et quidem totis:** supply *diebus:* "and even on days wholly busy."

18 **huic:** i.e., *philosophia.*

28 **eum:** direct object of an understood *impediet* supplied from *impediat.*

34 **exiret. . .intraret:** "if it entered [from without], it would depart from his soul."

34–35 **Aliquando. . .intervenit:** "sometimes from without [something] intervenes by which he is reminded of his mortality."

2 **liqueo, -ere, liqui,** 2, be clear
   edisco, -ere, -didici, 3, learn thoroughly
4 **situs, -us,** *m.*, mould, disuse
   cohaereo, -ere, -haesi, -haesus, 2, cling together
5 **explico,** 1, unroll
6 **subinde,** *adv.*, from time to time
   excutio, -ere, -cussi, -cussus, 3, shake out, examine
7 **exigo, -ere, -egi, -actus,** 3, demand
   in praesentia, for the present
   differo, -ferre, distuli, dilatus, *irr.*, postpone
10 **cisium, -i,** *n.*, light two-wheeled gig
11 **lectus, -i,** *m.*, couch
   desidero, 1, require
13 **succedo, -ere, -cessi, -cessus,** 3, follow, come along
14 **sero, -ere, sevi, satus,** 3, sow
15 **dilatio, -onis,** *f.*, delaying
   perago, -ere, -egi, -actus, 3, go through, accomplish
16 **incumbo, -ere, -cubui, -cubitus,** 3, devote one's self
17 **vaco,** 1, have leisure
20 **usque,** *adv.*, all the way
21 **refert,** *impers.*, it matters, it makes a difference
23 **intendo, -ere, -tendi, -tentus,** 3, stretch, stretch out
   dissilio, -ire, -silui, -sultus, 4, leap apart
25 **summoveo, -ere, -movi, -motus,** 2, remove
26 **studium, -i,** *n.*, study
27 **atqui,** *conj.*, and yet
   studeo, -ere, studui, 2, study
29 **alacer, -cris, -cre,** *adj.*, cheerful, lively
30 **adhuc,** *adv.*, still
   interscindo, -ere, -scidi, -scisus, 3, break
   contexo, -ere, -texui, -textus, 3, weave
33 **domesticus, -a, -um,** *adj.*, private, one's own
36 **cutis, -is,** *f.*, skin
   stringo, -ere, strinxi, strictus, 3, graze, touch lightly
   aliquo, *adv.*, somewhere
37 **adflo,** 1, blow on, breathe on
38 **extrinsecus,** *adv.*, from without
39 **interdum,** *adv.*, sometimes
   pustula, -ae, *f.*, blister, pimple
40 **ulcusculum, -i,** *n.*, little ulcer
   in alto, deep within

Epistle Seventy-two
THE PRIORITY OF PHILOSOPHY

Seneca Lucilio Suo Salutem

Quod quaeris a me liquebat mihi (sic rem edidiceram) per
se; sed diu non retemptavi memoriam meam, itaque non
facile me sequitur. Quod evenit libris situ cohaerentibus, hoc
evenisse mihi sentio: explicandus est animus et quaecumque   5
apud illum deposita sunt subinde excuti debent, ut parata
sint quotiens usus exegerit. Ergo hoc in praesentia differa-
mus; multum enim operae, multum diligentiae poscit. Cum
primum longiorem eodem loco speravero moram, tunc istud
in manus sumam. Quaedam enim sunt quae possis et in cisio   10
scribere, quaedam lectum et otium et secretum desiderant.
Nihilominus his quoque occupatis diebus agatur aliquid et
quidem totis. Numquam enim non succedent occupationes
novae: serimus illas, itaque ex una exeunt plures. Deinde
ipsi nobis dilationem damus: 'cum hoc peregero, toto animo   15
incumbam' et 'si hanc rem molestam composuero, studio me
dabo'. Non cum vacaveris philosophandum est, sed ut philosopheris vacandum est; omnia alia neglegenda ut huic ad-
sideamus, cui nullum tempus satis magnum est, etiam si a
pueritia usque ad longissimos humani aevi terminos vita   20
producitur. Non multum refert utrum omittas philosophiam
an intermittas; non enim ubi interrupta est manet, sed
eorum more quae intenta dissiliunt usque ad initia sua
recurrit, quod a continuatione discessit. Resistendum est
occupationibus, nec explicandae sed summovendae sunt.   25
Tempus quidem nullum est parum idoneum studio salutari;
atqui multi inter illa non student propter quae studendum
est. 'Incidet aliquid quod inpediat.' Non quidem eum cuius
animus in omni negotio laetus atque alacer est: inperfectis
adhuc interscinditur laetitia, sapientis vero contexitur gaudi-   30
um, nulla causa rumpitur, nulla fortuna; semper et ubique
tranquillus est. Non enim ex alieno pendet nec favorem
fortunae aut hominis expectat. Domestica illi felicitas est;
exiret ex animo si intraret: ibi nascitur. Aliquando extrinsecus quo admoneatur mortalitatis intervenit, sed id leve   35
et quod summam cutem stringat. Aliquo, inquam, incom-
modo adflatur; maximum autem illud bonum fixum est. Ita
dico, extrinsecus aliqua sunt incommoda, velut in corpore
interdum robusto solidoque eruptiones quaedam pustularum
et ulcuscula, nullum in alto malum est. Hoc, inquam, interest   40
inter consummatae sapientiae virum et alium procedentis
quod inter sanum et ex morbo gravi ac diutino emergentem,

43 **cui. . .accessio:** "for whom in place of health there is a lighter attack [of his illness]."

44 **in eadem:** supply *mala* or *incommoda.*

45 **ne. . .amplius:** "he cannot even fall [into illness] any more."

47 **excitatur:** supply *medicus* as subject.

57 **haec est quae:** "she it is who"; *haec* refers to *ratio.*

58 **Attalus:** Attalus, Stoic philosopher, teacher of Seneca.

61 **ad spem venturi:** i.e., in the hope of getting other pieces of bread or meat.

63–64 **ad rapinam. . .attoniti:** "aroused and frantic to snatch something else."

66–67 **Habet. . .summo:** "someone has good intentions, he has made progress, but lacks much to reach the top"; *summo* refers to the *summum bonum,* the highest good or virtue.

43 **adtendo, -ere, -tendi, -tentus,** 3, pay attention
    subinde, *adv.,* continually
45 **ad tempus,** for a period of time
47 **praesto, -are, -stiti, -stitus,** 1, guarantee
47 **excito,** 1, arouse from sleep
48 **semel,** *adv.,* once for all
    in totum, completely
51 **momentum, -i,** *n.,* importance
52 **accedo, -ere, -cessi, -cessus,** 3, be added
54 **inhio,** 1, gape
    ultro citroque, *adv.,* hither and thither
55 **mancipium, -i,** *n.,* property, permanent possession
58 **ingratus, -a, -um,** *adj.,* unpleasant, disagreeable
59 **aliquando,** *adv.,* at some time or other, ever
    frustum, -i, *n.,* bit
60 **protinus,** *adv.,* immediately
    integer, -gra, -grum, *adj.,* whole
61 **hio,** 1, open, open the mouth
63 **statim,** *adv.,* immediately
65 **obvenio, -ire, -veni, -ventus,** 4, come in the way of, fall to
    secure, *adv.,* calmly
68 **alternis,** supply *vicibus,* alternately
    modo, *adv.,* now
69 **inperitus, -a, -um,** *adj.,* inexperienced
    rudis, -e, *adj.,* uninstructed
    praecipitatio, -onis, *f.,* falling headlong
70 **inanis, -e,** *adj.,* void
71 **adhuc,** *adv.,* still
72 **adludo, -ere, -lusi, -lusus,** 3, play with
    contingo, -ere, -tigi, -tactus, 3, reach
73 **sub ictu,** within reach
    ne. . .quidem, not. . .even
74 **nondum,** *adv.,* not yet
    siccus, -a, -um, *adj.,* dry
    siccum, -i, *n.,* dry land
75 **discrimen, -inis,** *n.,* difference
77 **deterior, -ius,** *comp. adj.,* worse
80 **desino, -ere, -sivi (-sii), -situs,** 3, cease, stop

cui sanitatis loco est levior accessio: hic nisi adtendit, subinde gravatur et in eadem revolvitur, sapiens recidere non
potest, ne incidere quidem amplius. Corpori enim ad tempus   45
bona valetudo est, quam medicus, etiam si reddidit, non
praestat—saepe ad eundem qui advocaverat excitatur:
<animus> semel in totum sanatur. Dicam quomodo intellegas
sanum: si se ipse contentus est, si confidit sibi, si scit omnia
vota mortalium, omnia beneficia quae dantur petunturque,   50
nullum in beata vita habere momentum. Nam cui aliquid
accedere potest, id inperfectum est; cui aliquid abscedere
potest, id inperpetuum est: cuius perpetua futura laetitia est,
is suo gaudeat. Omnia autem quibus vulgus inhiat ultro
citroque fluunt: nihil dat fortuna mancipio. Sed haec quoque   55
fortuita tunc delectant cum illa ratio temperavit ac miscuit:
haec est quae etiam externa commendet, quorum avidis
usus ingratus est. Solebat Attalus hac imagine uti: 'vidisti
aliquando canem missa a domino frusta panis aut carnis
aperto ore captantem? quidquid excepit protinus integrum   60
devorat et semper ad spem venturi hiat. Idem evenit nobis:
quidquid expectantibus fortuna proiecit, id sine ulla voluptate demittimus statim, ad rapinam alterius erecti et attoniti.' Hoc sapienti non evenit: plenus est; etiam si quid
obvenit, secure excipit ac reponit; laetitia fruitur maxima,   65
continua, sua. Habet aliquis bonam voluntatem, habet pro-
fectum, sed cui multum desit a summo: hic deprimitur
alternis et extollitur ac modo in caelum adlevatur, modo
defertur ad terram. Inperitis ac rudibus nullus praecipita-
tionis finis est; in Epicureum illud chaos decidunt, inane   70
sine termino. Est adhuc genus tertium eorum qui sapientiae
adludunt, quam non quidem contigerunt, in conspectu tamen
et, ut ita dicam, sub ictu habent: hi non concutiuntur, ne
defluunt quidem; nondum in sicco, iam in portu sunt. Ergo
cum tam magna sint inter summos imosque discrimina, cum   75
medios quoque sequatur fluctus suus, sequatur ingens periculum ad deteriora redeundi, non debemus occupationibus
indulgere. Excludendae sunt: si semel intraverint, in locum
suum alias substituent. Principiis illarum obstemus: melius
non incipient quam desinent. *Vale.*   80

2–3 Hodierno. . .spectaculi: "Today I have leisure, thanks not so much to myself but to the show"; *beneficio* means "by the help, aid, support" and is equivalent to the colloquial English "thanks to."

5 hac ipsa fiducia: "because of this very assurance."

7 eunti. . .sequenti: supply *homini.*

19 non unius hominis: i.e., of more than one opponent.

25 Illis: i.e., the athletes, *quorum lacertos umerosque miramur* (lines 16–17).

31–32 Peculium. . .numerant: "in return for their liberty, they pay the money which they accumulated by depriving their bellies."

3 **sphaeromachia, -ae,** *f.,* boxing-match
5 **crepo, -are, crepui, crepitus,** 1, creak
  subinde, *adv.,* continually
6 **ostium, -i,** *n.,* door
  adlevo, 1, lift up, raise
  velum, -i, *n.,* curtain
  tuto, *adv.,* safely
8 **priores, -um,** *m.,* predecessors
9 **servio,** 4, be a slave to
  assentior, 4 *dep.,* give approval
11 **interpellator, -oris,** *m.,* interrupter
  secretum, -i, *n.,* solitude
12 **excutio, -ere, -cussi, -cussus,** 3, shake out, drive out
14 **ingenium, -i,** *n.,* mind
15 **fidelis, -e,** *adj.,* genuine
  lusorius, -a, -um, *adj.,* relating to play
17 **lacertus, -i,** *m.,* muscle
  umerus, -i, *m.,* shoulder
  revolvo, -ere, -volvi, -volutus, 3, ponder
18 **exercitatio, -onis,** *f.,* training
19 **pugnus, -i,** *m.,* fist
  pariter, *adv.,* at the same time, together
  calx, -cis, *f.,* heel
20 **pulvis, -eris,** *m.,* dust
21 **madeo, -ere, madui,** 2, be wet, drip
22 **conroboro (corroboro),** 1, strengthen
  ictus, -us, *m.,* blow
23 **conculco,** 1, trample under foot
24 **egeo, -ere, egui,** 2, be in need of
26 **contingo, -ere, -tigi, -tactus,** 3, befall
  apparatus, -us, *m.,* equipment
27 **inpensa, -ae,** *f.,* expense
30 **mancipium, -i,** *n.,* slave
  sordes, -is, *f.,* filth
31 **exuo, -ere, -ui, -utus,** 3, strip off, get rid of
34 **arca, -ae,** *f.,* money box
  emo, -ere, emi, emptus, 3, buy
35 **coicio (conicio), -ere, -ieci, -iectus,** 3, throw together, collect, record
38 **iugum, -i,** *n.,* yoke
40 **vultus, -us,** *m.,* face, expression
41 **sollicitudo, -inis,** *f.,* anxiety, trouble
  in alto, deep within
42 **fingo, -ere, finxi, fictus,** 3, feign

Epistle Eighty
VIRTUE IS WITHIN THE REACH OF THOSE WHO WISH IT

Seneca Lucilio Suo Salutem

Hodierno die non tantum meo beneficio mihi vaco sed spectaculi, quod omnes molestos ad sphaeromachian avocavit. Nemo inrumpet, nemo cogitationem meam inpediet, quae hac ipsa fiducia procedit audacius. Non crepabit subinde   5
ostium, non adlevabitur velum: licebit tuto vadere, quod magis necessarium est per se eunti et suam sequenti viam. Non ergo sequor priores? facio, sed permitto mihi et invenire aliquid et mutare et relinquere; non servio illis, sed assentior.

Magnum tamen verbum dixi, qui mihi silentium promitte-   10
bam et sine interpellatore secretum: ecce ingens clamor ex stadio perfertur et me non excutit mihi, sed in huius ipsius rei contemplationem transfert. Cogito mecum quam multi corpora exerceant, ingenia quam pauci; quantus ad spectacu- lum non fidele et lusorium fiat concursus, quanta sit circa   15
artes bonas solitudo; quam inbecilli animo sint quorum lacertos umerosque miramur. Illud maxime revolvo mecum: si corpus perduci exercitatione ad hanc patientiam potest qua et pugnos pariter et calces non unius hominis ferat, qua solem ardentissimum in ferventissimo pulvere sustinens   20
aliquis et sanguine suo madens diem ducat, quanto facilius animus conroborari possit ut fortunae ictus invictus excipiat, ut proiectus, ut conculcatus exsurgat. Corpus enim multis eget rebus ut valeat: animus ex se crescit, se ipse alit, se exercet. Illis multo cibo, multa potione opus est, multo oleo,   25
longa denique opera: tibi continget virtus sine apparatu, sine inpensa. Quidquid facere te potest bonum tecum est. Quid tibi opus est ut sis bonus? velle. Quid autem melius potes velle quam eripere te huic servituti quae omnes premit, quam mancipia quoque condicionis extremae et in his sordibus   30
nata omni modo exuere conantur? Peculium suum, quod comparaverunt ventre fraudato, pro capite numerant: tu non concupisces quanticumque ad libertatem pervenire, qui te in illa putas natum? Quid ad arcam tuam respicis? emi non potest. Itaque in tabellas vanum coicitur nomen libertatis,   35
quam nec qui emerunt habent nec qui vendiderunt: tibi des oportet istud bonum, a te petas. Libera te primum metu mortis (illa nobis iugum inponit), deinde metu paupertatis. Si vis scire quam nihil in illa mali sit, compara inter se pauperum et divitum vultus: saepius pauper et fidelius ridet;   40
nulla sollicitudo in alto est; etiam si qua incidit cura, velut nubes levis transit: horum qui felices vocantur hilaritas ficta

45 **agere felicem:** "to play the part of a happy man."

46 **ullo:** supply *exemplo.*

50–52 **en. . .Isthmos:** "Behold, I rule over Argos; Pelops left me a kingdom, where the Isthmus is lashed by the Hellespont and by the Ionian sea." The author of this passage is unknown; Quintilian (9.4.140) quotes it. Seneca wants to stress the point that life, like acting, often causes men to play roles which certainly do not become them. Here an actor who is a meager, poor slave in real life comes on stage playing the part of a mighty king. *Argis. . .Pelops:* Pelops, ruler of a large part of the Peloponnesus, including the cities of Argos and Mycenae. It is very likely that the role being played by this slave is that of King Atreus, Pelops' son, notorious for his boasting, his cruelty, and his treacherous seizure of power. *ponto. . .Helles:* the Hellespont, the sea named after Helle, a maiden drowned in that body of water.

55 **quod. . .occides:** the author of this passage is unknown. *quieris:* a syncopated form for *quieveris;* from *quiesco, -ere, quievi, quietus,* 3, keep quiet.

66 **insigni capitis decorum:** "adorned with royal headdress."

67 **fasciam solve:** "remove the diadem"; *fascia, -ae,* f ., literally means "band" or "bandage."

43 **eo,** *adv.*, for that reason, on that account
quidem, *adv.*, indeed

44 **interdum,** *adv.*, sometimes
palam, *adv.*, openly
aerumna, -ae, *f.*, trouble

45 **exedo, -ere, -edi, -esus,** 3, eat up, consume

45 **saepius,** *comp. adv.* (*of* **saepe**), rather often

47 **mimus, -i,** *m.*, mime, drama, farce

48 **latus, -a, -um,** *adj.*, broad, wide, proud

49 **resupinus, -a, -um,** *adj.*, with head thrown back, i.e., proudly

50 **linquo, -ere, liqui,** 3, leave

53 **modius, -i,** *m.*, measure of grain
denarius, -i, *m.*, denarius, a Roman coin

54 **superbus, -a, -um,** *adj.*, proud
inpotens, -entis, *adj.*, arrogant
tumidus, -a, -um, *adj.*, swollen

55 **occido, -ere, -cidi, -casus,** 3, fall, die

56 **diurnus, -a, -um,** *adj.*, daily
diurnum, -i, *n.*, daily allowance
centunculus, -i, *m.*, small patch or patchwork

58 **lectica, -ae,** *f.*, litter
personatus, -a, -um, *adj.*, masked

59 **contemno, -ere, -tempsi, -temptus,** 3, scorn
despolio, 1, strip

60 **stratum, -i,** *n.*, saddle
venalis, -e, *adj.*, for sale
venalis, -is, *m.*, slave for sale

61 **involvo, -ere, -volvi, -volutus,** 3, wrap up
mango, -onis, *m.*, slave dealer

62 **lenocinium, -i,** *n.*, ornament, finery

64 **sive. . .sive,** *conj.*, if. . .or if
crus, cruris, *n.*, leg
alligo, 1, bind
brachium, -i, *n.*, arm

68 **perpendo, -ere, -pendi, -pensus,** 3, weigh, examine
sepono, -ere, -posui, -positus, 3, lay aside

est aut gravis et suppurata tristitia, eo quidem gravior
quia interdum non licet palam esse miseros, sed inter aeru-
mnas cor ipsum exedentes necesse est agere felicem. Saepius   45
hoc exemplo mihi utendum est, nec enim ullo efficacius
exprimitur hic humanae vitae mimus, qui nobis partes quas
male agamus adsignat. Ille qui in scaena latus incedit et haec
resupinus dicit,

> en impero Argis; regna mihi liquit Pelops,   50
> qua ponto ab Helles atque ab Ionio mari
> urguetur Isthmos,

servus est, quinque modios accipit et quinque denarios. Ille
qui superbus atque inpotens et fiducia virium tumidus ait,

> quod nisi quieris, Menelae, hac dextra occides,   55

diurnum accipit, in centunculo dormit. Idem de istis licet
omnibus dicas quos supra capita hominum supraque turbam
delicatos lectica suspendit: omnium istorum personata
felicitas est. Contemnes illos si despoliaveris. Equum empturus
solvi iubes stratum, detrahis vestimenta venalibus ne qua   60
vitia corporis lateant: hominem involutum aestimas? Man-
gones quidquid est quod displiceat, id aliquo lenocinio
abscondunt, itaque ementibus ornamenta ipsa suspecta sunt:
sive crus alligatum sive brachium aspiceres, nudari iuberes et
ipsum tibi corpus ostendi. Vides illum Scythiae Sarmatiaeve   65
regem insigni capitis decorum? Si vis illum aestimare totum-
que scire qualis sit, fasciam solve: multum mali sub illa latet.
Quid de aliis loquor? si perpendere te voles, sepone pecuniam,
domum, dignitatem, intus te ipse considera: nunc qualis sis
aliis credis. *Vale.*   70

5   **aliena opera:** "by the toil of someone else," i.e., by the bearers of his *lectica* or litter.

    prosint: the subject of this verb is *itinera*.

6–7 **Sunt. . .necessariae:** supply *lectiones*.

10   **non sine studio tamen:** this seems to be Seneca's warning that any reading, to be profitable, must be accompanied by study. From the form the argument takes in the succeeding sentence, it appears that the word *studio* used with *fatigatum* refers to composition.

12   **de stilo dico:** "I'm talking about writing."

12–13 **Invicem. . .commeandum est:** "Alternately one must go from one to the other"; *invicem,* "by turns," "alternately," is an old accusative which came to be used as an adverb.

14   **stilus. . .corpus:** "the pen (or writing) may reduce to bodily form."

18–19 **liquentia. . .cellas:** Vergil, *Aeneid* 1.432–433. When Aeneas and Achates reach Carthage, they marvel at the activity of the inhabitants, who, like busy bees, work constantly to build their newly founded city.

20   **De illis:** i.e., the bees.

22   **Quibusdam:** supply *scriptoribus.*

23   **illis:** supply *apibus* (dative of possession). The infinitive clause is the subject of *placet.*

28   **animal:** here in the sense of "creature," which includes insects.

29   **in. . .verti:** "is changed into this substance" (i.e., honey); the subject of the infinitive *verti* is the following relative clause.

2   **segnitia, -ae,** *f.,* sluggishness
    excutio, -ere, -cussi, -cussus, 3, shake out
    valetudo, -inis, *f.,* health
3   **prosum, prodesse, profui,** *irr.,* be useful to
4   **piger, -gra, -grum,** *adj.,* lazy
6   **lectio, -onis,** *f.,* reading
9   **alo, -ere, alui, altus (alitus),** 3, nourish
10 **reficio, -ere, -feci, -fectus,** 3, restore
    tantum, *adv.,* only
11 **contristo,** 1, sadden, depress
12 **exhaurio, -ire, -hausi, -haustus,** 4, drain
    diluo, -ere, -lui, -lutus, 3, dilute
14 **apis, -is,** *f.,* bee
15 **vagor,** 1 *dep.,* wander
    mel, mellis, *n.,* honey
16 **carpo, -ere, carpsi, carptus,** 3, pluck
    dispono, -ere, -posui, -positus, 3, arrange
17 **favus, -i,** *m.,* honeycomb
    digero, -ere, -gessi, -gestus, 3, distribute
19 **stipo,** 1, pack close, crowd
20 **constat,** *impers.,* it is agreed
    sucus, -i, *m.,* juice
21 **protinus,** *adv.,* at once
    sapor, -oris, *m.,* flavor, savor
22 **proprietas, -atis,** *f.,* property
    spiritus, -us, *m.,* breath
24 **arundo, -inis,** *f.,* sugar-cane
25 **ros, roris,** *m.,* dew
    caelum, -i, *n.,* climate
    umor, -oris, *m.,* moisture, secretion
    pinguis, -e, *adj.,* rich
27 **contraho, -ere, -traxi, -tractus,** 3, draw together, collect
28 **conditura, -ae,** *f.,* preservation
29 **dispositio, -onis,** *f.,* arrangement
    tener, -era, -erum, *adj.,* tender
30 **virens, -entis,** *p. adj. (of vireo),* green
    decerpo, -ere, -cerpsi, -cerptus, 3, pluck, cull

Epistle Eighty-four
ON INTEGRATING KNOWLEDGE

Seneca Lucilio Suo Salutem

Itinera ista quae segnitiam mihi excutiunt et valetudini
meae prodesse iudico et studiis. Quare valetudinem adiuvent
vides: cum pigrum me et neglegentem corporis litterarum
amor faciat, aliena opera exerceor. Studio quare prosint   5
indicabo: a lectionibus <non> recessi. Sunt autem, ut existimo,
necessariae, primum ne sim me uno contentus, deinde ut,
cum ab aliis quaesita cognovero, tum et de inventis iudicem
et cogitem de inveniendis. Alit lectio ingenium et studio
fatigatum, non sine studio tamen, reficit. Nec scribere tantum   10
nec tantum legere debemus: altera res contristabit vires et
exhauriet (de stilo dico), altera solvet ac diluet. Invicem hoc
et illo commeandum est et alterum altero temperandum, ut
quidquid lectione collectum est stilus redigat in corpus. Apes,
ut aiunt, debemus imitari, quae vagantur et flores ad mel   15
faciendum idoneos carpunt, deinde quidquid attulere dis-
ponunt ac per favos digerunt et, ut Vergilius noster ait,

liquentia mella
stipant et dulci distendunt nectare cellas.

De illis non satis constat utrum sucum ex floribus ducant qui   20
protinus mel sit, an quae collegerunt in hunc saporem mixtura
quadam et proprietate spiritus sui mutent. Quibusdam enim
placet non faciendi mellis scientiam esse illis sed colligendi.
Aiunt inveniri apud Indos mel in arundinum foliis, quod aut
ros illius caeli aut ipsius arundinis umor dulcis et pinguior   25
gignat; in nostris quoque herbis vim eandem sed minus
manifestam et notabilem poni, quam persequatur et contra-
hat animal huic rei genitum. Quidam existimant conditura
et dispositione in hanc qualitatem verti quae ex tenerrimis
virentium florentiumque decerpserint, non sine quodam, ut   30
ita dicam, fermento, quo in unum diversa coalescunt.

44 **ne aliena sint:** "that they may not remain (be) foreign matter" to us or in us.

55–56 **omnibus. . .inpressit:** "has impressed his own form on all things which he drew from whatever model he chose."

58 **Aliqua illic:** supply *vox; illic,* i.e., in the chorus.

35 **adhibeo, -ere, -hibui, -hibitus,** 2, apply
    ingenium, -i, *n.,* nature
    facultas, -atis, *f.,* power
36 **libamentum, -i,** *n.,* libation
    confundo, -ere, -fudi, -fusus, 3, mix together
    unde, *adv.,* whence
39 **quamdiu,** *adv.,* as long as
40 **perduro,** 1, last, hold out
    innato, 1, flow
41 **demum,** *adv.,* at last
43 **praesto, -are, -stiti, -status** (**-status**), 1, guarantee
    haurio, -ire, hausi, haustus, 4, drain, take in
44 **concoquo, -ere, -coxi, -coctus,** 3, digest
    alioqui, *adv.,* otherwise
45 **adsentior, -sentiri, -sensus,** 4 *dep.,* welcome
47 **dissideo, -ere, -sedi, -sessus,** 2, be different
48 **conprendo, -ere, -prendi, -prensus,** 3, comprise, fasten together
49 **tantum,** *adv.,* only
51 **quomodo,** *adv.,* in what manner, even as
52 **imago, -inis,** *f.,* portrait
54 **aliquando,** *adv.,* sometimes
    ne. . .quidem, not. . .even
57 **conpeto, -ere, -petivi (-petii), -petitus,** 3, come together
    quam, *adv.,* how
59 **accedo, -ere, -cessi, -cessus,** 3, be added
60 **tibia, -ae,** *f.,* flute
62 **commissio, -onis,** *f.,* entertainment
63 **olim,** *adv.,* once
    via, -ae, *f.,* aisle
    ordo, -inis, *m.,* row
64 **cavea, -ae,** *f.,* theater
    aeneator, -oris, *m.,* trumpeter
    cingo, -ere, cinxi, cinctus, 3, surround
    pulpitum, -i, *n.,* stage
65 **tibia, -ae,** *f.,* flute
    organum, -i, *n.,* musical instrument
    concentus, -us, *m.,* harmony
68 **conspiro,** 1, breathe together, unite, blend

Sed ne ad aliud quam de quo agitur abducar, nos quoque
has apes debemus imitari et quaecumque ex diversa lectione
congessimus separare (melius enim distincta servantur), deinde
adhibita ingenii nostri cura et facultate in unum saporem   35
varia illa libamenta confundere, ut etiam si apparuerit unde
sumptum sit, aliud tamen esse quam unde sumptum est
appareat. Quod in corpore nostro videmus sine ulla opera
nostra facere naturam (alimenta quae accepimus, quamdiu
in sua qualitate perdurant et solida innatant stomacho, onera   40
sunt; at cum ex eo quod erant mutata sunt, tunc demum in
vires et in sanguinem transeunt), idem in his quibus aluntur
ingenia praestemus, ut quaecumque hausimus non patiamur
integra esse, ne aliena sint. Concoquamus illa; alioqui in
memoriam ibunt, non in ingenium. Adsentiamur illis fideliter   45
et nostra faciamus, ut unum quiddam fiat ex multis, sicut
unus numerus fit ex singulis cum minores summas et dissi-
dentes conputatio una conprendit. Hoc faciat animus noster:
omnia quibus est adiutus abscondat, ipsum tantum ostendat
quod effecit. Etiam si cuius in te comparebit similitudo quem   50
admiratio tibi altius fixerit, similem esse te volo quomodo
filium, non quomodo imaginem: imago res mortua est. 'Quid
ergo? non intellegetur cuius imiteris orationem? cuius argu-
mentationem? cuius sententias?' Puto aliquando ne intellegi
quidem posse, Si magni vir ingenii omnibus quae ex quo   55
voluit exemplari traxit formam suam inpressit, ut in unitatem
illa conpetant. Non vides quam multorum vocibus chorus
constet? unus tamen ex omnibus redditur. Aliqua illic acuta
est, aliqua gravis, aliqua media; accedunt viris feminae, inter-
ponuntur tibiae: singulorum illic latent voces, omnium   60
apparent. De choro dico quem veteres philosophi noverant:
in commissionibus nostris plus cantorum est quam in theatris
olim spectatorum fuit. Cum omnes vias ordo canentium
implevit et cavea aeneatoribus cincta est et ex pulpito omne
tibiarum genus organorumque consonuit, fit concentus ex   65
dissonis. Talem animum esse nostrum volo: multae in illo
artes, multa praecepta sint, multarum aetatum exempla,
sed in unum conspirata.

71 **Hanc:** "her," i.e., reason.

75–76 **tam. . .secum:** "it is as anxious to see no one ahead of itself as [to see] no one [on a par] with itself", *sollicita est* employs the same construction as is employed after verbs of fearing.

77 **duplici:** supply *invidia*.

77–78 **si is. . .et invidet:** "if he who is envied also feels envy." Verbs like *invideo* that govern the dative case become impersonal in the passive and the dative is retained; *cui invidetur* means literally "to whom it is envied."

79–80 **multum. . .intraveris:** "they impose [upon you] many insults when you enter, more when you have entered." The subjects of *habent* are *domus* and *limina; ut intres* and *cum intraveris* are used in the sense of "whenever." The subjunctive is frequently used in the second person singular to indicate an indefinite subject ("you" means "anyone").

81–82 **in praerupto. . .in lubrico:** adjectives used as substantives, "on a precipice. . .on slippery ground."

87 **dignitatis:** to be taken with *fastigium*, not with *via*.

88 **libet:** supply *tibi*.

88 **cui. . .summisit:** "to which Fortune has surrendered herself." I.e., Fortune has no control over the wise man, that man who has reached the height of dignity (*fastigium dignitatis*).

88–89 **omnia. . .aspicies:** "you will indeed see beneath you (i.e., at your feet) all things which are regarded as most lofty [by the crowd]."

---

69 **intentio, -onis,** *f.*, effort
70 **vito,** 1, avoid
72 **iamdudum,** *adv.*, at once
74 **mollio,** 4, soften
    ambitus, -us, *m.*, canvassing for office
75 **tumidus, -a, -um,** *adj.*, swollen
    ventosus, -a, -um, *adj.*, like the wind, fickle
78 **intueor, -eri, -tuitus,** 2 *dep.*, gaze upon
79 **rixa, -ae,** *f.*, quarrel, brawl
    limen, -inis, *n.*, threshold
80 **praetereo, -ire, -ivi (-ii), -itus,** *irr.*, go past, pass by
81 **gradus, -us,** *m.*, step
    adgestus, -us, *m.*, overcrowding
    suspensus, -a, -um, *p. adj.* (*of* **suspendo**), hanging, endangered
82 **istic,** *adv.*, there
    potius, *adv.*, rather
83 **simul,** *adv.*, at the same time
84 **emineo, -ere, -ui,** 2, stand out
85 **quamvis,** *adv.*, although
    pusillus, -a, -um, *adj.*, small
86 **trames, -itis,** *m.*, path
87 **confragosus, -a, -um,** *adj.*, broken, rough
    fastigium, -i, *n.*, height
    conscendo, -ere, -scendi, -scensus, 3, ascend
88 **vertex, -icis,** *m.*, height
    libet, -ere, libuit, *impers.*, 2, it is pleasing

'Quomodo' inquis 'hoc effici poterit?' Adsidua intentione:
si nihil egerimus nisi ratione suadente, nihil vitaverimus nisi   70
ratione suadente. Hanc si audire volueris, dicet tibi: relinque
ista iamdudum ad quae discurritur; relinque divitias, aut
periculum possidentium aut onus; relinque corporis atque
animi voluptates, molliunt et enervant; relinque ambitum,
tumida res est, vana, ventosa, nullum habet terminum, tam   75
sollicita est ne quem ante se videat quam ne secum, laborat
invidia et quidem duplici. Vides autem quam miser sit si is
cui invidetur et invidet. Intueris illas potentium domos, illa
tumultuosa rixa salutantium limina? multum habent con-
tumeliarum ut intres, plus cum intraveris. Praeteri istos   80
gradus divitum et magno adgestu suspensa vestibula: non in
praerupto tantum istic stabis sed in lubrico. Huc potius te ad
sapientiam derige, tranquillissimasque res eius et simul
amplissimas pete. Quaecumque videntur eminere in rebus
humanis, quamvis pusilla sint et comparatione humillimorum   85
exstent, per difficiles tamen et arduos tramites adeuntur.
Confragosa in fastigium dignitatis via est; at si conscendere
hunc verticem libet, cui se fortuna summisit, omnia quidem
sub te quae pro excelsissimis habentur aspicies, sed tamen
venies ad summa per planum. *Vale.*   90

4   **nos debere:** subject of *haberetur.*

5   **pro certo haberetur:** the phrase *pro certo habere* means "to regard as certain."

6–7 **cuius. . .omnibus:** "[the gods] have given to none the knowledge of philosophy [but] to all the potential [of acquiring such knowledge]."

10–11 **non obvenit:** "she does not accidentally fall to our lot."

12–13 **beneficiaria res:** "a thing bestowed as a favor," i.e., something acquired without effort on the part of the recipient.

18   **Quod:** i.e., *consortium.*

20   **fuit:** in the sense of "became."

20–21 **desierunt. . .propria:** this paradox indicates that one is impoverished when one becomes greedy for everything. Supply *omnia* before *propria.*

25   **praecedit:** "goes before as leader," just as the preceding *praesunt* means "are before or above as leader." The animal kingdom is a favorite source of illustrations for all who "would follow nature as a guide."

28   **pro maximo:** the preposition here means "takes the place of" or "is in the place of." i.e., among men, excellence of character takes the place of extreme size (*maximo*).

     Animo: ablative of cause, "for. . .," "because of. . ."

31   **potest:** supply the infinitive *facere* of which *quantum vult* will be the direct object. The same infinitive is to be supplied with the following *posse* and with *debet* also.

33   **Posidonius:** Posidonius of Rhodes (c. 135–51 B.C.), Stoic philosopher, scientist, historian, and pupil of Panaetius (director of the Stoic School in Athens). Posidonius acquired a renowned reputation for his brilliant writings, only fragments of which remain. He was visited in Rhodes by Romans of distinction, including Cicero and Pompey.

     manus: "bands" or "tribes," which the wise ruler restrained.

38   **regnum:** "royal authority," "despotism," "tyranny."

39   **per. . .posse:** lit., "through whom he had begun to have power"; we would say "from whom he had received his power."

12 **suspicio, -ere, -spexi, -spectus, 3,** look up to

14 **verum, -i,** *n.,* truth

15 **comitatus, -us,** *m.,* train, band, retinue
    consero, -ere, -serui, -sertus, 3, connect, join together

16 **cohaereo, -ere, -haesi, -haesus, 2,** cling together

17 **penes,** *prep. w. acc.,* with, in the possession or power of
    consortium, -i, *n.,* fellowship

18 **aliquamdiu,** *adv.,* for some time

20 **desino, -ere, -sivi (-sii), -situs, 3,** cease

23 **arbitrium, -i,** *n.,* judgment

24 **potior, -ius,** *comp. adj. (of* **potis),** more powerful
    deterior, -ius, *comp. adj.,* inferior, weaker

26 **armentum, -i,** *n.,* herd
    torus, -i, *m.,* muscle

27 **mas, maris,** *m.,* male

28 **rector, -oris,** *m.,* ruler

30 **tuto,** *adv.,* safely

32 **perhibeo, -ere, -hibui, -hibitus, 2,** assert, maintain

33 **contineo, -ere, -tinui, -tentus, 2,** hold in check, curb, subdue

34 **tueor, -eri, tuitus, 2** *dep.,* guard, protect

37 **arceo, -ere, arcui, 2,** keep off

39 **experior, -iri, expertus, 4** *dep.,* try

40 **in,** *prep. w. acc.,* to, towards, regarding, for

41 **minor, 1** *dep.,* threaten
    pareo, -ere, parui, paritus, 2, obey

42 **subrepo, -ere, -repsi, -reptus, 3,** creep in

Epistle Ninety
WISDOM, SKILL, AND THE GOLDEN AGE

Seneca Lucilio Suo Salutem

Quis dubitare, mi Lucili, potest quin deorum inmortalium munus sit quod vivimus, philosophiae quod bene vivimus? Itaque tanto plus huic nos debere quam dis quanto maius beneficium est bona vita quam vita pro certo haberetur, nisi ipsam philosophiam di tribuissent; cuius scientiam nulli dederunt, facultatem omnibus. Nam si hanc quoque bonum vulgare fecissent et prudentes nasceremur, sapientia quod in se optimum habet perdidisset, inter fortuita non esse. Nunc enim hoc in illa pretiosum atque magnificum est, quod non obvenit, quod illam sibi quisque debet, quod non ab alio petitur. Quid haberes quod in philosophia suspiceres si bene- ficiaria res esset? Huius opus unum est de divinis humanisque verum invenire; ab hac numquam recedit religio, pietas, iustitia et omnis alius comitatus virtutum consertarum et inter se cohaerentium. Haec docuit colere divina, humana diligere, et penes deos imperium esse, inter homines consor- tium. Quod aliquamdiu inviolatum mansit, antequam socie- tatem avaritia distraxit et paupertatis causa etiam iis quos fecit locupletissimos fuit; desierunt enim omnia possidere, dum volunt propria. Sed primi mortalium quique ex his geniti naturam incorrupti sequebantur eundem habebant et ducem et legem, commissi melioris arbitrio; naturaest enim potioribus deteriora summittere. Mutis quidem gregibus aut maxima corpora praesunt aut vehementissima: non praecedit armenta degener taurus, sed qui magnitudine ac toris ceteros mares vicit; elephantorum gregem excelsissimus ducit: inter homines pro maximo est optimum. Animo itaque rector eligebatur, ideoque summa felicitas erat gentium in quibus non poterat potentior esse nisi melior; tuto enim quantum vult potest qui se nisi quod debet non putat posse.

Illo ergo saeculo quod aureum perhibent penes sapientes fuisse regnum Posidonius iudicat. Hi continebant manus et infirmiorem a validioribus tuebantur, suadebant dissuade- bantque et utilia atque inutilia monstrabant; horum pru- dentia ne quid deesset suis providebat, fortitudo pericula arcebat, beneficentia augebat ornabatque subiectos. Officium erat imperare, non regnum. Nemo quantum posset adversus eos experiebatur per quos coeperat posse, nec erat cuiquam aut animus in iniuriam aut causa, cum bene imperanti bene pareretur, nihilque rex maius minari male parentibus posset quam ut abiret e regno. Sed postquam subrepentibus vitiis

44 **tulere:** *fero* is the regular word in Latin for introducing a law.

    Solon: Solon (c. 640 – c. 558 B.C.). renowned Athenian statesman, poet, and lawgiver, one of the seven wise men.

46 **Lycurgum:** Lycurgus, famous legendary Spartan lawgiver of the ninth century B.C. He is said to have framed the constitution responsible for the peculiar political system which grew up at Sparta.

47 **Zaleuci. . .Charondae:** Zaleucus of Magna Graecia (7th cent. B.C.) and Charondas of Sicily (6th cent. B.C.) were famous lawgivers and disciples of Pythagoras.

48 **atrio:** the atrium was the large reception room of the Roman house. Here it means the "waiting or consulting room" of the lawyers.

48 **Pythagorae:** see *Ep.* 52, line 58.

50 **per Italiam Graeciae:** one way of referring to Magna Graecia in Latin.

53 **sparsos:** supply *homines.*

56 **tectorum supra tecta:** "story on story."

57 **vivaria piscium:** "fishponds," constructed so that the fastidious might have their fish no matter what the weather might be. Otherwise, the storms of winter might interfere seriously with menus.

    in hoc: "for the purpose"; *hoc* is accusative.

61–62 **Quid. . .dare:** English idiom expects a *quam* ("than") in this form of statement.

62–63 **cum tanto. . .periculo:** i.e., of falling down.

63 **suspendit:** an architectural term meaning "build upon arches."

64 **enim:** ironical in tone.

66 **Ista:** i.e., *decidere et. . .scindere.*

68 **designata:** "the parts marked out" to show where the wood was to be cut.

69 **nam. . .lignum:** Vergil, *Georgics* 1.144. In the first book of the *Georgics,* Vergil celebrated and explained to farmers the "arts" of tilling the soil; nowadays skillful methods and labor are necessary, whereas, in the primitive Golden Age life was much simpler and nature yielded her bounties without requiring men to toil. Thus, in those early days, men did not use metal saws to cut wood fancily but required merely the simple wooden wedge to split wood.

76 **sed:** brackets indicate that Reynolds follows Axelson who omitted this word from the text.

48 **consultus, -i,** *m.,* lawyer
49 **secessus, -us,** *m.,* retreat
    disco, -ere, didici, 3, learn
51 **hactenus,** *adv.,* up to this point
    adsentior, 4 *dep.,* agree with
52 **cotidianus, -a, -um,** *adj.,* daily, **in cotidiano,** daily
53 **fabrica, -ae,** *f.,* artisan's trade
    spargo, -ere, sparsi, sparsus, 3, scatter
    casa, -ae, *f.,* hut
    tego, -ere, texi, tectus, 3, cover, protect
54 **suffodio, -ere, -fodi, -fossus,** 3, dig out, excavate
    exedo, -ere, -edi, -esus, 3, eat up, consume, destroy
55 **molior,** 4 *dep.,* build
56 **machinatio, -onis,** *f.,* mechanism, device
58 **gula, -ae,** *f.,* gullet, throat, gluttony
    quamvis, *adv.,* however much
60 **sagino,** 1, fatten
61 **clavis, -is,** *f.,* key
    sera, -ae, *f.,* bolt
63 **inmineo, -ere,** 2, hang down over
    parum, *adv.,* little, too little, not enough
67 **quadratum, -i,** *n.,* square
    tignum, -i, *n.,* timber, log
    serra, -ae, *f.,* saw
68 **trabs, trabis,** *f.,* beam
    scindo, -ere, scidi, scissus, 3, cut
69 **cuneus, -i,** *m.,* wedge
    fissilis, -e, *adj.,* that can be split
    lignum, -i, *n.,* wood
70 **tectum, -i,** *n.,* roof
    cenatio, -onis, *f.,* dining-hall
    epulum, -i, *n.,* public banquet
71 **abies, -etis,** *f.,* fir
72 **vicus, -i,** *m.,* street
    lacunar, -aris, *n.,* panelled ceiling
73 **furca, -ae,** *f.,* fork-shaped pole
    utrimque, *adv.,* on both sides
    fulcio, -ire, fulsi, fultus, 4, prop up, support
74 **spisso,** 1, thicken, pack closely
    ramale, -is, *n.,* twig, branch
    proclive, -is, *n.,* slope
75 **imber, imbris,** *m.,* rain
    quamvis, *adv.,* however
76 **culmus, -i,** *m.,* straw

in tyrannidem regna conversa sunt, opus esse legibus coepit,
quas et ipsas inter initia tulere sapientes. Solon, qui Athenas
aequo iure fundavit, inter septem fuit sapientia notos;   45
Lycurgum si eadem aetas tulisset, sacro illi numero accessisset
octavus. Zaleuci leges Charondaeque laudantur; hi non in
foro nec in consultorum atrio, sed in Pythagorae tacito illo
sanctoque secessu didicerunt iura quae florenti tunc Siciliae
et per Italiam Graeciae ponerent.   50
      Hactenus Posidonio adsentior: artes quidem a philosophia
inventas quibus in cotidiano vita utitur non concesserim, nec
illi fabricae adseram gloriam. 'Illa' inquit 'sparsos et aut casis
tectos aut aliqua rupe suffossa aut exesae arboris trunco docuit
tecta moliri.' Ego vero philosophiam iudico non magis ex-   55
cogitasse has machinationes tectorum supra tecta surgentium
et urbium urbes prementium quam vivaria piscium in hoc
clausa ut tempestatum periculum non adiret gula et quamvis acerrime pelago saeviente haberet luxuria portus suos in
quibus distinctos piscium greges saginaret. Quid ais? philo-   60
sophia homines docuit habere clavem et seram? Quid aliud
erat avaritiae signum dare ? Philosophia haec cum tanto
habitantium periculo inminentia tecta suspendit? Parum
enim erat fortuitis tegi et sine arte et sine difficultate naturale
invenire sibi aliquod receptaculum. Mihi crede, felix illud   65
saeculum ante architectos fuit, ante tectores. Ista nata sunt
iam nascente luxuria, in quadratum tigna decidere et serra
per designata currente certa manu trabem scindere;

      nam primi cuneis scindebant fissile lignum.

Non enim tecta cenationi epulum recepturae parabantur,   70
nec in hunc usum pinus aut abies deferebatur longo vehi-
culorum ordine vicis intrementibus, ut ex illa lacunaria auro
gravia penderent. Furcae utrimque suspensae fulciebant
casam; spissatis ramalibus ac fronde congesta et in proclive
disposita decursus imbribus quamvis magnis erat. Sub his   75
tectis habitavere [sed] securi: culmus liberos texit, sub mar-
more atque auro servitus habitat.

79 **isto. . .modo:** lit., "in that manner." We would say "according to that kind of argument or reasoning."

81–82 **tunc. . .saltus:** Vergil, *Georgics* 1.139–140. Men after the fall from the Golden Age had to work to capture their food, learning how to hunt with hounds, to set traps, to smear twigs with bird-lime (a sticky substance made from holly or mistletoe that captured small birds). Seneca contends that it was not intellectual or philosophic wisdom (*sapientia*) that taught men these tricks, but necessity, skillfulness, and shrewdness (*sagacitas*).

82 **inventum:** supply *est.*

84 **sapientes fuisse:** supply the words *quod iudicat* from the previous sentence.

85–86 **tellus. . .fudisset:** "the earth, having melted the veins [of ore] lying on the surface had poured [them] forth."

86–87 **tales. . .quales colunt:** "such men. . .as are concerned with (or interested in)."

90–91 **corpore. . .spectante:** Seneca is referring to the Platonic concept (*Republic* 586) that man's upright posture is more suited to contemplate heavenly than earthly affairs.

92 **facilis:** this word sometimes means "easy-going" and is followed by an ablative of specification, as here, or by *in* with the ablative.

94 **Diogenen. . .Daedalum:** Seneca again distinguishes between *sagacitas* and *sapientia*. Daedalus, on the one hand, is the archetype of "ingenuity," the legendary Athenian inventor and craftsman, said to have created the wedge, saw, ax, potter's wheel, and ship's sails. He is most renowned for having created the famous Cretan Labyrinth to incarcerate the monstrous Minotaur, half bull, half man. Diogenes of Sinope (c. 400–325 B.C.), on the other hand, was an early Cynic philosopher, noted for his austere life of simplicity, abstinence, and self-control. The symbol of his extreme self-abnegation was the famous earthenware tub in which he is reputed to have lived.

97 **cum:** not found in the manuscripts but supplied by Baehrens.

102–103 **versatilia. . .laquearia. . .coagmentat:** Seneca's description here of such luxurious excesses as the movable panelled ceiling recalls the rotating roof in the dining-hall of Nero's Golden House (Suetonius, *Nero* 31) as well as the banquet hall of Trimalchio in Petronius (*Satyricon* 60).

106 **posse nos habitare:** a verb of saying must be supplied before this and the following infinitive clauses.

78 **ferramentum, -i,** *n.*, tool
79 **fabrilis, -e,** *adj.*, mechanical
81 **laqueus, -i,** *m.*, snare, trap
    viscum, -i, *n.*, bird-lime
82 **saltus, -us,** *m.*, woods
85 **aduro, -ere, -ussi, -ustus, 3,** scorch
87 **ne. . .quidem,** not. . .even
88 **malleus, -i,** *m.*, hammer
89 **forceps, -cipis,** *m.* and *f.*, tongs
92 **victus, -us,** *m.*, manner of life, way of living
    quidni, *adv.*, why not?
93 **expeditus, -a, -um,** *p. adj.* (*of* **expedio**), unimpeded
    convenit, *impers.*, it is fitting, becoming, appropriate
94 **uter, utra, utrum,** *adj.*, which of the two
95 **comminiscor, -i, mentus, 3** *dep.*, invent
96 **protinus,** *adv.*, immediately
    eximo, -ere, -emi, -emptus, 3, take out
97 **perula, -ae,** *f.*, little wallet, pocket
    calix, -icis, *m.*, cup
    obiurgatio, -onis, *f.*, chiding, reproving
98 **supervacuus, -a, -um,** *adj.*, superfluous
    sarcina, -ae, *f.*, baggage
    conplico, -are, -avi (-plicui), -atus (-plicitus), 1, fold up
99 **dolium, -i,** *n.*, tub
    cubito, 1, lie down
101 **crocum, -i,** *n.*, and **crocus, -i,** *m.*, saffron
    latens, -entis, *p. adj.* (*of* **lateo**), hidden, concealed
    fistula, -ae, *f.*, pipe
    euripus, -i, *m.*, canal
102 **sicco, 1,** drain dry, empty
    versatilis, -e, *adj.*, movable, revolving
    cenatio, -onis, *f.*, dining-room
103 **laquear, -aris,** *n.*, panel
    coagmento, 1, join, cement
    subinde, *adv.*, continually
104 **succedo, -ere, -cessi, -cessus, 3,** enter, approach
    fericulum, -i, *n.*, course
106 **marmorarius, -i,** *m.*, worker in marble
107 **faber, fabri,** *m.*, carpenter, engineer
108 **serica, -orum,** *n.*, Seric (Chinese) garments, silks
109 **summum, -i,** *n.*, surface
111 **cocus, -i,** *m.*, cook

In illo quoque dissentio a Posidonio, quod ferramenta
fabrilia excogitata a sapientibus viris iudicat; isto enim modo
dicat licet sapientes fuisse per quos   80

    tunc laqueis captare feras et fallere visco
    inventum et magnos canibus circumdare saltus.

Omnia enim ista sagacitas hominum, non sapientia invenit.
In hoc quoque dissentio, sapientes fuisse qui ferri metalla
et aeris invenerint, cum incendio silvarum adusta tellus in   85
summo venas iacentis liquefacta fudisset: ista tales inveniunt
quales colunt. Ne illa quidem tam subtilis mihi quaestio
videtur quam Posidonio, utrum malleus in usu esse prius an
forcipes coeperint. Utraque invenit aliquis excitati ingenii,
acuti, non magni nec elati, et quidquid aliud corpore incur-   90
vato et animo humum spectante quaerendum est. Sapiens
facilis victu fuit. Quidni? cum hoc quoque saeculo esse quam
expeditissimus cupiat. Quomodo, oro te, convenit ut et
Diogenen mireris et Daedalum? Uter ex his sapiens tibi
videtur? qui serram commentus est, an ille qui, cum vidisset   95
puerum cava manu bibentem aquam, fregit protinus exem-
ptum e perula calicem <cum> hac obiurgatione sui: 'quamdiu
homo stultus supervacuas sarcinas habui!', qui se conplicuit
in dolio et in eo cubitavit? Hodie utrum tandem sapien-
tiorem putas qui invenit quemadmodum in immensam altitu-   100
dinem crocum latentibus fistulis exprimat, qui euripos subito
aquarum impetu implet aut siccat et versatilia cenationum
laquearia ita coagmentat ut subinde alia facies atque alia
succedat et totiens tecta quotiens fericula mutentur, an eum
qui et aliis et sibi hoc monstrat, quam nihil nobis natura   105
durum ac difficile imperaverit, posse nos habitare sine mar-
morario ac fabro, posse nos vestitos esse sine commercio
sericorum, posse nos habere usibus nostris necessaria si contenti fuerimus iis quae terra posuit in summo? Quem si
audire humanum genus voluerit, tam supervacuum sciet   110
sibi cocum esse quam militem.

113 **Simplici cura:** ablative of price translated by "of," "with." *Consto* occurs frequently in Latin as little more than the verb *to be.*

114 **in delicias laboratur:** "toil is expended on luxuries." The passive voice is sometimes employed for brief and compact expression.

115 **districtos:** a participial adjective in agreement with an understood *nos.*

120 **hodieque:** "even today"; -*que* is here used in the sense of *et*, meaning "even," "also."

121 **murum:** genitive plural of *mus.*

123 **de:** brackets indicate Reynolds' desire to omit this word from the text.

144 **contraria:** i.e., things which fight actively against the healthful and the normal.

145–146 **circitatur. . .strepit:** "is belabored and deafened"; the two verbs suggest that peddlers selling their wares fill the city with shouting and noise.

113 **expeditus, -a, -um,** *p. adj. (of* **expedio**), easy
117 **pellis, -is,** *f.*, skin
118 **queo, -ire, quivi (quii), quitus,** 4, be able
   cortex, -icis, *m.*, bark
118 **plerique, -aeque, -aque,** *adj.*, very many
120 **consero, -ere, -serui, -sertus,** 3, join together
   tergum, -i, *n.*, skin
121 **vulpes, -is,** *f.*, fox
   induo, -ere, -dui, -dutus, 3, clothe
   mus, muris, *c.*, mouse
   mollis, -e, *adj.*, soft
122 **quilibet, quae-, quid-,** *indef. pron.*, any
   virgeus, -a, -um, *adj.*, made of twigs or rods
   cratis, -is, *f.*, wicker-work, hurdle
123 **texo, -ere, texui, textus,** 3, weave
   oblino, -ere, -levi, -litus, 3, smear
   lutum, -i, *n.*, mud
   stipula, -ae, *f.*, straw, stubble
124 **operio, -ire, -ui, -ertus,** 4, cover
   fastigium, -i, *n.*, roof
   pluvia, -ae, *f.*, rain
   devexum, -i, *n.*, slope
125 **labor, -i, lapsus,** 3 *dep.*, fall, fall down
127 **abdo, -ere, -didi, -ditus,** 3, hide, conceal
128 **excavatus, -a, -um,** *p. adj. (of* **excavo**), hollowed out
   specus, -us, *m.*, cave
129 **defossus, -us,** *m.*, pit, dug-out
   nimius, -a, -um, *adj.*, excessive
131 **humus, -i,** *f.*, soil, earth
132 **actus, -us,** *m.*, part, role
134 **aegre,** *adv.*, painfully
136 **fastidium, -i,** *n.*, loathing, disdain
137 **fomentum, -i,** *n.*, warm application
138 **obvius, -a, -um,** *adj.*, at hand, easy to obtain
   modus, -i, *m.*, measure, limit
139 **prout,** *conj.*, in proportion as
141 **descisco, -ere, -scivi (-scii), -scitus,** 3, free one's self from, revolt from
142 **ingenium, -i,** *n.*, wit
143 **supervacuus, -a, -um,** *adj.*, superfluous
144 **novissime,** *superl. adv.*, lastly

Illi sapientes fuerunt aut certe sapientibus similes quibus
expedita erat tutela corporis. Simplici cura constant necessaria: in delicias laboratur. Non desiderabis artifices: sequere
naturam. Illa noluit esse districtos; ad quaecumque nos   115
cogebat instruxit. 'Frigus intolerabilest corpori nudo.' Quid
ergo? non pelles ferarum et aliorum animalium a frigore satis
abundeque defendere queunt? non corticibus arborum pleraae-
que gentes tegunt corpora? non avium plumae in usum vestis
conseruntur? non hodieque magna Scytharum pars tergis   120
vulpium induitur ac murum, quae tactu mollia et inpenetra-
bilia ventis sunt? Quid ergo? non quilibet virgeam cratem
texuerunt manu et vili obliverunt luto, deinde [de] stipula
aliisque silvestribus operuere fastigium et pluviis per devexa
labentibus hiemem transiere securi? 'Opus est tamen calorem   125
solis aestivi umbra crassiore propellere.' Quid ergo? non vetustas multa abdidit loca quae vel iniuria temporis vel alio quolibet casu excavata in specum recesserunt? Quid ergo? non in
defosso latent Syrticae gentes quibusque propter nimios solis
ardores nullum tegimentum satis repellendis caloribus soli-   130
dum est nisi ipsa arens humus? Non fuit tam iniqua natura
ut, cum omnibus aliis animalibus facilem actum vitae daret,
homo solus non posset sine tot artibus vivere; nihil durum
ab illa nobis imperatum est, nihil aegre quaerendum, ut
possit vita produci. Ad parata nati sumus: nos omnia nobis   135
difficilia facilium fastidio fecimus. Tecta tegimentaque et
fomenta corporum et cibi et quae nunc ingens negotium facta
sunt obvia erant et gratuita et opera levi parabilia; modus
enim omnium prout necessitas erat: nos ista pretiosa, nos
mira, nos magnis multisque conquirenda artibus fecimus.   140
Sufficit ad id natura quod poscit. A natura luxuria descivit,
quae cotidie se ipsa incitat et tot saeculis crescit et ingenio
adiuvat vitia. Primo supervacua coepit concupiscere, inde
contraria, novissime animum corpori addixit et illius deser-
vire libidini iussit. Omnes istae artes quibus aut circitatur   145

146 **negotium gerunt:** "carry on the business."

150 **infractos:** "broken," "weakened," comparable, no doubt, to our "effeminate."

153–162 **Incredibilest. . .in quo:** this is a difficult, run-on passage, atypical of Seneca's normally curt and lucid style. The more highly technical terms include: *stamen, - inis,* n., warp, tautened thread on an upright loom; *subtemen, -inis,* n., woof, threads woven and spun in weaving; *trama, -ae,* f., woof (web, weft), threads woven and spun in weaving; *spatha, -ae,* f., batten or spoon-shaped paddle used to interweave threads on the loom: *textrinum, -i,* n., weaving. The passage might be rendered as follows:

It is incredible, my Lucilius, how easily sweet oratory can lead even great men away from truth. Witness Posidonius—in my opinion, [one] of those who contributed most to philosophy—when he wants to describe initially how some threads are [wound and] turned, others are drawn from [a spool] that is loose and pliable, then how the threads by means of suspended weights stretch out this upright warp [on the loom], then how the inserted thread, which softens the harshness of the web that presses on both sides, is forced to come together and to be joined by means of the batten—he said that the art of weaving too was invented by [ancient] philosophers, having forgotten that this more subtle type [of weaving] was invented in later days, [the type] in which. . . .

163–165 **tela. . .dentes:** Ovid, *Metamorphoses* 11.55, 56, 58: lines 55 and 56 are cited here exactly from the Ovidian passage; line 58 is quoted rather freely. Seneca's version may be translated as follows:

The web is bound by the beam; the reed separates the warp. The woof by sharp shuttles is inserted between [the threads], And the apportioning teeth strike it with their broad comb.

169–170 **proscissum. . .iteratum:** *proscissum* refers to the initial ploughing and *iteratum* to additional ones.

---

146 **olim,** *adv.,* formerly, in times past
148 **textor, -oris,** *m.,* weaver
  officina, -ae, *f.,* workshop
149 **coquo, -ere, coxi, coctus,** 3, cook
  mollis, -e, *adj.,* soft, effeminate, unmanly
150 **recedo, -ere, -cessi, -cessus,** 3, retire, withdraw
151 **ops, opis,** *f.,* resources
  finio, 4, limit
157 **filum, -i,** *n.,* thread
158 **tela, -ae,** *f.,* web, thread
163 **iugum, -i,** *n.,* yoke
  vincio, -ire, vinxi, vinctus, 4, bind
  harundo, -inis, *f.,* reed
164 **radius, -i,** *m.,* shuttle, sharp piece of wood similar to a needle
166 **contingo, -ere, -tigi, -tactus,** 3, happen, fall to one's lot
167 **celo,** 1, conceal
169 **facunde,** *adv.,* eloquently
  proscindo, -ere, -di, -ssus 3, cut, plough
  aratrum, -i, *n.,* plough
  solum, -i, *n.,* ground
170 **itero,** 1, repeat, plough again
171 **herba, -ae,** *f.,* weeds
172 **succresco, -ere, -crevi, -cretus,** 3, spring up
  neco, 1, kill
  seges, -etis, *f.,* crop
173 **tamquam,** *adv.,* as if
175 **pistrinum, -i,** *n.,* mill
177 **panis, -is,** *m.,* bread
  fruges, -um, *f.,* grain
179 **umor, -oris,** *m.,* moisture
180 **lubricus, -a, -um,** *adj.,* slippery
181 **concoquo, -ere, -coxi, -coctus,** 3, cook, digest
182 **accedo, -ere, -cessi, -cessus,** 3, approach, be added
183 **ad,** *prep. w. acc.,* according to
184 **adtritus, -us,** *m.,* rubbing
186 **tero, -ere, trivi, tritus,** 3, rub
  spargo, -ere, sparsi, sparsus, 3, sprinkle
187 **tractatio, -onis,** *f.,* handling
  perdomo, -are, -domui, -domitus, 1, subdue
  fingo, -ere, finxi, fictus, 3, mould
188 **testa, -ae,** *f.,* earthen vessel
  furnus, -i, *m.,* oven
190 **sutrinum, -i,** *n.,* shoemaker's trade

civitas aut strepit corpori negotium gerunt, cui omnia olim
tamquam servo praestabantur, nunc tamquam domino paran-
tur. Itaque hinc textorum, hinc fabrorum officinae sunt, hinc
odores coquentium, hinc molles corporis motus docentium
mollesque cantus et infractos. Recessit enim ille naturalis   150
modus desideria ope necessaria finiens; iam rusticitatis et
miseriae est velle quantum sat est.
    Incredibilest, mi Lucili, quam facile etiam magnos viros
dulcedo orationis abducat a vero. Ecce Posidonius, ut mea
fert opinio, ex iis qui plurimum philosophiae contulerunt,   155
dum vult describere primum quemadmodum alia torquean-
tur fila, alia ex molli solutoque ducantur, deinde quemadmodum tela suspensis ponderibus rectum stamen extendat,
quemadmodum subtemen insertum, quod duritiam utrimque
conprimentis tramae remolliat, spatha coire cogatur et iungi,   160
textrini quoque artem a sapientibus dixit inventam, oblitus
postea repertum hoc subtilius genus in quo

> tela iugo vincta est, stamen secernit harundo,
> inseritur medium radiis subtemen acutis,
> quod lato paviunt insecti pectine dentes.   165

Quid si contigisset illi videre has nostri temporis telas, in
quibus vestis nihil celatura conficitur, in qua non dico nullum
corpori auxilium, sed nullum pudori est? Transit deinde ad
agricolas nec minus facunde describit proscissum aratro solum
et iteratum quo solutior terra facilius pateat radicibus, tunc   170
sparsa semina et collectas manu herbas ne quid fortuitum et
agreste succrescat quod necet segetem. Hoc quoque opus ait
esse sapientium, tamquam non nunc quoque plurima cultores
agrorum nova inveniant per quae fertilitas augeatur. Deinde
non est contentus his artibus, sed in pistrinum sapientem   175
summittit; narrat enim quemadmodum rerum naturam imi-
tatus panem coeperit facere. 'Receptas' inquit 'in os fruges
concurrens inter se duritia dentium frangit, et quidquid excidit ad eosdem dentes lingua refertur; tunc umore miscetur
ut facilius per fauces lubricas transeat; cum pervenit in ven-   180
trem, aequali eius fervore concoquitur; tunc demum corpori
accedit. Hoc aliquis secutus exemplar lapidem asperum aspero
inposuit ad similitudinem dentium, quorum pars immobilis
motum alterius expectat; deinde utriusque adtritu grana
franguntur et saepius regeruntur donec ad minutiam frequen-   185
ter trita redigantur; tum farinam aqua sparsit et adsidua
tractatione perdomuit finxitque panem, quem primo cinis
calidus et fervens testa percoxit, deinde furni paulatim reperti
et alia genera quorum fervor serviret arbitrio.' Non multum
afuit quin sutrinum quoque inventum a sapientibus diceret.   190

191 **ratio. . .recta ratio:** in the philosopher's judgment, *ratio* is to be distinguished from *recta ratio* as *vita* is from *bona vita* (a distinction which goes as far back as Plato, *Crito* 48). This distinction is called to our attention in the next line of this paragraph as well as in the very opening sentence of the epistle.

195 **a tergo:** "from behind," "in the rear."

197 **in utrumque:** "to one side or the other."

201 **hodieque:** see note to line 120.

208 **capacia populorum:** "able to hold crowds of people"; *capax* takes the genitive.

208 **verborum notas:** lit., "signs for words," i.e., shorthand.

209 **excipitur:** "is taken down"; *excipio* is the word regularly employed for taking notes.

219–220 **cui. . .serviunt:** "the ornaments of life are also slaves to that one to whom life is a slave."

226–227 **quid. . .perpetitae:** "what are the souls sought for the second class of godhood"; *perpetitae*, participial adjective from *per-* + *peto*. The passage is doubtless a reference to the demigods (for example, Hercules, Dionysus).

191 **comminiscor, -i, commentus,** 3 *dep.*, contrive, invent
192 **inventum, -i,** *n.*, invention
193 **amnis, -is,** *m.*, river
194 **velum, -i,** *n.*, sail
195 **gubernaculum, -i,** *n.*, rudder
197 **cauda, -ae,** *f.*, tail
    momentum, -i, *n.*, motion
198 **flecto, -ere, flexi, flexus,** 3, bend
200 **immo,** *adv.*, on the contrary
202 **specularia, -orum,** *n. pl.*, windows
    testa, -ae, *f.*, tile
203 **suspensura, -ae,** *f.*, vault
204 **paries, -etis,** *m.*, wall
    tubus, -i, *m.*, pipe
    circumfundo, -ere, -fudi, -fusus, 3, pour around
205 **simul,** *adv.*, at the same time
    simul ac, at the same time as, as well as
    foveo, -ere, fovi, fotus, 2, warm, heat
206 **fulgeo, -ere, fulsi,** 2, shine, gleam
207 **moles, -is,** *f.*, mass
    levis, -e, *adj.*, smooth, polished
208 **suscipio, -ere, -cepi, -ceptus,** 3, support, prop up
209 **quamvis,** *adv.*, however
    citatus, -a, -um, *p. adj. (of* **cito**), fast, rapid
210 **mancipium, -i,** *n.*, slave
    commentum, -i, *n.*, invention
212 **eruo, -ere, -ui, -utus,** 3, bring forth
213 **tuba, -ae,** *f.*, trumpet
    tibia, -ae, *f.*, flute
214 **excipio, -ere, -cepi, -ceptus,** 3, receive
    spiritus, -us, *m.*, breath
215 **vox, vocis,** *f.*, sound
216 **molior,** 4 *dep.*, devise
217 **opifex, -icis,** *m.*, artisan, workman
220 **ceterum,** *adv.*, but
    tendo, -ere, tetendi, tentus, 3, stretch, aim at, strive after
221 **illo,** *adv.*, to that place, thither
222 **exuo, -ere, -ui, -utus,** 3, strip
223 **vero,** *adv.*, but, indeed
224 **sino, -ere, sivi, situs,** 3, allow
    intersum, -esse, -fui, *irr.*, be different
    tumidus, -a, -um, *adj.*, swollen
226 **inferi, -orum,** *m. pl.*, gods of the lower world
    lares, -um (-ium), *m.*, household gods
    genius, -i, *m.*, guardian spirit

Omnia ista ratio quidem, sed non recta ratio commenta est. Hominis enim, non sapientis inventa sunt, tam mehercules quam navigia quibus amnes quibusque maria transimus, aptatis ad excipiendum ventorum impetum velis et additis a tergo gubernaculis quae huc atque illuc cursum   195
navigii torqueant. Exemplum a piscibus tractum est, qui cauda reguntur et levi eius in utrumque momento velocitatem suam flectunt. 'Omnia' inquit 'haec sapiens quidem invenit, sed minora quam ut ipse tractaret sordidioribus ministris dedit.' Immo non aliis excogitata ista sunt quam   200
quibus hodieque curantur. Quaedam nostra demum prodisse memoria scimus, ut speculariorum usum perlucente testa clarum transmittentium lumen, ut suspensuras balneorum et inpressos parietibus tubos per quos circumfunderetur calor qui ima simul ac summa foveret aequaliter. Quid loquar   205
marmora quibus templa, quibus domus fulgent? quid lapideas moles in rotundum ac leve formatas quibus porticus et capacia populorum tecta suscipimus? quid verborum notas quibus quamvis citata excipitur oratio et celeritatem linguae manus sequitur? Vilissimorum mancipiorum ista commenta   210
sunt: sapientia altius sedet nec manus edocet: animorum magistra est. Vis scire quid illa eruerit, quid effecerit? Non decoros corporis motus nec varios per tubam ac tibiam cantus, quibus exceptus spiritus aut in exitu aut in transitu formatur in vocem. Non arma nec muros nec bello utilia   215
molitur: paci favet et genus humanum ad concordiam vocat. Non est, inquam, instrumentorum ad usus necessarios opifex. Quid illi tam parvola adsignas? artificem vides vitae. Alias quidem artes sub dominio habet; nam cui vita, illi vitae quoque ornantia serviunt: ceterum ad beatum statum tendit,   220
illo ducit, illo vias aperit. Quae sint mala, quae videantur ostendit; vanitatem exuit mentibus, dat magnitudinem solidam, inflatam vero et ex inani speciosam reprimit, nec ignorari sinit inter magna quid intersit et tumida; totius naturae notitiam ac sui tradit. Quid sint di qualesque   225
declarat, quid inferi, quid lares et genii, quid in secundam numinum formam animae perpetitae, ubi consistant, quid

232 **hebes visus est:** "[our] vision is [too] dull."

236 **a corporibus. . .ad incorporalia:** i.e., "from the concrete to the abstract."

243 **Anacharsis:** Anacharsis, a Scythian philosopher who traveled extensively in Greece in the sixth century B.C. At Athens he made the friendship of Solon. He is said to have invented not only the potter's wheel but the true anchor with second fluke.

245 **apud Homerum invenitur:** *Iliad* 18.600–601.

247–248 **sapiens. . .sapiens:** "although he was a philosopher when he invented it, it was not the philosopher in him that invented it"; *tamquam = qua,* "in so far as," "in so much as."

249 **qua homines:** "in so far as they are men."

254 **Democritus:** Democritus of Abdera, atomistic philosopher (c. 460 – c. 360 B.C.). Since he laughed at the follies of mankind, he came to be known as the laughing philosopher in contrast to the melancholy Heraclitus (fl. c. 500 B.C.), who wept at human vanities.

256 **medio saxo:** "center-stone," "keystone."

258 **vobis:** dative after *excidit;* translate "it has escaped you." For *excidit* meaning "fall out of one's head or memory," see also *Ep.* 27, line 28.

261 **hodieque:** see note to line 120.

in: not found in the manuscripts but supplied by Schweighaeuser.

267 **tardis ad divina:** i.e., slow to see the divine.

228 **initiamenta, -orum,** *n. pl.,* rites of initiation
229 **sacrum, -i,** *n.,* shrine, temple
230 **resero,** 1, unlock
233 **indo, -ere, -didi, -ditus,** 3, impart, give to
234 **proprie,** *adv.,* properly, peculiarly, strictly for one's self
figuro, 1, shape, fashion
237 **excutio, -ere, -cussi, -cussus,** 3, shake out, strike out
238 **uterque, utraque, utrumque,** *adj.,* both
240 **abduco, -ere, -duxi, -ductus,** 3, withdraw, divorce one's self from
241 **omnino,** *adv.,* at all
243 **ponenda = deponenda**
244 **figulus, -i,** *m.,* potter
circuitus, -us, *m.,* circling, revolving
vas, vasis, *n.,* vessel
245 **apud,** *prep. w. acc.,* in the works of
251 **vitrearius, -i,** *m.,* glass-worker, glass-blower
252 **vitrum, -i,** *n.,* glass
habitus, -us, *m.,* shape
253 **effingo, -ere, -finxi, -fictus,** 3, fashion, mould
254 **desino, -ere, -sivi (-sii), -situs,** 3, cease
255 **fornix, -icis,** *m.,* arch
256 **alligo,** 1, bind, tie
258 **fere,** *adv.,* for the most part, usually
porro, *adv.,* then
259 **ebur, -oris,** *n.,* ivory
mollio, 4, soften
260 **decoquo, -ere, -coxi, -coctus,** 3, cook, boil
calculus, -i, *m.,* pebble
zmaragdus, -i, *m.,* emerald
261 **coctura, -ae,** *f.,* cooking, boiling
262 **licet,** although
264 **peritus, -a, -um,** *adj.,* skillful
exercitatus, -a, -um, *p. adj. (of exercito),* expert
268 **derigo (dirigo), -ere, -rexi, -rectus,** 3, arrange, direct
tantum, *adv.,* only
269 **aliter,** *adv.,* otherwise
excipio, -ere, -cepi, -ceptus, 3, receive, welcome

agant, quid possint, quid velint. Haec eius initiamenta sunt,
per quae non municipale sacrum sed ingens deorum omnium
templum, mundus ipse, reseratur, cuius vera simulacra   230
verasque facies cernendas mentibus protulit; nam ad spe-
ctacula tam magna hebes visus est. Ad initia deinde rerum
redit aeternamque rationem toti inditam et vim omnium
seminum singula proprie figurantem. Tum de animo coepit
inquirere, unde esset, ubi, quamdiu, in quot membra divisus.   235
Deinde a corporibus se ad incorporalia transtulit veritatem-
que et argumenta eius excussit; post haec quemadmodum
discernerentur vitae aut vocis ambigua; in utraque enim
falsa veris inmixta sunt.

    Non abduxit, inquam, se (ut Posidonio videtur) ab istis   240
artibus sapiens, sed ad illas omnino non venit. Nihil enim
dignum inventu iudicasset quod non erat dignum perpetuo
usu iudicaturus; ponenda non sumeret. 'Anacharsis' inquit
'invenit rotam figuli, cuius circuitu vasa formantur.' Deinde
quia apud Homerum invenitur figuli rota, maluit videri   245
versus falsos esse quam fabulam. Ego nec Anacharsim aucto-
rem huius rei fuisse contendo et, si fuit, sapiens quidem hoc
invenit, sed non tamquam sapiens, sicut multa sapientes
faciunt qua homines sunt, non qua sapientes. Puta velocissi-
mum esse sapientem: cursu omnis anteibit qua velox est, non   250
qua sapiens. Cuperem Posidonio aliquem vitrearium ostendere, qui spiritu vitrum in habitus plurimos format qui vix
diligenti manu effingerentur. Haec inventa sunt postquam
sapientem invenire desimus. 'Democritus' inquit 'invenisse
dicitur fornicem, ut lapidum curvatura paulatim inclina-   255
torum medio saxo alligaretur.' Hoc dicam falsum esse;
necesse est enim ante Democritum et pontes et portas fuisse,
quarum fere summa curvantur. Excidit porro vobis eundem
Democritum invenisse quemadmodum ebur molliretur,
quemadmodum decoctus calculus in zmaragdum conver-   260
teretur, qua hodieque coctura inventi lapides <in> hoc utiles
colorantur. Ista sapiens licet invenerit, non qua sapiens erat
invenit; multa enim facit quae ab inprudentissimis aut aeque
fieri videmus aut peritius atque exercitatius.

    Quid sapiens investigaverit, quid in lucem protraxerit   265
quaeris? Primum verum naturamque, quam non ut cetera
animalia oculis secutus est, tardis ad divina; deinde vitae
legem, quam ad universa derexit, nec nosse tantum sed sequi
deos docuit et accidentia non aliter excipere quam imperata.

275–276 **quae civem. . .voluptati:** a thrust at the Epicurean philosophy which asserted that it was unnecessary for the wise
man to take part in politics, that the gods were remote from
and indifferent to human affairs, and that pleasure was the
highest good.

276 **de:** not found in the manuscripts but supplied by Princianus.

282 **Sicut aut:** the daggers indicate a difficulty in the reading supplied by the manuscripts.

282–285 **cum. . .discurrere:** for the thought in this sentence, cf.
section 3 of this epistle; *docuere* is not found in the manuscripts but supplied by Reynolds, following Buecheler.

292 **fas erat:** i.e., right in the sight of the gods, whereas *ius est*
means right according to the legal standard of men.

in medium: "for the public good."

290–293 **nulli. . .ferebat:** Vergil, *Georgics* 1.125–128. Seneca
again, as earlier in this letter (lines 69 and 81–82) cites Vergil's
description of men in a natural state of grace in the Golden
Age. In those days, it was unnecessary for mankind to labor or
to till the soil; nature herself freely bestowed all earthly gifts.
Men had no need for boundaries or private property; all of
nature's munificence was mutually and benevolently shared.

295 **sufficiebat. . .in tutelam:** "she was sufficient for the
guardianship."

305 **per sua longam peregrinationem:** best understood by
remembering Trimalchio's desire (Petronius, *Satyricon* 48)
"to add Sicily to his possessions in order that, when he want-
ed to go to Africa, he might travel through his own boundaries (estate)."

306 **propagatio:** here means "extension," lit., "begetting."

313 **sibi iaceret:** "was lying idle for him." The verb *iaceo, -ere* is
sometimes used in the sense of "lie idle or unemployed"; *sibi*
is emphatic and means "for his own use."

270 **veto, -are, -ui, -itus,** 1, forbid
pareo, -ere, -ui, -itus, 2, obey
quisque, quaeque, quidque,
indef. pron., each one, each
thing
271 **perpendo, -ere, -pendi,**
-pensus, 3, weigh carefully,
consider
272 **palam,** *adv.*, openly, publicly
278 **delenio,** 4, charm, cajole
281 **artificium, -i,** *n.*, handicraft, art
disco, -ere, didici, 3, learn
283 **promiscue,** *adv.*, promiscuously, indiscriminately
284 **dissocio,** 1, separate from
fellowship, disunite
rapina, -ae, *f.*, plunder
284 **consortio, -onis,** *f.*, fellowship
285 **discurro, -ere, -cucurri**
(-curri), -cursus, 3, run in
different directions
287 **suspicio, -ere, -spexi,**
-spectus, 3, look up to
290 **subigo, -ere, -egi, -actus,** 3,
plough, cultivate
arvum, -i, *n.*, field
291 **signo,** 1, put a mark upon, mark
partior, 4 *dep.*, divide
limes, -itis, *m.*, boundary
293 **posco, -ere, poposci,** 3, demand
296 **ops, opis,** *f.*, resources
297 **locuples, -etis,** *adj.*, rich
299 **seduco, -ere, -duxi, -ductus,**
3, take away, carry off
300 **redigo, -ere, -egi, -actus,** 3,
drive back, reduce
302 **amitto, -ere, -misi, -missus,**
3, lose
licet, although
reparo, 1, get back, recover
303 **vicinus, -i,** *m.*, neighbor
pello, -ere, pepuli, pulsus, 3,
drive out, expel
306 **eo,** *adv.*, there
308 **diripio, -ere, -ripui, -reptus,**
3, plunder
309 **largus, -a, -um,** *adj.*,
abundant, copious
311 **concors, concordis,** *adj.*, of
the same mind, harmonious

Vetuit parere opinionibus falsis et quanti quidque esset   270
vera aestimatione perpendit; damnavit mixtas paenitentia
voluptates et bona semper placitura laudavit et palam fecit
felicissimum esse cui felicitate non opus est, potentissimum
esse qui se habet in potestate. Non de ea philosophia loquor
quae avem extra patriam posuit, extra mundum deos, quae   275
virtutem donavit voluptati, sed <de> illa quae nullum bonum
putat nisi quod honestum est, quae nec hominis nec fortunae
muneribus deleniri potest, cuius hoc pretium est, non posse
pretio capi.

Hanc philosophiam fuisse illo rudi saeculo quo adhuc   280
artificia deerant et ipso usu discebantur utilia non credo.
†Sicut aut† fortunata tempora, cum in medio iacerent beneficia naturae promiscue utenda, antequam avaritia atque
luxuria dissociavere mortales et ad rapinam ex consortio
<docuere> discurrere: non erant illi sapientes viri, etiam si   285
faciebant facienda sapientibus. Statum quidem generis humani non alium quisquam suspexerit magis, nec si cui per-
mittat deus terrena formare et dare gentibus mores, aliud
probaverit quam quod apud illos fuisse memoratur apud quos

> nulli subigebant arva coloni;   290
> ne signare quidem aut partiri limite campum
> fas erat: in medium quaerebant, ipsaque tellus
> omnia liberius nullo poscente ferebat.

Quid hominum illo genere felicius? In commune rerum
natura fruebantur; sufficiebat illa ut parens in tutelam   295
omnium; haec erat publicarum opum secura possessio. Quidni ego illud locupletissimum mortalium genus dixerim in quo
pauperem invenire non posses? Inrupit in res optime positas
avaritia et, dum seducere aliquid cupit atque in suum ver-
tere, omnia fecit aliena et in angustum se ex inmenso redegit. 300
Avaritia paupertatem intulit et multa concupiscendo omnia
amisit. Licet itaque nunc conetur reparare quod perdidit,
licet agros agris adiciat vicinum vel pretio pellens vel iniuria,
licet in provinciarum spatium rura dilatet et possessionem
vocet per sua longam peregrinationem: nulla nos finium   305
propagatio eo reducet unde discessimus. Cum omnia feceri-
mus, multum habebimus: universum habebamus. Terra ipsa
fertilior erat inlaborata et in usus populorum non diripien-
tium larga. Quidquid natura protulerat, id non minus invenisse quam inventum monstrare alteri voluptas erat; nec   310
ulli aut superesse poterat aut deesse: inter concordes divide-
batur. Nondum valentior inposuerat infirmiori manum, nondum avarus abscondendo quod sibi iaceret alium necessariis

322–323 **insigne. . .noctium:** in apposition with *mundus.*

323 **in praeceps agebatur:** lit., "was drawn headlong."

329 **instar:** an indeclinable noun meaning "image," "likeness." It is used with the possessive genitive in the sense "as big as" (lit., "the likeness of").

338 **hoc. . .est:** "this title now applies to those who attain the highest accomplishments." Seneca believes that, in the Golden Age (*aureum saeculum,* paragraph 5), the wise or better men naturally ruled. Yet because in that simple period all men followed nature and nature supplied every want and was herself virtuous, there was little need for the pursuit of wisdom. Only in later ages, when men had learned vices and had become divorced from their natural habitat, did it become necessary for the better men, by obvious struggle and effort of mind, to recover and consciously comprehend what had previously been innocently and unconsciously known—the rules for right reason and sound conduct and the principles for living a "life in accordance with nature." *Idem tibi de philosophia dico. Fuit aliquando simplicior inter minora peccantis et levi quoque cura remediabiles: adversus tantam morum eversionem omnia conanda sunt* (*Ep.* 95.29). Nowadays, because such knowledge must be discovered by strength of will and deliberate intellectual percipience, Seneca maintains that wisdom and philosophy are one and the same; hence, those who in this fallen world attain such insights are considered to have achieved the highest of accomplishments.

345 **lapides in:** not found in the manuscripts but supplied by Schweighaeuser.

314 **cesso,** 1, be idle, be at leisure
315 **incruentus, -a, -um,** *adj.,* without bloodshed, unstained
    in, *prep. w. acc.,* against
316 **fera, -ae,** *f.,* wild beast
317 **imber, -bris,** *m.,* rain
    vilis, -e, *adj.,* cheap
318 **tutus, -a, -um,** *adj.,* safe, secure
319 **suspirium, -i,** *n.,* sigh
321 **caelatus, -a, -um,** *p. adj.* (*of* **caelo**), carved
    laquear, -aris, *m.,* panelled ceiling
322 **superlabor, -i, lapsus,** 3 *dep.,* glide over
    insignis, -e, *adj.,* remarkable
324 **interdiu,** *adv.,* by day
325 **libet, -ere, libuit,** *impers.,* it is pleasing
    intueor, -eri, -tuitus, 2 *dep.,* observe, gaze upon
326 **vergo, -ere,** 3, bend, turn
327 **vagor,** 1 *dep.,* wander
    spargo, -ere, sparsi, sparsus, 3, strew, scatter
328 **paveo, -ere, pavi,** 2, tremble, quake
329 **increpo, -are, -crepui, -crepitus,** 1, make a noise
    attonitus, -a, -um, *adj.,* astonished, stunned
330 **spiritus, -us** *m.,* air
    perflatus, -us, *m.,* breeze
331 **rupes, -is,** *f.,* rock
    rivus, -i, *m.,* stream
332 **fistula, -ae,** *f.,* water-pipe
    iter, itineris, *n.,* path
    obsolefactus, -a, -um, *p. adj.* (*of* **obsolefacio**), worn out, spoiled
    sponte, *abl.,* at will, freely, of one's own accord
333 **agrestis, -e,** *adj.,* rural, rustic
    quamvis, *adv.,* however
    egregius, -a, -um, *adj.,* admirable, excellent
341 **quemadmodum,** *adv.,* just as
342 **indoles, -is,** *f.,* natural disposition, nature
343 **ingenium, -i,** *n.,* mental power, mind
    consummatus, -a, -um, *p. adj.* (*of* **consummo**), perfect, complete
345 **faex, faecis,** *f.,* dregs

quoque excluserat: par erat alterius ac sui cura. Arma cessa-
bant incruentaeque humano sanguine manus odium omne in   315
feras verterant. Illi quos aliquod nemus densum a sole pro-
texerat, qui adversus saevitiam hiemis aut imbris vili re-
ceptaculo tuti sub fronde vivebant, placidas transigebant sine
suspirio noctes. Sollicitudo nos in nostra purpura versat et
acerrimis excitat stimulis: at quam mollem somnum illis   320
dura tellus dabat! Non inpendebant caelata laquearia, sed in
aperto iacentis sidera superlabebantur et, insigne spectaculum
noctium, mundus in praeceps agebatur, silentio tantum
opus ducens. Tam interdiu illis quam nocte patebant prospectus huius pulcherrimae domus; libebat intueri signa ex   325
media caeli parte vergentia, rursus ex occulto alia surgentia.
Quidni iuvaret vagari inter tam late sparsa miracula? At vos
ad omnem tectorum pavetis sonum et inter picturas vestras,
si quid increpuit, fugitis attoniti. Non habebant domos instar
urbium: spiritus ac liber inter aperta perflatus et levis umbra   330
rupis aut arboris et perlucidi fontes rivique non opere nec
fistula nec ullo coacto itinere obsolefacti sed sponte currentes
et prata sine arte formosa, inter haec agreste domicilium
rustica politum manu—haec erat secundum naturam domus,
in qua libebat habitare nec ipsam nec pro ipsa timentem: 335
nunc magna pars nostri metus tecta sunt.

Sed quamvis egregia illis vita fuerit et carens fraude, non
fuere sapientes, quando hoc iam in opere maximo nomen est.
Non tamen negaverim fuisse alti spiritus viros et, ut ita
dicam, a dis recentes; neque enim dubium est quin meliora   340
mundus nondum effetus ediderit. Quemadmodum autem
omnibus indoles fortior fuit et ad labores paratior, ita non
erant ingenia omnibus consummata. Non enim dat natura
virtutem: ars est bonum fieri. Illi quidem non aurum nec
argentum nec perlucidos <lapides in> ima terrarum faece   345
quaerebant parcebantque adhuc etiam mutis animalibus:
tantum aberat ut homo hominem non iratus, non timens,

348 **tantum. . .occideret:** "that man neither angry nor fearful but merely for sport would kill his fellow-man was so far absent [from that age]"; *ut. . .occideret* is a substantive clause used as the subject of *aberat*. For Seneca's condemnation of human slaughter in the gladiatorial shows, see *Ep. 7.*

350 **est:** not found in the manuscripts but supplied by Feige.

348 **pingo, -ere, pinxi, pictus,** 3, paint, embroider
349 **texo, -ere, texui, textus,** 3, weave
eruo, -ere, -ui, -utus, 3, dig out
351 **interest,** *impers.*, it makes a difference
desum, -esse, -fui, *irr.*, be wanting, be lacking
354 **institutus, -a, -um,** *p. adj.* (*of* **instituo**), trained, educated
356 **erudio,** 4, educate, instruct

tantum spectaturus occideret. Nondum vestis illis erat picta, nondum texebatur aurum, adhuc nec eruebatur. Quid ergo <est>? Ignorantia rerum innocentes erant; multum autem 350 interest utrum peccare aliquis nolit an nesciat. Deerat illis iustitia, deerat prudentia, deerat temperantia ac fortitudo. Omnibus his virtutibus habebat similia quaedam rudis vita: virtus non contingit animo nisi instituto et edocto et ad summum adsidua exercitatione perducto. Ad hoc quidem, 355 sed sine hoc nascimur, et in optimis quoque, antequam erudias, virtutis materia, non virtus est. *Vale.*

8 **incucurrerunt:** supply *mihi.*

10 **cum maxime:** "just now"; see *Ep.* 7, lines 41–42.

18–19 **de capite:** "for your life."

23 **Videris:** the second person present and perfect subjunctives are sometimes used in commands and prohibitions instead of the more usual imperative mood.

32 **contumeliae causa:** "on account of [man's] contempt for them."

2 **indignor,** 1 *dep.,* be angry at
queror, -i, questus, 3 *dep.,* complain

7 **decumbo, -ere, -cubui,** 3, fall sick
fenus, -oris, *n.,* interest
crepo, -are, crepui, crepitus, 1, creak
damnum, -i, *n.,* loss

8 **parum,** *adv.,* too little, not enough

9 **decerno, -ere, -crevi, -cretus,** 3, decree

10 **adfectus, -us,** *m.,* emotion
detego, -ere, -texi, -tectus, 3, uncover, disclose

12 **adsentior, -iri, -sensus,** 4 *dep.,* agree with

13 **umquam,** *adv.,* ever
excipio, -ere, -cepi, -ceptus, 3, receive

14 **vultus, -us,** *m.,* face, expression
tributum, -i, *n.,* tax
invitus, -a, -um, *adj.,* unwilling

15 **gemo, -ere, gemui, gemitus,** 3, groan

17 **vesica, -ae,** *f.,* bladder

18 **propius,** *comp. adv.,* closer

20 **quomodo,** *adv.,* in what manner, even as

21 **pulvis, -eris,** *m.,* dust
lutum, -i, *n.,* mud
pluvia, -ae, *f.,* rain
careo, -ere, -ui, -itus, 2, lack
incommodum, -i, *n.,* inconvenience, trouble

23 **dedecet, -ere, -decuit,** *impers.,* 2, it is unbecoming
quemadmodum, *adv.,* how
votum, -i, *n.,* prayer, wish

24 **tantum,** *adv.,* only

25 **deliciae, -arum,** *f. pl.,* luxury

27 **macellum, -i,** *n.,* meat-market, provision-market
atqui, *conj.,* and yet

28 **operosus, -a, -um,** *adj.,* laborious

29 **sursum,** *adv.,* up
deorsum, *adv.,* down

30 **obeo, -ire, -ivi (-ii), -itus,** 4, travel through

31 **putidus, -a, -um,** *adj.,* rotten
molliter, *adv.,* softly, weakly
turturilla, -ae, *f.,* little turtle dove

32 **tutus, -a, -um,** *adj.,* safe

Epistle Ninety-six
ON PAYING THE MANLY TRIBUTE TO LIFE

Seneca Lucilio Suo Salutem

Tamen tu indignaris aliquid aut quereris et non intellegis
nihil esse in istis mali nisi hoc unum quod indignaris et
quereris? Si me interrogas, nihil puto viro miserum nisi
aliquid esse in rerum natura quod putet miserum. Non feram   5
me quo die aliquid ferre non potero. Male valeo: pars fati est.
Familia decubuit, fenus offendit, domus crepuit, damna,
vulnera, labores, metus incucurrerunt: solet fieri. Hoc parum
est: debuit fieri. Decernuntur ista, non accidunt. Si quid
credis mihi, intimos adfectus meos tibi cum maxime detego: 10
in omnibus quae adversa videntur et dura sic formatus sum:
non pareo deo sed adsentior; ex animo illum, non quia necesse
est, sequor. Nihil umquam mihi incidet quod tristis excipiam,
quod malo vultu; nullum tributum invitus conferam. Omnia
autem ad quae gemimus, quae expavescimus, tributa vitae   15
sunt: horum, mi Lucili, nec speraveris immunitatem nec
petieris. Vesicae te dolor inquietavit, epistulae venerunt
parum dulces, detrimenta continua—propius accedam, de
capite timuisti. Quid, tu nesciebas haec te optare cum optares
senectutem? Omnia ista in longa vita sunt, quomodo in   20
longa via et pulvis et lutum et pluvia. 'Sed volebam vivere,
carere tamen incommodis omnibus.' Tam effeminata vox
virum dedecet. Videris quemadmodum hoc votum meum
excipias; ego illud magno animo, non tantum bono facio:
neque di neque deae faciant ut te fortuna in deliciis habeat.   25
Ipse te interroga, si quis potestatem tibi deus faciat, utrum
velis vivere in macello an in castris. Atqui vivere, Lucili,
militare est. Itaque hi qui iactantur et per operosa atque
ardua sursum ac deorsum eunt et expeditiones periculosis-
simas obeunt fortes viri sunt primoresque castrorum; isti   30
quos putida quies aliis laborantibus molliter habet turturil-
lae sunt, tuti contumeliae causa. *Vale.*

5 **artificio:** *artificium, -ii,* n., profession, trade, handicraft. Translate here "hobby." Vine-growing was one of Seneca's favorite hobbies.

8 **eius:** "of it"; i.e., of the grafted part.

11 **mandas:** supply *quem:* "whom you entrust [to me]."

12 **Simul. . .induruit:** "at one and the same time he has become soft and hard"; *emarcuit* (from *emarcesco, -ere, emarcui,* wither away) and *induruit* (from *induresco, -ere, indurui,* become hard) recall *durus* and *mollis* of lines 3 and 4.

13 **At cupit ipse:** supply *rationem.*

15 **Stomachum. . .luxuria:** "luxury has caused him displeasure."

19–20 **nunc. . .convenit:** "at present there is disagreement between them" (i.e., between himself and luxury).

2 **ut,** *conj.,* as
3 **instituo, -ere, -ui, -utus,** 3, train
   valde, *adv.,* very
   immo, *adv.,* nay rather
5 **quilibet, quae-, quod-,** *indef. adj.,* any
6 **insitio, -onis,** *f.,* grafting
   vitis, -is, *f.,* vine
   exedo, -ere, -edi, -esus, 3, eat up
   gracilis, -e, *adj.,* slender
7 **surculus, -i,** *m.,* grafting
   alo, -ere, alui, alitus (altus), 3, nourish
9 **praecido, -ere, -cidi, -cisus,** 3, cut off
10 **iterum,** *adv.,* again
12 **indulgeo, -ere, -dulsi, -dultus,** 2, indulge in
14 **mentior, -iri, -itus,** 4 *dep.,* lie
15 **cito,** *adv.,* soon, quickly
17 **simul,** *adv.,* at the same time
18 **fides, -ei,** *f.,* promise
19 **invisus, -a, -um,** *adj.,* hateful

Epistle One Hundred Twelve
THE INTRANSIGENCE OF VICE

Seneca Lucilio Suo Salutem

Cupio mehercules amicum tuum formari ut desideras et
institui, sed valde durus capitur; immo, quod est molestius,
valde mollis capitur et consuetudine mala ac diutina fractus.
Volo tibi ex nostro artificio exemplum referre. Non quaelibet   5
insitionem vitis patitur: si vetus et exesa est, si infirma gracilis-
que, aut non recipiet surculum aut non alet nec adplicabit
sibi nec in qualitatem eius naturamque transibit. Itaque
solemus supra terram praecidere ut, si non respondit,
temptari possit secunda fortuna et iterum repetita infra   10
terram inseratur. Hic de quo scribis et mandas non habet vires:
indulsit vitiis. Simul et emarcuit et induruit; non potest
recipere rationem, non potest nutrire. 'At cupit ipse.' Noli
credere. Non dico illum mentiri tibi: putat se cupere.
Stomachum illi fecit luxuria: cito cum illa redibit in gratiam.   15
'Sed dicit se offendi vita sua.' Non negaverim; quis enim non
offenditur? Homines vitia sua et amant simul et oderunt.
Tunc itaque de illo feremus sententiam cum fidem nobis
fecerit invisam iam sibi esse luxuriam: nunc illis male
convenit. *Vale.*   20

9 **Hoc:** ablative of cause, "because of this," used in response to the repeated *quare.*

10–11 **talis. . .vita:** Cicero (*Tusculan Disputations* 5.47) attributes this saying to Socrates.

12 **dicendi:** the daggers indicate a difficulty in the manuscript reading.

18–19 **adflatur:** lit., "is inspired," i.e., "is infected," "is contaminated."

26 **Maecenas:** Gaius Maecenas, Roman knight, minister of Augustus, and renowned patron of learned men. His literary circle included Vergil and Horace. To him Vergil dedicated the *Georgics* and Horace the *Odes.* Both poets bestow highest praise upon him and express their gratitude for his generous support of their creative talents. Maecenas himself was a prolific writer, but only a few fragments of his work survive.

29 **discinctus:** here metaphorically in the sense of "loose," "dissolute."

31 **uxor:** Maecenas' wife, Terentia, is described by Seneca (*De Prov.* 3.10) as "wayward" (*morosa*).

31 **fuerat:** the indicative may be used in the apodosis of a contrary to fact condition.

34–35 **Maecenas. . .suo:** Reynolds, following Gruter, considers these words an interpolation.

4 **aliquando,** *adv.*, sometimes
explicatio, -onis, *f.*, unfolding, expounding, exposition
5 **infractus, -a, -um,** *p. adj.* (*of* **infringo**), broken, subdued
canticum, -i, *n.*, song
alias...alias, at one time...at another time
6 **egredior, -i, -gressus, 3** *dep.*, go out of, pass beyond
8 **translatio, -onis,** *f.*, metaphor
9 **inverecunde,** *adv.*, shamelessly
vulgo, *adv.*, everywhere
13 **deliciae, -arum,** *f.*, pleasure, luxury
14 **argumentum, -i,** *n.*, proof
15 **modo,** *adv.*, only
16 **ingenium, -i,** *n.*, character, nature
18 **siccus, -a, -um,** *adj.*, dry
vitio, 1, spoil
19 **pigre,** *adv.*, lazily
20 **incessus, -us,** *m.*, gait
21 **mollitia, -ae,** *f.*, softness, effeminacy
ferox, -ocis, *adj.*, high-spirited, courageous
gradus, -us, *m.*, step
24 **fingo, -ere, finxi, fictus, 3,** mould, shape
25 **pareo, -ere, parui, paritus, 2,** obey
26 **quam,** *adv.*, as
29 **discingo, -ere, -cinxi, -cinctus, 3,** ungird
30 **tam. . .quam,** so. . .as
insignitus, -a, -um, *p. adj.* (*of* **insignio**), striking, conspicuous
cultus, -us, *m.*, attire, appearance
comitatus, -us, *m.*, escort, attendant, retinue
33 **diffluo, -ere, -fluxi, -fluxus, 3,** flow in different directions
35 **amnis, -is,** *m.*, stream
comans, -antis, *p. adj.* (*of* **como**), having long hair
36 **ut,** *adv.*, how
alveus, -i, *m.*, channel
lynter (linter), -ris, *f.*, boat
aro, 1, plough
vadum, -i, *n.*, shallow water
38 **labrum, -i,** *n.*, lip
columbor, 1 *dep.*, bill or kiss like doves
ut, *adv.*, as
cervix, -icis, *f.*, neck
lassus, -a, -um, *adj.*, weary

Epistle One Hundred Fourteen
STYLE IS THE MAN

Seneca Lucilio Suo Salutem

Quare quibusdam temporibus provenerit corrupti generis
oratio quaeris et quomodo in quaedam vitia inclinatio ingeniorum facta sit, ut aliquando inflata explicatio vigeret,
aliquando infracta et in morem cantici ducta; quare alias   5
sensus audaces et fidem egressi placuerint, alias abruptae
sententiae et suspiciosae, in quibus plus intellegendum esset
quam audiendum; quare aliqua aetas fuerit quae transla-
tionis iure uteretur inverecunde. Hoc quod audire vulgo soles,
quod apud Graecos in proverbium cessit: talis hominibus   10
fuit oratio qualis vita. Quemadmodum autem uniuscuiusque
actio †dicendi† similis est, sic genus dicendi aliquando imitatur
publicos mores, si disciplina civitatis laboravit et se in delicias
dedit. Argumentum est luxuriae publicae orationis lascivia,
si modo non in uno aut in altero fuit, sed adprobata est et   15
recepta. Non potest alius esse ingenio, alius animo color. Si
ille sanus est, si compositus, gravis, temperans, ingenium
quoque siccum ac sobrium est: illo vitiato hoc quoque adflatur. Non vides, si animus elanguit, trahi membra et pigre
moveri pedes? si ille effeminatus est, in ipso incessu apparere   20
mollitiam ? si ille acer est et ferox, concitari gradum? si furit
aut, quod furori simile est, irascitur, turbatum esse corporis
motum nec ire sed ferri? Quanto hoc magis accidere ingenio
putas, quod totum animo permixtum est, ab illo fingitur,
illi paret, inde legem petit?   25

Quomodo Maecenas vixerit notius est quam ut narrari
nunc debeat quomodo ambulaverit, quam delicatus fuerit,
quam cupierit videri, quam vitia sua latere noluerit. Quid
ergo? non oratio eius aeque soluta est quam ipse discinctus?
non tam insignita illius verba sunt quam cultus, quam comita-   30
tus, quam domus, quam uxor? Magni vir ingenii fuerat si
illud egisset via rectiore, si non vitasset intellegi, si non etiam
in oratione difflueret. Videbis itaque eloquentiam ebrii
hominis involutam et errantem et licentiae plenam. [Mae-
cenas de cultu suo.] Quid turpius 'amne silvisque ripa coman-   35
tibus'? Vide ut 'alveum lyntribus arent versoque vado
remittant hortos'. Quid? si quis 'feminae cinno crispat et
labris columbatur incipitque suspirans, ut cervice lassa

46 **in:** included in the later manuscripts.

51 **spadones duo:** in apposition to *comitatus.*

52 **uxorem milliens duxit:** "married his wife a thousand times."
In *De Prov.* 3.10 Seneca mentions that Maecenas was daily
rejected by his wife but repeatedly restored to favor.

73–74 **illi. . .sunt:** "usual things are [regarded] as mean in its
eyes"; *illi* (dative of reference) refers to *animus.*

39 **fano,** 1, dedicate, consecrate
inremediabilis, -e, *adj.,*
   implacable
rimor, 1 *dep.,* pry into, search,
   explore
40 **lagona, -ae,** *f.,* flask, bottle
41 **festum, -i,** *n.,* festival, holiday
cereus, -i, *m.,* wax taper
filum, -i, *n.,* thread
crepax, -acis, *adj.,* sounding,
   creaking
42 **focus, -i,** *m.,* hearth
investio, 4, clothe, cover,
   surround
47 **pallium, -i,** *n.,* cloak
48 **utrimque,** *adv.,* on both sides
aliter, *adv.,* otherwise
fugitivus, -i, *m.,* fugitive slave
49 **strepo, -ere, -ui, -itus,** 3,
   make a noise, roar, resound
51 **spado, -onis,** *m.,* eunuch
53 **struo, -ere, struxi, structus,**
   3, arrange
56 **parco, -ere, peperci, parsus,**
   3, spare
58 **portentosus, -a, -um,** *adj.,*
   monstrous, unnatural
59 **deliciae, -arum,** *f.,*
   fastidiousness, fussiness
mollis, -e, *adj.,* soft, effeminate
mitis, -e, *adj.,* mellow, mature
60 **ambages, -is,** *f.,*
   circumlocution, ambiguity
transversus, -a, -um, *p. adj.*
   (*of* **transverto**), inverted
61 **quivis, quae-, quid-,** *indef.*
   pron., anyone
62 **nimius, -a, -um,** *adj.,* too
   much, excessive
63 **interdum,** *adv.,* sometimes
64 **fundo, -ere, fudi, fusus,** 3,
   pour, spread
cultus, -us, *m.,* care, cultivation
65 **supellex, -lectilis,** *f.,* furniture
66 **laxitas, -atis,** *f.,* roominess,
   spaciousness
67 **adveho, -ere, -vexi, -vectus,** 3,
   carry, bring
68 **lacunar, -aris,** *n.,* panelled
   ceiling
69 **lautitia, -ae,** *f.,* brightness,
   splendor
71 **includo, -ere, -clusi, -clusus,**
   3, end, close
72 **adsuesco, -ere, -suevi, -suetus,**
   3, become accustomed to
73 **fastidio,** 4, scorn, despise
74 **modo,** *adv.,* now
75 **exoletus, -a, -um,** *p. adj.* (*of*
   exolesco), obsolete

fanantur nemoris tyranni'. 'Inremediabilis factio rimantur
epulis lagonaque temptant domos et spe mortem exigunt.'   40
'Genium festo vix suo testem.' 'Tenuisve cerei fila et cre-
pacem molam.' 'Focum mater aut uxor investiunt.' Non
statim cum haec legeris hoc tibi occurret, hunc esse qui
solutis tunicis in urbe semper incesserit (nam etiam cum
absentis Caesaris partibus fungeretur, signum a discincto   45
petebatur); hunc esse qui <in> tribunali, in rostris, in omni
publico coetu sic apparuerit ut pallio velaretur caput exclusis
utrimque auribus, non aliter quam in mimo fugitivi divitis
solent; hunc esse cui tunc maxime civilibus bellis strepentibus
et sollicita urbe et armata comitatus hic fuerit in publico,   50
spadones duo, magis tamen viri quam ipse; hunc esse qui
uxorem milliens duxit, cum unam habuerit? Haec verba tam
inprobe structa, tam neglegenter abiecta, tam contra consuetudinem omnium posita ostendunt mores quoque non
minus novos et pravos et singulares fuisse. Maxima laus illi   55
tribuitur mansuetudinis: pepercit gladio, sanguine abstinuit,
nec ulla alia re quid posset quam licentia ostendit. Hanc
ipsam laudem suam corrupit istis orationis portentosissimae
delicis; apparet enim mollem fuisse, non mitem. Hoc istae
ambages compositionis, hoc verba transversa, hoc sensus   60
miri, magni quidem saepe sed enervati dum exeunt, cuivis
manifestum facient: motum illi felicitate nimia caput. Quod
vitium hominis esse interdum, interdum temporis solet. Ubi
luxuriam late felicitas fudit, cultus primum corporum esse
diligentior incipit; deinde supellectili laboratur; deinde in   65
ipsas domos inpenditur cura ut in laxitatem ruris excurrant,
ut parietes advectis trans maria marmoribus fulgeant, ut
tecta varientur auro, ut lacunaribus pavimentorum respon-
deat nitor; deinde ad cenas lautitia transfertur et illic commendatio ex novitate et soliti ordinis commutatione captatur,   70
ut ea quae includere solent cenam prima ponantur, ut quae
advenientibus dabantur exeuntibus dentur. Cum adsuevit
animus fastidire quae ex more sunt et illi pro sordidis solita
sunt, etiam in oratione quod novum est quaerit et modo
antiqua verba atque exoleta revocat ac profert, modo fingit   75

76 **et ignota ac:** the daggers indicate a difficulty in the manuscript reading.

76–77 **pro cultu habetur:** "is regarded as [a mark of] elegance."

96 **maximae famae:** supply *viros* before these words.

101–102 **duodecim tabulas:** The twelve tables, a code of Roman laws framed by a commission of ten magistrates (*decemviri*) in 451 B.C. These laws, written on twelve bronze tablets, were displayed in the forum where they were seen and read by all. Only fragments of this code, expressed in succinct, precise, clear language which revealed the Roman genius for legal expression, have come down to us.

102 **Gracchus. . .Crassus. . .Curio:** Gaius Sempronius Gracchus, tribune in 123 B.C.; he and his brother Tiberius became champions of the poor classes against the rich and won renown as eminent popular orators. L. Licinius Crassus was consul in 95 B.C.; Cicero fictively recreated him as one of the principal speakers in the *De Oratore*. C. Scribonius Curio, consul in 76 B.C., was an outstanding orator and intimate friend of Julius Caesar.

103 **Appium. . .Coruncanium:** Appius Claudius Caecus, outstanding orator and censor (312–308 B.C.), who built the first celebrated Roman road, the Via Appia, and also many aqueducts in Rome. J. Coruncanius was a consummate orator who served as consul in 280 B.C.

105 **in sordes incidunt:** "fall into a low style."

107 **in usu:** "in [daily] use."

109–110 **ille. . .vellit:** i.e., the former polishes the whole leg, the latter doesn't even shave the armpits.

118 **Quid illa:** "what [of] that," a colloquial expression.

76 **deflecto, -ere, -flexi, -flexus, 3**, vary the form of [a word]
increbresco, -ere, -crebui, 3, become frequent
77 **translatio, -onis, *f.***, metaphor
78 **praecido, -ere, -cidi, -cisus, 3**, cut off, abbreviate
79 **detineo, -ere, -tinui, -tentus, 2**, detain, delay
80 **porrigo, -ere, -rexi, -rectus, 3**, put forth, extend
usque, *adv.*, all the way
84 **descisco, -ere, -scivi (-scii), -scitus, 3**, revolt from, deviate from
85 **convivium, -i, *n.***, banquet
87 **procido, -cidere, -cidi, 3**, fall
88 **tantum, *adv.***, only
89 **corona, -ae, *f.***, crowd
92 **venia, -ae, *f.***, indulgence to faults, pardon
94 **ignosco, -ere, -novi, -notus, 3**, pardon, forgive
dissimulo, 1, conceal, keep secret
95 **prosum, prodesse, profui, *irr.***, help
102 **nimis, *adv.***, too much, over-much, excessively
104 **usitatus, -a, -um, *adj.***, common, ordinary
108 **pecco, 1**, commit a fault, make a mistake
109 **crus, cruris, *n.***, leg
ne. . .quidem, not. . .even
ala, -ae, *f.*, armpit
110 **vello, -ere, vulsi, vulsus, 3**, pluck out, pull out
112 **asper, -era, -erum, *adj.***, rough
113 **de industria**, purposely
114 **salebra, -ae, *f.***, jolt, roughness
iunctura, -ae, *f.*, joining
115 **percutio, -ere, -cussi, -cussus, 3**, strike
116 **blandior, 4 *dep.***, soothe, caress
molliter, *adv.*, softly, gently
labor, -i, lapsus, 3 *dep.*, glide
117 **differo, differre, distuli, dilatus, *irr.***, put off, delay
118 **clausula, -ae, *f.***, end of a clause
lentus, -a, -um, *adj.*, slow
119 **devexus, -a, -um, *adj.***, sweeping down
120 **pes, pedis, *m.***, rhythm, meter

†et ignota ac† deflectit, modo, id quod nuper increbruit, pro
cultu habetur audax translatio ac frequens. Sunt qui sensus
praecidant et hoc gratiam sperent, si sententia pependerit et
audienti suspicionem sui fecerit; sunt qui illos detineant et
porrigant; sunt qui non usque ad vitium accedant (necesse   80
est enim hoc facere aliquid grande temptanti) sed qui ipsum
vitium ament.

   Itaque ubicumque videris orationem corruptam placere,
ibi mores quoque a recto descivisse non erit dubium. Quomodo conviviorum luxuria, quomodo vestium aegrae civi-   85
tatis indicia sunt, sic orationis licentia, si modo frequens est,
ostendit animos quoque a quibus verba exeunt procidisse.
Mirari quidem non debes corrupta excipi non tantum a
corona sordidiore sed ab hac quoque turba cultiore; togis
enim inter se isti, non iudicis distant. Hoc magis mirari potes,   90
quod non tantum vitiosa sed vitia laudentur. Nam illud
semper factum est: nullum sine venia placuit ingenium. Da
mihi quemcumque vis magni nominis virum: dicam quid illi
aetas sua ignoverit, quid in illo sciens dissimulaverit. Multos
tibi dabo quibus vitia non nocuerint, quosdam quibus pro-   95
fuerint. Dabo, inquam, maximae famae et inter admiranda
propositos, quos si quis corrigit, delet; sic enim vitia virtutibus inmixta sunt ut illas secum tractura sint.

   Adice nunc quod oratio certam regulam non habet: consuetudo illam civitatis, quae numquam in eodem diu stetit,   100
versat. Multi ex alieno saeculo petunt verba, duodecim
tabulas loquuntur; Gracchus illis et Crassus et Curio nimis
culti et recentes sunt, ad Appium usque et Coruncanium
redeunt. Quidam contra, dum nihil nisi tritum et usitatum
volunt, in sordes incidunt. Utrumque diverso genere corru-   105
ptum est, tam mehercules quam nolle nisi splendidis uti ac
sonantibus et poeticis, necessaria atque in usu posita vitare.
Tam hunc dicam peccare quam illum: alter se plus iusto
colit, alter plus iusto neglegit; ille et crura, hic ne alas quidem
vellit.   110

   Ad compositionem transeamus. Quot genera tibi in hac
dabo quibus peccetur? Quidam praefractam et asperam
probant; disturbant de industria si quid placidius effluxit;
nolunt sine salebra esse iuncturam; virilem putant et fortem
quae aurem inaequalitate percutiat. Quorundam non est   115
compositio, modulatio est; adeo blanditur et molliter labitur.
Quid de illa loquar in qua verba differuntur et diu expectata
vix ad clausulas redeunt? Quid illa in exitu lenta, qualis
Ciceronis est, devexa et molliter detinens nec aiiter quam
solet ad morem suum pedemque respondens?   120

121 **Non tantum:** the asterisks indicate that the manuscripts omit some words necessary for a balanced structure of the sentence.

124 **nihil. . .sonant:** "[are] nothing more than they sound."

126 **Sallustio:** Gaius Sallustius Crispus, Roman historian (86–35 B.C.). Two of Sallust's works, the *Bellum Catilinae* and the *Bellum Jugurthinum* have come down to us. We also possess fragments of his *Historiae,* dealing with the period 78–67 B.C.

127–128 **ante expectatum cadentia:** "ending unexpectedly."

128 **Arruntius:** L. Arruntius, Roman orator and historian who became consul in A.D. 6. His historical writings dealt with the Punic Wars.

130 **apud Sallustium:** in citing an author, *apud*, "in the works of," "in the writings of," is regularly used.

133 **fugam nostris fecere:** "they put our men to flight."

134–135 **Panhormitanos. . .fecere:** "caused the inhabitants of Panormus (modern Palermo, Sicily) to surrender to the Romans." The use of the infinitive *dedere* with the verb *fecere* (rather than the more classical construction of *ut* plus the subjunctive) appears to be colloquial.

148 **Regulo:** M. Atilius Regulus, consul in 267 and 256 B.C., Roman hero during the First Punic War. Captured by the Carthaginians, he was sent to Rome to propose peace between the two hostile countries. If unsuccessful in his mission, he was bound by oath to return to Carthage for mortal punishment. Rather than argue for peace, he heroically urged his countrymen to continue the war and as a result suffered a most cruel death at the hands of the enemy.

155 **servata. . . parte:** "the remaining portion [of the hair] being preserved and hanging down" (i.e., allowed to grow long).

157 **oculis transire:** "to escape the eyes."

158–159 **dum conspici:** supply *possint.*

163 **quid aliud quam:** "what else is it," "what else than [this may I call it]."

121 **sententiae, -arum,** *f. pl.,* pointed thoughts
122 **pusillus, -a, -um,** *adj.,* petty, insignificant
  inprobus, -a, -um, *adj.,* bad, bold, shameless
123 **licet, -ere, licuit,** *impers.,* 2, it is permitted
  nitor, -i, nisus (nixus) 3 *dep.,* lean, rest, strive
136 **contexo, -ere, -texui, -textus,** 3, weave
138 **incido, -ere, -cidi, -cisus,** 3, fall upon accidentally
140 **hiemo,** 1, be wintry, stormy, cold
143 **oneraria, -ae,** *f.,* merchant-vessel
  praeter, *prep. w. acc.,* besides, in addition to
144 **aquilo, -onis,** *m.,* north wind
145 **desino, -ere, -sivi (-sii), -situs,** 3, cease, stop
  infulcio, -ire, -fulsi, -fultus, 4, put in, insert
147 **tempero,** 1, keep from, refrain from
150 **proprius, -a, -um,** *adj.,* one's own
151 **adfectus, -us,** *m.,* emotion
153 **fluxus, -a, -um,** *p. adj.* (*of* **fluo**), flowing, loose, slack
154 **intervello, -ere, -vulsi, -vulsus,** 3, pluck out here and there, thin
  labrum, -i, *n.,* lip
  pressius, *comp. adv.,* rather closely
  tondeo, -ere, totondi, tonsus, 2, shear
155 **adrado, -ere, -rasi, -rasus,** 3, shave
  lacerna, -ae, *f.,* cloak
156 **sumo, -ere, sumpsi, sumptus,** 3, put on, wear
  perlucens, -entis, *p. adj.* (*of* **perluceo**), transparent
158 **vel,** *conj.,* even
  reprehendo, -ere, -prehendi, -prehensus, 3, censure, blame
161 **titubo,** 1, falter, hesitate
162 **cedo, -ere, cessi, cessus,** 3, yield
  prodo, -ere, -didi, -ditus, 3, betray, surrender
164 **labo,** 1, totter, fall
165 **habitus, -us,** *m.,* appearance, demeanor
  incessus, -us, *m.,* gait

Non tantum * * * in genere sententiarum vitium est, si aut
pusillae sunt et pueriles aut inprobae et plus ausae quam pu-
dore salvo licet, si floridae sunt et nimis dulces, si in vanum
exeunt et sine effectu nihil amplius quam sonant.

Haec vitia unus aliquis inducit, sub quo tunc eloquentia   125
est, ceteri imitantur et alter alteri tradunt. Sic Sallustio
vigente anputatae sententiae et verba ante expectatum
cadentia et obscura brevitas fuere pro cultu. L. Arruntius, vir
rarae frugalitatis, qui historias belli Punici scripsit, fuit
Sallustianus et in illud genus nitens. Est apud Sallustium   130
'exercitum argento fecit', id est, pecunia paravit. Hoc
Arruntius amare coepit; posuit illud omnibus paginis. Dicit
quodam loco 'fugam nostris fecere', alio loco 'Hiero rex
Syracusanorum bellum fecit', et alio loco 'quae audita Panhormitanos dedere Romanis fecere'. Gustum tibi dare volui: 135
totus his contexitur liber. Quae apud Sallustium rara fuerunt
apud hunc crebra sunt et paene continua, nec sine causa; ille
enim in haec incidebat, at hic illa quaerebat. Vides autem
quid sequatur ubi alicui vitium pro exemplo est. Dixit
Sallustius 'aquis hiemantibus'. Arruntius in primo libro belli   140
Punici ait 'repente hiemavit tempestas', et alio loco cum
dicere vellet frigidum annum fuisse ait 'totus hiemavit
annus', et alio loco 'inde sexaginta onerarias leves praeter
militem et necessarios nautarum hiemante aquilone misit'.
Non desinit omnibus locis hoc verbum infulcire. Quodam   145
loco dicit Sallustius 'dum inter arma civilia aequi bonique
famas petit'. Arruntius non temperavit quominus primo
statim libro poneret ingentes esse 'famas' de Regulo. Haec
ergo et eiusmodi vitia, quae alicui inpressit imitatio, non
sunt indicia luxuriae nec animi corrupti; propria enim esse   150
debent et ex ipso nata ex quibus tu aestimes alicuius adfectus:
iracundi hominis iracunda oratio est, commoti nimis incitata,
delicati tenera et fluxa. Quod vides istos sequi qui aut vellunt
barbam aut intervellunt, qui labra pressius tondent et
adradunt servata et summissa cetera parte, qui lacernas   155
coloris inprobi sumunt, qui perlucentem togam, qui nolunt
facere quicquam quod hominum oculis transire liceat: inritant illos et in se avertunt, volunt vel reprehendi dum
conspici. Talis est oratio Maecenatis omniumque aliorum
qui non casu errant sed scientes volentesque. Hoc a magno   160
animi malo oritur: quomodo in vino non ante lingua titubat
quam mens cessit oneri et inclinata vel prodita est, ita ista
orationis quid aliud quam ebrietas nulli molesta est nisi
animus labat. Ideo ille curetur: ab illo sensus, ab illo verba
exeunt, ab illo nobis est habitus, vultus, incessus. Illo sano   165

168–169 Rege. . .fidem: Vergil. *Georgics* 4.212–213. In describing the *modus vivendi* of bees, Vergil employs these lines to emphasize their absolute allegiance to their queen and their confused behavior when she is lost.

173 conatus: a noun modified by *omnis:* "every effort."

191–192 Numquid. . .furor est: *numquid* is an interrogative adverb used to introduce a question and need not be translated; Reynolds inserts *non* to give the negative force: "is there not madness in this?"

198 consulum: the Romans employed the names of the consuls to designate given years. For example, "in the consulships of Caesar and Bibulus" would refer to the year 59 B.C.

167 **procumbo, -ere, -cubui, -cubitus,** 3, fall down
168 **incolumis, -e,** *adj.*, unharmed
171 **pareo, -ere, parui, paritus,** 2, obey
   obtempero, 1, obey, conform to
172 **simul,** *adv.*, at once
173 **marceo, -ere,** 2, be weak, languid
174 **similitudo, -inis,** *f.*, simile
175 **modo,** *adv.*, now
   intueor, -eri, -tuitus, 2 *dep.*, look upon, contemplate
177 **inpotens, -entis,** *adj.*, weak, immoderate, uncontrolled
178 **dirus, -a, -um,** *adj.*, awful
179 **excipio, -ere, -cepi, -ceptus,** 3, take hold of, capture
181 **haurio, -ire, hausi, haustus,** 4, drink up, consume
   contrecto, 1, touch, handle
182 **exedo, -ere, -edi, -esus,** 3, consume
   medulla, -ae, *f.*, marrow
184 **pro,** *prep. w. abl.*, in place of
185 **sumministrator, -oris,** *m.*, promoter
186 **aufero, auferre, abstuli, ablatus,** *irr.*, take away, remove
187 **quod,** *conj.*, because
189 **exoletus, -a, -um,** *p. adj.* (*of* **exolesco**), grown out of use, obsolete, emasculated
   convoluto, 1, whirl or roll round rapidly
190 **maereo, -ere,** 2, be sad, grieve
191 **cesso,** 1, cease, stop, be idle, do nothing
193 **inbecillus, -a, -um,** *adj.*, weak
194 **culina, -ae,** *f.*, kitchen
195 **cocus, -i,** *m.*, cook
196 **veterarius, -a, -um,** *adj.*, old, mature
197 **vindemia, -ae,** *f.*, vintage
   horreum, -i, *n.*, granary, storehouse
199 **colonus, -i,** *m.*, settler
   aro, 1, plough
   fodio, -ere, fodi, fossus, 3, dig
200 **sero, -ere, sevi, satus,** 3, sow

ac valente oratio quoque robusta, fortis, virilis est: si ille
procubuit, et cetera ruinam sequuntur.

> Rege incolumi mens omnibus una est:
> amisso rupere fidem.

Rex noster est animus; hoc incolumi cetera manent in   170
officio, parent, obtemperant: cum ille paulum vacillavit,
simul dubitant. Cum vero cessit voluptati, artes quoque eius
actusque marcent et omnis ex languido fluidoque conatus est.
　Quoniam hac similitudine usus sum, perseverabo. Animus
noster modo rex est, modo tyrannus: rex cum honesta intue-   175
tur, salutem commissi sibi corporis curat et illi nihil imperat
turpe, nihil sordidum; ubi vero inpotens, cupidus, delicatus
est, transit in nomen detestabile ac dirum et fit tyrannus.
Tunc illum excipiunt adfectus inpotentes et instant; qui
initio quidem gaudet, ut solet populus largitione nocitura   180
frustra plenus et quae non potest haurire contrectans; cum
vero magis ac magis vires morbus exedit et in medullas
nervosque descendere deliciae, conspectu eorum quibus se
nimia aviditate inutilem reddidit laetus, pro suis voluptatibus
habet alienarum spectaculum, sumministrator libidinum   185
testisque, quarum usum sibi ingerendo abstulit. Nec illi tam
gratum est abundare iucundis quam acerbum quod non
omnem illum apparatum per gulam ventremque transmittit,
quod non cum omni exoletorum feminarumque turba con-
volutatur, maeretque quod magna pars suae felicitatis exclusa 190
corporis angustiis cessat. Numquid enim, mi Lucili, <non> in
hoc furor est, quod nemo nostrum mortalem se cogitat,
quod nemo inbecillum? immo quod nemo nostrum unum
esse se cogitat? Aspice culinas nostras et concursantis inter
tot ignes cocos: unum videri putas ventrem cui tanto tumultu 195
comparatur cibus? Aspice veteraria nostra et plena multorum saeculorum vindemiis horrea: unum putas videri ventrem cui tot consulum regionumque vina cluduntur? Aspice
quot locis terra vertatur, quot millia colonorum arent, fodiant:
unum videri putas ventrem cui et in Sicilia et in Africa seritur? 200

201 **unusquisque, unaquaeque, unumquidque,** *indef. pron.,* each one
202 **metior, -iri, mensus,** 4 *dep.,* measure
    simul, *adv.,* at the same time, at once
203 **prosum, prodesse, profui,** *irr.,* be of use, benefit
205 **aevum, -i,** *n.,* life
    respicio, -ere, -spexi, -spectus, 3, look to, have regard for

Sani erimus et modica concupiscemus si unusquisque se numeret, metiatur simul corpus, sciat quam nec multum capere nec diu possit. Nihil tamen aeque tibi profuerit ad temperantiam omnium rerum quam frequens cogitatio brevis aevi et huius incerti: quidquid facies, respice ad mortem. *Vale.*   205

VOCABULARY

A

a, ab, *prep. w. abl.*, from, away from, by

abditum, -i, *n.*, hiding, concealment

abditus, -a, -um, *p. adj.* (*of* **abdo**), concealed, secret

abdo, -ere, -didi, -ditus, 3, hide

abduco, -ere, -duxi, -ductus, 3, lead or take away, withdraw

abeo, -ire, -ivi (-ii), -itus, 4, go away

aberro, 1, wander, lose one's way

abicio, -ere, -ieci, -iectus [ab-iacio], 3, throw away or down

abiectus, -a, -um, *p. adj.* (*of* **abicio**), low, common, abject

abies, -etis, *f.*, fir

abigo, -ere, -egi, -actus [ab-ago], 3, drive away

abrumpo, -ere, -rupi, -ruptus, 3, break off

abruptus, -a, -um, *p. adj.* (of **abrumpo**), broken, disconnected, abrupt

abscedo, -ere, -cessi, -cessus, 3, go away, depart

abscondo, -ere, -di (-didi), -ditus, 3, hide

absens, -entis, *adj.*, absent

absolute, *adv.*, absolutely, perfectly, completely

absolutus, -a, -um, *p. adj.* (*of* **absolvo**), perfect, complete

absolvo, -ere, -solvi, -solutus, 3, loosen, free; complete, finish

abstineo, -ere, -tinui, -tentus [abs-teneo], 2, hold or keep away from, abstain from

abstraho, -ere, -traxi, -tractus, 3, draw away

absum, abesse, afui, afuturus, *irr.*, be away, be absent

abunde, *adv.*, copiously, abundantly

abundo, 1, abound

abutor, -uti, -usus, 3 *dep.*, abuse

ac, *reduced form of* **atque,** *conj.*, and

accedo, -ere, -cessi, -cessus [ad-cedo], 3, go towards, approach; be added

accendo, -ere, -cendi, -census, 3, kindle, set on fire, light

acceptus, -a, -um, *p. adj.* (*of* **accipio**), received, taken

accerso, *see* **arcesso**

accessio, -onis, *f.*, approach, access, attack

accido, -ere, -cidi [ad-cado], 3, fall to, happen

accipio, -cipere, -cepi, -ceptus [ad-capio], 3, take, receive

accusator, -oris, *m.*, accuser

acer, acris, acre, *adj.*, sharp, keen

acerbitas, -atis, *f.*, bitterness

acerbus, -a, -um, *adj.*, bitter, harsh

Achilles, -is, *m.*, Achilles

Achivus, -a, -um, *adj.*, Greek

accolo, -ere, -colui, -cultus, 3, dwell by or near, inhabit

acquiro, -ere, -quisivi, -quisitus [ad-quaero], 3, add to, acquire

acta, -orum, *n. pl.*, actions

actio, -onis, *f.*, action

actus, -us, *m.*, doing or performing a thing, action, role

acuo, -ere, acui, acutus, 3, sharpen, spur on, incite

acutus, -a, -um, *p. adj.* (*of* **acuo**), sharpened, sharp, acute

ad, *prep. w. acc.*, to, toward, against; for; according to

adclamo, 1, cry out at

addico, -ere, -dixi, -dictus, 3, give up or over, attach

addo, -ere, -didi, -ditus, 3, give to, give, add

adduco, -ere, -duxi, -ductus, 3, draw to oneself, lead, bring

adeo, -ire, -ii (-ivi), -itus, 4, go to or towards, approach

adeo, *adv.*, to that point, so far, so much, so, to such an extent

adfecto, 1, strive after

adfectus, -us, *m.*, emotion

adfero, -ferre, -tuli, -latus, *irr.*, bring to, bring

adficio, -ere, -feci, -fectus [ad-facio], 3, affect

adfigo, -ere, -fixi, -fixus, 3, fasten to, fix to or in

adfirmatio, -onis, *f.*, affirmation, assertion

adfirmo, 1, assert

adflo, 1, blow on, breathe on

adfrico, -are, -fricui, -fricatus, 1, rub on

adfundo, -ere, -fudi, -fusus, 3, pour on, spread on

adgestus, -us, *m.*, carrying to, accumulation, overcrowding

adgredior, -i, -gressus [ad-gradior], 3 *dep.*, go to, approach; attack; undertake

adhaereo, -ere, -haesi, -haesus, 2, cling to

adhibeo, -ere, -ui, -itus [ad-habeo], 2, have by or near, summon; apply

adhortor, 1 *dep.*, urge

adhuc, *adv.*, up to this point, thus far, until now, still

adicio, -ere, -ieci, -iectus [ad-iacio], 3, throw to or at; add

adiungo, -ere, -iunxi, -iunctus, 3, add

adiutor, -oris, *m.*, assistant, helper

adiutorium, -i, *n.*, assistance

adiutus, -a, -um, *p. adj.* (*of* **adiuvo**), aided, helped

adiuvo, -are, -iuvi, -iutus, 1, help, assist

adlevo, 1, lift up, raise

adlino, -ere, -levi, -litus, 3, smear on

adloquor, -i, -locutus, 3 *dep.*, address, exhort, encourage

adludo, -ere, -lusi, -lusus, 3, play with

adminiculum, -i, *n.,* support

admiratio, -onis, *f.,* admiration, wonder, astonishment

admiror, 1 *dep.,* wonder at, be surprised; admire

admitto, -ere, -misi, -missus, 3, admit

admoneo, -ere, -monui, -monitus, 2, advise, admonish

admoveo, -ere, -movi, -motus, 2, move to, place near

adolesco, -ere, -olevi (-ui), -ultus, 3, grow up, mature

adoro, 1, worship, honor

adpeto, -ere, -petivi, -petitus, 3, seek

adplico, -are, -avi (-ui), -atus (-itus), attach

adprehendo, -ere, -hendi, -hensus, 3, seize upon

adprobo, 1, approve, prove, establish

adquiesco, -ere, -quievi, -quietus, 3, rest, repose, find rest or comfort

adquiro, -ere, -quisivi, -quisitus [ad-quaero], 3, add to, acquire

adquisitus, -a, -um, *p. adj.* (*of* **adquiro**), acquired

adrado, -ere, -rasi, -rasus, 3, shave

adrisor, -oris, *m.,* one who smiles approvingly, flatterer

adrogantia, -ae, *f.,* arrogance

adrosor, -oris, *m.,* gnawer, parasite

adsensio, -onis, *f.,* agreement; applause

adsentior, -sentiri, -sensus, 4 *dep.,* assent to, agree with; welcome

adsequor, -i, -secutus, 3 *dep.,* attain

adsero, -ere, -serui, -sertus, 3, claim

adsideo, -ere, -sedi, -sessus [ad-sedeo], 2, sit near

adsiduus, -a, -um, *adj.,* continual, constant

adsigno, 1, assign

adsisto, -ere, -stiti, 3, stand at, by, or near

adsuesco, -ere, -suevi, -suetus, 3, become accustomed to

adsum, -esse, -fui, -futurus, *irr.,* be at, near, be present

adtendo, -ere, -tendi, -tentus, 3, pay attention

adtribuo, -ere, -ui, -utus, 3, assign

adtritus, -us, *m.,* rubbing

adulatio, -onis, *f.,* flattery

adulescens, -entis, *adj.,* young; *subst. m.,* young man

adulescentia, -ae, *f.,* youth

adultera, -ae, *f.,* adulteress

adultus, -a, -um, *p. adj.* (*of* **adolesco**), grown up, adult

aduro, -ere, -ussi, -ustus, 3, scorch

adustus, -a, -um, *p. adj.* (*of* **aduro**), scorched

advectus, -a, -um, *p. adj.* (*of* **adveho**), carried, brought

adveho, -ere, -vexi, -vectus, 3, carry, bring

advenio, -ire, -veni, -ventus, 4, arrive

adventicius, -a, -um, *adj.,* foreign, strange; accidental, external

adversus, -a, -um, *adj.,* hostile, adverse

adversus, *prep. w. acc.,* to, towards, against

adverto, -ere, -verti, -versus, 3, turn towards, turn

advoco, 1, call, summon

aedificium, -i, *n.,* building

aedituus, -i, *m.,* keeper of a temple

aeger, -ra, -rum, *adj.,* sick

aegre, *adv.,* painfully, with difficulty

aegritudo, -inis, *f.,* sickness, malady

aegroto, 1, be sick

Aegyptius, -i, *m.,* an Egyptian

Aeneas, -ae, *m.,* hero of Vergil's Aeneid

aeneator, -oris, *m.,* trumpeter

aequalis, -e, *adj.,* equal

aequalitas, -atis, *f.,* evenness, smoothness; calm; equality

aequaliter, *adv.,* equally

aeque, *adv.,* equally

aequitas, -atis, *f.,* fairness, justice, equanimity

aequo, 1, equal

aequus, -a, -um, *adj.,* even, equal, level, fair, just

aerumna, -ae, *f.,* trouble, toil

aes, aeris, *n.,* copper, bronze; **aes alienum,** debt

aestimatio, -onis, *f.,* valuation, appraisement, estimation

aestimo, 1, value, estimate, judge

aestivus, -a, -um, *adj.,* pertaining to summer, summer-like, summer

aestuo, 1, boil, be hot

aestus, -us, *m.,* heat

aetas, -atis, *f.,* age

aeternus, -a, -um, *adj.,* everlasting, eternal

Aetna, -ae, *f.,* Mount Aetna in Sicily

aevum, -i, *n.,* age, time, life

affero, afferre, attuli, allatus [ad-fero], *irr.,* carry, bring

Africa, -ae, *f.,* Africa

ager, agri, *m.,* field, piece of land

agilis, -e, *adj.,* light, nimble, active

agito, 1, stir, agitate

agmen, -inis, *n.,* line of march, army

agnosco, -ere, -novi, -nitus, 3, know, understand, recognize, acknowledge

ago, -ere, egi, actus, 3, do, drive, discuss, live, spend, pay attention to, be concerned with; **age, agite,** used as an interjection, come now! **gratias agere,** give thanks, thank

agrestis, -e, *adj.,* wild, rustic, rural

agricola, -ae, *m.,* farmer

Agrippa, -ae, *m.,* Agrippa, son-in-law of Atticus, Cicero's intimate friend

aio, *def. verb,* say, assert

ala, -ae, *f.*, wing; shoulders and armpits of a man
alacer, -cris, -cre, *adj.*, cheerful, lively
Alexander, -dri, *m.*, Alexander the Great (356-323 B.C.), king of Macedonia
alias, *adv.*, at another time; **alias. . .alias,** at one time. . .at another time
alicubi, *adv.*, somewhere, anywhere
alienus, -a, -um, *adj.*, of or belonging to another, another's; strange, foreign
alimentum, -i, *n.*, food
alioqui (alioquin), *adv.*, otherwise
alipilus, -i, *m.*, hair plucker
aliquamdiu, *adv.*, for some time
aliquando, *adv.*, at some time or other, now and then, sometimes, finally
aliquis, -quid, *indef. subst.*, someone, something; also **aliqui, -qua, -quod,** *indef. adj.*, some
aliquo, *adv.*, somewhere
aliquot, *indecl. adj.*, several, some
aliter, *adv.*, otherwise, differently; **aliter atque aliter,** now in one way, now in another
alius, alia, aliud, *adj.*, other, another; **alius. . .alius,** one, another; **alii. . .alii,** some, . .others; **alio. . .alio,** in one direction. . .in another
alligo, 1, bind
alo, -ere, alui, alitus (altus), 3, nourish
Alpes, -ium, *f.*, the Alps
alter, -era, -erum, *adj.*, other (of two), the other; another; **alter. . .alter,** the one. . .the other
alternus, -a, -um, *adj.*, one after the other, by turns, alternately; **alternis** (*abl. pl.*, supply *vicibus*), alternately, by turns
altilis, -e, *adj.*, fattened; **altilis** (supply *avis*), *f.*, fowl
altitudo, -inis, *f.*, height, altitude; depth
altus, -a, -um, *adj.*, high, deep; **ex alto,** from deep down within; **in alto,** deep within; *subst.*, **altum, -i,** *n.*, depth, deep sea
alumnus, -i, *m.*, pupil
alveus, -i, *m.*, channel
alvus, -i, *f.*, belly
amaritudo, -inis *f.*, bitterness
ambages, -is, *f.*, circumlocution, ambiguity
ambigo, -ere [amb-ago], 3, wander about; doubt, dispute
ambiguus, -a, -um, *adj.*, uncertain, doubtful, ambiguous
ambitio, -onis, *f.*, canvassing for office; ambition, ostentation
ambitiosus, -a, -um, *adj.*, ambitious
ambitus, -us, *m.*, going around, canvassing for office
ambo, -ae, -o, *adj.*, both
ambulatio, -onis, *f.*, walking
ambulo, 1, walk
amicitia, -ae, *f.*, friendship

amicus, -a, -um, *adj.*, friendly; **amicus, -i,** *m.*, friend
amissus, -a, -um, *p. adj.* (*of* **amitto**), lost
amitto, -ere, -misi, -missus, 3, let go, lose
amnis, -is, *m.*, stream, river
amo, 1, love
amoenitas, -atis, *f.*, pleasantness
amoenus, -a, -um, *adj.*, pleasant, charming
amor, -oris, *m.*, love
ample, *adv.*, amply; *comp.*, **amplius,** more
amplector, -plecti, -plexus 3 *dep.*, embrace
amplius, *comp.* (*of* **ample**), more, longer
amplus, -a, -um, *adj.*, large, great, ample
an, *conj.*, or, whether
Anacharsis, -is, *m.*, Anacharsis, renowned Scythian philosopher, 6th cent. B.C., friend of Solon
analecta, -ae, *m.*, a slave who picked up crumbs after a meal
anceps, -ipitis, *adj.*, ambiguous, dangerous; doubtful, uncertain
ancillula, -ae, *f.*, maid-servant
ancora, -ae, *f.*, anchor
ango, -ere, anxi, anctus and anxus, 3, cause pain
angulus, -i, *m.*, corner
angustia, -ae, *f.*, narrowness
angustus, -a, -um, *adj.*, narrow; slight, meager, small
anhelitus, -us, *m.*, panting
anicula, -ae, *f.*, a little old woman
animal, -alis, *n.*, living creature, animal
animus, -i, *m.*, mind, soul, spirit, breath; thought
annus, -i, *m.*, year
anputatus, -a, -um, *p. adj.* (*of* **anputo**), cut off, amputated
anputo, 1, cut off, amputate
ante, *adv.* and *prep. w. acc.*, before, in front of
antecedo, -ere, -cessi, -cessus, 3, go before, precede
antecessus, -us, *m.*, a going before; **in antecessum,** in advance
anteeo, -ire, -ivi (-ii), 4, go before, excel, surpass
antequam, *adv.*, before
anticipo, 1, anticipate
antiquus, -a, -um, *adj.*, ancient
antistes, -itis, *m.* and *f.*, high priest
anxius, -a, -um, *adj.*, anxious, uneasy
aperio, -ire, -ui, -ertus, 4, uncover, lay bare, reveal
apertus, -a, -um, *adj.*, open, obvious
apis, -is, *f.*, bee
apologo, 1, reject
apparatus, -us, *m.*, equipment, apparatus, provision
appareo, -ere, -ui, -itus [ad-pareo], 2, appear
appello, 1, call, name
Appius, -i, *m.*, Appius Claudius Caecus, outstanding orator and censor (312–308 B.C.) who built the Via Appia
applico [ad-plico], 1, fasten, attach, apply

Vocabulary A

aptatus, -a, -um, *p. adj.* (*of* apto), fitted, adapted
apto, 1, fit, adapt
aptus, -a, -um, *adj.*, fit, suited
apud, *prep. w. acc.*, at, with, by, near, among; at one's house, in one's possession, in the works of; in the case of
aqua, -ae, *f.*, water
aquilo, -onis, *m.*, north wind
ara, -ae, *f.*, altar
aratrum, -i, *n.*, plow
arbiter, -tri, *m.*, witness, judge
arbitrium, -i, *n.*, judgment, decision
arbor, -oris, *f.*, tree
arca, -ae, *f.*, money box
arcanus, -a, -um, *adj.*, secret
arceo, -ere, -cui, -ctus, 2, keep off, ward off
arcesso, -ere, -ivi, -itus, 3, summon
architectus, -i, *m.*, architect
ardens, -entis, *p. adj.* (*of* ardeo), hot, glowing
ardeo, -ere, arsi, arsus, 2, burn, glow
ardor, -oris, *m.*, heat, burning
arduus, -a, -um, *adj.*, steep, difficult, arduous
area, -ae, *f.*, open space, site for a house
arens, -entis, *p. adj.* (*of* areo), dry, arid
areo, -ere, 2, be dry
argentum, -i, *n.*, silver
Argi, -orum, *m.*, Argos
argumentatio, -onis, *f.*, argumentation
argumentum, -i, *n.*, argument, proof
aridus, -a, -um, *adj.*, dry, arid
arieto, 1, strike violently
Aristoteles, -is, *m.*, Aristotle of Stagira, 384–322 B.C., the renowned Greek philosopher, founder of the Peripatetic School
arma, -orum, *n.*, arms
armentum, -i, *n.*, herd
armo, 1, arm
aro, 1, plough
arripio, -ere, arripui, arreptus [ad-rapio], 3, seize upon, snatch
Arruntius, -i, *m.*, L. Arruntius, Roman orator and historian, consul in A.D. 6
ars, artis, *f.*, art, skill
articulus, -i, *m.*, joint
artifex, -ficis, *m.*, artist, artisan, worker
artificium, -i, *n.*, occupation, trade, profession, skill, art
arundo, -inis, *f.*, reed, sugar-cane
arvum, -i, *n.*, field
as, assis, *m.*, the as, a Roman coin
ascendo, -ere, -scendi, -scensus, 3, climb, ascend
Asia, -ae, *f.*, Asia
aspectus, -us, *m.*, sight
asper, -era, -erum, *adj.*, rough, harsh
aspicio, -ere, -spexi, -spectus [ad-specio], 3, look at, see

assentior, -iri, -sensus, 4 *dep.*, agree with, give approval
at, *conj.*, but, moreover
Athenae, -arum, *f.*, Athens
atque, *conj.*, and
atqui, *conj.*, and yet
atrium, -i, *n.*, open court in a Roman house, atrium, reception room
Attalus, -i, *m.*, Stoic philosopher, teacher of Seneca
Atticus, -i, *m.*, Atticus, intimate friend of Cicero, to whom the orator addressed one of his four collections of letters
attingo, -ere, -tigi, -tactus [ad-tango], 3, arrive at a place, approach, reach
attollo, -ere, 3, raise up, lift up
attonitus, -a, -um, *p. adj.* (*of* attono), thunderstruck, stunned, astonished, confounded, senseless; frantic
attono, -ere, -tonui, -tonitus, 3, strike with thunder, stun, make senseless
auctor, -oris, *m.*, author, authority, voucher
auctoramentum, -i, *n.*, oath
auctoritas, -atis, *f.*, influence, authority
auctus, -us, *m.*, increase, growth
audaciter (audacter), *adv.*, boldly
audax, -acis, *adj.*, bold, audacious
audeo, -ere, ausus, 2 *semi-dep.*, dare
audio, -ire, -ivi, -itus, 4, hear, listen
auditor, -oris, *m.*, hearer, auditor
auditorium, -i, *n.*, lecture-room
aufero, auferre, abstuli, ablatus, *irr.*, take away, remove
augeo, -ere, auxi, auctus, 2, increase, augment
aura, -ae, *f.*, breeze
auratus, -a, -um, *adj.*, golden
aureus, -a, -um, *adj.*, golden
auris, -is, *f.*, ear
aurum, -i, *n.*, gold
auspicor, 1 *dep.*, take the auspices; begin, enter upon; attain, receive
austeritas, -atis, *f.*, harshness, austerity
ausus, -a, -um, *p. adj.* (*of* audeo), having dared, having ventured
aut, *conj.*, or; **aut. . .aut,** either. . .or
autem, *conj.*, but, however, moreover
auxilium, -i, *n.*, help, aid
avaritia, -ae, *f.*, greed, avarice
avarus, -a, -um, *adj.*, greedy, avaricious
aversus, -a, -um, *p. adj.* (*of* averto), turned away
averto, -ere, -verti, -versus, 3, turn away
aviditas, -atis, *f.*, vehement desire, avarice
avidus, -a, -um, *adj.*, greedy
avis, -is, *f.*, bird
avocatio, -onis, *f.*, distraction
avoco, 1, call away, distract

Vocabulary A

B

Baba, -ae, *m.*, Baba, a court fool in the age of Seneca

bacchor, 1 *dep.*, revel, rave

Baiae, -arum, *f.*, Baiae, a luxurious resort in Campania

Baianus, -a, -um, *adj.*, belonging to Baiae

balineum, -i, *n.*, *see* balneum

balneum, -i, *n.*, bath, bathhouse

barba, -ae, *f.*, beard

barbarus, -a, -um, *adj.*, foreign, barbarian

beatus, -a, -um, *adj.*, happy, blessed, wealthy

bellum, -i, *n.*, war

bene, *adv.*, well, rightly

beneficentia, -ae, *f.*, kindness, beneficence

beneficiarius, -a, -um, *adj.*, relating to a favor, bestowed as a favor

beneficium, -i, *n.*, kindness, benefit

biberarius, -i, *m.*, the man selling drinks

bibo, -ere, bibi, bibitus, 3, drink

bilis, -is, *f.*, gall, bile

blandimentum, -i, *n.*, allurement, blandishment

blandior, -iri, -itus, 4 *dep.*, flatter, soothe, caress

blandus, -a, -um, *adj.*, enticing

bonitas, -atis, *f.*, goodness

bonus, -a, -um, *adj.*, good; *comp.*, melior, -ius, better; *superl.*, optimus, -a, -um, best

bos, bovis, *c.*, ox, cow

botularius, -i, *m.*, sausage-maker

brachium, -i, *n.*, arm

bratteatus, -a, -um, *adj.*, gilded

brevis, -e, *adj.*, short, brief

bubulcus, -i, *m.*, herdsman

C

cadaver, -eris, *n.*, dead body, cadaver

cado, -ere, cecidi, casus, 3, fall

caecus, -a, -um, *adj.*, blind

caedes, -is, *m.*, slaughter

caelatura, -ae, *f.*, carving

caelatus, -a, -um, *p. adj.* (*of* caelo), carved, engraved

caelestis, -e, *adj.*, heavenly, celestial

caelo, 1, carve, engrave

caelum, -i, *n.*, sky, heaven, atmosphere, climate

Caesar, -aris, *m.*, C. Julius Caesar (c. 102–44 B.C.), the renowned general, statesman, and author, assassinated by Brutus and Cassius

calco, 1, trample upon

calculus, -i, *m.*, pebble

calens, -entis, *p. adj.* (*of* caleo), hot

caleo, -ere, -ui, 2, be warm, hot

calidus, -a, -um, *adj.*, hot

calix, -icis, *m.*, cup, goblet

Callistus, -i, *m.*, Callistus, a slave who later became a master and scorned his former master

calor, -oris, *m.*, warmth, heat

calx, -cis, *f.*, heel

Campania, -ae, *f.*, Campania, a district of Central Italy

campus, -i, *m.*, field, plain

candidatus, -i, *m.*, candidate

candidus, -a, -um, *adj.*, glistening, white, pure

canis, -is, *c.*, dog

cano, -ere, cecini, 3, sing, sound, play

Canopus, -i, *m.*, Canopus, a city of Egypt, twelve miles from Alexandria, whose inhabitants were known for their debauchery

canticum, -i, *n.*, song

canto, 1, sing, play on an instrument

cantor, -oris, *m.*, singer

cantus, -us, *m.*, song

capax, -acis, *adj.*, able to hold

capio, -ere, cepi, captus, 3, take, seize

capitalis, -e, *adj.*, capital

Capitolium, -i, *n.*, the Capitol

capto, 1, seize, catch, capture

caput, -itis, *n.*, head, top, summit, source

carcer, -eris, *m.*, prison

cardiacus, -a, -um, *adj.*, suffering from a disease of the stomach

careo, -ere, -ui, -itus, 2, *w. abl.*, be without, lack

carmen, -inis, *n.*, poem, song

caro, carnis, *f.*, flesh, meat

carpo, -ere, carpsi, carptus, 3, pluck

carus, -a, -um, *adj.*, dear

casa, -ae, *f.*, hut, cottage

castigatio, -onis, *f.*, punishment, chastisement

castigo, 1, punish, check, restrain

castrum, -i, *n.*, castle, fort; *pl.*, castra, -orum, camp

casus, -us, *m.*, falling down, fall; occurrence, accident, chance; casu = forte, by chance

catena, -ae, *f.*, chain

Cato, -onis, *m.*, M. Cato, the Younger (95–46 B.C.), political opponent of Julius Caesar

cauda, -ae, *f.*, tail

causa, -ae, *f.*, cause, reason; causa (*abl. used as prep.*), for the sake of

cavea, -ae, *f.*, hollow place, cavity; theater

caveo, -ere, cavi, cautus, 2, be on one's guard, take care, take heed, beware

cavus, -a, -um, *adj.*, hollow

cedo, -ere, cessi, cessus, 3, go, depart; yield

celebro, 1, visit frequently

celer, -eris, -e, *adj.*, swift, quick

celeritas, -atis, *f.*, speed, swiftness

cella, -ae, *f.*, hut, cell

celo, 1, conceal

cena, -ae, *f.*, dinner

cenatio, -onis, *f.*, dining-hall

ceno, 1, dine

censeo, -ere, -sui, -sus, 2, express an opinion

censura, -ae, *f.*, rating

census, -us, *m.*, census, censor's list

centeni, -ae, -a, *num. adj.*, a hundred each, a hundred

centunculus, -i, *m.*, a small patch or patchwork

cereus, -a, -um, *adj.*, waxen, of wax; cereus, -i, *m.*, wax taper

cerno, -ere, crevi, cretus, 3, see, perceive, discern

certe, *adv.*, certainly, surely

certus, -a, -um, *adj.*, sure, fixed, certain

cervix, -icis, *f.*, neck, back of the neck, back or shoulders

cesso, 1, leave off, cease, delay; be idle, be negligent, do nothing

ceterus, -a, -um, *adj.*, the rest of, the remaining; ceterum, *adv.*, for the rest, moreover, but

chaos, *n.*, chaos

Charinus, -i, *m.*, Charinus, archon in 308–307 B.C.

Charondas, -ae, *m.*, a famous lawgiver of the 6th cent. B.C., disciple of Pythagoras

chorus, -i, *m.*, chorus

Chrysippus, -i, *m.*, Chrysippus (280–207 B.C.), successor of Cleanthes as head of the Stoic School

cibus, -i, *m.*, food

cicatrix, -icis, *f.*, scar

Cicero, -onis, *m.*, M. Tullius Cicero, the renowned orator and philosopher, 106–43 B.C.

cingo, -ere, cinxi, cinctus, 3, surround

cinis, -eris, *m.*, ashes

cinnus, -i, *m.*, mixed drink of spelt-grain and wine

circa, *adv. and prep. w. acc.*, around, about, concerning

circito, 1, make busy

circuitus, -us, *m.*, circling, revolving

circulor, 1 *dep.*, collect people around one's self

circumdo, -dare, -dedi, -datus, 1, put around, place around, surround

circumfero, -ferre, -tuli, -latus, *irr.*, carry around

circumfodio, -ere, -fodi, -fossus, 3, dig around

circumfundo, -ere, -fudi, -fusus, 3, pour around

circumscribo, -ere, -scripsi, -scriptus, 3, draw together, circumscribe, restrain

circumsono, -are, -sonui, -sonatus, 1, sound around

circumspicio, -ere, -spexi, -spectus, 3, look around, survey, ponder upon, consider

circumsto, -are, -steti, -status, 1, stand around

circumstrepo, -ere, -strepui, -strepitus, 3, roar, make a noise around

cisium, -i, *n.*, a light two-wheeled gig

citatus, -a, -um, *p. adj. (of* cito), fast, rapid

cito, 1, put in quick motion, move rapidly; cite, summon

cito, comp, citius, superl, citissime, *adv.*, quickly, speedily

citro, *adv. (found only in combination with* ultro), hither and thither

citus, -a, -um, *p. adj. (of* cieo), quick, speedy

civilis, -e, *adj.*, civil

civis, -is, *c.*, citizen

civitas, -atis, *f.*, citizenship; state

clamo, 1, shout, cry aloud

clamor, -oris, *m.*, loud shouting, noise

clare, *adv.*, in a loud voice

clarus, -a, -um, *adj.*, clear, loud; famous, renowned

classicum, -i, *n.*, war-trumpet

claudo, -ere, clausi, clausus, 3, close

clausula, -ae, *f.*, conclusion, close, end

clausus, -a, -um, *p. adj. (of* claudo), closed, enclosed

clavis, -is, *f.*, key

Cleanthes, -is, *m.*, Cleanthes (331–232 B.C.), successor to Zeno as head of the Stoic School

clementer, *adv.*, kindly, affably

cliens, -entis, *m.*, client, dependent

cludo, -ere, clusi, clusus, 3, shut, close

clunis, -is, *m. and f.*, rump

coactor, -oris, *m.*, one who forces

coactus, -a, -um, *p. adj. (of* cogo), forced, compelled

coagmento, 1, join, cement

coalesco, -ere, -alui, -alitus, 3, grow together, coalesce, unite

coarguo, -ere, -argui, 3, convict, expose

coctura, -ae, *f.*, cooking, boiling

cocus, -i, *m.*, cook

coeo, -ire, -ivi (-ii), -itus, 4, go or come together

coepi, coepisse, coeptus (used only in perf. tenses), have begun, began

coetus, -us, *m.*, meeting, assembly

cogitatio, -onis, *f.*, thought

cogitatus, -a, -um, *p. adj. (of* cogito), thought, deliberated, reflected

cogito, 1, think, reflect

cognitio, -onis, *f.*, knowledge, acquaintance

cognosco, -ere, -gnovi, -gnitus, 3, recognise, learn

cogo, -ere, coegi, coactus [con-ago], 3, drive together, collect; force, compel

cohaereo, -ere, -haesi, -haesus, 2, cling together

coicio, -ere, -ieci, -iectus [con-iacio], 3, throw together, unite

collido, -ere, -lisi, -lisus [con-laedo], 3, dash together

colligo, -ere, -legi, -lectus [con-lego], 3, bring together, collect

Vocabulary C

colo, -ere, colui, cultus, 3, cultivate, worship, honor, cherish

colonus, -i, *m.*, settler

color, -oris, *m.*, color, hue; class, kind

coloratus, -a, -um, *p. adj.* (*of* coloro), colored, specious

coloro, 1, color

columbor, 1 *dep.*, bill or kiss like doves

comans, -antis, *p. adj.* (*of* como), having long hair, hairy

comes, -itis, *c.*, companion, comrade

comessatio, -onis, *f.*, revel

comitatus, -us, *m.*, retinue, band, train

comiter, *adv.*, affably

commeatus, -us, *m.*, respite, furlough

commemoro, 1, recall to mind, mention, relate

commendatio, -onis, *f.*, recommendation, commendation, praise

commendo, 1, recommend

commentum, -i, *n.*, invention, fabrication

commeo, 1, come and go

commercium, -i, *n.*, trade, commerce, intercourse, exchange

comminiscor, -i, commentus, 3 *dep.*, contrive, invent

commissio, -onis, *f.*, contest, entertainment, concert

commissus, -a, -um, *p. adj.* (*of* committo), entrusted

committo, -ere, -misi, -missus, 3, entrust

commodo, 1, lend

commodus, -a, -um, *adj.*, advantageous, convenient

commonefacio, -ere, -feci, -factus, 3, admonish

commotus, -a, -um, *p. adj.* (*of* commoveo), moved, aroused, excited

commoveo, -ere, -movi, -motus, 2, move, arouse, excite

communico, 1, share, communicate

communis, -e, *adj.*, common

commutatio, -onis, *f.*, charge

como, 1, be furnished with hair

comparatio, -onis, *f.*, comparison

compareo, -ere, -parui, 2, appear

comparo, 1, prepare, obtain

comparo, 1, compare

compendiarius, -a, -um, *adj.*, short, compendious; compendiaria, -ae, *f.*, (supply *via*), short way, short cut

compesco, -ere, -pescui, 3, check, restrain

complector, -i, -plexus, 3 dep., embrace

complexus, -us, *m.*, embrace

complico, -are, -avi (-ui), -atus (-itus), 1, fold together, fold up

compono, -ere, -posui, -positus, 3, put together, collect; put in order, arrange, settle

compositio, -onis, *f.*, composition, arrangement

compositus, -a, -um, *p. adj.* (*of* compono), put in order, arranged, settled

conatus, -us, *m.*, attempt, effort, undertaking

concavus, -a, -um, *adj.*, hollow

concedo, -ere, -cessi, -cessus, 3, grant, allow, concede

concentus, -us, *m.*, singing together, harmony, harmonious music

conceptus, -a, -um, *p. adj.* (*of* concipio), conceived

conchyliatus, -a, -um, *adj.*, purple, clothed in purple

concinno, 1, fit together carefully, arrange

concipio, -ere, -cepi, -ceptus [con-capio], 3, take, receive, conceive

concitatus, -a, -um, *p. adj.* (*of* concito), stirred up, aroused

concito, 1, stir up, excite

conclamo, 1, shout together

concoquo, -ere, -coxi, -coctus, 3, digest

concordia, -ae, *f.*, harmony, concord

concors, concordis, *adj.*, of the same mind, united, agreeing, harmonious

conculco, 1, trample under foot

concupisco, -ere, -pivi (-pii), -pitus, 3, desire eagerly, covet

concurro, -ere, -curri, -cursus, 3, run together

concursatio, -onis, *f.*, running about, restlessness

concurso, 1, rush together, run about

concutio, -ere, -cussi, -cussus, 3, shake, agitate

condicio, -onis, *f.*, condition

conditivum, -i, *n.*, tomb

conditua, -ae, *f.*, preservation

condo, -ere, -didi, -ditus, 3, found, establish; store away, conceal

confero, -ferre, -tuli, -latus, *irr.*, bring together, contribute, grant, bestow; **confer**, converse; **se conferre**, betake oneself, flee

confessio, -onis, *f.*, confession

conficio, -ere, -feci, -fectus, 3, make, complete, accomplish

confido, -ere, -fisus, 3, *w. dat.* and *abl.*, trust, confide

confirmo, 1, strengthen

confiteor, -eri, -fessus, 2 *dep.*, confess, admit

confragosus, -a, -um, *adj.*, broken, rugged, rough

confugio, -ere, -fugi, 3, flee for refuge

confundo, -ere, -fudi, -fusus, 3, pour together, mix together, confuse

congero, -ere, -gessi, -gestus, 3, carry or bring together, collect, amass

congestus, -a, -um, *p. adj.* (*of* congero), brought together, collected, amassed

congregatio, -onis, *f.*, assembling together, sociability

congrego, 1, collect, join, unite

congruo, -ere, -ui, 3, harmonize

conicio, -ere, -ieci, -iectus [con-iacio], 3, throw

coniectus, -a, -um, *p. adj. (of* conicio), thrown

coniungo, -ere, -iunxi, -iunctus, 3, join together, unite

conloco, 1, place

conloquor, -i, -locutus, 3 *dep.*, converse with

conluctor, 1 *dep.*, struggle

conor, 1 *dep.*, try, attempt

conpello, -ere, -puli, -pulsus, 3, compel

conpesco, -ere, -pescui, 3, check, restrain

conpeto, -ere, -petivi, -petitus, 3, come together

conplico, -are, -avi (-ui), -atus (-itus), 1, fold up

conploro, 1, bewail, weep

conprendo, -ere, -prendi, -prensus, 3, comprise, fasten together

conprimo, -ere, -pressi, -pressus, 3, press together

conputatio, -onis, *f.*, reckoning, computation

conputo, 1, reckon, calculate, compute

conquiro, -ere, -quisivi, -quisitus, 3, seek for

conroboro (corroboro), 1, strengthen

conscendo, -ere, -scendi, -scensus [con-scando], 3, ascend, mount

conscientia, -ae, *f.*, a sharing of knowledge; knowledge in oneself; consciousness of right or wrong; conscience

consector, 1 *dep.*, follow, pursue

consenesco, -ere, -senui, 3, grow old

consequor, -i, -secutus, 3 *dep.*, attain

consero, -ere, -serui, -sertus, 3, connect, join together

conservus, -i, *m.*, fellow slave, servant

considero, 1, consider, reflect upon

consilium, -i, *n.*, plan, purpose, advice, counsel

consisto, -ere, -stiti, -status, 3, stand still, halt, stay in one place, stop, dwell

consolatio, -onis, *f.*, consolation

consolator, -oris, *m.*, consoler

consono, -are, -sonui, 1, sound together

consortium, -i, *n.*, fellowship

consors, -sortis, *adj.*, sharing in, partaking of

conspectus, -us, *m.*, sight, view

conspicio, -ere, -spexi, -spectus, 3, look at, notice

conspiro, 1, breathe together, unite, blend

constans, -antis, *p. adj. (of* consto), firm, constant

constituo, -ere, -stitui, -stitutus [con-statuo], 3, set up, establish, settle upon

consto, -are, -stiti, -status, 1, stand together, stand; stand firm, be consistent; stand at the price of, cost; **constat**, *impers.*, it is agreed

constringo, -ere, -strinxi, -strictus, 3, bind

consuetudo, -inis, *f.*, custom, habit

consul, -ulis, *m.*, consul

consularis, -e, *adj.*, consular

consultus, -i, *m.*, lawyer

consummatus, -a, -um, *p. adj. (of* consummo), complete, perfect, consummate

consummo, 1, add together, sum up; complete

consumo, -ere, -sumpsi, -sumptus, 3, consume, spend

consuo, -ere, -sui, -sutus, 3, sew

contemno, -ere, -tempsi, -temptus, 3, scorn

contemplatio, -onis, *f.*, contemplation

contemptus, -us, *m.*, scorn, contempt

contendo, -ere, -di, -tus, 3, hasten, contend; maintain, assert

contentus, -a, -um, *p. adj. (of* contineo), content, satisfied

contexo, -ere, -texui, -textus, 3, weave

conticesco, -ere, -ticui, 3, become silent

contineo, -ere, -tinui, -tentus, 2, hold together, hold in check, curb, subdue

contingo, -ere, -tigi, -tactus [con-tango], 3, touch; befall; fall to one's lot, attain

continuatio, -onis, *f.*, continuity

continuo, 1, continue

continuus, -a, -um, *adj.*, continuous

contio, -onis, *f.*, assembly, meeting, speech

contra, *prep. w. acc.*, against; *adv.*, on the contrary

contraho, -ere, -traxi, -tractus, 3, draw together, collect

contrarius, -a, -um, *adj.*, opposite, opposed, contrary

contrecto (contracto), 1, touch, handle

contristo, 1, sadden, depress

contubernalis, -is, *c.*, comrade, companion

contubernium, -i, *n.*, dwelling together, companionship, intimacy

contumaciter, *adv.*, obstinately

contumelia, -ae, *f.*, insult

contumeliosus, -a, -um, *adj.*, insulting, abusive

convalesco, -ere, -valui, 3, become strong

conveniens, -entis, *p. adj. (of* convenio), agreeing; fit for, suitable

convenio, -ire, -veni, -ventus, 4, come together, be fitting, be suitable; **convenit**, *impers.*, it is agreed upon

conversatio, -onis, *f.*, association, conversation

converso, 1, turn around; **converser**, 1 *dep.*, live with, associate with

converto, -ere, -verti, -versus, 3, turn round, direct towards

convicium, -i, *n.*, loud cry, shout, clamor

convictor, -oris, *m.*, one who lives with another, constant associate, companion

convictus, -us, *m.*, a living together, intimacy, social life

conviva, -ae, *c.*, guest

convivium, -i, *n.*, feast, banquet

Vocabulary C

convoluto, 1, whirl or roll round rapidly

copia, -ae, *f.*, supply, abundance; resources, troops, forces

copulo, 1, link

coquo, -ere, -xi, -ctus, 3, cook

cor, cordis, *n.*, heart

coram, *prep. w. abl.*, in the presence of

corona, -ae, *f.*, wreath, crown; crowd

corporalis, -e, *adj.*, relating to the body, corporeal

corpus, -oris, *n.*, body

corpusculum, -i, *n.*, tiny body, corpuscle, atom

corrigo, -ere, -rexi, -rectus [con-rego], 3, make straight, correct

corripio, -ere, -ripui, -reptus [con-rapio], 3, seize, catch

corrumpo, -ere, -rupi, -ruptus, 3, break, destroy, corrupt, entice

Coruncanius, -i, *m.*, T. Coruncanius, orator and consul (280 B.C.)

corruptus, -a, -um, *p. adj.* (*of* corrumpo), corrupted, bad

cortex, -icis, *m.*, bark, rind

cotidianus, -a, -um, *adj.*, daily

cotidie, *adv.*, daily

crassus, -a, -um, *adj.*, thick, dense

Crassus, -i, *m.*, L. Licinius Crassus, consul in 95 B.C.

crastinus, -a, -um, *adj.*, of the morrow, tomorrow's; *subst.*, crastinum, -i, *n.*, the morrow, tomorrow; in crastinum, for tomorrow

cratis, -is, *f.*, wicker-work, hurdle

creber, -bra, -brum, *adj.*, frequent

creditor, -oris, *m.*, creditor

credo, -ere, -didi, -ditus, 3, believe, trust

crepax, -acis, *adj.*, sounding, creaking

crepitus, -us, *m.*, noise

crepo, -are, crepui, crepitus, 1, creak

cresco, -ere, crevi, cretus, 3, grow

crispo, 1, curl, crisp

crocum, -i, *n.*, and crocus, -i, *m.*, saffron

Croesus, -i, *m.*, Croesus, the wealthy and renowned king of Lydia (560–546 B.C.,)

crudelis, -e, *adj.*, cruel

crudelitas, -atis, *f.*, cruelty

cruor, -oris, *m.*, blood

crus, cruris, *n.*, leg

crustularius, -i, *m.*, confectioner

cubiculum, -i, *n.*, bedroom

cubile, -is, *n.*, bed, couch

cubito, 1, lie down

culina, -ae, *f.*, kitchen

culmen, -inis, *n.*, height

culmus, -i, *m.*, straw

cultor, -oris, *m.*, cultivator

cultus, -us, *m.*, care, cultivation, culture; attire, appearance

cultus, -a, -um, *p. adj.* (*of* colo), cultivated, tilled, cultured

cum, *prep. w. abl.*, with

cum, *conj.*, when, since, although; cum maxime, to the greatest extent, however much; just now; cum primum, as soon as, as soon as possible

cumba, -ae, *f.*, boat

cunctus, -a, -um, *adj.*, whole, all, entire

cuneus, -i, *m.*, wedge

cupiditas, -atis, *f.*, eager desire, passionate longing, avarice

cupidus, -a, -um, *adj.*, desirous, eager; avaricious

cupio, -ere, -ivi (-ii), -itus, 3, desire

cur, *interrog. adv.*, why?

cura, -ae, *f.*, care, concern

curatio, -onis, *f.*, cure

curia, -ae, *f.*, senate, senate-house

Curio, -onis, *m.*, C. Scribonius Curio, consul in 76 B.C.

curiosus, -a, -um, *adj.*, full of care, anxious; curious

curo, 1, care for, pay attention to; cure, heal

curro, -ere, cucurri, cursus, 3, run

cursim, *adv.*, hastily, quickly

cursus, -us, *m.*, running, course

curvatura, -ae, *f.*, bending, curving

curvo, 1, bend, curve

custodia, -ae, *f.*, watching, guarding, custody; prisoner

custodio, -ire, -ivi, -itus, 4, guard, watch

custos, -odis, *c.*, guard, watch, protector

cutis, -is, *f.*, skin

D

Daedalus, -i, *m.*, Daedalus, the legendary Athenian inventor, father of Icarus, renowned for having created the Cretan labyrinth to incarcerate the monstrous Minotaur, half bull, half man

damno, 1, condemn

damnosus, -a, -um, *adj.*, harmful

damnum, -i, *n.*, loss

Dareus, -i, *m.*, Darius III, the last king of Persia, whose mother, Sisigambis, was taken prisoner by Alexander the Great

de, *prep. w. abl.*, from, down from; about, concerning

dea, -ae, *f.*, goddess

debello, 1, wage war, conquer, overcome

debeo, -ere, -ui, -itus, 2, owe, ought

debitum, -i, *n.*, debt

decedo, -ere, -cessi, -cessus, 3, go away, depart; depart from life, die

December, -bris, *m.*, December

decenter, *adv.*, properly

decerno, -ere, -crevi, -cretus, 3, decide, decree

Vocabulary C–D

decerpo, -ere, -cerpsi, -cerptus [de-carpo], 3, pluck off, cull

decet, -ere, decuit, *impers.*, 2, it fits, it becomes

decido, -ere, -cidi [de-cado], 3, fall down

decido, -ere, -cidi, -cisus [de-caedo], 3, cut down

decipio, -ere, -cepi, -ceptus [de-capio], 3, cheat, deceive

declaro, 1, make clear, demonstrate, disclose

declino, 1, avoid, decline

decoctus, -a, -um, *p. adj.* (*of* decoquo), cooked, boiled

decoquo, -ere, -xi, -ctus, 3, cook, boil

decor, -oris, *m.*, charm, grace, glory

decorus, -a, -um, *adj.*, decorous, adorned

decrepitus, -a, -um, *adj.*, very old, decrepit

decretus, -a, -um, *p. adj.* (*of* decerno), decreed

decumbo, -ere, -cubui, 3, fall down, fall sick

decuria, -ae, *f.*, class, division, group

decurro, -ere, -curri (-cucurri), -cursus, 3, run down, maneuver, charge, go through military exercises

decursus, -us, *m.*, running down, downward course; drainage

dedecet, -decere, -decuit, *impers.*, it is unbecoming

dedico, 1, dedicate, devote

dedo, -ere, -didi, -ditus, 3, give up, surrender

deduco, -ere, -duxi, -ductus, 3, lead, bring, lead down, drag

defendo, -ere, -di, -sus, 3, guard, protect, defend

defero, -ferre, -tuli, -latus, *irr.*, bring, bear, carry down; technically, bring to market to sell, sell

defetigo, 1, wear out

deficio, -ere, -feci, -fectus [de-facio], 3, fail, become less, disappear; revolt; passive voice, be wanting in, lack

deflecto, -ere, -flexi, -flexus, 3, bend downwards, turn aside; inflect, vary the form of [a word]

defluo, -ere, -fluxi, -fluxus, 3, flow down

defossus, -us, *m.*, cave, pit, dug-out

defunctus, -a, -um, *p. adj.* (*of* defungor), dead

defungor, -i, -functus, 3 *dep.*, finish, complete; depart, die

degener, -eris, *adj.*, degenerate, unworthy, base

degusto, 1, taste

deicio, -ere, -ieci, -iectus, 3, throw down, cast down

deiectus, -us, *m.*, fall

deinde, *adv.*, then

delabor, -i, -lapsus, 3 *dep.*, fall down

delecto, 1, delight

delegatio, -onis, *f.*, substitution, delegation of one person by another

delego, 1, transfer, entrust, assign

delenio, -ire, -ivi, -itus, 4, charm, cajole

deleo, -ere, -levi, -letus, 2, destroy

delibero, 1, weigh carefully, consider

delicatus, -a, -um, *adj.*, soft, delicate, luxurious, effeminate

deliciae, -arum, *f. pl.*, pleasure, luxury, delight, fastidiousness, fussiness

deliciolum, -i, *n.*, little darling or sweetheart

delicium, -i, *n.*, little darling, sweetheart

deliro, 1, be crazy, be mad

demens, -mentis, *adj.*, mad, insane

dementia, -ae, *f.*, madness

demergo, -ere, -mersi, -mersus, 3, sink

Demetrius, -i, *m.*, Demetrius of Sunium, renowned Cynic philosopher who taught in Rome during Caligula's reign

deminutio, -onis, *f.*, lessening, diminution

demissus, -a, -um, *p. adj.* (*of* demitto), sent down

demitto, -ere, -misi, -missus, 3, send down, bring down

demo, -ere, dempsi, demptus, 3, take away, remove

Democritus, -i, *m.*, Democritus (c. 460 – c. 360 B.C.), atomic philosopher, to whom Epicurus was indebted

demonstro, 1, show, demonstrate, point out

demum, *adv.*, at length, at last

denarius, -i, *m.*, Roman coin

denique, *adv.*, finally

dens, dentis, *m.*, tooth

densitas, -atis, *f.*, thickness, density

densus, -a, -um, *adj.*, thick, close, dense

deorsum, *adv.*, downwards; sursum deorsum, up and down, topsy-turvy

depello, -ere, -puli, -pulsus, 3, drive out

dependeo, -ere, 2, hang from, hang down

depono, -ere, -posui, -positus, 3, put down, lay aside

depravo, 1, pervert, distort; corrupt, deprave

deprecator, -oris, *m.*, one who begs off, an intercessor

deprehendo (deprendo), -ere, -prehendi (-prendi), -prehensus (-prensus), 3, catch off guard, catch, seize, detect, discover

deprehensus, -a, -um, *p. adj.* (*of* deprehendo), caught off guard, caught, seized

deprensus, *see* deprehensus

deprimo, -ere, -pressi, -pressus, 3, press down, depress

derideo, -ere, -risi, -risus, 2, laugh at, mock, deride

derigo (dirigo), -ere, -rexi, -rectus [dis-rego], 3, set straight out, set straight; arrange, direct

derisor, -oris, *m.*, mocker

descendo, -ere, -scendi, -scensus, 3, go down, descend

descisco, -ere, -scivi (-ii), -scitus, 3, free one's self from, revolt from, deviate from

Vocabulary D

describo, -ere, -scripsi, -scriptus, 3, describe
deservio, -ire, -ivi, -itus, 4, serve, be a slave to
desiderium, -i, *n.*, desire, longing, loss
desidero, 1, desire, long for, require
desidia, -ae, *f.*, sloth
desido, -ere, -sedi, 3, settle down
designatus, -a, -um, *p. adj.* (*of* designo), marked out
designo, 1, mark out, designate
desino, -ere, -sivi (-sii), -situs, 3, cease, stop, desist
desisto, -ere, -stiti, -stitus, 3, cease, desist
despero, 1, be without hope, despair of, give up
despoliatus, -a, -um, *p. adj.* (*of* despolio), plundered, despoiled
despolio, 1, plunder, despoil, strip
destino, 1, choose, appoint
desudo, 1, perspire
desuesco, -ere, -suevi, -suetus, 3, become unaccustomed to
desuetus, -a, -um, *p. adj.* (*of* desuesco), unaccustomed
desum, -esse, -fui, -futurus, *irr.*, fail, be lacking
desumo, -ere, -sumpsi, 3, take for one's self, choose
detego, -ere, -texi, -tectus, 3, uncover, disclose
detergeo, -ere, -tersi, -tersus, 2, wipe up
deterior, -ius, *comp. adj.*, worse, inferior
deterreo, -ere, -terrui, -territus, 2, frighten, deter
detestabilis, -e, *adj.*, detestable
detineo, -ere, -tinui, -tentus [de-teneo], 2, hold back, detain, delay
detraho, -ere, -traxi, -tractus, 3, draw off or from, take away
detrimentum, -i, *n.*, detriment, injury
deus, -i, *m.*, *nom. pl.*, dei, dii, di, god, deity
deversorium, -i, *n.*, resort
deverto, -ere, -verti, -versus, 3, turn aside
devexum, -i, *n.*, slope
devexus, -a, -um, *adj.*, moving downward, sweeping down
devito, 1, avoid
devoro, 1, swallow, devour
dexter, -tra, -trum, *adj.*, right; dextra, -ae, *f.*, right hand
di, *see* deus
dico, -ere, dixi, dictus, 3, say, tell
dicto, 1, dictate
dictum, -i, *n.*, word, saying
dies, -ei, *m.* and *f.*, day, daylight; time
differo, differre, distuli, dilatus [dis-fero], *irr.*, bear apart, scatter; put off, postpone, delay
difficilis, -e, *adj.*, difficult
difficultas, -atis, *f.*, difficulty
difficulter, *adv.*, with difficulty

diffluo, -ere, -fluxi, -fluxus, 3, flow in different directions, be loose
diffundo, -ere, -fudi, -fusus, 3, spread
digero, -ere, -gessi, -gestus, 3, distribute
dignatio, -onis, *f.*, dignity, reputation
dignitas, -atis, *f.*, worth, worthiness; rank, position, honor, dignity
dignus, -a, -um, *adj.*, worthy
dilabor, -i, -lapsus, 3 *dep.*, glide apart, fall down
dilatio, -onis, *f.*, delaying
dilato, 1, spread out, extend
diligens, -entis, *adj.*, careful, diligent
diligenter, *adv.*, carefully, diligently
diligentia, -ae, *f.*, diligence
diligo, -ere, -lexi, -lectus [dis-lego, choose out], 3, love, esteem
diluo, -ere, -lui, -lutus, 3, dilute
dimidium, -i, *n.*, half
dimitto, -ere, -misi, -missus, 3, send away, dismiss
dinumero, 1, count up, enumerate
Diogenes, -is, *m.*, Diogenes, famous philosopher of the Cynic School (c. 400 – c. 325 B.C.)
dipondium, -i, *n.*, the sum of two asses
diripio, -ere, -ripui, -reptus, 3, plunder
dirus, -a, -um, *adj.*, awful
discedo, -ere, -cessi, -cessus, 3, go apart, go away, withdraw, depart
discerno, -ere, -crevi, -cretus, 3, separate, set apart, distinguish, discern
discerpo, -ere, -cerpsi, -cerptus, 3, tear to pieces
discinctus, -a, -um, *p. adj.* (*of* discingo), ungirt, loose, dissolute
discingo, -ere, -cinxi, -cinctus, 3, ungird
disciplina, -ae, *f.*, discipline
discipulus, -i, *m.*, pupil, disciple
disco, -ere, didici, 3, learn, take lessons in
discordo, 1, be at discord, disagree
discrimen, -inis, *n.*, difference
discumbo, -ere, -cubui, -cubitus, 3, recline
discurro, -ere, -cucurri (-curri), -cursus, 3, run apart, run hither and thither
discutio, -ere, -cussi, -cussus, 3, shake off, dash to pieces
disertus, -a, -um, *p. adj.* (*of* dissero), eloquent, well-expressed
dispicio, -ere, -spexi, -spectus, 3, see through
displiceo, -ere, -plicui, -plicitus [dis-placeo], 2, displease
dispono, -ere, -posui, -positus, 3, arrange
dispositio, -onis, *f.*, arrangement
dispositus, -a, -um, *p. adj.* (*of* dispono), arranged
disputatio, -onis, *f.*, argument, debate
disputo, 1, discuss, debate, argue
dissentio, -ire, -sensi, -sensus, 4, disagree
dissero, -ere, -serui, -sertus, 3, treat of, discuss a subject

Vocabulary D

dissicio, -ere, -ieci, -iectus, 3, throw aside
dissideo, -ere, -sedi, -sessus [dis-sedeo], 2, sit apart, be at variance, be different
dissilio, -ire, -silui, -sultus [dis-salio], 4, leap apart
dissimilis, -e, *adj.*, unlike
dissimilitudo, -inis, *f.*, lack of similarity
dissimulo, 1, conceal, hide, keep secret
dissocio, 1, separate from fellowship, disunite
dissolutio, -onis, *f.*, breaking up, dissolution, destruction; want of energy, lethargy
dissonus, -a, -um, *adj.*, dissonant, discordant
dissuadeo, -ere, -suasi, -suasus, 2, advise against, dissuade
distendo, -ere, -tendi, -tentus, 3, stretch apart, expand; fill full, distend
distentus, -a, -um, *p. adj. (of* **distendo**), distended, full
distinctus, -a, -um, *p. adj. (of* **distinguo**), separated, distinct
distinguo, -ere, -stinxi, -stinctus, 3, separate, distinguish
disto, -are, -stiti, 1, stand apart, differ
distorqueo, -ere, -torsi, -tortus, 2, twist apart, distort
distortus, -a, -um, *p. adj. (of* **distorqueo**), distorted, disformed
distraho, -ere, -traxi, -tractus, 3, tear asunder, distract
districtus, -a, -um, *p. adj. (of* **distringo**), distracted, occupied
distringo, -ere, -trinxi, -trictus, 3, draw apart, distract
disturbo, 1, throw into confusion, disturb
diu, *adv.*, long, a long time
diurnus, -a, -um, *adj.*, daily; **diurnum, -i,** *n.*, daily allowance
diutinus, -a, -um, *adj.*, lasting a long time, long
diutius, diutissime, *comp.* and *superl.* of **diu**
divello, -ere, -velli, -vulsus, 3, tear asunder
diversus, -a, -um, *adj.*, various, different, diverse
dives, -itis, *adj.*, rich, wealthy
divido, -ere, -visi, -visus, 3, divide
divinus, -a, -um, *adj.*, divine
divitiae, -arum, *f. pl.*, wealth
do, dare, dedi, datus, 1, give
doceo, -ere, docui, doctus, 2, teach
doleo, -ere, dolui, doliturus, 2, suffer pain, grieve, sorrow
dolium, -i, *n.*, large earthenware jar or wooden cask, tub
dolor, -oris, *m.*, pain, sorrow, grief
domesticus, -a, -um, *adj.*, domestic, private
domicilium, -i, *n.*, dwelling, home
domina, -ae, *f.*, mistress, ruler
dominicus, -a, -um, *adj.*, of or belonging to a master

dominor, 1 *dep.*, rule, be master
dominium, -i, *n.*, rule, power
dominus, -i, *m.*, master
domus, -us, or **-i,** *f.*, house, home
donec, *conj.*, until; as long as, while
dono, 1, grant, bestow
dormio, -ire, -ivi (-ii), -itus, 4, sleep
dos, dotis, *f.*, dowry, gift
Drusus, -i, *m.*, Drusus Caesar, great-grandson of Atticus, Cicero's intimate friend
dubius, -a, -um, *adj.*, doubting, doubtful, dubious; **sine dubio,** without doubt
dubito, 1, doubt, hesitate
duco, -ere, duxi, ductus, 3, lead, draw out, extend, build
ductus, -us, *m.*, drawing, carving
ductus, -a, -um, *p. adj. (of* **duco**), led, drawn out
dudum, *adv.*, a little while ago, lately, recently
dulcedo, -inis, *f.*, sweetness, pleasantness, charm
dulcis, -e, *adj.*, sweet, pleasant
dum, *conj.*, while, so long as, until
dummodo, *conj.*, provided that
dumtaxat, *adv.*, only
duo, -ae, -o, *num. adj.*, two
duplex, -icis, *adj.*, double
duritia, -ae, *f.*, harshness, hardness
duro, 1, make hard, become hard, last, remain
durus, -a, -um, *adj.*, hard
dux, ducis, *c.*, leader

E

e, *prep. w. abl., see* **ex**
ebrietas, -atis, *f.*, drunkenness
ebrius, -a, -um, *adj.*, drunk, intoxicated
ebur, -oris, *n.*, irovy
ecce, *interj.*, lo!, behold!
ecquis, -qua, -quid, *indef. interrog. pron.*, (whether) any? anyone? anything?
edax, -acis, *adj.*, greedy
edisco, -ere, -didici, 3, learn thoroughly
editus, -a, -um, *p. adj. (of* **edo**), high, lofty
edo, -ere, edi, esus, 3, eat
edo, -ere, -didi, -ditus, 3, give out, bring forth
edoceo, -ere, -cui, -ctus, 2, teach, instruct
edoctus, -a, -um, *p. adj. (of* **edoceo**), taught, instructed
educo, 1, bring up, rear, educate
educo, -ere, -duxi, -ductus, 3, lead out
effectus, -us, *m.*, effect
effeminatus, -a, -um, *p. adj. (of* **effemino**), effeminate
effemino, 1, make effeminate, enervate
effero, efferre, extuli, elatus [ex-fero], *irr.*, bring forth or out, carry out, bury
effetus, -a, -um, *adj.*, weakened, effete, worn out

efficax, -acis, *adj.,* effective, efficient, efficacious

efficio, -ere, -feci, -fectus, 3, bring about, effect, make, accomplish

effingo, -ere, -finxi, -fictus, 3, fashion, mould

effluo, -ere, -fluxi, -fluxus [ex-fluo], 3, flow out, vanish, disappear

effugio, -ere, -fugi, -fugitus, 3, flee, escape

effundo, -ere, -fudi, -fusus [ex-fundo], 3, pour out

effusus, -a, -um, *p. adj.* (*of* **effundo**), poured out, immoderate, unrestrained

egeo, -ere, egui, 2, be in need of

egero, -ere, -gessi, -gestus, 3, carry or bring out, vomit

ego, mei, *gen.,* **mihi,** *dat.,* **me,** *acc.* and *abl., pers. pron.,* I

egredior, -i, -gressus [ex-gradior], 3 *dep.,* go beyond

egregie, *adv.,* excellently, admirably

egregius, -a, -um, *adj.,* excellent, distinguished

egressus, -a, -um, *p. adj.* (*of* **egredior**), having gone beyond

eicio, -ere, eieci, eiectus [ex-iacio], 3, throw out, eject

eiusmodi (**is** and **modus**), of this kind, such

elabor, -i, elapsus, 3 *dep.,* slip away

elaboro, 1, work out, elaborate

elanguesco, -ere, -gui, 3, grow faint, feeble

elapsus, -a, -um, *p. adj.* (*of* **elabor**), having slipped forth

elatus, -a, -um, *p. adj.* (*of* **effero**), brought forth, carried out, buried; exalted, elevated

elegantia, -ae, *f.,* elegance

elephantus, -i, *c.,* elephant

elevo, 1, lift up, raise

elido, -ere, -lisi, -lisus, 3, shatter, crush

eligo, -ere, -legi, -lectus, 3, choose, select

eloquentia, -ae, *f.,* eloquence

eludo, -ere, -lusi, -lusus, 3, delude, deceive

emarcesco, -ere, emarcui, 3, wither away

emendatio, -onis, *f.,* improvement, emendation

emendo, 1, improve

emergo, -ere, -mersi, -mersus, 3, rise, emerge

emineo, -ere, -ui, 2, stand out

emitto, -ere, -misi, -missus, 3, send forth, send out

emo, -ere, emi, emptus, 3, buy

emollio, -ire, -ivi, -itus, 4, soften

emptor, -oris, *m.,* buyer

en, *interj.,* lo! behold!

enervatus, -a, -um, *p. adj.* (*of* **enervo**), weakened, enervated

enervo, 1, weaken, enervate

enim, *conj.,* for

enuntio, 1, tell, divulge, disclose

eo, ire, ii (ivi), itus, 4, go

eo, *adv.,* thither, to that place; so far, to such a pitch; on that account, therefore, for that reason; **eo magis. . .quo magis,** the more. . .the more

Epicureus, -a, -um, *adj.,* Epicurean

Epicurus, -i, *m.,* Epicurus, 341–270 B.C., founder of the Epicurean School

epistula, -ae, *f.,* letter, epistle

epulum, -i, *n.,* public banquet

eques, -itis, *c.,* horseman, rider, knight

equus, -i, *m.,* horse

erado, -ere, -rasi, -rasus, 3, scratch out, eradicate

erectus, -a, -um, *p. adj.* (*of* **erigo**), lifted up, upright, erect, aroused

erepo, -ere, -repsi, 3, creep

ergo, *adv.,* therefore, then

erigo, -ere, -rexi, -rectus [ex-rego], 3, place upright, lift up, erect, arouse

eripio, -ere, -ripui, -reptus [ex-rapio], 3, snatch away, steal

erro, 1, make a mistake, wander, err

error, -oris, *m.,* error

erubesco, -ere, erubui, 3, redden, blush

erudio, -ire, -ivi (-ii), -itus, 4, educate, instruct, teach

eruditio, -onis, *f.,* learning, erudition

eruditus, -a, -um, *p. adj.* (*of* **erudio**), learned, erudite, skilled

erumpo, -ere, -rupi, -ruptus, 3, break out

eruo, -ere, -ui, -utus, 3, bring forth, dig out

eruptio, -onis, *f.,* bursting or breaking forth, eruption

esseda, -ae, *f.,* chariot, carriage

esurio, -ire, -ivi, -itus, 4, be hungry, long for

et, *conj.,* and, also, even; **et. . .et,** both. . .and

etiam, *conj.,* also, even, still, yet; **etiamnunc,** moreover

euripus, -i, *m.,* canal

evado, -ere, -vasi, -vasus, 3, go out, go forth

evello, -ere, -velli, -vulsus, 3, tear out

evenio, -ire, -veni, -ventus, 4, come out, turn out, happen

evito, 1, avoid

evoco, 1, call forth

evolvo, -ere, -volvi, -volutus, 3, roll out

evomo, -ere, -ui, -itus, 3, vomit forth

evulsus, -a, -um, *p. adj.* (*of* **evello**), torn out

ex or **e,** *prep. w. abl.,* out of, from

exagitatus, -a, -um, *adj.,* stirred up, agitated

exanimo, 1, deprive of life, terrify greatly

exardesco, -ere, -arsi, -arsus, 3, burn, kindle, break out

exaudio, -ire, -ivi, -itus, 4, hear plainly

excandesco, -ere, -candui, 3, grow hot

excavatus, -a, -um, *p. adj.* (*of* **excavo**), hollowed out

excavo, 1, hollow out

Vocabulary E

excellens, -entis, *p. adj.* (*of* **excello**), high, lofty, excellent
excello, -ere, -cellui, -celsus, 3, excel, be distinguished
excelsus, -a, -um, *p. adj.* (*of* **excello**), lofty, elevated
exceptio, -onis, *f.*, exception, restriction
exceptus, -a, -um, *p. adj.* (*of* **excipio**), received
excerpo, -ere, -cerpsi, -cerptus [ex-carpo], 3, pick out, choose, withdraw, separate
excido, -ere, -cidi [ex-cado], 3, fall out, root out, slip out unawares, escape; stumble
excido, -ere, -cidi, -cisus [ex-caedo], 3, cut or root out
excipio, -ere, -cepi, -ceptus [ex-capio], 3, take out, except; receive, welcome, continue; take hold of, capture
excitatus, -a, -um, *p. adj.* (*of* **excito**), aroused, excited
excito, 1, arouse, stir up, excite; erect
exclamatio, -onis, *f.*, exclamation
exclamo, 1, shout, cry aloud
excludo, -ere, -clusi, -clusus [ex-claudo], 3, shut out, exclude
exclusus, -a, -um, *p. adj.* (*of* **excludo**), shut out, excluded
excogito, 1, scheme, devise
excurro, -ere, -cucurri (-curri), -cursus, 3, run out
excutio, -ere, -cussi, -cussus, 3, shake out, cut off
execratio, -onis, *f.*, curse, execration
exedo, -ere, -edi, -esus, 3, eat up, consume
exemplar, -aris, *n.*, copy, model, exemplar
exemplum, -i, *n.*, example
exeo, -ire, -ivi (-ii), -itus, *irr.*, go out
exerceo, -ere, -ui, -itus, 2, exercise, train, practice
exercitatio, -onis, *f.*, exercise, training
exercitatus, -a, -um, *p. adj.* (*of* **exercito**), practiced, exercised
exercito, 1, exercise diligently, practice
exercitus, -us, *m.*, army
exero (exsero), -ere, -erui, -ertus, 3, thrust out
exesus, -a, -um, *p. adj.* (*of* **exedo**), eaten up
exhaurio, -ire, -hausi, -haustus, 4, drain out, exhaust
exhibeo, -ere, -hibui, -hibitus, 2, exhibit, display
exhortatio, -onis, *f.*, exhortation, encouragement
exhortor, 1 *dep.*, encourage, exhort
exigo, -ere, -egi, -actus [ex-ago], 3, spend, pass; demand, measure, weigh, deliberate, consult
exiguus, -a, -um, *adj.*, small
eximius, -a, -um, *adj.*, extraordinary
eximo, -ere, -emi, -emptus, 3, take away, take out, remove
existimo, 1, think
exitus, -us, *m.*, going out, exit; outcome, result, end

exolesco, -ere, -olevi, -oletus, 3, grow up, grow out of use or out of date, become obsolete
exoletus, -a, -um, *p. adj.* (*of* **exolesco**), grown out of use, obsolete
exonero, 1, unload
exoro, 1, beg, implore
expavesco, -ere, -pavi, 3, fear, dread
expectatio, -onis, *f.*, waiting for, expectation
expectatus, -a, -um, *p. adj.* (*of* **expecto**), awaited, expected, longed for; **ante expectatum,** unexpectedly
expecto, 1, wait for, await, expect
expedio, -ire, -ivi (-ii), -itus, 4, set free, liberate
expeditio, -onis, *f.*, expedition
expeditus, -a, -um, *p. adj.* (*of* **expedio**), unimpeded, free, easy
expello, -ere, -puli, -pulsus, 3, drive out, expel
expergiscor, -i, -perrectus, 3 *dep.*, awake, rouse one's self
experimentum, -i, *n.*, experiment
experior, -iri, expertus, 4 *dep.*, try, test, find
explanatio, -onis, *f.*, explanation
explicatio, -onis, *f.*, unfolding, expounding, exposition
explico, -are, -plicavi (-plicui), -plicatus (-plicitus), 1, unfold
explorator, -oris, *m.*, explorer
expono, -ere, -posui, -positus, 3, put out, expose
expositus, -a, -um, *p. adj.* (*of* **expono**), exposed
exprimo, -ere, -pressi, -pressus, 3, press out, express, model, portray
expugno, 1, take by storm, conquer
exsecutio, -onis, *f.*, execution; discussion, following out
exspiro, 1, breathe out, expire
exstimulo, 1, excite, stimulate
exsto, 1, stand out
exstruo, -ere, -struxi, -structus, 3, build, construct
exsurgo, -ere, -surrexi, 3, rise up
extendo, -ere, -di, -tus, 3, stretch out, extend
extenuo, 1, make thin, reduce
exter and exterus, -a, -um, *adj.*, outward, foreign, strange
externus, -a, -um, *adj.*, external, foreign
extinguo, -ere, -tinxi, -tinctus, 3, put out, extinguish
extollo, -ere, extuli, and rarely exsustuli, 3, lift up, raise up
extorqueo, -ere, -torsi, -tortus, 2, twist out, wrest
extra, *prep. w. acc.*, outside of
extraho, -ere, -traxi, -tractus, 3, draw out, drag out
extraordinarius, -a, -um, *adj.*, extraordinary
extremum, -i, *n.*, end

Vocabulary E

extremus, -a, -um, *adj., superl.* (*of* exter and exterus), outermost, extreme, last

extrinsecus, *adv.*, from without, outside, external

exturbo, 1, thrust out, drive away

exulo, 1, live in exile

exulto, 1, rejoice

exuo, -ere, -ui, -utus, 3, strip off, shake off, get rid off

F

faber, fabri, *m.*, carpenter, metal-worker, engineer

Fabianus, -i, *m.*, Fabianus, of the Sextian School of philosophy, one of Seneca's teachers

fabrica, -ae, *f.*, art or trade of an artisan

fabrico, 1, fashion, form

fabrilis, -e, *adj.*, belonging to an artificer, mechanical

fabula, -ae, *f.*, story

facies, -ei, *f.*, face

facilis, -e, *adj.*, easy

facilitas, -atis, *f.*, easiness, ease

facio, -ere, feci, factus, 3, make, do

factio, -onis, *f.*, faction

factum, -i *n.*, deed, act

facultas, -atis, *f.*, power, ability

fecunde, *adv.*, eloquently

faeneror (feneror), 1 *dep.*, lend on interest

faex, faecis, *f.*, dregs

fallo, -ere, fefelli, falsus, 3, deceive, beguile

falsus, -a, -um, *p. adj.* (*of* fallo), feigned, false

fama, -ae, *f.*, fame, reputation

fames, -is, *f.*, hunger

familia, -ae, *f.*, household of slaves, household, the entire household or family

familiaris, -e, *adj.*, familiar, intimate

familiaritas, -atis, *f.*, intimacy, familiarity

familiariter, *adv.*, intimately, familiarly

fano, 1, dedicate, consecrate

farina, -ae, *f.*, meal, flour

fas, *indecl., n.*, divine law and right; fas est, it is right, it is lawful

fascia, -ae, *f.*, band, bandage, diadem

fastidio, -ire, -ivi, -itus, 4, dislike, loath; cause nausea; scorn, despise; fastidiens, -entis, *p. adj.*, squeamish

fastidiose, *adv.*, fastidiously

fastidiosus, -a, -um, *p. adj.*, fastidious

fastidium, -i, *n.*, loathing, disdain

fastigium, -i, *n.*, height, summit, high position; roof

fateor, -eri, fassus, 2 *dep.*, confess, admit

fatigo, 1, tire out, weary

fatum, -i, *n.*, fate

fatuus, -a, -um, *adj.*, foolish, fatuous; fatuus, -i, *m.*, fool

fauces, -ium, *f.*, throat

faveo, -ere, favi, fautus, 2, favor

favor, -oris, *m.*, favor, goodwill, partiality

favus, -i, *m.*, honeycomb

febris, -is, *f.*, fever

Felicio, -onis, *m.*, Felicio, Seneca's pet slave, son of the steward Philositus mentioned in Ep. 12.3

felicitas, -atis, *f.*, happiness, felicity, good fortune, prosperity

feliciter, *adv.*, happily

felix, -icis, *adj.*, happy

femina, -ae, *f.*, woman

fenero (faenero), 1, lend on interest

fenus, -oris, *n.*, interest

fera, -ae, *f.*, wild beast

fere, *adv.*, almost, nearly, for the most part, usually

fericulum, -i, *n.*, tray, course

fermentum, -i, *n.*, fermentation

fero, ferre, tuli, latus, *irr.*, carry, bear, endure, tolerate

ferox, -ocis, *adj.*, bold, courageous, high-spirited

ferramentum, -i, *n.*, tool

ferreus, -a, -um, *adj.*, made of iron

ferrum, -i, *n.*, iron; sword

fertilis, -e, *adj.*, fruitful, fertile

fertilitas, -atis, *f.*, fruitfulness, fertility

fervens, -entis, *p. adj.* (*of* ferveo), glowing, hot

ferveo, -ere, ferbui, 2, be hot, seethe, boil

fervor, -oris, *m.*, heat

festino, 1, hasten, hurry

festum, -i, *n.*, holiday, festival, feast

festus, -a, -um, *adj.*, festive

fetus, -us, *m.*, bearing, breeding, offspring

fictile, -is, *n.*, earthenware

fictus, -a, -um, *p. adj.* (*of* fingo), feigned

fidelis, -e, *adj.*, faithful, loyal, genuine, lasting

fideliter, *adv.*, faithfully, honestly

fidens, -entis, *p. adj.* (*of* fido), confident

fides, -ei, *f.*, trust, confidence; promise; bona fide, genuinely, truly

fido, -ere, fisus, 3 *semi-dep.*, trust, confide

fiducia, -ae, *f.*, confidence, trust

figo, -ere, fixi, fixus, 3, fix, fasten

figulus, -i, *m.*, potter

figuro, 1, shape, fashion

filius, -i, *m.*, son

filum, -i, *n.*, thread

fingo, -ere, finxi, fictus, 3, fashion, form, mould

finio, -ire, -ivi (-ii), -itus, 4, limit, bound

finis, -is, *m.* and *f.*, boundary, limit, end

fio, fieri, factus sum, *pass.* of facio, be made of, be done, become, happen

firmitas, -atis, *f.*, firmness

firmo, 1, make firm, strengthen

firmus, -a, -um, *adj.*, firm, strong

fissilis, -e, *adj.*, that may be split

fistula, -ae, *f.*, pipe
Flaccus, -i, *m.*, Flaccus, friend of Lucilius
flecto, -ere, flexi, flexus, 3, bend, twist
fleo, -ere, flevi, fletus, 2, weep, lament
fletus, -us, *m.*, weeping
flexibilis, -e, *adj.*, that can be bent, flexible
flexus, -a, -um, *p. adj.* (*of* flecto), bent, twisted
flexus, -us, *m.*, turning
florens, -entis, *p. adj.* (*of* floreo), blooming, fresh
floreo, -ere, florui, 2, bloom, flower
floridus, -a, -um, *adj.*, flowery
flos, floris, *m.*, flower
fluctuo, 1, move up and down, fluctuate, vacillate
fluctus, -us, *m.*, wave
fluidus, -a, -um, *adj.*, flowing, fluid, moist, loose
flumen, -inis, *n.*, river, stream
fluo, -ere, fluxi, fluxus, 3, flow
fluvidus, -a, -um, *adj.*, moist
fluvito, 1, flow
fluxus, -a, -um, *p. adj.* (*of* fluo), flowing, loose, slack
focus, -i, *m.*, fireplace, hearth
fodio, -ere, fodi, fossus, 3, dig
folium, -i, *n.*, leaf
fomentum, -i, *n.*, warm application, warm baths; pampering
fons, fontis, *m.*, fountain
foras, *adv.*, out of doors, out
forceps, -cipis, *m.* and *f.*, tongs
forensis, -e, *adj.*, relating to the market or forum
foris, *adv.*, out of doors, outside, without
forma, -ae, *f.*, form, shape
formido, 1, fear
formo, 1, form, shape, fashion
formonsus, -a, -um (formosus, -a, -um), *adj.*, beautiful, handsome
formula, -ae, *f.*, rule
fornix, -icis, *m.*, arch, vault
forsitan, *adv.*, perhaps
fortasse, *adv.*, perhaps
forte, *adv.*, by chance
fortitudo, -inis, *f.*, bravery, fortitude
fortis, -e, *adj.*, brave, strong
fortuitus, -a, -um, *adj.*, accidental, fortuitous
fortuna, -ae, *f.*, fortune, fate, chance
fortunatus, -a, -um, *adj.*, fortunate
forum, -i, *n.*, forum, market place
foveo, -ere, fovi, fotus, 2, nurse, nourish, fondle
fractus, -a, -um, *p. adj.* (of frango), broken down
fragilitas, -atis, *f.*, frailty, weakness
fragor, -oris, *m.*, noise, din
frango, -ere, fregi, fractus, 3, break
fraudo, 1, cheat, defraud
fraus, fraudis, *f.*, deceit, deception
fremitus, -us, *m.*, loud noise
fremo, -ere, fremui, fremitus, 3, roar

freneticus, -a, -um, *adj.*, frantic
frenum, -i, *n.*, (*pl.* = freni, *m.* or frena, *n.*), bit, bridle
frequens, -entis, *adj.*, crowded, filled, frequent
frequenter, *adv.*, frequently
frequento, 1, visit frequently, frequent, repeat often
frigidus, -a, -um, *adj.*, cold, frigid
frigus, -oris, *n.*, cold
frons, frondis, *f.*, leaf
frons, frontis, *f.*, forehead, brow; outward appearance
fructuosus, -a, -um, *adj.*, profitable
fructus, -us, *m.*, fruit; profit, yield
frugalitas, -atis, *f.*, frugality, economy
frugi, *indecl. adj.*, temperate
fruor, frui, fructus, 3 *dep.*, enjoy
frustra, *adv.*, in vain
frustrum, -i, *n.*, bit, piece
frux, frugis, and more frequently in *pl.* fruges, -um, *f.*, fruit, produce, grain
fuga, -ae, *f.*, flight
fugax, -acis, *adj.*, fleeting, swift
fugio, -ere, fugi, fugitus, 3, flee, run away
fugitivus, -i, *m.*, fugitive, fugitive slave
fugo, 1, put to flight
fulcio, -ire, fulsi, fultus, 4, prop up, support
fulgeo, -ere, fulsi, 2, shine, gleam
fulgor, -oris, *m.*, glitter, gleam
fullonius, -a, -um, *adj.*, of or belonging to a fuller or laundryman
fumosus, -a, -um, *adj.*, smokey, full of smoke
fundamentum, -i, *n.*, foundation
fundo, 1, found, lay the foundation of
fundo, -ere, fudi, fusus, 3, pour, pour out, spread
fundus, -i, *m.*, bottom, foundation
fungor, -i, functus, 3 *dep.*, perform
fur, furis, *c.*, thief
furca, -ae, *f.*, fork-shaped poles
furiosus, -a, -um, *adj.*, mad, furious
furnus, -i, *m.*, oven
furo, -ere, -ui, 3, be mad, furious
furor, -oris, *m.*, madness
futurus, -a, -um, *fut. p.* of sum

G

galea, -ae, *f.*, helmet
gaudeo, -ere, gavisus, 2 *semi-dep.*, rejoice
gaudium, -i, *n.*, joy
gausapatus, -a, -um, *adj.*, clad in a cloak
gemitus, -us, *m.*, groan, grunt
gemo, -ere, gemui, gemitus, 3, groan
gener, -eri, *m.*, son-in-law
genero, 1, beget, produce

Vocabulary F G

generosus, -a, -um, *adj.*, noble, magnanimous

genitus, -a, -um, *p. adj.* (*of* gigno), born, begotten

genius, -i, *m.*, guardian spirit

gens, -tis, *f.*, people, tribe, nation

genu, -us, *n.*, knee

genus, -eris, *n.*, race, family, birth; tribe, species; kind, sort

gero, -ere, gessi, gestus, 3, bear, carry on, wage

gestatio, -onis, *f.*, riding

gigno, -ere, genui, genitus, 3, beget, bring forth, bear

glaber, -bra, -brum, *adj.*, without hair, beardless

gladius, -i, *m.*, sword

glomero, 1, gather together

gloria, -ae, *f.*, glory, fame, renown

glorior, 1 *dep.*, boast

grabbatus, -i, *m.*, pallet, small couch

Gracchus, -i, *m.*, Gaius Sempronius Gracchus, tribune in 123 B.C.

gracilis, -e, *adj.*, thin, slender

gradior, -i, gressus, 3 *dep.*, step, walk

gradus, -us, *m.*, step, step towards something, rank

Graecia, -ae, *f.*, Greece

Graecus, -a, -um, *adj.*, Greek

grammaticus, -a, -um, *adj.*, grammatical; *subst.*, grammaticus, -i, *m.*, grammarian

granum, -i, *n.*, grain

gratia, -ae, *f.*, gratitude, thankfulness; favor, grace

gratis, *adv.*, free of charge

gratuitus, -a, -um, *adj.*, gratuitous, free

gratulatio, -onis, *f.*, congratulation

gratus, -a, -um, *adj.*, pleasing, agreeable; grateful, thankful

gravis, -e, *adj.*, heavy, serious

gravitas, -atis, *f.*, weight, heaviness

gravo, 1, burden, trouble

grex, gregis, *m.*, herd, flock, litter

gubernaculum, -i, *n.*, rudder

gubernator, -oris, *m.*, helmsman, steersman, pilot

gula, -ae, *f.*, gullet, palate, appetite

gustus, -us, *m.*, taste

H

habeo, -ere, -ui, -itus, 2, have, hold, possess

habito, 1, dwell, inhabit

habitus, -us, *m.*, appearance, condition, disposition, demeanor

hac, *adv.*, (*abl.* of hic, supply parte or via), here, this way

hactenus, *adv.*, up to this point

haereo, -ere, haesi, haesus, 2, cling

haesitatio, -onis, *f.*, hesitation

Hannibal, -is, *m.*, Hannibal, the renowned

Carthaginian general of the Second Punic War (218–201 B.C.), son of Hamilcar

harena, -ae, *f.*, sand, sandy place, arena

Harpaste, *f.*, female clown of Seneca's wife

harundo, -inis, *f.*, reed

haurio, -ire, hausi, haustus, 4, drain, take in, drink up, consume

hebes, -etis, *adj.*, dull

Hecato, -onis, *m.*, Hecato of Rhodes, Stoic philosopher of the first cent. B.C., pupil of Panaetius

Hecuba, -ae, *f.*, Hecuba, wife of King Priam of Troy

Hellespontus, -i, *m.*, the Hellespont

herba, -ae, *f.*, grass, herb, weeds

hereditarius, -a, -um, *adj.*, hereditary, inherited

Hermarchus, -i, *m.*, Hermarchus, successor of Epicurus as head of the Epicurean School

Hesiodus, -i, *m.*, Hesiod, the oldest Greek poet after Homer, author of the *Works and Days* and the *Theogony*

hibernus, -a, -um, *adj.*, of winter, wintry, winter; *subst.*, hibernum, -i, *n.*, winter

hic, haec, hoc, *dem. adj.* and *pron.*, this; he, she, it; the latter

hic, *adv.*, here

hiemo, 1, be wintry, stormy, cold

hiems (hiemps), -emis, *f.*, winter

Hiero, -onis, *m.*, Hiero, king of Syracuse (478–467 B.C.)

hilariculus, -a, -um, *adj.*, cheerful

hilaris, -e, *adj.*, cheerful, merry

hilaritas, -atis, *f.*, cheerfulness, mirth, hilarity

hinc, *adv.*, from here, hence; on this side; hinc atque illinc, on this side and on that

hio, 1, open, open the mouth

historia, -ae, *f.*, history

hodie, *adv.*, today

hodiernus, -a, -um, *adj.*, of or relating to today

Homerus, -i, *m.*, Homer, the renowned Greek epic poet, author of the *Iliad* and *Odyssey*

homicidium, -i, *n.*, murder, homicide

homo, -inis, *m.*, human being, man

honeste, *adv.*, honorably

honestus, -a, -um, *adj.*, honorable

honor, -oris, *m.*, honor, distinction, office of dignity

hora, -ae, *f.*, hour, time

hordeacius, -a, -um, *adj.*, of or relating to barley

horreum, -i, *n.*, granary, storehouse

horridus, -a, -um, *adj.*, rough, coarse, dreadful, horrid

hortor, 1 *dep.*, urge

hortulus, -i, *m.*, garden

hortus, -i, *m.*, garden

hospes, -itis, *c.*, host, guest, stranger

Vocabulary G–H

hospitalis, -e, *adj.*, hospitable
hospitium, -i, *n.*, hospitality, hospitable reception; guest's lodging, inn
hostis, -is, *c.*, enemy
huc, *adv.*, hither, here
humanitas, -atis, *f.*, humanity, human feeling, kindness
humanus, -a, -um, *adj.*, human, humane
humilis, -e, *adj.*, humble
humus, -i, *f.*, ground; **humi**, on the ground

I

ibi, *adv.*, there, then
ictus, -us, *m.*, blow, stroke, hit; **sub ictu**, within reach
idem, eadem, idem, *dem. adj.* and *pron.*, the same
ideo, *adv.*, for this reason, therefore
Idomeneus, -ei, *m.*, Idomeneus, a Greek writer and statesman in the age of Epicurus
idoneus, -a, -um, *adj.*, suitable, fit
ignis, -is, *m.*, fire
ignorantia, -ae, *f.*, ignorance
ignoro, 1, not know, be ignorant of
ignosco, -ere, -novi, -notus [in-(g)nosco], 3, pardon, forgive
ignotus, -a, -um, *adj.*, unknown
ille, illa, illud, *dem. adj.* and *pron.*, that; he, she, it
illic, *adv.*, there, at that place
illinc, *adv.*, from that place, thence
illo, *adv.*, to that place, thither; to that situation
illuc, *adv.*, thither, there
imago, -inis, *f.*, image, statue
imber, -bris, *m.*, rain
imitatio, -onis, *f.*, imitation
imitor, 1 *dep.*, imitate
immensus, -a, -um, *adj.*, immense, vast
immineo, -ere, 2, hang over, threaten
immo, *adv.*, nay, nay rather, on the contrary
immobilis, -e, *adj.*, immovable
immodicus, -a, -um, *adj.*, immoderate, excessive
immunitas, -atis, *f.*, immunity, exemption
imperator, -oris, *m.*, commander, leader
imperium, -i, *n.*, command, rule
impero, 1, order, command
impetus, -us, *m.*, violent impulse, violence, attack, impetus
impleo, *see* inpleo
imus, -a, -um, *superl.* (*of* inferus), lowest
in, *prep. w. abl.*, in, on, upon; *w. acc.*, into, among, to, towards, against, at, regarding, for
inaequalitas, -atis, *f.*, inequality, irregularity
inaequaliter, *adv.*, unequally, unevenly
inanis, -e, *adj.*, empty, void; **inane, -is**, *n.*, void, emptiness

inbecillitas, -atis, *f.*, weakness
inbecillus, -a, -um, *adj.*, weak, powerless
incedo, -ere, -cessi, -cessus, 3, go, march along, proceed
incendium, -i, *n.*, conflagration, fire
incertus, -a, -um, *adj.*, uncertain
incessus, -us, *m.*, gait
inchoo, 1, begin
incido, -ere, -cidi, -casus [in-cado], 3, fall upon, happen upon, happen, meet
incido, -ere, -cidi, -cisus [in-caedo], 3, cut into, engrave
incipio, -ere, -cepi, -ceptus [in-capio], 3, begin, undertake
incitatus, -a, -um, *p. adj.* (*of* incito), aroused
incito, 1, incite, arouse
inclinatio, -onis, *f.*, leaning, bending, inclination; alteration, change
inclinatus, -a, -um, *p. adj.* (*of* inclino), bent, inclined
inclino, 1, bend, lean, incline
includo, -ere, -clusi, -clusus [in-claudo], 3, shut in, enclose, end, close
incolumis, -e, *adj.*, uninjured, safe and sound
incommodus, -a, -um, *adj.*, disadvantageous, inconvenient, unsuitable; *subst.*, **incommodum, -i**, *n.*, inconvenience, disadvantage
incomptus, -a, -um, *adj.*, inelegant, rude
inconcussus, -a, -um, *adj.*, unshaken, firm
incorporalis, -e, *adj.*, bodiless, incorporeal
incorruptus, -a, -um, *adj.*, uncorrupted
increbresco, -ere, -crebrui, 3, become frequent
incredibilis, -e, *adj.*, incredible
incrementum, -i, *n.*, growth, increase, gain
increpo, -are, -crepui, -crepitus, 1, make a noise
incruentus, -a, -um, *adj.*, unstained, bloodless
inculco [in-calco], 1, trample in, impress upon, inculcate
incultus, -a, -um, *adj.*, unadorned, wild
incumbo, -ere, -cubui, -cubitus, 3, lean upon, apply or devote one's self
incurro, -ere, -curri (-cucurri), -cursus, 3, run upon or against
incurvatus, -a, -um, *p. adj.* (*of* incurvo), bent
incurvo, 1, bend
inde, *adv.*, thence, from there; from that time
indecens, -entis, *adj.*, unbecoming
Indi, -orum, *m. pl.*, Indians
indicium, -i, *n.*, mark, sign, indication
indico, -ere, -dixi, -dictus, 3, declare, make known, proclaim
indigeo, -ere, -ui, 2, need, be in need of
indignor, 1 *dep.*, be angry at
indo, -ere, -didi, -ditus, 3, impart, give to
indoles, -is, *f.*, natural disposition, nature, mind
indomitus, -a, -um, *adj.*, unsubdued

induco, -ere, -duxi, -ductus, 3, lead on, lead, bring in

indulgeo, -ere, -dulsi, -dultus, 2, indulge, give oneself up to

induo, -ere, -dui, -dutus, 3, put on, assume, clothe

induresco, -ere, -durui, 3, harden, become hard

induro, 1, make hard, harden

industria, -ae, f., industry, diligence; de industria, purposely

ineptiae, -arum, f. pl., absurdities

iners, -ertis, adj., sluggish, inert

inertia, -ae, f., unskillfulness, sluggishness

inexercitatus, -a, -um, adj., inexperienced, unexercised

inexorabilis, -e, adj., inexorable

inexpertus, -a, -um, adj., inexperienced, untried

infelix, -icis, adj., unhappy

infero, inferre, intuli, illatus, irr., bring, carry; introduce

inferus, -a, -um, comp., inferior, superl., infimus or imus, adj., low, below; in imo, in the bottom; inferi, -orum, m. pl., gods of the lower world

infestus, -a, -um, adj., hostile

infigo, -ere, -fixi, -fixus, 3, fix in, fasten in

infirmitas, -atis, f., weakness, infirmity

infirmus, -a, -um, adj., weak, infirm

infixus, -a, -um, p. adj. (of infigo), fixed to or in, fastened to or in

inflatus, -a, -um, p. adj. (of inflo), inflated

inflo, 1, blow into or upon, inflate

influo, -ere, -fluxi, -fluxus, 3, flow or rush upon

infra, adv. and prep. w. acc., below

infractus, -a, -um, p. adj. (of infringo), broken, weakened, subdued

infringo, -ere, -fregi, -fractus [in-frango], 3, break, weaken

infulcio, -ire, -fulsi, -fultus, 4, put in, insert

ingemesco, -ere, -ui, 3, groan

ingenitus, -a, -um, p. adj. (of ingigno), inborn, innate

ingenium, -i, n., nature, character, cleverness, wit, mind, talent, genius

ingens, -entis, adj., vast, immense, huge

ingenue, adv., freely, nobly; frankly

ingenuus, -a, -um, adj., native, not foreign; free-born, noble, honorable; frank, sincere

ingero, -ere, -gessi, -gestus, 3, heap on, carry in or upon

ingigno, -ere, -genui, -genitus, 3, implant by birth or nature

ingratus, -a, -um, adj., unpleasing, ungrateful

inhabilis, -e, adj., unfit

inhio, 1, gape

inhumanus, -a, -um, adj., cruel, inhuman

inicio, -ere, -ieci, -iectus [in-iacio], 3, throw upon, cast upon

iniectus, -a, -um, p. adj. (of inicio), thrown upon, cast upon

inimicus, -a, -um, adj., unfriendly, hostile; inimicus, -i, m., enemy

iniquitas, -atis, f., unevenness, unfairness, injustice, inequity

iniquus, -a, -um, adj., unequal, unfair, unjust

initiamenta, -orum, n. pl., rites of initiation

initium, -i, n., beginning

iniuria, -ae, f., injury

iniussus, -a, -um, adj., unbidden

inlaboratus, -a, -um, adj., not labored, uncultivated

inlido, -ere, -lisi, -lisus, 3, beat against

inligo, 1, fasten, bind

inlustris, -e, adj., famous, noble, illustrious

inmensus, -a, -um, adj., immense, vast

inmerito, adv., undeservedly

inmineo, -ere, 2, hang over, threaten

inmisceo, -ere, -scui, -xtus, 2, mix in, intermix, intermingle

inmitto, -ere, -misi, -missus, 3, send in, cause or allow to go in

inmoror, 1, stay, remain, linger

inmortalis, -e, adj., immortal

inmotus, -a, -um, adj., unmoved, motionless, fixed

innato, 1, flow

innocens, -entis, adj., guiltless, innocent

innumerabilis, -e, adj., innumerable, countless

innutrio, -ire, -ivi, -itus, 4, bring up, educate with or among

inoffense, adv., without stumbling, without hindrance

inopia, -ae, f., want, need, poverty

inpango, -ere, -pegi, -panctus, 3, fix upon

inparatus, -a, -um, adj., unprepared

inpatiens, -entis, adj., unable to bear or endure, impatient

inpedimentum, -i, n., hindrance, impediment

inpedio, -ire, -ivi, -itus, 4, hinder, impede

inpello, -ere, -puli, -pulsus, 3, drive on, urge on, impel; strike, overthrow

inpendeo, -ere, 2, hang over, hang over menacingly, threaten

inpendo, -ere, -pendi, -pensus, 3, expend

inpenetrabilis, -e, adj., impenetrable

inpensa, -ae, f., expense, cost

inperfectus, -a, -um, adj., imperfect

inperitus, -a, -um, adj., unskilled, inexperienced, ignorant

inpetro, 1, gain one's request, obtain, demand

inpingo, -ere, -pegi, -pactus, 3, drive

inpleo, -ere, -plevi, -pletus, 2, fill up, satisfy

inplico, -are, -plicui (-plicavi), -plicitus (-plicatus), 1, enfold, entangle

inpono, -ere, -posui, -positus, 3, place upon, impose

inportuosus, -a, -um, *adj.,* without harbors

inpotens, -entis, *adj.,* weak, unrestrained, arrogant

inpotenter, *adv.,* weakly, powerlessly, intemperately

inpressus, -a, -um, *p. adj.* (*of* inprimo), pressed upon

inprimo, -ere, -pressi, -pressus [in-premo], 3, press upon

inprobus, -a, -um, *adj.,* bad, wicked; bold, impudent

inprudens, -entis, *adj.,* not knowing, ignorant, imprudent

inpudicus, -a, -um, *adj.,* shameless, loud, impudent

inpulsus, -a, -um, *p. adj.* (*of* inpello), driven on, urged on, impelled; stricken, overthrown

inputo, 1, to impute to, to charge to one's account

inquam, -is, -it, *v., def.,* I say

inquieto, 1, disturb

inquietus, -a, -um, *adj.,* unquiet, restless

inquilinus, -i, *m.,* inhabitant of a place which is not one's own, tenant, lodger

inquino, 1, pollute, contaminate

inquiro, -ere, -quisivi, -quisitus [in-quaero], 3, seek, investigate, inquire into

inquis, *see* inquam

inremediabilis, -e, *adj.,* incurable, irremediable; implacable

inrepo, -ere, -repsi, -reptus, 3, creep into

inrigo, 1, irrigate

inritamentum, -i, *n.,* incentive

inrito, 1, stir up, incite

inritus, -a, -um, *adj.,* in vain, useless

inrumpo, -ere, -rupi, -ruptus, 3, break in, interrupt

insania, -ae, *f.,* madness, insanity

insatiabilis, -e, *adj.,* that cannot be satisfied, insatiable

inscribo, -ere, -scripsi, -scriptus, 3, write upon, inscribe

inscriptus, -a, -um, *p. adj.* (*of* inscribo), written upon, inscribed

inseco, -are, -cui, -ctus, 1, cut into, cut up

insectus, -a, -um, *p. adj.* (*of* inseco), cut into, cut up

insero, -ere, -serui, -sertus, 3, put in, insert

insertus, -a, -um, *p. adj.* (*of* insero), inserted

insideo, -ere, -sedi, -sessus, 2, sit or settle on

insidiosus, -a, -um, *adj.,* deceitful, treacherous, insidious

insido, -ere, -sedi, -sessus, 3, sit or settle on

insigne, -is, *n.,* mark, sign, sign or badge of honor, decoration

insignio, -ire, -ivi, -itus, 4, put a mark or sign upon, distinguish one's self

insignis, -e, *adj.,* marked, distinguished, renowned, remarkable

insignitus, -a, -um, *p. adj.* (*of* insignio), marked, striking

insitio, -onis, *f.,* grafting

insomnium, -i, *n.,* dream

inspicio, -ere, -spexi, -spectus [in-specio], 3, look in or on, see in or on, inspect, contemplate, observe, see

instabilis, -e, *adj.,* unstable, changeable

instar, *n., indecl.,* image, likeness

instigatus, -a, -um, *p. adj.* (*of* instigo), stimulated, incited

instigo, 1, goad on, stimulate, incite

institor, -oris, *m.,* huckster, pedlar

instituo, -ere, -ui, -tutus [in-statuo], 3, train, establish, institute

institutus, -a, -um, *p. adj.* (*of* instituo), trained, educated

insto, -are, -stiti, -staturus, 1, stand in or on, press upon, urge

instructus, -a, -um, *p. adj.* (*of* instruo), set up, furnished, equipped

instrumentum, -i, *n.,* tool, instrument, means

instruo, -ere, -struxi, -structus, 3, set up, furnish, equip

intactus, -a, -um, *adj.,* untouched

integer, -gra, -grum, *adj.,* whole, entire

intellectus, -us, *m.,* understanding

intellego, -ere, -lexi, -lectus [inter-lego], 3, understand

intemperantia, -ae, *f.,* intemperance, want of moderation

intempestivus, -a, -um, *adj.,* untimely

intendo, -ere, -tendi, -tentus, 3, stretch out, extend, direct towards, intend

intentio, -onis, *f.,* attention, application, effort

intento, 1, stretch out

intentus, -a, -um, *p. adj.* (*of* intendo), stretched out, extended; anxious, intent, attentive to, unceasing

inter, *prep. w. acc.,* between, among

interdico, -ere, -dixi, -dictus, 3, forbid

interdiu, *adv.,* by day

interdum, *adv.,* sometimes

interest, *impers.,* it concerns, it matters, it is of importance

interfector, -oris, *m.,* murderer, slayer

interficio, -ere, -feci, -fectus [inter-facio], 3, kill

interim, *adv.,* meanwhile, in the meantime

interior, -ins, *comp. adj.,* inner, inside; **intimus, -a, -um,** *superl.,* inmost, farthest

intermitto, -ere, -misi, -missus, 3, interrupt, neglect

interpellator, -oris, *m.,* interrupter

interpello, 1, interrupt

interpono, -ere, -posui, -positus, 3, put or place between, insert; set aside

Vocabulary I

interpretor, 1 *dep.*, explain, interpret
interritus, -a, -um, *adj.*, unterrified
interrogo, 1, ask, interrogate
interrumpo, -ere, -rupi, -ruptus, 3, interrupt
interruptus, -a, -um, *p. adj.* (*of* interrumpo), interrupted
interscindo, -ere, -scidi, -scissus, 3, cut off, break
intersum, -esse, -fui, *irr.*, be between, be in the midst of; be different; be present, take part in; *impers.*, interest, it concerns, it matters, it is of importance, it makes a difference
intervallum, -i, *n.*, interval, distance
intervello, -ere, -vulsi, -vulsus, 3, pluck out here and there, thin
intervenio, -ire, -veni, -ventus, 4, come between, intervene
intimus, -a, -um, *superl. adj.*, *see* interior
intolerabilis, -e, *adj.*, intolerable, unbearable
intonsus, -a, -um, *adj.*, unshorn
intra, *adv.* and *prep. w. acc.*, within
intremo, -ere, -ui, 3, tremble, shake
intrepide, *adv.*, without trembling, undauntedly, intrepidly
intrepidus, -a, -um, *adj.*, not trembling, undaunted, intrepid
intro, 1, enter
introrsus, *adv.*, inwards, inwardly, within
intueor, -eri, -tuitus, 2 *dep.*, look at, contemplate, consider
intus, *adv.*, within
inutilis, -e, *adj.*, useless
invado, -ere, -vasi, -vasus, 3, go in, come in, invade, attack
invecticius, -a, -um, *adj.*, imported, not genuine
invenio, -ire, -veni, -ventus, 4, come upon, find
inventum, -i, *n.*, invention
inventus, -us, *m.*, invention
inverecunde, *adv.*, shamelessly
investigo, 1, track out, investigate
investio, -ire, -ivi, -itus, 4, clothe, cover
inveteratus, -a, -um, *adj.*, old, inveterate
invicem, *adv.*, in turn, by turns, alternately
invictus, -a, -um, *adj.*, unconquered
invideo, -ere, -vidi, -visus, 2, envy
invidia, -ae, *f.*, envy, hostility
invidiosus, -a, -um, *adj.*, full of envy, causing envy, envied; odious
inviolatus, -a, -um, *adj.*, unhurt, inviolate
invisus, -a, -um, *adj.*, hateful
invitus, -a, -um, *adj.*, unwilling, against one's will
invoco, 1, call upon, invoke
involvo, -ere, -volvi, -volutus, 3, roll upon, roll about, wrap up, involve
involutus, -a, -um, *p. adj.* (*of* involvo), wrapped up, involved, tangled

Ionius, -a, -um, *adj.*, Ionian
ipse, -a, -um, *intens. pron.*, self, very
ira, -ae, *f.*, anger
iracundus, -a, -um, *adj.*, irascible, angry
irascor, -i, iratus, 3 *dep.*, be angry, become angered
iratus, -a, -um, *p. adj.* (*of* irascor), angry, enraged
is, ea, id, *dem. adj.* and *pron.*, this, that; he, she, it
Isio, -onis, *m.*, Isio, a court fool in the age of Seneca
iste, ista, istud (istuc), *dem. adj.* and *pron.*, this or that; that of yours, that sort
Isthmus, -i, *m.*, the Isthmus
istic, *adv.*, there
ita, *adv.*, thus, so
itaque, *adv.*, and so, therefore, for that reason
iter, itineris, *n.*, journey, way, road, path
itero, 1, do a second time, repeat; plough again
iterum, *adv.*, again, a second time, repeatedly

I CONSONANT

iaceo, -ere, iacui, iacitus, 2, lie, lie down
iacio, -ere, ieci, iactus, 3, throw, throw up
iactatio, -onis, *f.*, tossing, restlessness
iacto, 1, toss about
iactura, -ae, *f.*, a throwing away, loss
iam, *adv.*, now, already, presently, soon
iamdudum, *adv.*, at once
ianitor, -oris, *m.*, door-keeper, porter
ianua, -ae, *f.*, door
ieiunus, -a, -um, *adj.*, fasting
iocus, -i, *m.*, joke, jest
iuba, -ae, *f.*, the mane of an animal
iubeo, -ere, iussi, iussus, 2, order
iucundus, -a, -um, *adj.*, pleasant, agreeable
iudex, -icis, *m.*, judge
iudicium, -i, *n.*, judgment
iudico, 1, judge
iugerum, -i, *n.*, acre
iugulo, 1, cut the throat, slay, kill
iugum, -i, *n.*, yoke, team, pair of horses; ridge or summit of a mountain
iumentum, -i, *n.*, beast of burden
iunctura, -ae, *f.*, joining
iungo, -ere, -nxi, -nctus, 3, join
iuro, 1, swear, take an oath
ius, iuris, *n.*, right, law; ius dicere, to administer justice
iussus, -a, -um, *p. adj.* (*of* iubeo), ordered
iustitia, -ae, *f.*, justice
iustus, -a, -um, *adj.*, just, right
iuvenis, -is, *adj.*, young, youthful; *subst.*, iuvenis, -is, *c.*, young man, young woman
iuvo, -are, iuvi, iutus, 1, help, aid; please, delight

Vocabulary I-I CONSONANT

L

labo, 1, totter, fall
labor, -oris, *m.*, work, labor, effort
labor, labi, lapsus, 3 *dep.*, fall, fall down, glide
laboriosus, -a, -um, *adj.*, full of toil, laborious
laboro, 1, work,
labrum, -i, *n.*, lip
labyrinthus, -i, *m.*, labyrinth
lacerna, -ae, *f.*, cloak
lacertus, -i, *m.*, generally *pl.*, muscles
lacrima, -ae, *f.*, tear
lacrimo, 1, weep
lacunar, -aris, *n.*, panelled ceiling
lacunarium, -i, *n.*, panelled ceiling
lacus, -us, *m.*, lake
laedo, -ere, laesi, laesus, 3, hurt, injure
Laelius, -i, *m.*, Laelius, well-known philosopher,
    surnamed the "Wise," personal friend of Scipio
    Africanus the Younger, conqueror of Carthage
    (146 B.C.)
laetitia, -ae, *f.*, joy, happiness
laetor, 1 *dep.*, rejoice
laetus, -a, -um, *adj.*, joyous, happy
lagona, -ae, *f.*, flask, bottle
lamentatio, -onis, *f.*, lamentation
languesco, -ere, -gui, 3, become weak, languid,
    decrease
languidus, -a, -um, *adj.*, weak, languid, dull,
    gentle
languor, -oris, *m.*, languor, weariness
lanio, 1, rend, tear
lapideus, -a, -um, *adj.*, of stone
lapis, -idis, *m.*, stone
laquear, -aris, *n.*, panel in a ceiling
laqueus, -i, *m.*, snare, trap
lar, -is, *m.*, usually *pl.*, lares, -um (-ium),
    household gods
large, *adv.*, largely, plentifully, abundantly
largitio, -onis, *f.*, largess
largus, -a, -um, *adj.*, large, abundant, plentiful
lascivia, -ae, *f.*, wantonness, licentiousness
lascivio, -ire, -ii, -itus, 4, sport, play, be wanton
lassitudo, -inis, *f.*, weariness, lassitude
lasso, 1, make weary, exhaust
lassus, -a, -um, *adj.*, weary
late, *adv.*, widely, broadly, far and wide
latebra, -ae, *f.*, hiding, hiding-place
latens, -entis, *p. adj.* (*of* lateo), concealed, hidden
lateo, -ere, -ui, 2, lie hidden
latito, 1, hide
latro, -onis, *m.*, thief, robber
latrocinium, -i, *n.*, robbery, highway robbery
latus, -a, -um, *adj.*, wide, broad
latus, -eris, *n.*, side
laudatio, -onis, *f.*, praise

laudo, 1, praise
laus, laudis, *f.*, praise, glory
lautitia, -ae, *f.*, splendor, elegance
laxamentum, -i, *n.*, relaxation
laxitas, -atis, *f.*, roominess, width, spaciousness
laxo, 1, stretch out, expand
laxus, -a, -um, *adj.*, wide, spacious
lectica, -ae, *f.*, litter
lectio, -onis, *f.*, reading
lectus, -i, *m.*, small bed, couch
legitimus, -a, -um, *adj.*, lawful, legal, legitimate
lego, -ere, legi, lectus, 3, collect, gather together,
    choose; read
lenio, -ire, -ivi, -itus, 4, assuage
lenis, -e, *adj.*, smooth, mild, gentle
lenocinium, -i, *n.*, ornament, finery
lente, *adv.*, slowly
lentus, -a, -um, *adj.*, slow
leo, -onis, *m.*, lion
levis, -e, *adj.*, light, fickle, unstable
levis, -e, *adj.*, smooth, polished
levo, 1, raise, lift up
lex, legis, *f.*, law
libamentum, -i, *n.*, libation
libens, -entis, *p. adj.* (*of* libeo), willing, gladly
libenter, *adv.*, willingly, gladly
liber, -era, -erum, *adj.*, free
liber, libri, *m.*, book
liberalis, -e, *adj.*, liberal, generous
libere, *adv.*, freely
libero, 1, set free, liberate
libertas, -atis, *f.*, freedom, liberty
libertinus, -i, *m.*, freedman
libet, libere, libuit or libitum est, *impers.*, 2, it is
    pleasing
libido, -inis, *f.*, unrestrained desire, wantonness,
    lust
licentia, -ae, *f.*, license, freedom from restraint
licet, licere, licuit or licitum est, *impers.*, 2, it is
    allowed, it is permitted; licet *w. subj.*, granting
    that, even if, although
lignum, -i, *n.*, wood
limen, -inis, *n.*, threshold, door
limes, -itis, *m.*, boundary
lingua, -ae, *f.*, tongue; language
linquo, -ere, liqui, 3, leave
linter, lintris, *f.*, boat
liquefacio, -ere, -feci, -factus, 3, *pass.*, liquefio,
    -fieri, -factus, melt
liquens, -entis, *p. adj.* (*of* liqueo), flowing, liquid
liqueo, -ere, liqui (licui), 2, be fluid, liquid; be
    clear
Liternum, -i, *n.*, Liternum, a town in Campania
litigo, 1, quarrel, dispute
littera, -ae, *f.*, letter (*of the alphabet*); *pl.*, letter,
    epistle; literature; learning

Vocabulary L

litteratus, -a, -um, *adj.*, learned, liberally educated

litus, -oris, *n.*, shore

loco, 1, place, put; contract for having a thing done; lease or hire out

locuples, -etis, *adj.*, rich, wealthy

locus, -i, *m.*, (*pl. m.* **loci** or *n.* **loca**), place; topic, point

longe, *adv.*, far, far away, by far; long

longinquus, -a, -um, *adj.*, distant

longius, *comp. of* **longe**

longissime, *superl. of* **longe**

longus, -a, -um, *adj.*, long; distant

loquor, loqui, locutus, 3 *dep.*, speak

lubricus, -a, -um, *adj.*, slippery

lucellum, -i, *n.*, small profit

luceo, -ere, luxi, 2, shine, gleam

lucerna, -ae, *f.*, lamp

Lucilius, -i, *m.*, Lucilius, Seneca's friend, to whom the philosopher addressed the *Epistulae Morales*

lucrifico, 1, gain

luctor, 1 *dep.*, wrestle

luctus, -us, *m.*, mourning, grief

locus, -i, *m.*, grove

ludo, -ere, lusi, lusus, 3, play, play with, amuse oneself

lusus, -i, *m.*, game, sport, joke, jest

lugeo, -ere, luxi, luctus, 2, mourn

lumen, -inis, *n.*, light

luo, -ere, lui, 3, pay for

lusorius, -a, -um, *adj.*, relating to play

lusus, -us, *m.*, play, sport, game, amusement, entertainment

lutum, -i, *n.*, mud, mire

lux, lucis, *f.*, light

luxuria, -ae, *f.*, luxury

luxuriosus, -a, -um, *adj.*, luxurious, immoderate

Lycurgus, -i, *m.*, Lycurgus, legendary Spartan lawgiver of the ninth century B.C.

lyricus, -a, -um, *adj.*, lyric; *subst.*, **lyricus, -i,** *m.*, lyric poet

M

macellum, -i, *n.*, meat-market

machinatio, -onis, *f.*, mechanism, device

madeo, -ere, madui, 2, be wet, drip

Maecenas, -atis, *m.*, Maecenas, Roman knight, minister of Augustus, renowned patron of learned men

maereo, -ere, 2, mourn, grieve, lament

maeror, -oris, *m.*, mourning, grief

magis, *comp. adv.*, more, rather

magister, -tri, *m.*, teacher, master

magisterium, -i, *n.*, office of instructor of youth, tutorship, teaching

magistra, -ae, *f.*, mistress

magistratus, -us, *m.*, office, magistracy; magistrate

magnificus, -a, -um, *adj.*, magnificent

magnitudo, -inis, *f.*, greatness, magnitude

magnus, -a, -um, *comp.*, **maior,** *superl.*, **maximus,** *adj.*, great, large; **magno,** at a great price; **maior,** older; **maiores,** ancestors; **maximus,** oldest, eldest

maiestas, -atis, *f.*, dignity, majesty

maior, maiores, *comp.* (*of* **magnus**), greater, larger, older; **maiores,** ancestors

male, *adv.*, badly

maligne, *adv.*, maliciously, malignantly; stingily, hardly, scarcely

malignitas, -atis, *f.*, maliciousness, malignity

malignus, -a, -um, *adj.*, malicious, malignant, wicked

malitia, -ae, *f.*, wickedness, evil

malleus, -i, *m.*, hammer

malo, malle, malui, *irr.*, prefer

malus, -a, -um, *comp.*, **peior,** *superl.*, **pessimus,** *adj.*, bad, evil, wicked

malum, -i, *n.*, punishment

mancipium, -i, *n.*, slave; property

mando, 1, entrust, recommend

mane, *adv.*, in the morning

maneo, -ere, mansi, mansus, 2, remain

mango, -onis, *m.*, slave dealer

manifestus, -a, -um, *adj.*, clear, evident, manifest

mansuetudo, -inis, *f.*, mildness, clemency, gentleness

manus, -us, *f.*, hand, band

marceo, -ere, 2, wither, be weak, be languid

mare, -is, *n.*, sea

Marius, -i, *m.*, C. Marius (157–86 B.C.), the conqueror of Jugurtha, seven times consul, rival of Sulla, leader of the popular party at Rome

marmor, -oris, *n.*, marble

marmorarius, -i, *m.*, worker in marble, marble-mason

mas, maris, *m.*, male

mater, -tris, *f.*, mother

materia, -ae, *f.*, matter, material

maxime, *adv., superl.* (*of* **magis**), in the highest degree, most of all, especially

maximus, -a, -um, *superl.* (*of* **magnus**), greatest, largest

medicamentum, -i, *n.*, drug, medicine, remedy

medicina, -ae, *f.*, medicine

medicus, -i, *m.*, doctor

mediocris, -e, *adj.*, moderate; mediocre

meditatio, -onis, *f.*, meditation, preparation for anything, practicing

meditor, 1 *dep.*, meditate

medium, -i, *n.*, the midst of all, the public

medius, -a, -um, *adj.*, middle, middle of, midst

medulla, -ae, *f.*, marrow

megistanes, -um, *m.*, grandees, magnates, nobles

mehercules, as an oath, by Hercules

mel, mellis, *n.*, honey

melior, -ius, *comp.* (*of* bonus), better

membrum, -i, *n.*, member, part, limb

memini, -isse, *pf. in sense of pres.*, remember, recollect

memor, -oris, *adj.*, mindful, remembering

memoria, -ae, *f.*, memory

memoro, 1, mention, call to mind, recount, relate

mens, mentis, *f.*, mind

mensa, -ae, *f.*, table; food, meal

mensis, -is, *m.*, month

mentior, -iri, -itus, 4 *dep.*, lie, cheat

mercedula, -ae, *f.*, small reward

merces, -edis, *f.*, pay, wages, reward; merchandise

mereo, -ere, -ui, -itus, 2, deserve, merit

mergo, -ere, mersi, mersus, 3, sink, immerse

meridie, *adv.*, in the afternoon

merito, *adv.*, deservedly

merus, -a, -um, *adj.*, pure

merx, mercis, *f.*, merchandise, goods, wares

Messala, -ae, *m.*, Marcus Valerius Messala Corvinus, renowned orator, author, and literary patron of the Augustan Age

meta, -ae, *f.*, conical columns set in the ground at each end of the Roman Circus; goal, turning point

metallum, -i, *n.*, mine, quarry, metal

metior, -iri, mensus, 4 *dep.*, measure

meto, -ere, messui, 3, reap

Metrodorus, -i, *m.*, Metrodorus, disciple of Epicurus, 331–278 B.C.

metus, -us, *m.*, fear

meus, -a, -um, *poss. adj. and pron.*, my, mine

migro, 1, remove from one place to another, move, migrate

mihi, *see* ego

miles, -itis, *m.*, soldier

militaris, -e, *adj.*, of or relating to a soldier, military

militia, -ae, *f.*, military service

milito, 1, be a soldier, wage war

mille, milia, -ium, *num. adj.*, a thousand; mille (passuum), 1000 paces; *in the pl.*, milia (passuum)

miliens, *adv.*, a thousand times

mimus, -i, *m.*, mime, drama, farce

minime, *superl. adv.*, least, very little, not at all, by no means

minimus, -a, -um, *superl.* (*of* parvus), smallest, least

minister, -tri, *m.*, servant, attendant, assistant

ministerium, -i *n.*, service, duty

minor, 1 *dep.*, threaten

minor, minus, *comp.* (*of* parvus), smaller, less

minutatim, *adv.*, in small pieces, little by little, gradually

minutia, -ae, *f.*, smallness, minuteness

miraculum, -i, *n.*, marvel, wonder

mire, adv., wonderfully

miror, 1 *dep.*, look at, admire, wonder, be astonished

mirus, -a, -um, *adj.*, surprising, wondrous, astonishing

misceo, -ere, miscui, mixtus, 2, mix, mingle

miser, -era, -erum, *adj.*, wretched

miseria, -ae, *f.*, wretchedness, misery

misericordia, -ae, *f.*, pity

missio, -onis, *f.*, discharge

mitis, -e, *adj.*, gentle, mild

mitto, -ere, misi, missus, 3, let go, send

mixtura, -ae, *f.*, mixture

mixtus, -a, -um, *p. adj.* (*of* misceo), mixed, mingled

mobilis, -e, *adj.*, moveable, excitable, pliable

moderatio, -onis, *f.*, moderation

moderatus, -a, -um, *adj.*, moderate, modest

modeste, *adv.*, moderately, modestly

modicus, -a, -um, *adj.*, moderate

modius, -i, *m.*, measure of grain

modo, *adv.*, only; now, but now

modulatio, -onis, *f.*, modulation, rhythmical measure, singing and playing

modus, -i, *m.*, measure, limit, boundary; moderation, control; manner, way, method

mola, -ae, *f.*, coarse meal, flour

moles, -is, *f.*, mass, heap

molestia, -ae, *f.*, annoyance, trouble

molestus, -a, -um, *adj.*, annoying, troublesome

molior, -iri, -itus, 4 *dep.*, build, devise

mollis, -e, *adj.*, soft, gentle, mild, effeminate

mollio, -ire, -ivi, -itus, 4, soften

mollitia, -ae, *f.*, softness, effeminacy

molliter, *adv.*, softly, gently, mildly

momentum, -i, *n.*, movement, motion; change; importance

moneo, -ere, -ui, -itus, 2, warn, admonish

mons, montis, *m.*, mountain

monstro, 1, show, point out

mora, -ae, *f.*, delay

morbus, -i, *m.*, disease

morior, mori, mortuus, 3 *dep.*, die

moror, 1 *dep.*, linger, dwell, delay

mors, mortis, *f.*, death

morsus, -us, *m.*, biting, sting

mortalis, -e, *adj.*, mortal

mortalitas, -atis, *f.*, mortality

mortuus, -a, -um, *p. adj.* (*of* morior), dead

mos, moris, *m.*, custom, habit; *pl.*, mores, morum, character motiuncula, -ae, *f.*, slight motion; in medicine, attack of fever

motus, -us, *m.*, motion, movement

motus, -a, -um, *p. adj.* (*of* moveo), moved

moveo, -ere, movi, motus, 2, move, change

mulceo, -ere, mulsi, mulsus, 2, soothe

muliebris, -e, *adj.*, of a woman, womanly

muliercula, -ae, *f.*, little woman

mulio, -onis, *m.*, mule-driver, muleteer

multa, -ae, *f.*, punishment, fine, cost

multitudo, -inis, *f.*, large number, multitude

multo, *adv.*, much; by far

multus, -a, -um, *adj.*, much, many; *comp.*, **plus, pluris**, more; *superl.*, **plurimus, -a, -um**, very much, very many

munditia, -ae, *f.*, cleanliness, neatness

mundus, -i, *m.*, world

municipalis, -e, *adj.*, belonging to a town, municipal

munimentum, -i, *n.*, protection

munio, -ire, -ivi, -itus, 4, fortify, protect

munus, -eris, *n.*, duty, office, service; gift

munusculum, -i, *n.*, small present, small gift

murus, -i, *m.*, wall

mus, muris, *c.*, mouse

murmur, -uris, *n.*, murmur

mutatio, -onis, *f.*, change

muto, 1, change, alter

mutuo, *adv.*, mutually, reciprocally

mutus, -a, -um, *adj.*, mute, silent

mutuus, -a, -um, *adj.*, mutual

N

nam, *conj.*, for

nanciscor, nancisci, nanctus (nactus), 3 *dep.*, get, obtain, come upon

narro, 1, narrate, tell, relate

nascor, nasci, natus, 3 *dep.*, be born, spring up, arise

natura, -ae, *f.*, nature; **ex natura**, naturally

naturalis, -e, *adj.*, natural

natus, -a, -um, *p. adj.* (*of* nascor), born

naufragium, -i, *n.*, shipwreck

nauseabundus, -a, -um, *adj.*, nauseated

nausia, -ae, *f.*, sea-sickness, nausea

nausiator, -oris, *m.*, one who is apt to feel nausea, who vomits easily

nauta, -ae, *m.*, sailor

navigium, -i, *n.*, ship

navigo, 1, *sail*, navigate

navis, -is, *f.*, ship

ne, *adv.*, not, that. . .not

-ne, *interrogative suffix*

nec (neque), *conj.*, and not, neither, nor

necdum, *adv.*, and not yet

necessarius, -a, -um, *adj.*, necessary

necesse, *adj., n.*, necessary, fated; *with* est, it is necessary

necessitas, -atis, *f.*, need, necessity

neco, 1, kill, slay

necque, *see* nec

nectar, -aris, *n.*, nectar

nedum, *adv.*, not to mention

neglegens, -entis, *adj.*, negligent, careless

neglegentia, -ae, *f.*, carelessness, negligence

negligenter, *adv.*, carelessly

neglego, -ere, -lexi, -lectus, 3, neglect

nego, 1, deny

negotium, -i, *n.*, business, occupation; trouble

nemo, -inis, *m.*, no one, nobody; *adj.*, no

nemus, -oris, *n.*, woods, grove

nempe, *conj.*, to be sure, certainly, truly

neque, *see* nec

nequeo, -ire, -ivi (-ii), -itus, 4, be unable

nequitia, -ae, *f.*, wickedness

nervus, -i, *m.*, sinew, nerve

nescio, -ire, -ivi (-ii), -itus, 4, not know, be ignorant

Nesis, -idis, *f.*, Nesis, an island on the coast of Campania

nitor, -oris, *m.*, brightness, splendor

neu, *see* neve

neuter, -era, -rum, *adj.*, neither (of two)

neve (neu), *conj.*, or not, and not, nor; **neve. . .neve**, neither. . .nor

nihil, *n., indecl.*, nothing; *adv.*, not at all, not in the least

nihilominus, *adv.*, nevertheless

Nilus, -i, *m.*, the river Nile

nimis, *adv.*, too much, too

nimius, -a, -um, *adj.*, too much, excessive

Nioba, -ae, *f.*, Niobe, daughter of Tantalus and mother of seven sons and seven daughters

nisi, *conj.*, unless, if not, except

niteo, -ere, 2, shine

nitidus, -a, -um, *adj.*, glittering, shining

nitor, nisi, nisus (nixus), 3 *dep.*, lean, rest, strive

nix, nivis, *f.*, snow

nobilis, -e, *adj.*, well-known, famous, noble

nobilitas, -atis, *f.*, nobility

noceo, -ere, nocui, nocitus, *w. dat.*, 2, harm, injure

nodosus, -a, -um, *adj.*, knotty

nolo, nolle, nolui, *irr.*, be unwilling, not wish

nomen, -inis, *n.*, name; account

nomenclator, -oris, *m.*, nomenclator, a slave who announced to his master the names of guests at large gatherings

non, *adv.*, no, not

nondum, *adv.*, not yet

nonne, *interrog. adv. introducing a question expecting an affirmative answer*

nos, *pl. of* ego

nosco, -ere, novi, notus, 3, know

noster, -tra, -trum, *poss. adj.* and *pron.*, our, ours

nota, -ae, *f.*, mark, note, sign, stamp

notabilis, -e, *adj.*, notable, striking, ostentatious

notitia, -ae, *f.*, knowledge

notus, -a, -um, *p. adj.* (*of* nosco), known

novem, *indecl. num. adj.*, nine

novissime, *superl. adv.*, lastly

novitas, -atis, *f.*, newness

novus, -a, -um, *adj.*, new, strange; *superl.*, novissimus, -a, -um, *adj.*, latest, last

nox, noctis, *f.*, night

nubes, -is, *f.*, cloud

nudo, 1, lay bare, strip, expose

nudus, -a, -um, *adj.*, bare, nude

nugae, -arum, *f.*, trifles, nonsense

nullus, -a, -um, *adj.*, no, none

num, *interrog. adv. expecting a negative answer; w. indir. questions*, whether

numen, -inis, *n.*, divine will, divinity

numeratio, -onis, *f.*, payment

numero, 1, count

numerus, -i, *m.*, number

numquam, *adv.*, never

numquid, *interrog. adv., used to introduce a direct question.* There is no corresponding term in English.

nunc, *adv.*, now

nuper, *adv.*, recently, lately

nusquam, *adv.*, nowhere

nutrio, -ire, -ivi (-ii), -itus, 4, nourish

nutrix, -icis, *f.*, nurse

O

o and oh, *interj.*, oh! O!

obeo, -ire, -ivi (-ii), -itus, 4, go to, travel through; offer

obicio, -ere, -ieci, -iectus [ob-iacio], 3, throw in the way of, throw before, expose

obirascor, -irasci, -iratus, 3 *dep.*, be angry

obiratus, -a, -um, *p. adj.* (*of* obirascor), angry, wrathful

obiurgatio, -onis, *f.*, chiding, blaming

oblectamentum, -i, *n.*, delight, pleasure

oblectatio, -onis, *f.*, pleasure, amusement

oblino, -ere, -levi, -litus, 3, smear

oblitus, -a, -um, *p. adj.* (*of* obliviscor), having forgotten

oblivio, -onis, *f.*, forgetfulness, oblivion

obliviscor, oblivisci, oblitus, 3 *dep.*, forget

oboediens, -entis, *p. adj.* (*of* oboedio), obedient

oboedio, -ire, -ivi, -itus, 4, give ear to, obey

obscurus, -a, -um, *adj.*, dark, obscure

obsecro, 1, beg, pray, implore

obsequens, -entis, *p. adj.* (*of* obsequor), yielding, obedient

obsequor, -sequi, -secutus, 3 *dep.*, comply with, obey

observator, -oris, *m.*, observer, watcher

observo, 1, watch, observe

obsolefacio, -ere, -feci, -factus, 3, wear out, spoil

obsolefactus, -a, -um, *p. adj.* (*of* obsolefacio), worn out, spoiled

obsonator, -oris, *m.*, purchaser of victuals

obsto, -stare, -stiti, -status, 1, stand in the way of, oppose, resist

obstrepo, -ere, -strepui, -strepitus, 3, make a loud noise, roar

obtempero, 1, obey, conform to, comply with

obvenio, -ire, -veni, -ventus, 4, come in the way of, occur to, happen, fall to, fall to the lot of

obverto, -ere, -verti, -versus, 3, turn towards

obvius, -a, -um, *adj.*, in the way, exposed, meeting; at hand, easy to obtain

occasio, -onis, *f.*, opportunity, occasion

occido, -ere, -cidi, -cisus [ob-caedo], 3, kill, slay

occido, -ere, -cidi, -casus [ob-cado], 3, fall, fall down; die

occulo, -ere, -cului, -cultus, 3, hide, conceal

occultus, -a, -um, *p. adj.* (*of* occulo), hidden, secret, occult

occupatio, -onis, *f.*, occupation

occupatus, -a, -um, *p. adj.* (*of* occupo), busy, occupied

occupo, 1, occupy, take possession of, lay hold of, seize

occurro, -ere, -curri, -cursus [ob-curro], 3, run to meet; occur

oculus, -i, *m.*, eye

odi, odisse, osurus, *def.*, hate

odiosus, -a, -um, *adj.*, odious, hateful

odium, -i, *n.*, hatred

odor, -oris, *m.*, smell, odor

offendo, -ere, -fendi, -fensus, 3, strike or knock against; punish; offend

offensa, -ae, *f.*, harm

officina, -ae, *f.*, workshop

officio, -ere, -feci, -fectus [ob-facio], 3, hinder

officium, -i, *n.*, duty

oleum, -i, *n.*, oil

olim, *adv.*, once, formerly, some time ago

omitto, -ere, -misi, -missus, 3, let go, omit

omnino, *adv.*, altogether, entirely, at all

omnis, -e, *adj.*, all, every

oneraria, -ae, *f.*, ship of burden, merchant-vessel

onero, 1, load

onerosus, -a, -um, *adj.*, burdensome

onus, -eris, *n.*, burden, load

opacitas, -atis, *f.*, shade

opera, -ae, *f.,* effort, labor; **operam dare,** give attention to, pay attention, see to it
operio, -ire, -ui, -ertus, 4, cover
operosus, -a, -um, *adj.,* laborious
opifex, -icis, *m.,* artisan, workman
opimus, -a, -um, *adj.,* rich, fat
opinio, -onis, *f.,* opinion
oportet, -ere, oportuit, 2, *impers.,* it is necessary, one ought
oppono, -ere, -posui, -positus [ob-pono], 3, put or place towards, before, against
opprimo, -ere, -pressi, -pressus [ob-premo], 3, press against, overwhelm, crush, oppress
ops, opis, *f.,* wealth, means, aid
optimus, -a, -um, *superl. adj. (of* **bonus),** best
opto, 1, wish, desire
opulens, -entis, *adj.,* rich
opus, indecl. n., need, necessity; **opus est,** it is necessary, there is need, one needs, one requires
opus, -eris, *n.,* work, labor
oratio, -onis, *f.,* speech, style
ordinarius, -a, -um, *adj.,* regular, ordinary
ordino, 1, set in order, settle, arrange
ordior, -iri, orsus, 4 *dep.,* begin
ordo, -inis, *m.,* series, row, order
organum, -i, *n.,* musical instrument
origo, -inis, *f.,* origin, source
orior, -iri, ortus, 4 *dep.,* rise, be born, spring
ornamentum, -i, *n.,* ornament, decoration
orno, 1, adorn, ornament
oro, 1, beg
ortus, -us, *m.,* rising, dawn, beginning
os, oris, *n.,* mouth, face
osculor, 1, kiss
ostendo, -ere, -tendi, -tentus, 3, show, display
ostentatio, -onis, *f.,* ostentation
ostium, -i, *n.,* entrance, door
otiosus, -a, -um, *adj.,* idle, at leisure
otium, -i, *n.,* leisure, peace, repose

P

paedagogus, -i, *m.,* pedagogue, teacher, guide
paene, *adv.,* almost, nearly
paenitentia, -ae, *f.,* repentance, penitence, dissatisfaction
paeniteo, -ere, 2, repent
pagina, -ae, *f.,* page
palam, *adv.,* openly, publicly
palatum, -i, *n.,* and **palatus, -i,** *m.,* palate, taste
pallidus, -a, -um, *adj.,* pale, pallid
pallium, -i, *n.,* cloak, mantle
palmes, -itis, *f.,* young branch or shoot of a vine
paluster, -tris, -tre, *adj.,* marshy
Panhormitanus, -i, *m.,* inhabitant of Panormus (modern Palermo, Sicily)

panis, -is, *m.,* bread
pantomimus, -i, *m.,* ballet-dancer
par, paris, *adj.,* equal, even; subst., pair
parabilis, -e, *adj.,* that can be easily obtained
paratus, -a, -um, *p. adj. (of* **paro),** prepared, ready
parco, -ere, peperci, parsus, 3, save, spare
parens, -entis, *c.,* parent
pareo, -ere, parui, paritus, 2, appear; obey
paries, -etis, *m.,* wall
pariter, *adv.,* equally, alike, together, at the same time
paro, 1, get, obtain, prepare
pars, partis, *f.,* part, role
parsimonia, -ae, *f.,* thriftiness, parsimony
Parthenope, -es, *f.,* Parthenope, the ancient name for Naples
partior, -iri, -itus, 4 *dep.,* divide
parum, *adv.,* little, too little, not enough
parvulus or **parvolus, -a, -um,** *adj.,* very small, very little
parvus, -a, -um, *comp.,* **minor;** *superl.,* **minimus,** small, little; *adj.,* **minor** (supply *natu*), younger
pasco, -ere, pavi, pastus, 3, feed, pasture, graze
pascuus, -a, -um, *adj.,* fit for pasture; **pascuum, -i,** *n.,* pasture
passim, *adv.,* everywhere
passus, -a, -um, *p. adj. (of* **patior),** suffered, endured
pastor, -oris, *m.,* shepherd
pateo, -ere, patui, 2, lie open
pater, -tris, *m.,* father
patientia, -ae, *f.,* endurance, patience
patior, pati, passus, 3 *dep.,* suffer, allow, endure
patria, -ae, *f.,* fatherland
patricius, -a, -um, *adj.,* patrician, noble
patrimonium, -i, *n.,* patrimony
pauci, -ae, -a, *adj.,* few; *subst.,* **pauci, -orum,** *m. pl.,* few
paulatim, *adv.,* gradually, little by little
paulus, -a, -um, *adj.,* little, small; **paulo,** *abl. as adv.,* a little; **paulum,** *acc. as adv.,* a little
pauper, -eris, *adj.,* poor
paupertas, -atis, *f.,* poverty
pausarius, -i, *m.,* commander of the rowers, boatswain
paveo, -ere, pavi, 2, tremble
pavimentum, -i, *n.,* pavement
pavio, -ire, -ivi, -itus, 4, beat, strike
pavor, -oris, *m.,* fear
pax, pacis, *f.,* peace
peccatum, -i, *n.,* sin, fault
pecco, 1, sin, err, do wrong, make a mistake
pecten, -inis, *m.,* comb
pectus, -oris, *n.,* heart, breast
peculium, -i, *n.,* property in cattle, property; allotment, allowance

Vocabulary O-P

pecunia, -ae, *f.*, money

peior, peius, *comp.* (*of* malus), worse

pelagus, -i, *n.*, sea

pellis, -is, *f.*, skin

Pelops, -opis, *m.*, Pelops, son of Tantalus, father of Atreus and Thyestes

pendeo, -ere, pependi, 2, hang, hover; depend

pendo, -ere, pependi, pensus, 3, weigh, pay

penes, *prep. w. acc.*, with, in the possession or power of

penetralia, -ium, *n. pl.*, the inner part, interior, sanctuary

penitus, *adv.*, deep within, thoroughly

penso, 1, weigh, consider; pay for, purchase

per, *prep. w. acc.*, through

percoquo, -ere, -xi, -ctus, 3, boil or cook thoroughly; heat

percurro, -ere, -cucurri (-curri), -cursus, 3, run through

percutio, -ere, -cussi, -cussus, 3, strike, stamp

perdo, -ere, -didi, -ditus, 3, destroy, ruin; lose, waste

perdomo, -are, -ui, -itus, 1, subdue

perduco, -ere, -duxi, -ductus, 3, lead or bring to

perduro, 1, last, hold out

peregrinatio, -onis, *f.*, wandering, peregrination, traveling

peregrinor, 1 *dep.*, travel

pereo, -ire, -ii (-ivi), -itus, 4, perish

perfecte, *adv.*, perfectly, completely

perfectus, -a, -um, *adj.*, perfect, complete

perfero, -ferre, -tuli, -latus, *irr.*, carry through, deliver

perflatus, -us, *m.*, blowing through, wind, breeze

perfusorius, -a, -um, *adj.*, slight, superficial

perhibeo, -ere, -ui, -itus, 2, assert, maintain

periculosus, -a, -um, *adj.*, dangerous

periculum, -i, *n.*, danger

peritus, -a, -um, *adj.*, skilled

perlucens, -entis, *p. adj.* (*of* perluceo), shining through, transparent

perluceo, -ere, -xi, 2, shine through, be transparent

perlucidus, -a, -um, *adj.*, shining, very clear

permaneo, -ere, -mansi, -mansus, 2, remain, stay; last, abide

permisceo, -ere, -miscui, -mixtus, 2, mix, mingle, confuse

permitto, -ere, -misi, -missus, 3, give up, allow, permit

perniciosus, -a, -um, *adj.*, dangerous, pernicious

perpendo, -ere, -pendi, -pensus, 3, weigh, examine, consider

perperam, *adv.*, wrongly, falsely

perpessicius, -a, -um, *adj.*, one who can endure much

perpetitus, -a, -um, *p. adj.* (*of* perpeto), sought

perpeto, -ere, -ivi, -itus, 3, seek

perpetuus, -a, -um, *adj.*, continuous, perpetual

persaluto, 1, greet one by one

persequor, -sequi, -secutus, 3 *dep.*, pursue, proceed against

persevero, 1, persevere

persona, -ae, *f.*, person, character

personatus, -a, -um, *adj.*, masked; fictitious, not genuine

perspicio, -ere, -spexi, -spectus [per-specio], 3, see through, behold

persto, -stare, -stiti, -status, 1, stand firm, stand fixed

persuadeo, -suadere, -suasi, -suasus, 2, persuade

persuasio, -onis, *f.*, persuasion; conviction

pertinaciter, *adv.*, constantly, pertinaciously

pertinax, -acts, *adj.*, persistent

pertineo, -ere, -tinui, 2, pertain to

pertritus, -a, -um, *adj.*, worn out, very trite

perula, -ae, *f.*, little wallet, pocket

pervenio, -ire, -veni, -ventus, 4, come to, reach

perversus, -a, -um, *adj.*, perverted

pervideo, -ere, -vidi, -visus, 2, see clearly

pervigilo, 1, watch, remain awake

pes, pedis, *m.*, foot; metrical foot, meter

pessimus, -a, -um, *superl.* (*of* malus), worst

pestifer, -fera, -ferum and pestiferus, -a, -um, *adj.*, deadly, pestiferous

pestis, -is, *f.*, plague, pestilence

peto, -ere, petivi, petitus, 3, seek, ask, beg

Philositus, -i, *m.*, Philositus, steward of Seneca, mentioned in *Ep.* 12,3

philosophia, -ae, *f.*, philosophy

philosophor, 1 *dep.*, philosophize

philosophus, -i, *m.*, philosopher

phoenix, -icis, *m.*, phoenix

pictura, -ae, *f.*, painting

pictus, -a, -um, *p. adj.* (*of* pingo), painted, embroidered

pietas, -atis, *f.*, dutiful conduct, loyalty, piety

piger, -gra, -grum, *adj.*, lazy

piget, pigere, piguit or pigitum est, *impers.*, 2, it displeases, it grieves

pigre, *adv.*, lazily

pila, -ae, *f.*, ball

pilicrepus, -i, *m.*, ball-player

pilleatus, -a, -um, *adj.*, wearing the **pilleus** or felt cap

pilleus, -i, *m.*, and pilleum, -i, *n.*, a felt cap worn by slaves when liberated

pilus, -i, *m.*, hair

pingo, -ere, pinxi, pictus, 3, paint, embroider

pinguis, -e, *adj.*, fat, rich

pinna, -ae, *f.*, wing

pinus, -i and -us, *f.*, pine

piscina, -ae, *f.*, pool

piscis, -is, *m.*, fish

pistrinum, -i, *n.*, mill

placenta, -ae, *f.*, cake

placeo, -ere, placui, placitus, 2, please, delight, give pleasure

placidus, -a, -um, *adj.*, calm, placid

placo, 1, soothe, calm

plaga, -ae, *f.*, blow

planus, -a, -um, *adj.*, level, flat

platanus, -i, *f.*, plane-tree

Platon, -onis, *m.*, Plato, 427–347 B.C., the renowned Greek philosopher, disciple of Socrates, and founder of the Academy

plebeius, -a, -um, *adj.*, common, plebeian, low, cheap

plenus, -a, -um, *adj.*, full

plerumque, *adv.*, for the most part, usually, generally

plerusque, -aque, -umque, generally *pl.*, plerique, -aeque, -aque, *adj.*, very many, a large part, the majority

ploro, 1, wail, lament

pluma, -ae, *f.*, feather

plumbum, -i, *n.*, lead, leaden-weight

plurimus, -a, -um, *superl.* (*of* multus), very much, very many

plus, pluris, *comp.* (*of* multus), more

pluvia, -ae, *f.*, rain

podagra, -ae, *f.*, gout

poena, -ae, *f.*, punishment, penalty

poeta, -ae, *m.*, poet

poeticus, -a, -um, *adj.*, poetic

polenta, -ae, *f.*, barley

polio, -ire, -ivi (-ii), -itus, 4, polish, adorn

Polyaenus, -i, *m.*, Polyaenus, a mathematician who followed the tenets of Epicurus

Pompeius, -i, *m.*, Cn. Pompey, consul in 70 B.C. In 60 B.C., he joined the First Triumvirate, consisting of himself, Caesar, and Crassus

Pomponius, -i, *m.*, Pomponius, one of Seneca's contemporaries who wrote letters and tragedies

pomum, -i, *n.*, fruit

pondus, -eris, *n.*, weight

pono, -ere, posui, positus, 3, put, place

pons, -ntis, *m.*, bridge

popina, -ae, *f.*, eating-house

popularis, -e, *adj.*, popular

populus, -i, *m.*, people

porrigo, -ere, -rexi, -rectus, 3, put forth, extend; offer

porro, *adv.*, further, then, moreover

porta, -ae, *f.*, gate

portentosus, -a, -um, *adj.*, monstrous, unnatural

porticus, -us, *f.*, portico, colonnade

porto, 1, carry

portorium, -i, *n.*, tax

portus, -us, *m.*, harbor, port

posco, -ere, poposci, 3, demand

Posidonius, -i, *m.*, Posidonius, c. 135–151 B.C., Stoic philosopher, pupil of Panaetius

positus, -a, -um, *p. adj.* (*of* pono), placed

possessio, -onis, *f.*, possession

possideo, -ere, -sedi, -sessus, 2, possess

possum, posse, potui, *irr.*, be able, can, have power, can do

post, *prep. w. acc.* and *adv.*, after, behind

postea, *adv.*, afterwards

posterus, -a, -um, *adj.*, coming after, following; *subst.*, posteri, -orum, *m. pl.*, posterity

postquam, *adv.*, after

postulaticius, -a, -um, *adj.*, demanded, requested

potens, -entis, *p. adj.* (*of* possum), powerful, mighty

potentia, -ae, *f.*, power

potestas, -atis, *f.*, power, opportunity

potio, -onis, *f.*, drink, potion

potior, -ius, *comp. adj.* (*of* potis), preferable, better; potius, *n. as adv.*, rather, more

potis, -e, *adj.*, able, powerful

potius, *see* potior

praebeo, -ere, -ui, -itus, 2, offer, furnish.

praecedo, -ere, -cessi, -cessus, 3, go before, precede

praeceps, -cipitis, *adj.*, headlong, declining, fallen; hasty, quick

praceps, -itis, *n.*, precipice, extreme danger

praeceptum, -i, *n.*, instruction, teaching, precept

praecido, -ere, -cidi, -cisus [prae-caedo], 3, cut off, abbreviate

praecipio, -ere, -cepi, -ceptus [prae-capio], 3, take beforehand, anticipate; tell beforehand, instruct, advise

praecipitatio, -onis, *f.*, falling headlong

praecipito, 1, cast down headlong, hurl, hasten

praecipue, *adv.*, especially, particularly

praecipuus, -a, -um, *adj.*, especial

praeco, -onis, *m.*, public crier, herald

praedium, -i, *n.*, estate

praefero, -ferre, -tuli, -latus, *irr.*, carry before, prefer

praefractus, -a, -um, *p. adj.* (*of* praefringo), broken, abrupt

praefringo, -ere, -fregi, -fractus [prae-frango], 3, break to pieces

praemitto, -ere, -misi, -missus, 3, send forth or ahead

praemium, -i, *n.*, reward

praenavigo, 1, sail by or past

praeoccupo, 1, seize beforehand

praeparo, 1, make ready, prepare

praeposterus, -a, -um, *adj.*, reversed, inverted, perverted

praerumpo, -ere, -rupi, -ruptus, 3, break off

praeruptus, -a, -um, *p. adj.* (*of* praerumpo), broken off; steep, precipitous

praesens, -entis, *adj.*, present, in person, at hand; *subst.*, praesentia, -ium, *n. pl.*, the present; in praesentia, for the present

praesto, -are, -stiti, -status (-status), 1, fulfill keep one's promise; offer, show, render; guarantee

praesum, -esse, -fui, *irr.*, preside or rule over, be in charge of

praeter, *adv.* and *prep. w. acc.*, beyond, beside, in addition to

praeterea, *adv.*, furthermore, besides, moreover

praetereo, -ire, -ivi (-ii), -itus, 4, go by, pass by

praeteritus, -a, -um, *p. adj.* (*of* praetereo), gone by, past

praetermitto, -mittere, -misi, -missus, 3, pass over, neglect, omit

pratum, -i, *n.*, meadow, lawn

pravitas, -atis, *f.*, depravity

pravus, -a, -um, *adj.*, crooked, perverse

precario, *adv.*, by entreaty or request

premo, -ere, pressi, pressus, 3, press

presse, *adv.*, with pressure; closely, tightly

pressus, -a, -um, *p. adj.* (*of* premo), pressed, compressed, concise

pretiosus, -a, -um, *adj.*, costly, precious

pretium, -i, *n.*, price, worth, value

Priamus, -i, *m.*, Priam, King of Troy during the Trojan War, as reported in the *Iliad*

primo, *adv.*, at first

primor, -oris, *m.*, first in rank, most distinguished

primum, *adv.*, first, in the first place; cum primum, as soon as; quam primum, as soon as possible

primus, -a, -um, *superl. adj., see* prior

principium, -i, *n.*, beginning, origin

prior, -ius, *comp. adj.*, former, first; *subst.*, priores, -um, *m.*, ancestors; primus, -a, -um, *superl. adj.*, first, foremost; in primis, especially, chiefly

prius, *adv.*, before, sooner, first

privatus, -a, -um, *adj.*, private

pro, *prep. w. abl.*, before, in front of; in defense of, on behalf of, for, for the sake of; in place of; as, as good as

probatus, -a, -um, *p. adj.* (*of* probo), approved, excellent

probo, 1, try, test, prove, examine, approve

probus, -a, -um, *adj.*, good, upright

procedo, -ere, -cessi, -cessus, 3, go forth, proceed

procella, -ae, *f.*, storm

proceritas, -atis, *f.*, tallness

procido, -ere, -cidi [pro-cado], 3, fall

procido, -ere, [no perf.], -cisus [pro-caedo], 3, strike down

procisus, -a, -um, *p. adj.* (*of* procido), struck down

proclive, -is, *n.*, slope

procul, *adv.*, far, at a distance

procumbo, -ere, -cubui, -cubitus, 3, fall, sink

prodeo, -ire, -ii, -itus, 4, go, come forth

prodigium, -i, *n.*, prodigy, portent, omen; monster, monstrosity

prodo, -ere, -didi, -ditus, 3, betray, surrender

produco, -ere, -duxi, -ductus, 3, lead or bring forth, prolong, produce, expose or put up for sale

profectus, -us, *m.*, progress

profero, -ferre, -tuli, -latus, *irr.*, carry forth; offer

professio, -onis, *f.*, acknowledgment, profession, promise

professus, -a, -um, *p. adj.* (*of* profiteor), professed

proficio, -ere, -feci, -fectus [pro-facio], 3, make progress, advance; assist, help

profiteor, -eri, -fessus, 2 *dep.*, profess

profugio, -ere, -fugi, -fugitus, 3, flee away from, escape

profundus, -a, -um, *adj.*, deep, profound

progener, -eri, *m.*, granddaughter's husband

progressus, -a, -um, *p. adj.* (*of* progredior), go forth, proceed

prohibeo, -ere, -hibui, -hibitus [pro-habeo], 2, hold off, forbid

proicio, -ere, -ieci, -iectus [pro-iacio], 3, throw forth, throw down

prolabor, -labi, -lapsus, 3 *dep.*, fall

promitto, -ere, -misi, -missus, 3, promise

promiscue, *adv.*, promiscuously, indiscriminately

pronepos, -otis, *m.*, great-grandson

pronus, -a, -um, *adj.*, inclined, forward

propagatio, -onis, *f.*, begetting, propagating; extension

prope, *adv.* and *prep.*, near, near by, close to

propello, -ere, -puli, -pulsus, 3, drive forth, drive away, keep off, ward off

propemodum, *adv.*, nearly, almost

propero, 1, hasten

propior, propius, *comp. adj.*, nearer, closer; *superl.*, proximus, nearest, next

propono, -ere, -posui, -positus, 3, put forth, propose

propositum, -i, *n.*, plan

propositus, -a, -um, *p. adj.* (*of* propono), put forth, proposed

proprie, *adv.*, properly, peculiarly, strictly for oneself

proprietas, -atis, *f.*, property, peculiarity

proprius, -a, -um, *adj.*, one's own, peculiar, characteristic of

propter, *prep. w. acc.*, on account of, for the sake of

prora, -ae, *f.*, prow

prorito, 1, incite, tempt

prorsus, *adv.*, utterly, absolutely, wholly

prospicio, -ere, -spexi, -spectus, 3, look forward, look out upon

prospectus, -us, *m.*, view, sight

prostituo, -ere, -ui, -utus, 3, expose publicly to prostitution, prostitute

prosum, prodesse, profui, *irr.*, help, be of use

protego, -ere, -texi, -tectus, 3, cover, protect

protinus, *adv.*, at once, immediately, straightway

protraho, -ere, -traxi, -tractus, 3, drag forth, bring forth or out

prout, *conj.*, just as, according as, in proportion as

proveho, -ere, -xi, -ctus, 3, carry forward

provenio, -ire, -veni, -ventus, 4, come forth

proverbium, -i, *n.*, proverb

providentia, -ae, *f.*, foresight, forethought, providence

provideo, -ere, -vidi, -visus, 2, see to, look after, provide

provincia, -ae, f., province

proximus, -a, -um, *superl.* (*of* propior), nearest, next

prudens, -entis, *adj.*, wise, prudent

prudentia, -ae, *f.*, wisdom, prudence

psychroluta, -ae, *m.*, one who bathes in cold water

publice, *adv.*, publicly, by the crowd

publico, 1, make public

publicus, -a, -um, *adj.*, public, common, ordinary

pudet, -ere, -uit, *impers.*, 2, it makes ashamed

pudor, -oris, *m.*, shame, modesty, decency

puer, pueri, *m.*, boy

puerilis, -e, *adj.*, childish, puerile

pueritia, -ae, *f.*, boyhood

pugillares, -ium, *m. pl.*, writing tablets

pugna, -ae, *f.*, fight, battle

pugno, 1, fight

pugnus, -i, *m.*, fist

pulcher, -chra, -chrum, *adj.*, beautiful

pulpitum, -i, *n.*, platform, stage

pulvis, -eris, *m.*, dust

punctiuncula, -ae, *f.*, pricking pain

Punicus, -a, -um, *adj.*, Punic, Carthaginian

pupulus, -i, *m.*, little boy

purpura, -ae, *f.*, purple

purus, -a, -um, *adj.*, clean, pure

pusillus, -a, -um, *adj.*, very small, tiny; *subst.*, pusillum, -i, *n.*, small amount

pustula, -ae, *f.*, blister

Puteoli, -orum, *m.*, Puteoli, a town in Campania, between Baiae and Naples

putidus, -a, -um, *adj.*, rotten, putrid

puto, 1, think

putris, -e, *adj.*, rotten

Pythagoras, -ae, *m.*, Pythagoras, Greek philosopher of the 6th cent. B.C., founder of the Pythagorean School of philosophy

Pythocles, *m.*, Pythocles, friend of Idomeneus in the age of Epicurus

Q

qua, *adv.*, on which side, where

quadratum, -i, *n.*, square

quaero, -ere, quaesivi, quaesitus, 3, seek, ask, ask for, inquire

quaesitus, -a, -um, *p. adj.* (*of* quaero), sought out

quaestio, -onis, *f.*, question

qualis, -e, *adj.*, of what sort, what kind of; talis. . .qualis, such. . .as

qualiscumque, qualecumque, *adj.*, of whatever sort

qualitas, -atis, *f.*, quality, property

quam, *interrog. adv.*, how, how much; *rel. adv.*, as much, as, than; quam primum, as soon as possible; (*with superl.*) as. . .as possible

quamdiu, *interrog. adv.*, how long; *rel. adv.*, as long as

quamvis, *adv.*, however much, however; although

quando, *adv. and conj.*, when, at any time, since

quandoque, *adv.*, at some time or other

quantulus, -a, -um, *adj.*, how little

quantuluscumque, -acumque, -umcumque, *adj.*, how little soever, however small

quantus, -a, -um, *adj.*, how great, how much, as great as, as; quantum, *acc. as adv.*, how much, how, as much, as, as far as, as much as

quantuscumque, -acumque, -umcumque, *adv.*, how great soever

quantuslibet, -alibet, -umlibet, *adj.*, as great as you will, however great

quare, *interrog. and rel. adv.*, on what account, why, wherefore

quasi, *adv.*, as if, as if it were

quatriduum, -i, *n.*, a space of four days

quattuordecim, *num. adj.*, fourteen

quemadmodum, *interrog. and rel. adv.*, in what manner, how, just as

queo, -ire, -ivi (-ii), -itus, 4, be able

queror, queri, questus, 3 *dep.*, complain

qui, quae, quod, *rel. adj. and pron.*, who, which, what

quia, *conj.*, because

quicumque, quae-, quid-, *indef. rel. pron.* and quicumque, quae-, quod -, *indef. adj.*, whoever, whatever

quid, *adv.*, why; *see also* quis

quidam, quaedam, quoddam, *indef. adj.*, certain, some; quidam, quaedam, quiddam, *indef. pron.*, a certain one or thing

quidem, *adv.*, truly, indeed, to be sure; ne. . .quidem, not even, nor. . .either quidni? *adv.*, why not?, of course

quies, quietis, *f.*, quiet, repose

quiesco, -ere, quievi, quietus, 3, rest, repose, be quiet

quietus, -a, -um, *adj.*, quiet, peaceful

quiete, *adv.*, quietly, peaceably

quilibet, quae-, quid-, *indef. pron.* and quilibet, quae-, quod-, *indef. adj.*, anyone you please, anyone, any, some

quin, *conj.*, that, but that; *adv.*, why not

quingentesimus, -a, -um, *adj.*, five hundredth

quinque, *num. adj.*, five

quis, quid, *interrog. pron.*, who, what; quid, why

quis, quid, *indef. pron.*, any, anyone, anything; someone, something

quisquam, quae-, quid- (quic-), *indef. pron.*, anyone, anything

quisque, quaeque, quidque, *indef. pron.* and quisque, quaeque, quodque, *indef. adj.*, each one, each thing, every

quisquis, quidquid, *indef. rel. pron.*, whoever, whatever

quivis, quaevis, quidvis, *indef. pron.* and quivis, quaevis, quodvis, *indef. adj.*, anyone, anything

quo, *adv.*, whither, to what end, for what purpose; *with comp. introducing a* quo *purpose clause*, in order that; eo magis. . .quo magis, the more. . .the more

quo. . .hoc = quanto. . .tanto, the. . .the

quocumque, *adv.*, wherever

quod, *conj.*, that, because, in that, the fact that

quominus, *conj.*, that not, from, *after verbs of hindering, preventing, etc.*

quomodo, *adv.*, in what way, in which manner, as

quoniam, *conj.*, since

quoque, *conj.*, also, too

quot, *indecl. adj.*, how many; tot. . .quot, so many. . .as

quotiens, *adv.*, whenever, as often as, how many times, how often; totiens. . .quotiens, so often. . .as

quotusquisque, -quaeque, - quodque, *adj.*, -quidque, *pron.*, how many; *ironically*, how few

quousque, *adv.*, how long

R

rabies, -ei, *f.*, rage, fury

radius, -i, *m.*, ray; shuttle (sharp piece of wood similar to a needle)

radix, -icis, *f.*, root

ramale, -is, *n.*, usually *pl.*, twigs, branches

ramus, -i, *m.*, branch, twig

rapina, -ae, *f.*, plundering, robbery, pillage

rapio, -ere, rapui, raptus, 3, snatch

raritas, -atis, *f.*, fewness, rarity

rarus, -a, -um, *adj.*, rare

ratio, -onis, *f.*, reckoning, account, way, means; reason

rationalis, -e, *adj.*, of or belonging to reason, reasonable, rational

recalesco, -ere, -calui, 3, become warm, glow

recedo, -ere, -cessi, -cessus, 3, go back, recede, retreat, retire, withdraw

recens, -entis, *adj.*, new, fresh, young, recent

receptaculum, -i, *n.*, receptacle, shelter, retreat

receptus, -us, *m.*, drawing back, retreat

receptus, -a, -um, *p. adj.* (*of* recipio), received, taken

recido, -ere, -cidi, -casurus [re-cado], 3, fall back

recipio, -ere, -cepi, -ceptus [re-capio], 3, take, receive

recito, 1, read aloud or publicly, recite

recondo, -ere, -didi, -ditus, 3, conceal, hide

recordatio, -onis, *f.*, recollection, remembrance

recordor, 1 *dep.*, remember

recorrigo, -ere, -correxi, -correctus [re-con-rego], 3, amend, reform

recreo, 1, refresh, restore

recrudesco, -ere, recrudui, 3, become raw again; break out again

rector, -oris, *m.*, ruler, leader

recurro, -ere, -curri, -cursus, 3, run back

recte, *adv.*, rightly

rectus, -a, -um, *p. adj.* (*of* rego), right, straight, erect

recuso, 1, refuse, reject

reddo, -ere, -didi, -ditus, 3, give back, return, render, restore

redeo, -ire, -ii (-ivi), -itus [re-eo], 4, go back, return

redigo, -ere, -egi, -actus [re-ago], 3, drive back, reduce

redimo, -ere, -emi, -emptus [re-emo], 3, pay for

reduco, -ere, -duxi, -ductus, 3, bring back

redundo [re-undo], 1, overflow, be very abundant, abound

refero, -ferre, -tuli, -latus, *irr.*, bring back, repeat

refers, referre, retulit, *irr. impers.*, it is important, it matters, it makes a difference

reficio, -ere, -feci, -fectus [re-facio], 3, make afresh, restore

reformido, 1, fear

refrigesco, -ere, -frixi, 3, grow cold

refugio, -ere, -fugi, -fugitus, 3, flee away, escape

regero, -ere, -gessi, -gestus, 3, bring back

regio, -onis, *f.*, region

regius, -a, -um, *adj.*, royal

regnum, -i, *n.*, royal power, rule, authority; despotism, tyranny

rego, -ere, rexi, rectus, 3, direct, rule

Vocabulary Q -R

regula, -ae, *f.*, rule, pattern, model; ruler

Regulus, -i, *m.*, M. Atilius Regulus, consul in 267 and 256 B.C., Roman hero during the First Punic War

reicio, -ere, -ieci, -iectus [re-iacio], 3, throw back, reject

reiculus, -a, -um, *adj.*, worthless

relatus, -a, -um, *p. adj.* (*of* refero), brought back

relictus, -a, -um, *p. adj.* (*of* relinquo), abandoned, relinquished

religio, -onis, *f.*, respect for what is sacred, religion

relinquo, -ere, -liqui, -lictus, 3, leave behind, abandon, relinquish

reliquiae, -arum, *f.*, remains

remaneo, -ere, -mansi, -mansus, 2, remain

remedium, -i, *n.*, remedy

remex, -igis, *m.*, rower, oarsman

remissio, -onis, *f.*, breaking off, interrupting, relaxation, recovery

remissus, -a, -um, *p. adj.* (*of* remitto), mild

remitto, -ere, -misi, -missus, 3, send back, return, leave behind; give up, let go, yield, relax

remollio, -ire, -ivi, -itus, 4, soften

reparabilis, -e, *adj.*, that can be repaired or restored, reparable

reparo, 1, acquire again, get back, recover

repello, -ere, repuli (reppuli), -pulsus, 3, drive back, repel

repente, *adv.*, suddenly

repentinus, -a, -um, *adj.*, sudden, unexpected

reperio, -ire, repperi, repertus, 4, find, find out, discover

repeto, -ere, -petivi (-ii), -petitus, 3, seek again

repono, -ere, -posui, -positus, 3, put back, return

repraesento, 1, represent, show

reprehendo, -ere, -prehendi, -prehensus, 3, blame, reprehend, censure

reprimo, -ere, -pressi, -pressus [re-premo], 3, hold back, restrain, repress

repugnans, *p. adj.* (*of* repugno), contrary, opposed

repugno, 1, oppose, resist

res, rei, *f.*, thing, matter, event, circumstance; res publica, state, republic

resero, 1, unlock, open

resideo, -ere, -sedi, -sessus [re-sedeo], 2, quiet down

resisto -ere, -stiti, 3, stand back, resist

resolvo, -ere, -solvi, -solutus, 3, unbind, loosen

resono, -are, -sonui (-sonavi), 1, resound

respicio, -ere, -spexi, -spectus [re-specio], 3, look back, reflect upon, have respect for, look to

respiratio, -onis, *f.*, respiration

respondeo, -ere, -spondi, -sponsus, 2, answer, respond

responsum, -i, *n.*, answer

respuo, -ere, -spui, -sputus, 3, spit back, reject, refuse

resto, -are, -stiti, 1, remain, be left

resupinus, -a, -um, *adj.*, with head thrown back, i.e., proudly

retardo, 1, delay, retard

retempto, 1, test

retentus, -a, -um, *p. adj.* (*of* retineo), held back

retineo, -ere, -tinui, -tentus [re-teneo], 2, hold back

retorridus, -a, -um, *adj.*, dried up

retractatio, -onis, *f.*, remembrance

retractus, -a, -um, *p. adj.* (*of* retracto), drawn back or away

retraho, -ere, -traxi, -tractus, 3, draw back, take back

retritus, -a, -um, *adj.*, worn down, rubbed down

retro, *adv.*, back, backwards, behind

retundo, -ere, -tudi, -tusus (-tunsus), 3, beat, blunt

revello, -ere, -velli, -vulsus, 3, tear out or away

revertor, -i, -versus, 3 *dep.*, return

revoco, 1, call back, recall

revolvo, -ere, -volvi, -volutus, 3, roll back, revolve, return; ponder

rex, regis, *m.*, king, ruler

rideo, -ere, risi, risus, 2, laugh

ridiculus, -a, -um, *adj.*, ridiculous, laughable

rigeo, -ere, 2, be stiff

rigo, 1, water

rimor, 1, pry into, search, explore

ripa, -ae, *f.*, bank

risus, -us, *m.*, laughter

rivus, -i, *m.*, stream

rixa, -ae, *f.*, quarrel, brawl

rixor, 1 *dep.*, quarrel

robur, -oris, *n.*, strength; hard wood

robustus, -a, -um, *adj.*, strong, robust

rogo, 1, ask, beg

rogus, -i, *m.*, funeral pile

Roma, -ae, *f.*, Rome

Romanus, -a, -um, *adj.*, Roman

ros, roris, *m.*, dew

rosa, -ae, *f.*, rose

rostra, -orum, *n. pl.*, the speaker's platform

rota, -ae, *f.*, wheel

rotundus, -a, -um, *adj.*, rotund, round

rubesco, -ere, rubui, 3, redden, blush

rubigo, -inis, *m.*, rust

rubor, -oris, *m.*, redness, blush

rudis, -e, *adj.*, rough, rude, raw, untrained, uninstructed

ruina, -ae, *f.*, fall, ruin, disaster

rumor, -oris, *m.*, rumor, gossip

rumpo, -ere, rupi, ruptus, 3, break

Vocabulary R

ruo, -ere, rui, rutus, 3, rush, hasten
rupes, -is, *f.*, rock, cliff
rursus and rursum, *adv.*, on the other hand, again
rus, ruris, *n.*, country, farm
rusticitas, -atis, *f.*, rustic manners, rusticity

S

Sabinus, -i, *m.*, Calvisius Sabinus, an example of the vulgar *nouveaux riches* in the age of Seneca
sacer, -era, -crum, *adj.*, sacred, holy
sacramentum, -i, *n.*, oath
sacro, 1, make holy, consecrate
sacrum, -i, *n.*, shrine, temple
saeculum, -i, *n.*, age, generation, century
saepe, *adv.*, often, frequently
saevio, -ire, -ii, -itus, 4, rage
saevitia, -ae, *f.*, ferocity, cruelty, severity
saevus, -a, -um, *adj.*, cruel, fierce, savage
sagacitas, -atis, *f.*, shrewdness, skillfulness, keenness
sagina, -ae, *f.*, stuffing
sagino, 1, fatten
sagum, -i, *n.*, coarse cloak
sal, -is, *n.* and *m. in sing., m. always in pl.*, salt, wit
salebra, -ae, *f.*, roughness, harshness
saliaris, -e, *adj.*, of or belonging to the Salii (priests of Mars)
salio, -ire, salui, 4, leap
Sallustianus, -a, -um, *adj.*, of or like Sallust, Sallustian
Sallustius, -i, *m.*, Sallust, Roman historian (86–35 B.C.)
saltus, -us, *m.*, jumping
saltus, -us, *m.*, forest, woods
salubris, -e, *adj.*, healthy, healthful, salubrious
salus, -utis, *f.*, health, safety; greeting, salutation
salutaris, -e, *adj.*, healthful, wholesome, salutary
salutatio, -onis, *f.*, good morning greeting
saluto, 1, greet, salute
salutor, -oris, *m.*, one who greets, a caller, a visitor
salvus, -a, -um, *adj.*, safe, sound
sancio, -ire, sanxi, sanctus, 4, make sacred, make inviolable
sanctus, -a, -um, *p. adj.* (*of* sancio), sacred, holy, inviolable
sanguis, -inis, *m.*, blood
sane, *adv.*, indeed, to be sure
sanitas, -atis, *f.*, sound state of mind, sanity, health
sano, 1, heal, cure
sanus, -a, -um, *adj.*, sound, healthy
sapiens, -entis, *p. adj.* (*of* sapio), wise; subst., wise man

sapientia, -ae, *f.*, wisdom
sapio, -ere, -ii, 3, be wise
sapor, -oris, *m.*, taste, flavor, savor
sarcina, -ae, *f.*, burden, load
Sarmatia, -ae, *f.*, Sarmatia, the name for what is now modern Poland
sat, *see* satis
Satellius Quadratus, -i, *m.*, a parasite, fawner, and mocker of wealthy men in the age of Seneca
satietas, -atis, *f.*, abundance, satiety
satio, 1, satisfy, satiate
satio, -onis, *f.*, sowing, planting
satis (*abbreviated* sat), *adj.* and *adv.*, enough, sufficient; satius, *comp.*, better, preferable
satrapes, -ae and -is, satrapa, -ae, *m.*, satraps, -apis, *m.*, the governor of a Persian province, satrap
satur, -ura, -urum, *adj.*, full, satiated
saturitas, -atis, *f.*, fullness, satiety
Saturnalia, -ium, *n.*, Saturnalia, a festival celebrated Dec. 15–17, in honor of Saturn, god of planting. It was a period of general rejoicing during which presents were exchanged and slaves were waited upon by their masters
saxum, -i, *n.*, stone, rock
scaena, -ae, *f.*, stage, scene
scaenicus, -a, -um, *adj.*, of the stage, theatrical
scapulae, -arum, *f.*, shoulders, back
scelus, -eris, *n.*, crime, wickedness
schola, -ae, *f.*, leisure, learned leisure; school
scientia, -ae, *f.*, knowledge
scilicet, *adv.*, of course, evidently
scindo, -ere, scidi, scissus, 3, cut
scintilla, -ae, *f.*, spark
scio, -ire, scivi, scitus, 4, know, know how to
Scipio, -onis, *m.*, Publius Cornelius Scipio Africanus Major, who brought the Second Punic War to an end by his victory at Zama (202 B.C.)
scordalus, -i, *m.*, quarrelsome fellow
scribo, -ere, scripsi, scriptus, 3, write
scrinium, -i, *n.*, bookcase
Scytha, -ae, *m.*, Scythian
Scythia, -ae, *f.*, Scythia, country north of the Black and the Caspian Seas
scrutor, 1, scrutinize
scutum, -i, *n.*, shield
se, *see* sui
secedo, -ere, -cessi, -cessus, 3, go away, withdraw, retire
secessus, -us, *m.*, retirement, retreat
seco, -are, secui, sectus, 1, cut
secretum, -i, *n.*, secret; solitude
sector, 1 *dep.*, follow, pursue
secundum, *prep. w. acc.*, following, according to, next to

Vocabulary R–S

secundus, -a, -um, *adj.*, following, following the first, second

secure, *adv.*, safely, securely, without care

securitas, -atis, *f.*, freedom from care, security, calm

securus, -a, -um, *adj.*, free from care, secure, calm

sed, *conj.*, but

sedeo, -ere, sedi, sessus, 2, sit, settle

sedes, -is, *f.*, seat, abode, habitation

seditio, -onis, *f.*, dissension, sedition

sedo, 1, settle, soothe, calm

seduco, -ere, -duxi, -ductus, 3, take away, carry off

seges, -etis, *f.*, crop

segnis, -e, *adj.*, slow, sluggish

segnitia, -ae, *f.*, sluggishness

semel, *num. adv.*, once, a single time, once for all

semen, -inis, *n.*, seed

seminudus, -a, -um, *adj.*, half-naked

semper, *adv.*, always

senatorius, -a, -um, *adj.*, senatorial

senatus, -us, *m.*, senate

senectus, -utis, *f.*, old age

senex, -is, *adj.*, old; *subst. m.*, old man

sensus, -us, *m.*, feeling, sense, meaning, thought

sententia, -ae, *f.*, thought, opinion

sentio, -ire, sensi, sensus, 4, feel, perceive, see

separo, 1, separate

sepono, -ere, -posui, -positus, 3, set aside

sepositus, -a, -um, *p. adj.* (*of* sepono), set aside, withdrawn

septem, *num. adj. indecl.*, seven

sequor, sequi, secutus, 3 *dep.*, follow

sera, -ae, *f.*, lock, bolt

Serenus, -i, *m.*, Annaeus Serenus, Seneca's intimate friend to whom he dedicated the dialogues *De Constantia Sapientis, De Otio* and *De Tranquillitate Animi*

serica, -orum, *n. pl.*, Seric (Chinese) garments, silks

series (no gen. or dat.), -em, -e, *f.*, row, succession, series

serius, -a, -um, *adj.*, serious

sermo, -onis, *m.*, talk, conversation

sero, -ere, sevi, satus, 3, sow, plant

serpens, -entis, *c.*, snake, serpent

serra, -ae, *f.*, saw

serrarius, -i, *m.*, one who saws

serus, -a, -um, *adj.*, late

servatus, -a, -um, *p. adj.* (*of* servo), preserved, saved

servilis, -e, *adj.*, slavish, servile

servio, -ire, -ivi, -itus, 4, be a slave, serve

servitus, -utis, *f.*, slavery, servitude

servo, 1, keep, preserve, save

servus, -i, *m.*, slave

severus, -a, -um, *adj.*, serious, severe

sexaginta, *num. adj.*, sixty

si, *conj.*, if

sibilus, -i, *m.*, hissing, whistling

sic, *adv.*, thus, so

sicco, 1, drain, dry, empty

siccus, -a, -um, *adj.*, dry, temperate; siccum,; -i, *n.*, dry land

Sicilia, -ae, *f.*, Sicily

sicut, *adv.*, just as, as

sidus, -eris, *n.*, star

sigillaria, -orum, *n. pl.*, small images or figures

signo, 1, put a mark upon, mark

signum, -i, *n.*, sign, mark, signal; watchword

silentium, -i, *n.*, silence

silva, -ae, *f.*, woods, forest

silvester, -tris, -tre, *adj.*, belonging to a woods or forest

similis, -e, *adj.*, like, similar

similitudo, -inis, *f.*, likeness, similitude; simile

simplex, -icis, *adj.*, single, simple, pure

simul, *adv.*, at once, at the same time; simul ac, at the same time as, as well as

simulacrum, -i, *n.*, image, portrait, statue

simulatus, -a, -um, *p. adj.* (*of* simulo), feigned

simulo, 1, feign, pretend, simulate

sine, *prep. w. abl.*, without

singularis, -e, *adj.*, singular, unique, extraordinary, exceptional

singuli, -ae, -a, *adj.*, one at a time, separate, single, each

singultus, -us, *m.*, sobbing; hiccuping

sino, -ere, sivi, situs, 3, allow, permit

sinus, -us, *m.*, bending, curve, fold

Sirena, -ae, *f.*, usually *pl.*, Sirens, birds with the faces of women

sitis, -is, *f.*, thirst

situs, -us, *m.*, mould, disuse

sive and seu, *conj.*, or if; sive. . .sive, seu. . .seu, whether. . .or, if. . .or if

sobrius, -a, -um, *adj.*, sober

societas, -atis, *f.*, society, companionship, association

socius, -i, *m.*, ally, comrade, companion

Socrates, -is, *m.*, Socrates, 469–399 B.C., the celebrated Greek philosopher

sol, solis, *m.*, sun

solacium, -i, *n.*, consolation, solace

soleo, -ere, solitus, 2 *semi-dep.*, be accustomed, be wont

solidus, -a, -um, *adj.*, solid

solitudo, -inis, *f.*, solitude

solitus, -a, -um, *p. adj.* (*of* soleo), usual, customary

sollicito, 1, disturb

sollicitudo, -inis, *f.*, anxiety, solicitude, care

Vocabulary S

sollicitus, -a, -um, *adj.,* full of anxiety, anxious, solicitous, stirred up, disturbed

Solon, -onis, *m.,* Solon, c. 640–c. 558 B.C., renowned Athenian statesman, poet, and lawgiver, one of the seven wise men

solum, *adv.,* alone, only; **non solum. . .sed etiam,** not only. . .but also

solum, -i, *n.,* ground

solus, -a, -um, *adj.,* alone, only, sole

solutus, -a, -um, *p. adj. (of* **solvo),** loosened, set free

solvo, -ere, solvi, solutus, 3, loosen, set free, solve, pay a debt, pay

somnium, -i, *n.,* dream

somnus, -i, *m.,* sleep

sono, -are, sonui, sonitus, 1, resound, make a noise

sonus, -i, *m.,* noise, sound

sopor, -oris, *m.,* sleep

sordeo, -ere, sordui, 2, be dirty

sordes, -is, *f.,* generally *pl.,* **sordes, -ium,** *f.,* dirt, filth, meanness, sordidness

sordidus, -a, -um, *adj.,* dirty, sordid, mean; small, paltry

sors, sortis, *f.,* lot, fate, chance; order, rank

spado, -onis, *m.,* eunuch

spargo, -ere, sparsi, sparsus, 3, scatter, sprinkle

sparsus, -a, -um, *p. adj. (of* **spargo),** scattered

spatha, -ae, *f.,* batten or spoon-shaped paddle used to interweave threads on the loom

spatium, -i, *n.,* space, period of time, interval

species, -ei, *f.,* sight, look, appearance; vision

speciosus, -a, -um, *adj.,* showy, good-looking

spectaculum, -i, *n.,* show, sight, spectacle

spectator, -oris, *m.,* spectator

specto, 1, look at, look to as an aim or object, aim

spector, -oris, *m.,* spectator

specularia, -orum, *n.,* window panes, windows

speculor, 1 *dep.,* examine, explore

specus, -us, *m.,* cave

spero, 1, hope

spes, spei, *f.,* hope

sphaeromachia, -ae, *f.,* boxing-match

spiritus, -us, *m.,* breath, air, spirit, soul

spiro, 1, breathe

spisso, 1, thicken, pack closely

splendeo, -ere, -ui, 2, shine

splendidus, -a, -um, *adj.,* bright, splendid

splendor, -oris, *m.,* brilliance, splendor

(spons), -tis, *f.,* free-will (only found in gen. and abl.); **sponte,** of one's own accord, voluntarily, freely

sponte, *see* **spons**

sputum, -i, *n.,* spittle

squalidus, -a, -um, *adj.,* squalid, dirty

squalor, -oris, *m.,* filthiness, squalor

stabilis, -e, *adj.,* firm, stable

stagnum, -i, *n.,* standing water, pool, pond, bath

stamen, -inis, *n.,* warp, tautened thread on an upright loom

statim, *adv.,* at once, immediately

statio, -onis, *f.,* station, office, position

statua, -ae, *f.,* statue

status, -us, *m.,* condition, state

stemma, -atis, *n.,* crown, chaplet, nobility, pedigree

sternumentum, -i, *n.,* sneezing

stilus, -i, *m.,* pen; writing

stimulus, -i, *m.,* goad, spur, stimulus

stipo, 1, pack close, crowd

stipula, -ae, *f.,* straw

sto, stare, steti, status, 1, stand

stomachor, 1 *dep.,* be angry or vexed

stomachus, -i, *m.,* stomach; good digestion; taste, liking; dislike, distaste

strangulo, 1, choke, strangle

stratum, -i, *n.,* saddle

strepens, -entis, *p. adj. (of* **strepo),** noisy

strepitus, -us, *m.,* noise

strepo, -ere, -ui, -itus, 3, make a loud noise, creak, clash

stridulus, -a, -um, *adj.,* creaking, shrill

stringo, -ere, strinxi, strictus, 3, graze

structus, -a, -um, *p. adj. (of* **struo),** arranged

struo, -ere, struxi, structus, 3, arrange

studeo, -ere, studui, 2, be eager, study

studium, -i, *n.,* zeal, eagerness, study, pursuit

stultitia, -ae, *f.,* foolishness, folly

stultus, -a, -um, *adj.,* foolish

stupeo, -ere, -ui, 2, be amazed, be astonished

stupor, -oris, *m.,* stupidity; astonishment, amazement

suadeo, -ere, suasi, suasus, 2, advise, persuade

suaviter, *adv.,* sweetly, agreeably, pleasantly

sub, *prep. w. abl.,* under, beneath

subdo, -ere, -didi, -ditus, 3, put, place at, near, under

subditus, -a, -um, *p. adj. (of* **subdo),** placed at or near

subduco, -ducere, -duxi, -ductus, 3, draw from under, take away, steal, withdraw

subeo, -ire, -ii, -itus, 4, go under, come under, come upon

subicio, -ere, -ieci, -iectus [sub-iacio], 3, throw under, place under, subdue, subject

subiectus, -a, -um, *p. adj. (of* **subicio),** lying beneath

subigo, -ere, -egi, -actus [sub-ago], 3, plough, cultivate

subinde, *adv.,* continually, repeatedly

subito, *adv.,* suddenly

subitus, -a, -um, *adj.,* sudden, unexpected

submissus, -a, -um, *p. adj. (of* **submitto**), lowered, low, soft

submitto, -ere, -misi, -missus, 3, let down, lower

subrepo, -ere, -repsi, -reptus, 3, creep in

subripio, -ere, -ripui, -reptus [sub-rapio], 3, take away secretly, steal

subsicivus, -a, -um, *adj.,* that is cut off and left remaining, remaining over, occasional, incidental

subsido, -ere, -sedi, -sessus, 3, sink, settle down

substituo, -ere, -stitui, -stitutus [sub-statuo], 3, substitute

subtemen, -inis, *n.,* woof, threads woven in weaving

subtero, -ere, -trivi, -tritus, 3, wear out, bruise

subtilis, -e, *adj.,* thin, fine, acute, subtle

subtilitas, -atis, *f.,* accuracy, subtlety

suburbanum, -i, *n.,* suburban villa

subveho, -ere, -vexi, -vectus, 3, carry, convey

succedo, -ere, -cessi, -cessus [sub-cedo], 3, go beneath; follow, come along, enter, approach

succresco, -ere, -crevi, -cretus [sub-cresco], 3, spring up

succurro, -ere, -curri, -cursus [sub-curro], 3, run to aid, help, succor; occur [to one's mind]

sucus, -i, *m.,* juice

sudatorium, -i, *n.,* sweating-room

sudo, 1, perspire, sweat

sudor, -oris, *m.,* sweat

sufficio, -ere, -feci, -fectus [sub-facio], 3, be sufficient, suffice; be fit for

suffocatio, -onis, *f.,* suffocation

suffodio, -ere, -fodi, -fosus, 3, dig out, excavate

suffosus, -a, -um, *p. adj. (of* **suffodio**), dug out, excavated

suffragium, -i, *n.,* vote

suffundo, -ere, -fudi, -fusus [sub-fundo], 3, pour beneath, spread through, suffuse

suggero, -ere, -gessi, -gestus, 3, furnish, supply

sui, *gen.,* **sibi,** *dat.,* **se** or **sese,** *acc.* and *abl., reflex. pron. 3rd pers.,* himself, herself, itself, themselves

Sulla, -ae, *m.,* Sulla, distinguished leader of the aristocratic party, opponent of Marius, head of the democratic party. Sulla became dictator of Rome in 32 B.C.

sum, esse, fui, futurus, *irr.,* be, exist

summa, -ae, *f.,* main thing, chief point; sum, sum total, sum of money

sumministrator, -oris, *m.,* one who aids or assists, promoter

summissus, -a, -um, *p. adj. (of* **summitto**), let down, lowered, hanging down

summitto, -ere, -misi, -missus [sub-mitto], 3, lower; subject, submit; send

summoveo, -ere, -movi, -motus [sub-moveo], 2, remove

summus, -a, -um, *superl. adj. (of* **superus**), highest, very high, uppermost; last, extreme; **summum, -i,** *n.,* top, highest place, surface

sumo, -ere, sumpsi, sumptus, 3, take, take up, put on, wear

sumptuosus, -a, -um, *adj.,* costly, expensive, sumptuous; extravagant

supellex, -lectilis, *f., abl.* **-lectile** and **-lectili,** *f.,* furniture

super, *prep. w. acc.,* above, upon

superbia, -ae, *f.,* pride, haughtiness

superbus, -a, -um, *adj.,* proud, haughty

superior, -oris, *comp. (of* **superus**)

superiacio, -ere, -ieci, -iectus, 3, throw over, exceed, outstrip

superlabor, -labi, -lapsus, 3 *dep.,* glide over

supero, 1, surpass, excel

supersum, -esse, -fui, *irr.,* be over and above; be left, remain

superus, -a, -um, *comp.,* **superior,** *superl.,* **supremus, summus,** *adj.,* upper, higher, above, on high, high

supervacuus, -a, -um, *adj.,* superfluous, useless

supervenio, -ire, -veni, -ventus, 4, come over, come along

supplicium, -i, *n.,* punishment

supprimo, -ere, -pressi, -pressus [sub-premo], 3, press down, suppress

suppuratus, -a, -um, *adj.,* full of sores

supra, *adv.* and *prep.,* above, over

surculus, -i, *m.,* young shoot, sprout, scion, graft

surdus, -a, -um, *adj.,* deaf

surgo, -ere, surrexi, surrectus, 3, rise

sursum, *adv.,* upwards, on high; **sursum deorsum,** up and down, topsy-turvy

suscipio, -ere, -cepi, -ceptus [sub-capio], 3, support, hold up, prop up

suspendo, -ere, -pendi, -pensus, 3, hang up; support, suspend

suspensura, -ae, *f.,* vault, arch

suspensus, -a, -um, *p. adj. (of* **suspendo**), suspended, hanging, endangered, uncertain, anxious

suspicio, -ere, -spexi, -spectus [sub-specio], 3, look up to

suspicio, -onis, *f.,* suspicion; notion, idea, conception

suspicor, 1 *dep.,* suspect

suspiciosus, -a, -um, *adj.,* suspicious

suspirium, -i, *n.,* sigh, shortness of breath, asthma

suspiro [sub-spiro], 1, breathe deeply, sigh

sustineo, -ere, -tinui, -tentus [sub-teneo], 2, hold up, support, sustain, endure, bear

sutrinum, -i, *n.,* shoemaker's trade

suus, -a, -um, *poss. adj.* and *pron.,* his, her, its, their own

symphonia, -ae, *f.*, concert, musical performance

Syrticus, -a, -um, *adj.*, of or belonging to the Syrtes

T

tabella, -ae *f.*, flat board, tablet

tabula, -ae, *f.*, tablet for writing; XII tabulae, the Twelve Tables, a code of Roman laws framed by a commission of ten magistrates in 451 B.C.

taceo, -ere, -ui, -itus, 2, be silent

tacitus, -a, -um, *p. adj.* (*of* taceo), silent, tacit

tactus, -us, *m.*, touch

taedium, -i, *n.*, weariness, tedium

taeter, -ra, -rum, *adj.*, foul, offensive, nauseating

talaria, -ium, *n. pl.*, ankles

talis, -e, *adj.*, of such a kind, such; talis. . .qualis, such. . .as

talus, -i, *m.*, ankle

tam, *adv.*, so, so much, as, as much; tam. . .quam, so. . .as

tamen, *adv.*, yet, still, however, nevertheless

tamquam, *adv.*, as, just as, as if

tango, -ere, tetigi, tactus, 3, touch

tantum, *acc. as adv.*, only, merely

tantummodo, *adv.*, only

tantundem, *acc. as adv.*, just so much, as much

tantus, -a, -um, *adj.*, so great, so much

tantusdem, tantadem, tantundem, *adj.*, just so much; tantundem, *acc. as adv.*, just so much, as much

tardus, -a, -um, *adj.*, slow, tardy

taurus, -i, *m.*, bull

tector, -oris, *m.*, builder

tectum, -i, *n.*, roof, dwelling

tectus, -a, -um, *p. adj.* (*of* tego), 3, covered, protected

tegimentum, -i, *n.*, covering

tego, -ere, texi, tectus, 3, cover, protect

tegula, -ae, *f.*, roofing-tile, roof

tela, -ae, *f.*, web, that which is woven

telum, -i, *n.*, weapon

tellus, -uris, *f.*, earth

temperans, -antis, *p. adj.* (*of* tempero), moderate, temperate

temperantia, -ae, *f.*, self-control, temperance

temperatura, -ae, *f.*, temperature

tempero, 1, keep from, refrain from; regulate, temper

tempestas, -atis, *f.*, storm, tempest

templum, -i, *n.*, temple

tempto, 1, try, attempt, test

tempus, -oris, *n.*, time, occasion, circumstance

temulentus, -a, -um, *adj.*, drunken, intoxicated

tenax, -acis, *adj.*, holding fast, tenacious

tendo, -ere, tetendi, tentus, 3, stretch, extend; strive, aim at

tenebricosus, -a, -um, *adj.*, dark

teneo, -ere, tenui, tentus, 2, hold, possess

tener, -era, -erum, *adj.*, tender, young

tenor, -oris, *m.*, uninterrupted course, tenor

tenuis, -e, *adj.*, thin, slender

tergum, -i, *n.*, rear, back, hide, skin

terminus, -i, *m.*, limit, bound, boundary

tero, -ere, trivi, tritus, 3, rub

terra, -ae, *f.*, earth, ground, land

terrenus, -a, -um, *adj.*, earthly

territo, 1, frighten, terrify

tertius, -a, -um, *adj.*, third

testa, -ae *f.*, earthen vessel, tile

testis, -is, *c.*, witness

testor, 1 *dep.*, bear witness, testify; show, prove

texo, -ere, -xui, -xtus, 3, weave

textor, -oris, *m.*, weaver

textrinum, -i, *n.*, weaving

theatrum, -i, *n.*, theatre, audience

Theophrastus, -i, *m.*, Theophrastus, disciple of Aristotle who succeeded him as head of the Lyceum

Tiberius, -i, *m.*, Tiberius, husband of the granddaughter of Atticus, Cicero's intimate friend

tibia, -ae, *f.*, flute

tignum, -i, *n.*, timber

timeo, -ere, -ui, 2, be afraid, fear

timide, *adv.*, timidly, fearfully

timidus, -a, -um, *adj.*, fearful, timid

Timoneus, -a, -um, *adj.* (*of* Timon), Athenian misanthrope and miser

timor, -oris, *m.*, fear

titubo, 1, falter

titulus, -i, *m.*, label, title; sales-tag; glory, honor

toga, -ae, *f.*, toga

tolerabiliter, *adv.*, bearably, tolerably

tollo, -ere, sustuli, sublatus, 3, lift up, remove

tondeo, -ere, totondi, tonsus, 2, shear, clip

tormentum, -i, *n.*, torment

torpeo, -ere, 2, be numb, be sluggish, be torpid

torqueo, -ere, torsi, tortus, 2, twist, torment

torrens, -entis, *p. adj.* (*of* torreo), burning, hot; rushing

torreo, -ere, torrui, tostus, 2, burn, scorch

tortor, -oris, *m.*, torturer

torus, -i, *m.*, couch, bed; muscle

tot, *indecl. adj.*, so many

totidem, *indecl. adj.*, just so many, just as many

totiens, *adv.*, so often; totiens. . .quotiens, so often. . .as

totus, -a, -um, *adj.*, all, the whole, entire; in totum, completely

trabs, trabis, *f.*, a beam of wood

tractatio, -onis, *f.*, handling, management

tracto, 1, treat, handle, draw, conduct
trado, -ere, -didi, -ditus [trans-do], 3, hand over, surrender
traho, -ere, traxi, tractus, 3, draw, drag
traicio, -ere, -ieci, -iectus [trans-iacio], 3, throw over or across
trama, -ae, f., woof, web, weft
trames, -itis, m., road, path
tranquillitas, -atis, f., calmness, tranquillity
tranquillus, -a, -um, adj., calm, tranquil
trans, prep. w. acc., across
transcurro, -ere, -cucurri (-curri), -cursus, 3, run across, pass over, pass by
transeo, -ire, -ivi (-ii), -itus, 4, cross over, pass over, pass through
transfero, -ferre, -tuli, -latus, irr., carry over, transfer
transfiguro, 1, transform, transfigure
transfuga, -ae, c., deserter
transfundo, -ere, -fudi, -fusus, 3, pour, heap
transigo, -ere, -egi, -actus [trans-ago], 3, pass time, spend
transilio, -ire, -ivi (-ui) [trans-salio], 4, leap across
transitus, -us, m., passing over or across, going through
translatio, -onis, f., metaphor
translatus, -a, -um, p. adj. (of transfero), carried over, transferred
transmitto, -ere, -misi, -missus, 3, send across, pass through
transverto, -ere, -verti, -versus, 3, turn across or athwart
transversus, -a, -um, p. adj. (of transverto), turned across, lying across, athwart, crosswise, inverted
tremo, -ere, -ui, 3, tremble
trepidatio, -onis, f., alarm, trepidation
trepido, 1, tremble
trepidus, -a, -um, adj., trembling
tribunale, -alis, n., tribunal
tribuo, -ere, -ui, -utus, 3, assign, bestow
tribus, -us, f., tribe, mob
tributum, -i, n., tax, contribution
triduum, -i, n., a space of three days
triginta, indecl. num., thirty
tristis, -e, adj., sad, sorrowful
tristitia, -ae, f., sadness
tritus, -a, -um, p. adj. (of tero), rubbed, much trodden; common, trite
Troianus, -a, -um, adj., Trojan
trudo, -ere, trusi, trusus, 3, push, shove
truncus, -i, m., trunk
tu, tui, pers. pron., you
tuba, -ae, f., trumpet
tubule, -ae, f., small trumpet

tubus, -i, m., pipe
tueor, -eri, tuitus, 2 dep., defend, protect, guard
tum, adv., then, at that time
tumidus, -a, -um, adj., swollen
tumultus, -us, m., confusion, tumult
tumultuosus, -a, -um, adj., tumultuous
tunc, adv., then, at that time
tunica, -ae, f., tunic
turba, -ae, f., crowd
turbatus, -a, -um, p. adj. (of turbo), disturbed, thrown into confusion
turbidus, -a, -um, adj., confused, disordered, tumultuous
turbo, 1, disturb, throw into confusion
turbo, -inis, m., whirlpool, whirlwind
turbulentus, -a, -um, adj., restless, disturbed, turbulent
turpis, -e, adj., base, foul
turturilla, -ae, f., little turtledove
tussis, -is, f., cough
tutela, -ae, f., guarding, protection, care
tuto, adv., safely
tutus, -a, -um, adj., safe, secure; tutum, -i, n., safety; tuto, adv., safely, securely
tuus, -a, -um, poss. adj. and pron., your, yours
tyrannis, -idis, f., tyranny
tyrannus, -i, m., tyrant

U

ubi, adv., where, when
ubicumque, adv., wherever
ubique, adv., everywhere
ulcusculum, -i, n., a little ulcer
Ulixes, -is, m., Ulysses
ullus, -a, -um, adj., any
ulterior, -ius, comp. adj., farther, further
ultimus, -a, -um, superl. adj., farthest, most distant, last
ultra, adv. and prep., beyond
ultro, adv., on the other side, beyond; ultro citro, hither and thither
umbra, -ae f., shade, shadow
umerus, -i, m., shoulder
umor, -oris, m., liquid, moisture
umquam, adv., ever
unctio, -onis, f., anointing, massage
unctus, -a, -um, p. adj. (of ungo), anointed
unda, -ae, f., wave
unde, adv., whence, from where
undique, adv., on all sides, everywhere
ungo (unguo), -ere, unxi, unctus, 3, anoint
ungula, -ae, f., hoof, claw
unicus, -a, -um, adj., sole, only, unique
unitas, -atis, f., unity, oneness
universum, -i, n., whole world, universe

unus, -a, -um, *num. adj.*, one, alone, only

unusquisquc, unaquaeque, unumquidque, *indef. pron.*, each one, each

urbanus, -a, -um, *adj.*, urbane, refined, elegant

urbs, -is, *f.*, city

urgeo, -ere, ursi, 2, push, press, urge

uro, -ere, ussi, ustus, 3, burn

ursa, -ae, *f.*, bear

usitatus, -a, -um, *adj.*, customary, common, ordinary

usque, *adv.*, all the way, as far as

usus, -us, *m.*, use, practice, experience, treatment

ut (or **uti**), *adv.* and *conj.; with indic.*, as, when, how; *with subj.*, in order that, so that, that; although

utcumque, *adv.*, in what manner soever, however

uter, utra, utrum, *adj.*, which (of two)

uterque, utraque, utrumque, *adj.*, each (of two), both

utilis, -e, *adj.*, useful

utilitas, -atis, *f.*, usefulness, utility, advantage, interest

utique, *adv.*, in any case, certainly, especially

utor, uti, usus, 3 *dep.*, use, enjoy

utrimque, *adv.*, on either side, on both sides

utrum, *conj.*, whether; **utrum. . .an,** whether. . .or

uva, -ae, *f.*, cluster, bunch of grapes

uxor, -oris, *f.*, wife, spouse

V

vacillo, 1, vacillate, waver

vaco, 1, be empty, have time for, be at leisure

vadimonium, -i, *n.*, bail, security (for appearance on a particular day before a court of law)

vado, -ere, 3, go

vadum, -i, *n.*, shallow water

vagor, 1 *dep.*, wander

vagus, -a, -um, *adj.*, wandering, roaming, vague

valde, *adv.*, exceedingly, very

valens, -entis, *p. adj. (of* **valeo**), strong, powerful

valeo, -ere, -ui, -itus, 2, be strong, be well, have power, have force; **vale,** farewell

valetudinarium, -i, *n.*, hospital

valetudo, -inis, *f.*, health

Valgius, -i, *m.*, Valgius Rufus, a distinguished poet of the Augustan Age and intimate friend of Horace

validus, -a, -um, *adj.*, strong, powerful

vallum, -i, *n.*, rampart, wall, fortification

vanitas, -atis, *f.*, emptiness, vanity

vanus, -a, -um, *adj.*, empty; vain, fickle

vapor, -oris, *m.*, vapor, steam

Varianus, -a, -um, *adj.*, of Varus; Quintilius Varus, commander of the Roman armies of Germany

varie, *adv.*, diversely, in various ways

varietas, -atis, *f.*, variety

vario, 1, vary, change, alter

varius, -a, -um, *adj.*, various, manifold, diverse; varying, changing

vas, vasis, *n.*, vessel

vastus, -a, -um, *adj.*, huge, immense, vast

vates, -is, *c.*, soothsayer, prophet, seer

-ve (shortened form of **vel**), *enclit. conj.*, or

vehemens, -entis, *adj.*, violent, vehement

vehementer, *adv.*, vehemently

vehiculum, -i, *n.*, vehicle

veho, -ere, -xi, -ctus, 3, carry

vel, *conj.*, or, even; **vel. . .vel,** either. . .or

velamentum, -i, *n.*, cover, screen

vellico, 1, sting

vello, -ere, vulsi, vulsus, 3, pluck

velo, 1, cover, veil

velocitas, -atis, *f.*, quickness, rapidity, velocity

velox, -ocis, *adj.*, swift, rapid

velum, -i, *n.*, covering, curtain, sail

velut, *adv.*, just as, as if

vena, -ae, *f.*, vein

venalis, -e, *adj.*, for sale, on sale; **venalis, -is,** *m.*, slave offered for sale

vendo, -ere, vendidi, venditus, 3, sell

venenum, -i, *n.*, poison

veneratio, -onis, *f.*, respect, veneration

veneror, 1 *dep.*, reverence, venerate

venia, -ae, *f.*, indulgence to faults, pardon

venio, -ire, veni, ventus, 4, come

venter, -tris, *m.*, belly, stomach

ventosus, -a, -um, *adj.*, like the wind, fickle

venturus, -a, -um, *fut. p. of* **venio**

ventus, -i, *m.*, wind

ver, veris, *n.*, spring

verber, -eris, *n.*, lash, blow

verbero, 1, lash, beat

verbum, -i, *n.*, word

verecundia, -ae, *f.*, modesty

vereor, -eri, veritus, 2 *dep.*, fear, respect

Vergilius, -i, *m.*, Vergil, great Roman poet of the Augustan Age

vergo, -ere, 3, bend, turn, incline

veritas, -atis, *f.*, truth

verna, -ae, *c.*, slave born in the master's house, home-born slave

vero, *adv.*, truly, indeed; but, yet

versatilis, -e, *adj.*, turning round, revolving

verso, 1, turn, turn over; turn over in one's mind, think over, consider; **versor,** 1 *dep.*, associate

versus, -a, -um, *p. adj. (of* **verto**), turned

versus, -us, *m.*, verse

vertex, -icis, *m.*, height

verto, -ere, verti, versus, 3, turn

verus, -a, -um, *adj.*, true, real

vescor, vesci, 3 *dep.*, feed, eat
vesica, -ae, *f.*, bladder
vestibulum, -i, *n.*, entrance-court, entrance
vestigium, -i, *n.*, foot-step
vestimentum, -i, *n.*, clothing, garment
vestio, -ire, -ivi, -itus, 4, clothe
vestis, -is, *f.*, garment, clothing, clothes
veteranus, -a, -um, *a*dj., old, veteran
veterarius, -a, -um, *adj.*, old, mature
veto, -are, -ui, -itus, 1, avoid, forbid
vetulus, -a, -um, *adj.*, old
vetus, -eris, *adj.*, old, ancient
vetustas, -atis, *f.*, old age, age
vetustus, -a, -um, *adj.*, old, ancient
vexatio, -onis, *f.*, trouble, vexation
vexo, 1, annoy, molest, vex
via, -ae *f.*, way, road
vibro, 1, vibrate, brandish
vicensimus, -a, -um, *adj.*, twentieth
vicinia, -ae, *f.*, neighborhood, vicinity
vicinus, -a, -um, *adj.*, near, neighboring; subst.,
    vicinus, -i, *m.*, vicina, -ae, *f.*, neighbor;
    vicinum, -i, *n.*, neighborhood, vicinity
vicis, gen., vices, *nom. pl., f.*, change, alternation,
    vicissitude
victor, -oris, *m.*, victor
victus, -us, *m.*, food, manner of life, way of living
vicus, -i, *m.*, street
videlicet, *adv.*, clearly
video, -ere, vidi, visus, 2, see; pass., be seen,
    seem, appear
vigeo, -ere, 2, be vigorous, thrive
vigesco, -ere, vigui, 3, become vigorous, thrive
vigilia, -ae, f., sleeplessness, wakefulness
vigilo, 1, be awake, watch
vigor, -oris, *m.*, vigor
vilicus, -i, *m.*, steward
vilis, -e, *adj.*, cheap, common, base
villa, -ae, *f.*, country-house, estate
vincio, -ire, vinxi, vinctus, 4, bind
vinco, -ere, vici, victus, 3, conquer, overcome,
    subdue
vinculum, -i, *n.*, bond
vindemia, -ae, *f.*, grapes, wine, vintage
vindico, 1, claim, set free
vinum, -i, *n.*, wine
violentus, -a, -um, *adj.*, violent
vir, viri, *m.*, man
virens, -entis, *p. adj. (of* vireo), green, blooming
vireo, -ere, 2, be green

virga, -ae, *f.*, rod
virgeus, -a, -um, *adj.*, made of twigs or rods
virilis, -e, *adj.*, manly, virile
virtus, -utis, *f.*, manliness, courage, virtue
vis, vis, *f.*, power, strength, force
viscum, -i, *n.*, bird-lime
viscus, -eris, *n.*, usually *pl.*, viscera, -um, entrails,
    viscera
visum, -i, *n.*, something seen, sight
vita, -ae, *f.*, life
vitio, 1, spoil
vitiosus, -a, -um, *adj.*, faulty, bad, corrupt
vitis, -is, *f.*, vine
vitium, -i, *n.*, fault, weakness, vice
vito, 1, avoid
vitrearius, -i, *m.*, glass-worker, glass-blower
vitrum, -i, *n.*, glass
vivarium, -i, *n.*, an enclosure in which game, fish,
    etc. are kept alive
vivo, -ere, vixi, victus, 3, live
vivus, -a, -um, *adj.*, alive, living
vix, *adv.*, scarcely, hardly
voco, 1, call, summon
volaticus, -a, -um, *adj.*, fleeting, flighty
volens, -entis, *p. adj. (of* volo), willing, glad
volo, velle, volui, *irr.*, wish, be willing, want
volumen, -inis, *n.*, volume
voluntarius, -a, -um, *adj.*, voluntary
voluntas, -atis, *f.*, wish, will, desire
voluptas, -atis, *f.*, pleasure
volvo, -ere, volvi, volutus, 3, roll, revolve, turn
vomito, 1, vomit
votum, -i, *n.*, vow, wish, prayer
vox, vocis, *f.*, voice, word, saying
vulgaris, -e, *adj.*, common, ordinary, vulgar
vulgo, *adv.*, commonly, generally, in public
vulgus, -i, *n.*, rarely m., crowd, people
vulnus, -eris, *n.*, wound
vulpes, -is, *f.*, fox
vultus, -us, *m.*, expression of the face, countenance,
    face

Z

Zaleucus, -i, *m.*, Zaleucus, a famous lawgiver of
    the 7th cent. B.C., disciple of Pythagoras
Zeno, -onis, *m.*, Zeno (335–263 B.C.), founder of
    the Stoic School at Athens
zmaragdus, -i, *m.*, emerald

Cicero
Pro Archia Poeta Oratio

Steven M. Cerutti

A Structural Analysis of the Speech

✦ Historical introduction

✦ Running vocabulary on facing pages

✦ Complete text

✦ Full apparatus of notes

✦ Glossary of proper names and places

✦ Appendix clarifying rhetorical terms and political offices

✦ Complete lexicon

✦ Bibliography

Student Text
160 pp.
(1998, Revised Reprint 1999)
Paperback, ISBN 0-86516-402-9

Cicero's
First Catilinarian Oration
Karl Frerichs

Cicero's First Catilinarian speech is now available in a practical and inexpensive annotated edition for third-year Latin students. In light of existing textbooks, Karl Frerichs' edition has several important and distinguishing strengths:

✦ Clear, tripartite page layout for text, vocabulary and notes on facing pages
✦ Running vocabulary separate from notes and complete vocabulary at the end
✦ Introduction and Glossary of Terms and Figures of Speech provide basic biographical, historical, and rhetorical background
✦ Maps and illustrations

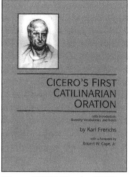

80 pp., (1997, Reprint 2000)
Paperback, ISBN 0-86516-341-3

Vergil's Aeneid
Selections from Books 1, 2, 4, 6, 10, and 12

Barbara Weiden Boyd

The divinely sanctioned plight of Rome's founding hero Aeneas, a Trojan's view of the fall of Troy, the divinely finagled love affair of Aeneas and Phoenician queen Dido, Dido's angry suicide when Aeneas leaves her, their encounter in the Underworld, the death of Aeneas' young charge Pallas at Turnus' hands, the revenge killing of Turnus by Aeneas—all these stories are found within these selections.

xviii + 413 pp. (December 2001)
Paperback, ISBN 0-86516-480-0, Hardbound, ISBN 0-86516-538-6

Embers of the Ancient Flame
Latin Love Poetry Selections from Catullus, Horace, and Ovid

Carol A. Murphy, Daniel G. Thiem, and Ryan T. Moore

Embers of the Ancient Flame is a user-friendly introduction to the Latin love poetry of Catullus, Horace, and Ovid. Each poet has his distinctive voice. Catullus, Horace, and Ovid lived during two of Rome's most dynamic eras, the late Republic and the early Empire. Their poetry provides a glimpse into the most personal parts of Roman life during historically and literarily singular times.

ix + 114 pp. (December 2001)
Paperback, ISBN 0-86516-505-X

Bolchazy-Carducci Publishers, Inc.

1000 Brown Street, Unit 101
Wauconda, IL 60084
Phone: 847/526-4344
www.bolchazy.com

WWW.BOLCHAZY.COM

AP Textbooks   AP Ancillaries

Latin Studies   Greek Studies

Artes Latinae   Gilgamesh

Classical Bulletin   Myth

Slavic Studies   WWII

Website Galleries   Modern History